Instant InDesign

Designing templates for fast and efficient page layout

Gabriel Powell

Adobe

Instant InDesign: Designing templates for tast and efficient page layout
By Gabriel Powell

This Adobe Press book is published by Peachpit.
Peachpit
1249 Eighth Street
Berkeley, CA 94710
510/524-2178
510/524-2221 (fax)

For the latest on Adobe Press books, go to www.adobepress.com
To report errors, please send a note to errata@peachpit.com
Peachpit is a division of Pearson Education

Acquisition Editor: Pamela Pfiffner
Project Editor: Susan Rimerman
Developmental Editor: Anne Marie Walker
Production Editor: Kate Reber
Tech Editors: Adam Pratt, Lynn Grillo
Indexer: FireCrystal Communications
Compositor: Danielle Foster
Interior design & cover: Mimi Heft
Cover art: StockLayouts LLC (newsletter);
Family Circle Magazine © 2007 Meredith Corporation (template)

ISBN-13: 978-0-321-49571-6
ISBN-10: 0-321-49571-3

9 8 7 6 5 4 3 2 1

Printed and bound in the United States of America

Dedication

To Lonny, the woman of my dreams, whose unconditional support and patience made this book possible. You're the best.

Acknowledgments

There are several individuals to whom I owe a great deal of thanks and recognition for the successful completion of this book. First, I would like to extend my deepest appreciation to all the Peachpit staff members who helped make this book possible. They really care about quality, are thorough in the work they do, and enjoy it at the same time. It's a pleasure working with each of you. Thanks to my family and friends for their encouragement and inspiration. And special thanks to Tech Editor Adam Pratt. The timely completion of this book would not have been possible without him writing Chapters 9 and 12.

Table of Contents

Introduction vii

SECTION 1 The Zen of Template Design 1

1 Understanding Templates 3
What Is a Template? 4
Benefits of Using Templates 5
Suitable Projects for Templating 8
Basic Elements of a Template 9
Beyond the Basic Elements 16

2 Seven Principles of Great Template Design 23
Know Your Tools 24
Design with a Goal in Mind 24
Speed Is a Priority 25
Design for Ease of Use 25
Employ Good Production Practices 26
Continually Test and Explore Other Solutions 26
Choose Between Flexibility and Rigidity 27

3 Step-by-step Approach to Designing Templates 29
Step 1: Define Your Objectives 30
Step 2: Create a Mock-up Layout 33
Step 3: Construct the Template 34
Step 4: Test the Template 35
Step 5: Implement the Template 36

4 Getting Your Feet Wet with InDesign CS3 Templates 37
Exploring the Templates that Ship with InDesign 38
Customizing Predesigned InDesign Templates 41

SECTION 2 Setting Up InDesign to Do the Work 59

5 The Anatomy of a Frame 61
Understanding the Terminology 62
Three Types of Frames 64
Redefining a Frame's Content 72

6 Frames in Action 73
Understanding the Rulers 74
Measuring, Positioning, and Transforming Frames 78
Grouping, Nesting, Anchoring, and Stacking 88

7 Setting Up the Framework of a Template 93
Study the Mock-up Layout 94
Setting Up the Page 94
Constructing a Layout Grid 97
Taking Advantage of Layout Adjustment 120

8 Setting Up Master Pages, Libraries, and Layers 123
Setting Up Master Pages 124
Setting Up Object Libraries 142
Setting Up Layers 145

9 Working with Color 149
Creating Color Swatches 150

10 Formatting Type and Generating Style Sheets 165
Essential Character Formatting 166
Essential Paragraph Formatting 174
Paragraph and Character Styles 190

11 Formatting Frames and Generating Object Styles 199
Essential Frame Formatting 200
Creating Object Styles 222
Productivity Tips 225
Importing Object Styles 226

12 Formatting Tables and Generating Table and Cell Styles 227
Creating Tables 228
Selecting Tables 229
Formatting Essential Cell Options 229
Creating Cell Styles 234
Formatting Essential Table Options 235
Creating Table Styles 239

13 Adding Support for Long Documents 247
Creating Running Lists 248
Creating Multilevel Lists 250

Setting the Document Footnote Options 251
Creating a Table of Contents Style 255

14 Preparing Your Template for Success 261
Finalizing Your Template 262
Testing Your Template 270
Implementing Your Template 272
Creating a Style Guide 279

15 Managing Templates with Adobe Bridge CS3 283
Launching Bridge 284
Exploring the Interface 284
Organizing Files 289
Finding Files 294
Saving and Using Collections 295

16 Automating Layouts with XML 297
What Is XML? 298
XML Terminology and Markup Rules 298
InDesign's XML Tools 304
Understanding the Workflow 305
Setting Up an XML-ready Template 309
Importing the XML Document 318

Index 322

Introduction

Beneath just about every publication is a template at work. From the time man began to record information as a series of symbols, written material has always required some sort of basic framework. The ancient Egyptian scribes utilized columns to compose hieroglyphs on sheets of papyrus. Later, the scribes of the Middle Ages set many of the standards—in terms of margins, columns, and spacing—which the Western world continues to use. The invention of printing with moveable type further established a regular system of control over lines and columns of type. And now, with the advent of computers and desktop publishing software, templates are being used in households and businesses worldwide to create all kinds of publications.

What makes templates so important? First, they guide the placement of text and graphics, and provide a well-established starting point from which a publication can be easily created. Second, and most important, they save a lot of setup time, ensure design consistency, and significantly minimize the possibility for error.

Designing a template is expert work, demanding all of your attention, skill, good judgment, and experience. As a template designer, you must choose among an array of production methods and tools, carefully considering the most optimal use of grids, master pages, color, style sheets, and so on. You must carefully balance your attention to the minutest detail with the big picture objectives of each project. *Instant InDesign* is dedicated to teaching you the tricks of the trade and provides you with the knowledge you need to create exceptional templates.

Who Should Read This Book?

This book is for anyone who wants to learn how to design a template from the ground up with Adobe InDesign. By leveraging the concepts covered in this book and InDesign's amazing toolset, you can create a wide range of templates—from basic templates for business cards and newsletters to incredibly sophisticated templates that automate entire catalogs.

Many books have been written on InDesign, but what makes this book unique is its exclusive focus on template design. You'll learn how to translate your great designs into production-viable templates, using the best tools for the job in the most productive ways.

If you're responsible for producing any kind of printed material—including newsletters, books, magazines, newspapers, catalogs, and so on—this book is designed for you. And it's not a book to read once and forget about. You can keep coming back to it as your guide for future projects.

Once you're accustomed to designing templates, you'll be able to quickly spot the most efficient solutions. And you'll be completely confident in the templates you create, knowing that you've made the best choices in their construction.

How This Book Is Organized

This book is arranged into three sections; each building on the knowledge of the previous section:

- Section 1, "The Zen of Template Design," introduces you to the world of template design. You'll first learn what a template is and become familiar with the various elements that make up a template. You'll then discover the most important principles of great template design. Thereafter, each step in the template construction process is outlined for you in detail. And before jumping into the second section, you'll get a chance to put the theory into practice and get your feet wet with template design by learning to modify the templates that ship with InDesign.
- Section 2, "Setting Up InDesign to Do the Work," makes up the bulk of this book. You'll learn the most effective use of each tool and technology, and how to combine them to achieve the most productive results. This section is organized in the same order in which a template is designed, so it's best to read the chapters in this section consecutively instead of skipping around.

What's on the Web Site?

As a complement to the book, additional learning material is available on the companion Peachpit Web site at www.peachpit.com/InstantInDesign. You'll find a bonus chapter on Data Merge to automate your layouts, as well as a collection of sample templates, with detailed explanation, that demonstrate the use of various tools and techniques. By studying real-world examples, you'll gain an even better understanding of template design. And keep checking back because more content will be added.

Section 1

The Zen of Template Design

1

Understanding Templates

TEMPLATES EXCEL AT HELPING YOU TO ACHIEVE A HIGH-LEVEL OF EFFICIENCY and maintain a consistent look throughout a document. They harness the processing power of computers to automate production—freeing designers from mundane and repetitive tasks.

Most designers use some form of a template on a regular basis. In some cases, they may just pick up an older project that has already been produced and use it as a template for a new project. In other cases, they might specifically design a template that is intended for a particular publication. For small projects and one in which a solo designer is producing an entire layout, it may be sufficient to use an existing project as a template. But in larger organizations—where many people are collaborating on projects—strategically designed templates are a vital component of project consistency and an efficient workflow.

This chapter introduces you to the world of template design. It explains what a template is and what its main benefits are, and identifies the various elements that compose a template.

What Is a Template?

A template serves as a pattern for the sequence of assembly of a publication. More specifically, it is a document that is preset with the various elements that make up a design—a model that provides a useful starting point for frequently published documents. For example, if you publish a monthly newsletter, you can create a template that contains the layout of a typical issue (**Figure 1.1**). Each month, you would simply start from the template and import new content into it, saving countless hours of repetitive labor.

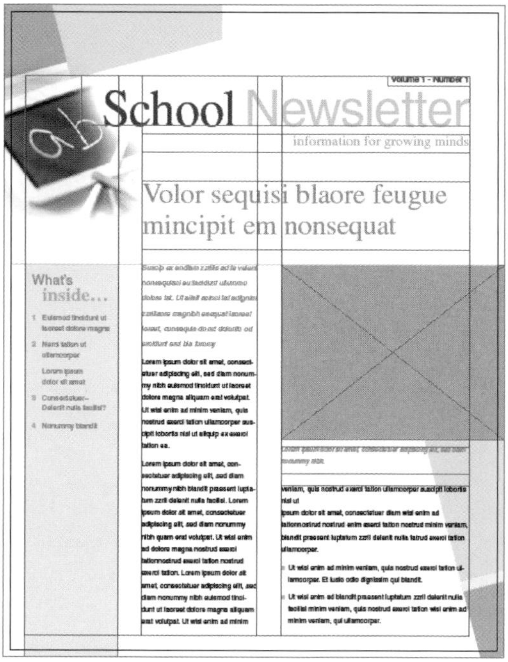
Volume 1 - Number 1
School Newsletter
information for growing minds
Volor sequisi blaore feugue mincipit em nonsequat
What's inside...

Figure 1.1 This newsletter template by Stocklayouts contains all the placeholders and repeating objects of a typical layout, giving you a good starting point for each new issue.

As designers, we may have a hard time accepting the idea of using templates, because we assume we are locked into a restricting layout. We are accustomed to having supreme control over the type, color, and layout choices of the publications we produce. And, within reason, we can expect to deliver reliable results throughout the production process. But imagine what design would be if everything we produced for a client looked different. Imagine how time-consuming the production process would be if we had to re-create a newsletter from scratch every month.

Although templates can limit our layout choices, it's definitely not always the case. Templates should be regarded as an aid to design, uniformity, and efficient production—never as a straitjacket. A well-designed template saves time and facilitates creative freedom as much as possible.

Benefits of Using Templates

The principal function of a template is to facilitate efficient page production while maintaining a consistent design. As more thought goes into the design of a template, it can ultimately develop into an intelligent design aid and a powerful production tool. The benefits of a great template—perhaps too many to list—fall into three main categories:

- Productivity
- Consistency
- Profitability

Productivity

In this day and age, speed is critical. Well-built templates respond to this requisite by minimizing the stress of manual repetitive formatting and automating routine tasks. With a standardized template, the variables of complex routine are reduced to a more predictable and productive system. Without a template, you can plan on spending hours of unproductive time on a project.

When you start from a template, a large bulk of the work has already been done. Then, all you have to do is import, arrange, and format the new content. This process is facilitated by the use of master pages, style sheets, and predefined colors. In many cases, the process can be further automated by using one of InDesign's built-in automation tools, such as Data Merge, XML, or scripting. All types of projects—from envelopes and labels to product sheets and 500 page catalogs—can be automated with one of these valuable tools. However, even without the assistance of an automated solution, the most basic template will save you hours of setup time (**Figure 1.2**).

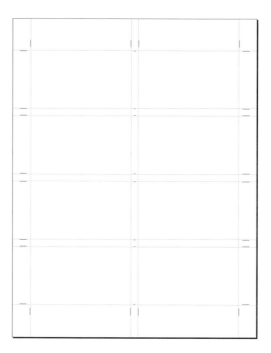

Figure 1.2 The simplicity of this business card template makes it versatile enough for many layout variations and saves a lot of setup time.

In addition to speeding up productivity, well-built templates enforce consistent and reliable production habits. In a team environment, several designers can work cooperatively from the same template to produce different sections of a publication. Although each designer is working on his or her own section, each is using the same production procedure—ensuring that the final publication is built reliably. This significantly reduces the possibility for design errors and printing issues. It also makes it easier for another designer to pick up the work that someone else has already started and finish it.

Consistency

The most essential ingredient in efficient page production is consistency. The more systematic a template is, the easier it is to use and the more productive it becomes. Without it, the possibility for errors increases and the time required to produce a page can easily multiply. Imagine if you had to first draw out the margins, columns, and baseline grid on each page before you could start placing text and art. It would take forever to complete a document, and it wouldn't be long before you or someone on your team unintentionally diverged from the design.

Consistency is not only of benefit to designers. With magazines, newspapers, books, and collections of promotional material, it is desirable and often required to establish a corporate identity. It also creates a coherent reading experience, allowing readers to find the material they are looking for without ambiguity. Therefore, a template should be regarded as an aid to readability, recognition, and understanding in addition to its productive nature.

Consistency is achieved in two ways. First, a well thought out design can make similar pages in a multiple page layout look the same, or it can give a collection of single page layouts a uniform look. Second, it is attained by the intelligent use of formatting tools—such as master pages and style sheets—to increase productivity.

One of the hallmarks of a well-built template is its use of standard naming conventions. Every style sheet, master page, and color swatch is methodically named and organized (**Figure 1.3**). Such a template is user friendly, productive, and ultimately consistent.

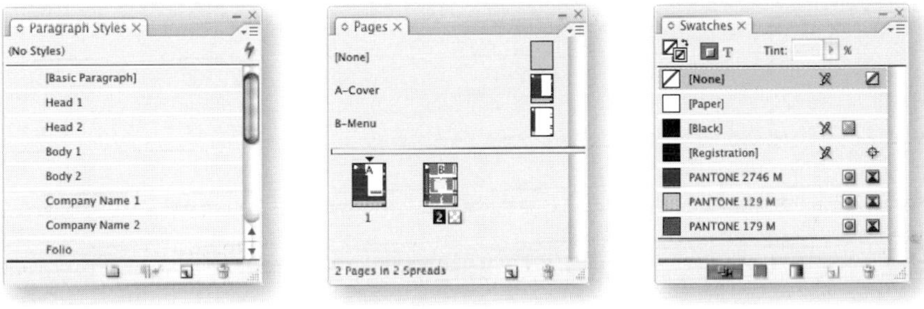
Paragraph Styles
(No Styles)
[Basic Paragraph]
Head 1
Head 2
Body 1
Body 2
Company Name 1
Company Name 2
Folio
Pages
[None]
A-Cover
B-Menu
1
2 Pages in 2 Spreads
Swatches
Tint:
%
[None]
[Paper]
[Black]
[Registration]
PANTONE 2746 M
PANTONE 129 M
PANTONE 179 M

Figure 1.3 Consistently named style sheets, master pages, and color swatches make templates easier to use and designers more productive.

Profitability

Perhaps the biggest advantage of a template is its profitability. Graphic design and print production are costly. By standardizing a design and constructing a template, the process becomes much more affordable.

Well-built templates allow multiple designers to collaborate on projects without wasting time. They make it easier to manage workflow systems and enforce good production habits. The more consistent and productive a template is, the more profitable you become.

As you might imagine, a substantial amount of time is invested in making a template perfect, because any errors in it will be endlessly repeated. One small change to a template can mean substantial time and money savings. For example, by carefully organizing paragraph styles into style groups, you can make them easy to find and use (**Figure 1.4**). Even something as simple as setting a ruler guide can save time and effort: If an imported graphic or heading requires consistent placement throughout a document, you can set a ruler guide on the master page and save yourself a lot of hassle.

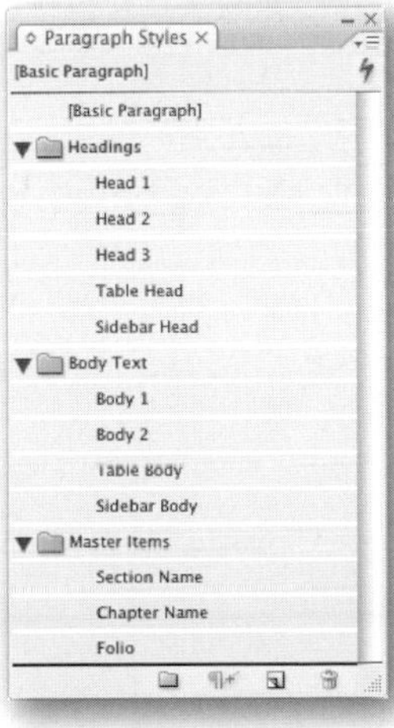
Paragraph Styles
[Basic Paragraph]
[Basic Paragraph]
Headings
Head 1
Head 2
Head 3
Table Head
Sidebar Head
Body Text
Body 1
Body 2
Table Body
Sidebar Body
Master Items
Section Name
Chapter Name
Folio

Figure 1.4 The paragraph styles in this template have been categorized into style groups to make them easier to find.

Suitable Projects for Templating

Templates are suitable for many projects, but they are definitely not always necessary. Essentially, any document that has some design consistency and that you create often enough is worth constructing a template for.

On the other hand, documents with a unique design that you don't plan on using again are likely not suitable for templating. Why waste time and effort on constructing a template for a design that you'll only use once? Documents that fall into this category are posters, flyers, advertisements, and so on. However, in some circumstances you might want to create a series of posters or flyers that call for a uniform identity. In that case, building a simple and flexible template may be just the ticket you need to save a lot of production time.

Templates can range from being very flexible to being extremely rigid. Flexible templates allow for more creative freedom, whereas rigid templates are more consistent, increasing the possibility to automate production tasks.

Types of Templates

- Catalogs and Product Sheets
- Magazines
- Newsletters
- Brochures
- Reports and Proposals
- Business Cards
- Flyers and Direct Mail
- Advertisements
- Packaging
- Business Forms
- Books and Booklets
- Posters and Signs
- Labels

Basic Elements of a Template

A template is a mechanism, and like all mechanisms is most easily understood when broken down into its component parts. Each part can then be focused on and mastered separately. Like every other mechanism, a template is constructed from its smallest part to its most complex assembly. Each part plays a unique role. The parts then work together to serve the template as a whole. The purpose of each part is best understood by maintaining reference to the overall purpose of a template—to facilitate efficient page production while maintaining a consistent design.

With that in mind, let's take a look at the elements that compose a template and the roles of each. Since the detail of a template can be quite comprehensive, let's begin with the most essential elements.

Page Framework

The foundation of any template is its framework—page size, margins, and number of columns. The page size is specified first, usually in American sizes—letter, legal, and tabloid. ISO (International Standards Organization) sizes—A1, A3, and A5—are also commonly used. Then margins are applied at the head, foot, binding, and foredge of the page to define the print area. This area can then be divided into any combination of columns. Together, page size, margins, and columns form the setup of a page (**Figure 1.5**).

Additional structure can, if necessary, be added to the template by establishing a bleed area, slug area, ruler guides, or a baseline grid (Figure 1.5). A bleed area is a margin that extends past the edge of the page. When you want an image or other element to print completely to the edge of a page, place it into the bleed area. A slug area may also be defined if the template requires space for special instructions, descriptions, or for other information. Objects positioned in the bleed or slug area can be printed but will be eliminated when the printed document is trimmed to its final page size.

A baseline grid looks like ruled notebook paper and is used to align columns of text. It can be customized to your exact specifications. Ruler guides are different from a baseline grid in that they can be positioned freely on a page. With their assistance, you can quickly and consistently arrange text and graphics.

A

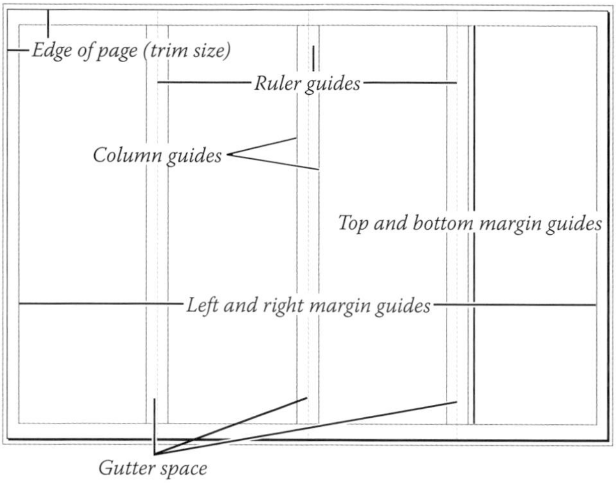
Edge of page (trim size)
Ruler guides
Column guides
Top and bottom margin guides
Left and right margin guides
Gutter space

B

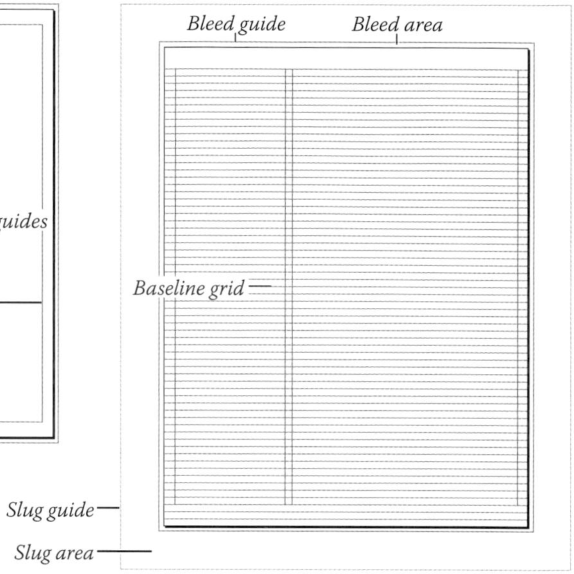
Bleed guide
Bleed area
Baseline grid
Slug guide
Slug area

Figure 1.5 (**A**) This brochure is composed of four panels and a bleed area. The gutter space between each column is wide enough to keep the information away from the folds. Additional ruler guides have been drawn to indicate the fold lines. (**B**) This table of contents page is composed of two irregular columns, a bleed area, and a slug area. The top and bottom margins are slightly bigger than the left and right margins.

Master Pages

Master pages are at the core of every template. They lay out the necessary groundwork to achieve a high level of consistency and productivity. By default, every InDesign document has at least one master page, though it is possible to create more as the template requires.

A master page is like a background that you can easily apply to many pages. When you place an object on a master page, it automatically appears on all the pages that have that master applied. If you make a change to a master page object, that change is instantly applied throughout its associated pages. This eliminates the need for manual repetitive page formatting and reduces the possibility for error.

MASTER PAGE COMPONENTS

Master pages commonly contain the template's framework as well as all repeating objects and placeholders (**Figure 1.6**).

A

Agna Feum Alit
Eliquatum
Velis!

B

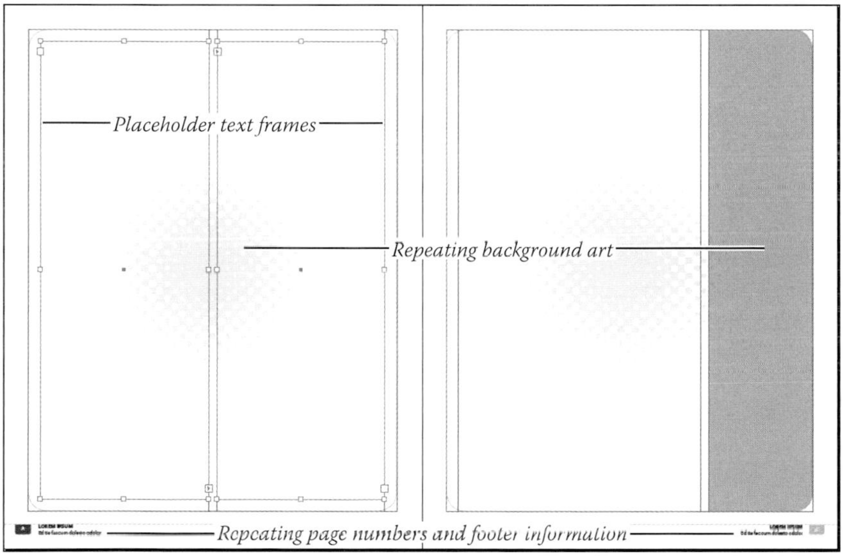
Placeholder text frames
Repeating background art
Repeating page numbers and footer information

Figure 1.6 This publication (**A**) is using this master page (**B**) as its foundation for the design. The master page contains the template's framework, repeating background art, and placeholder text frames.

Page framework: Margins, columns, ruler guides, and baseline grids all shape the framework of a template. They are essentially visual aids that determine where the different elements of a design are to be placed on the page. It's possible for each master page in a template to have its own page framework.

For example, you might use one master page for a three column layout and another for a two column layout.

Repeating objects: Whenever an object needs to be repeated throughout a document, simply place it on a master page. Objects such as background art, logos, page numbers, headers and footers, and dividing rules are typically placed for replication.

Placeholders: Templates use placeholders to demonstrate type specifications and to display the position of graphics. Text placeholders are extremely useful for demonstrating font selection, size, and spacing. They are also frequently used to represent the position of repeating page numbers, section markers, chapter headings, running headers and footers, folios, and any other text element that repeats throughout the design. Graphics placeholders indicate the position where graphical elements and images are to be placed. They are also useful for defining a preferred size, height, and width. When producing pages, simply replace each placeholder with your own text and artwork.

Type, Graphic, and Table Specifications

Once the page dimensions have been established, the remaining ingredients can be defined. All the typographic, graphical, and table formatting that constitutes the design must be clearly defined and represented in the template.

Typographic specs include the following characteristics:

- Font, including size, weight, and type style
- Leading and paragraph spacing
- Word and letter spacing
- Paragraph indentation and text alignment
- Horizontal and vertical scaling
- Text fill and stroke color

Graphical specs include the following characteristics:

- Height, width, scale attributes, and rotation angle
- X and Y position
- Transparency effects, including drop shadow, feathering, blending mode, and opacity level
- Text wrap requirements
- Stroke weight and style
- Fill and stroke color

Table specs include the following characteristics:

- Table and cell dimensions
- Table spacing
- Cell spacing
- Fill and stroke settings for rows, columns, and cells
- Diagonal lines

Style Sheets

Like master pages, style sheets are another core component of every template. They serve as a master control instrument that regulates formatting. A style sheet is a collection of attributes that can be applied to text, frames, or tables with a single click. Also, when you change the formatting of a style sheet, each element to which it has been applied will instantly update with the new changes. InDesign gives you the ability to control text formatting with character styles and paragraph styles; control frame formatting with object styles; and control table formatting with cell styles and table styles (**Figure 1.7**).

Character styles consist of character-level formatting. They are applied to a selected character or range of text within a paragraph.

Paragraph styles contain both character-level and paragraph-level formatting. They are applied to a selected paragraph or range of paragraphs. They can also contain nested styles, which are character styles applied to a specified range of text within the paragraph. Any number of nested styles can be sequenced within a paragraph style. The best part is that they are applied at the same time you apply the paragraph style, all in one mouse click.

Object styles contain frame-level formatting, such as color, stroke attributes, transparency effects, text wrap, and more. They are applied to selected graphics and frames.

Cell styles consist of cell-level formatting. They are applied to a selected cell or range of cells within a table.

Table styles contain both cell-level and table-level formatting. They are applied to a selected table.

Figure 1.7 This book template defines and illustrates the use of each of its permitted style sheets, including all character styles, paragraph styles, object styles, cell styles, and table styles.

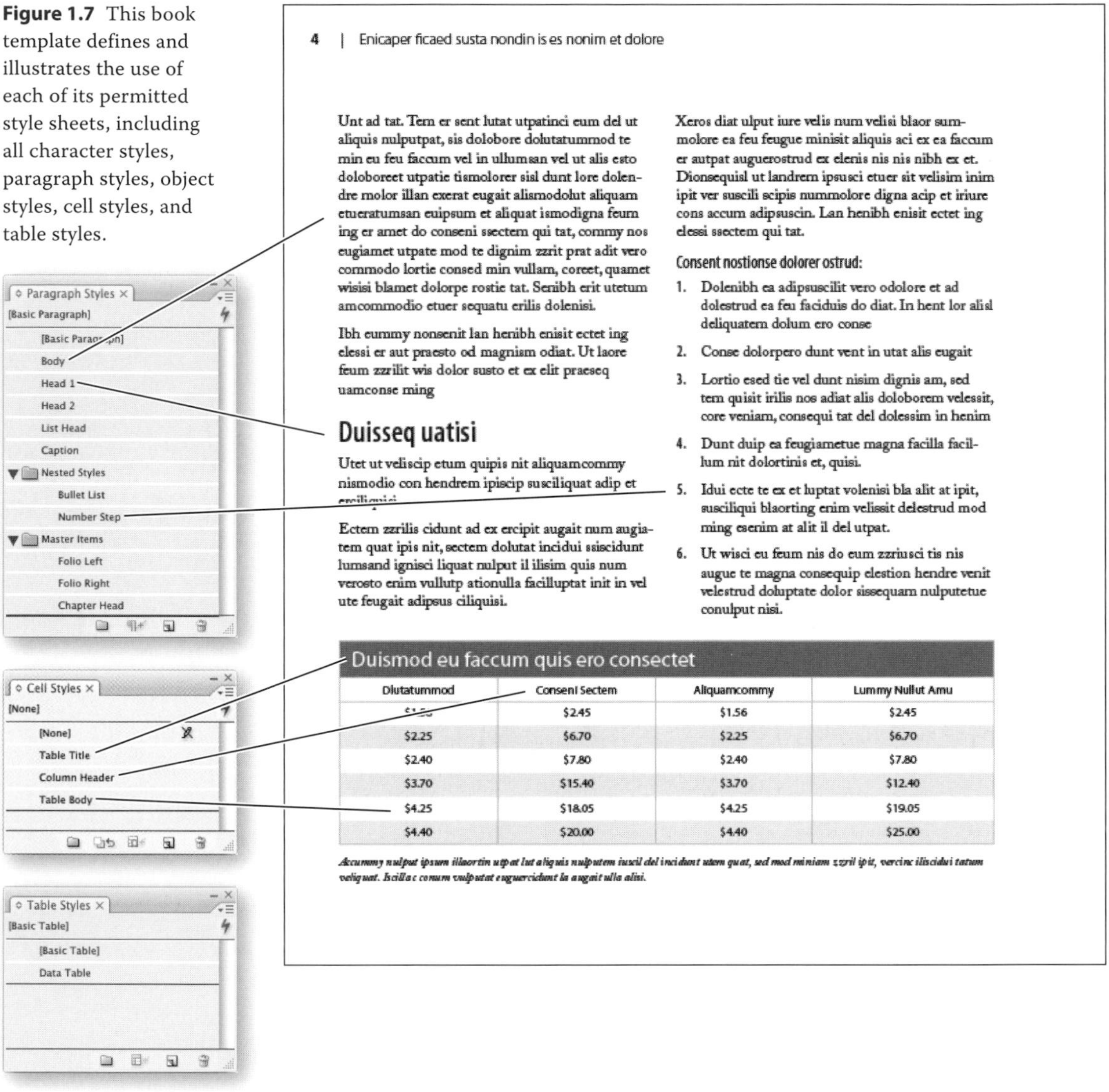
Paragraph Styles
[Basic Paragraph]
Body
Head 1
Head 2
List Head
Caption
Nested Styles
Bullet List
Number Step
Master Items
Folio Left
Folio Right
Chapter Head
Cell Styles
[None]
Table Title
Column Header
Table Body
Table Styles
[Basic Table]
Data Table
4 | Enicaper ficaed susta nondin is es nonim et dolore
Unt ad tat. Tem er sent lutat utpatinci eum del ut aliquis nulputpat, sis dolobore dolutatummod te min eu feu faccum vel in ullumsan vel ut alis esto doloboreet utpatie tismolorer sisl dunt lore dolendre molor illan exerat eugait alismodolut aliquam etueratumsan euipsum et aliquat ismodigna feum ing er amet do conseni ssectem qui tat, commy nos eugiamet utpate mod te dignim zzrit prat adit vero commodo lortie consed min vullam, coreet, quamet wisisi blamet dolorpe rostie tat. Senibh erit utetum amcommodio etuer sequatu erilis dolenisi.
Ibh eummy nonsenit lan henibh enisit ectet ing elessi er aut praesto od magnism odiat. Ut laore feum zzrilit wis dolor susto et ex elit praeseq uamconse ming
Duisseq uatisi
Utet ut veliscip etum quipis nit aliquamcommy nismodio con hendrem ipiscip susciliquat adip et
Ectem zzrilis cidunt ad ex ercipit augait num augiatem quat ipis nit, sectem dolutat incidui ssiscidunt lumsand ignisci liquat nulput il ilisim quis num verosto enim vullutp ationulla facilluptat init in vel ute feugait adipsus ciliquisi.
Xeros diat ulput iure velis num velisi blaor summolore ea feu feugue minisit aliquis aci ex ea faccum er autpat augueróstrud ex elenis nis nis nibh ex et. Dionsequisl ut landrem ipsusci etuer sit velisim inim ipit ver suscili scipis nummolore digna acip et iriure cons accum adipsuscin. Lan henibh enisit ectet ing elessi ssectem qui tat.
Consent nostionse dolorer ostrud:
1. Dolenibh ea adipsuscilit vero odolore et ad dolestrud ea feu faciduis do diat. In hent lor alisl deliquatem dolum ero conse
2. Conse dolorpero dunt vent in utat alis eugait
3. Lortio esed tie vel dunt nisim dignis am, sed tem quisit irilis nos adiat alis doloborem velessit, core veniam, consequi tat del dolessim in henim
4. Dunt duip ea feugiametue magna facilla facillum nit dolortinis et, quisi.
5. Idui ecte te ex et luptat volenisi bla alit at ipit, susciliqui blaorting enim velissit delestrud mod ming esenim at alit il del utpat.
6. Ut wisci eu feum nis do eum zzriusci tis nis augue te magna consequip elestion hendre venit velestrud doluptate dolor sissequam nulputetue conulput nisi.
Duismod eu faccum quis ero consectet
Dlutatummod | Conseni Sectem | Aliquamcommy | Lummy Nullut Amu
$2.45 | $1.56 | $2.45
$2.25 | $6.70 | $2.25 | $6.70
$2.40 | $7.80 | $2.40 | $7.80
$3.70 | $15.40 | $3.70 | $12.40
$4.25 | $18.05 | $4.25 | $19.05
$4.40 | $20.00 | $4.40 | $25.00

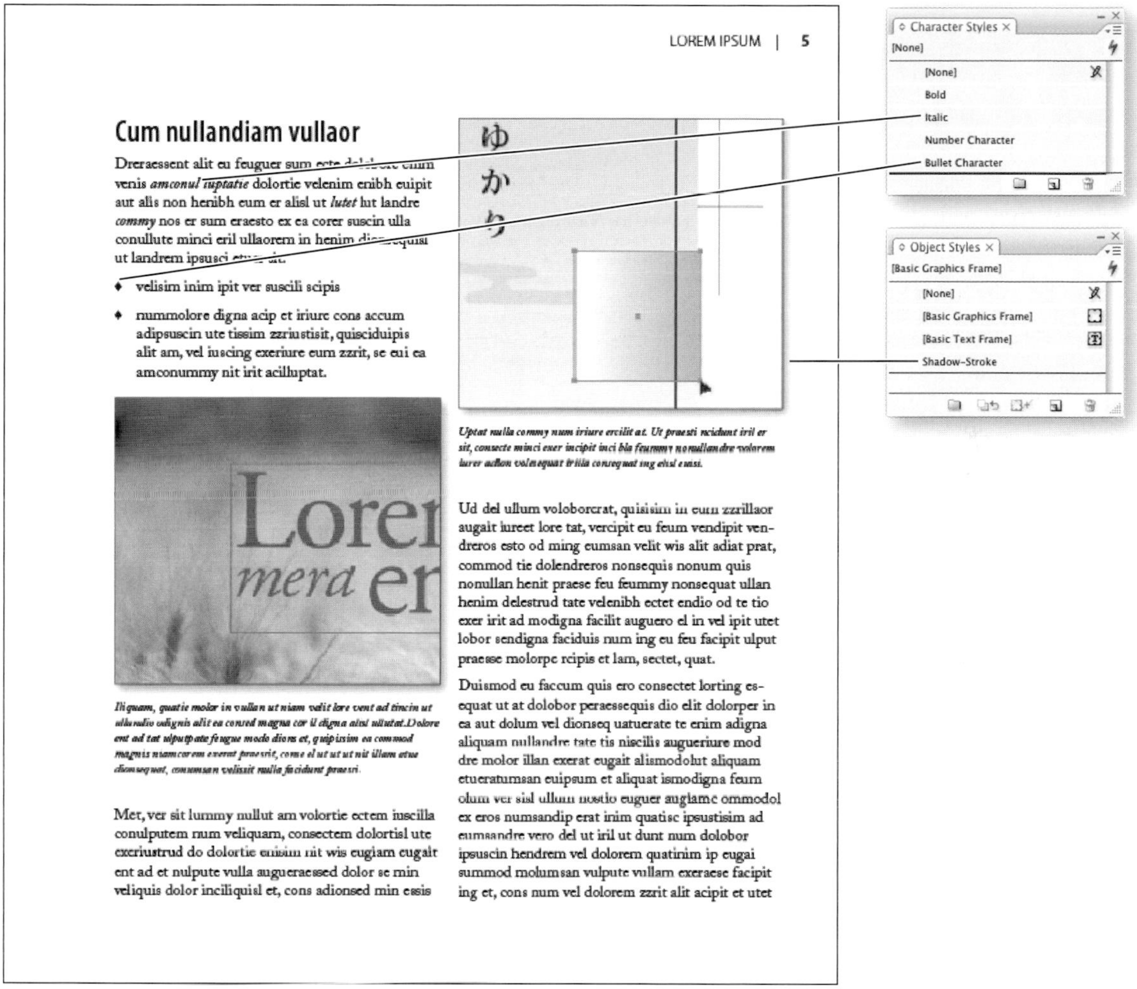
LOREM IPSUM | 5
Cum nullandiam vullaor
Character Styles
[None]
[None]
Bold
Italic
Number Character
Bullet Character
Object Styles
[Basic Graphics Frame]
[None]
[Basic Graphics Frame]
[Basic Text Frame]
Shadow-Stroke

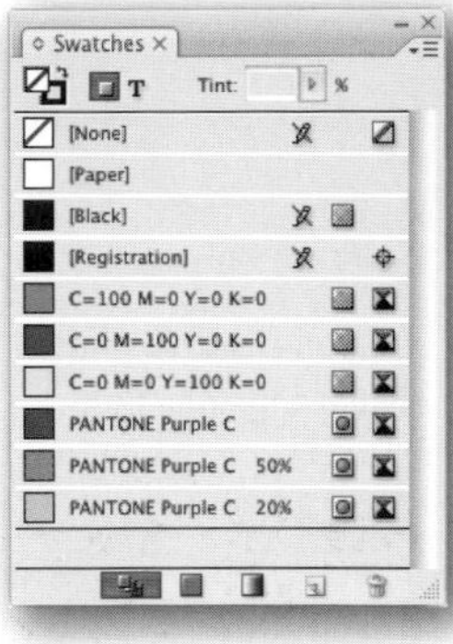
Swatches
Tint: %
[None]
[Paper]
[Black]
[Registration]
C=100 M=0 Y=0 K=0
C=0 M=100 Y=0 K=0
C=0 M=0 Y=100 K=0
PANTONE Purple C
PANTONE Purple C 50%
PANTONE Purple C 20%

Figure 1.8 Templates contain frequently used colors in the Swatches panel.

Color Swatches

Color swatches serve as a master control instrument for regulating color. All frequently used colors should be saved as a color swatch. This ensures that the same color is consistently applied throughout a document and makes it easier to globally update the color when necessary.

Once a color swatch is created, it can easily be found and applied to objects and text. When you modify a color swatch, each element to which it has been applied will instantly update with the new changes—just like style sheets and master pages (**Figure 1.8**).

Layers

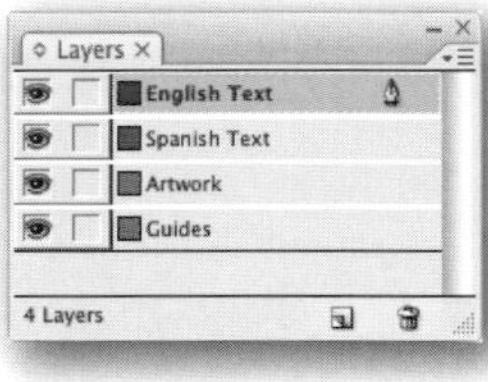
Layers
English Text
Spanish Text
Artwork
Guides
4 Layers

Figure 1.9 The Layers panel can contain any number of layers to make it easier to organize and manage the various elements of a template.

Every InDesign document contains at least one layer by default. By using multiple layers, you can keep specific items, such as artwork, text, and guides, on separate layers (**Figure 1.9**). You can then more easily manage, create, and edit objects on each layer without affecting other objects in the layout. For instance, you can use one layer for just the text in your document and—when it's time to proofread the text—simply hide all the other layers and quickly print just that layer. Layers are also useful for displaying different design ideas, maintaining production notes, and managing different language versions within a layout.

Beyond the Basic Elements

Some templates might contain additional elements depending on their design and workflow requirements. By utilizing even one of the following elements, a whole new level of power and automation can be achieved—making for an even more productive experience.

Object Libraries

Object libraries help you organize the type and graphic elements you use most often. Instead of placing frequently used items on the pasteboard, it's much more efficient to add them to an object library. Libraries are a perfect repository for elements that repeat often but not consistently enough to be placed on a master page. You can add many different types of items, including boilerplate text, commonly used graphics and logos, and even ruler guides to a library (**Figure 1.10**).

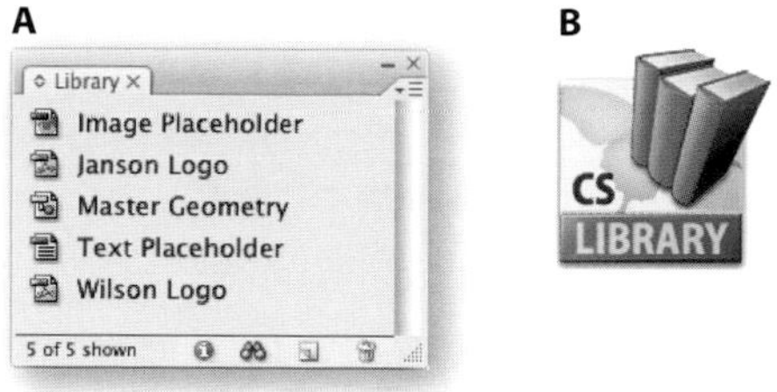
A
B
Library
Image Placeholder
Janson Logo
Master Geometry
Text Placeholder
Wilson Logo
5 of 5 shown
CS
LIBRARY

InDesign CS3 Library file

Figure 1.10 This object library contains several different types of items (**A**). An object library is a separate file from an InDesign document (**B**) that can be shared across computers and operating systems, making them a perfect companion to templates.

It's a good idea to create a library of common elements for your template and share it with your production team. This helps to enforce consistency and good production standards.

Table of Contents Styles

When your publication requires a table of contents (TOC), InDesign can automatically generate one for you. This saves a lot of time, especially when the text in your document is constantly reflowing between pages. Each time the headings and subheadings move, the TOC needs to be updated as well. Fortunately, InDesign can keep track of where they move for you.

The process for creating a TOC requires two elements. First, paragraph styles must be applied to all the text that will be used to create the TOC. Second, you need to specify which paragraph styles are to be used in the TOC and how its entries and page numbers are to be formatted. After all the settings have been defined, you can save them as a TOC style. The style will follow the template wherever it goes (**Figure 1.11**).

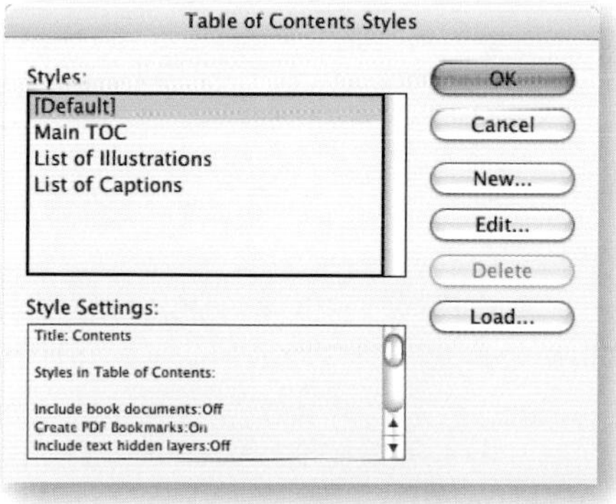
Table of Contents Styles
Styles:
[Default]
Main TOC
List of Illustrations
List of Captions
OK
Cancel
New...
Edit...
Delete
Load...
Style Settings:
Title: Contents
Styles in Table of Contents:
Include book documents:Off
Create PDF Bookmarks:On
Include text hidden layers:Off

Figure 1.11 Saved TOC styles can be viewed and edited by choosing Layout > Table of Contents Styles.

When you are ready to create a TOC, simply activate the saved style. InDesign does the rest of the work for you. If a change occurs in the document—such as a relocated heading—all you have to do is update the TOC with a click of the mouse. It's really that easy.

It's possible for one document to contain multiple TOC styles. You might use one for the overall document and another to display a list of illustrations or any other information that helps readers to find information easily.

User Dictionary

DICT.

Figure 1.12 InDesign User Dictionary file.

Some templates are used for producing publications within a particular industry. In such cases, it's often necessary to create a custom dictionary that contains all the words used in that industry. InDesign lets you create a user dictionary and easily share it with a work group (**Figure 1.12**). With everyone connected to the same dictionary, you can be certain that each document created properly adheres to the same spelling and hyphenation rules.

Style Guide

Depending on how complex a template is and who will be using it, you might need to set up an accompanying style guide that identifies the components of the template and demonstrates the appropriate use of each design element (**Figure 1.13**). Style guides can range from simple to very detailed. Most importantly, a style guide provides all the information necessary for a designer to accurately create a publication with the template.

ITC AMERICAN TYPE
165/12 -25
DIN BLACK
7/17 TT 300
SL STYLE frontice
3pt Butt Cap.
style
hed tk
¶ DIN Med9/12
AL Frontis Txt Bumps
UREET LA FACIPIS NOS
UREET LA FACIPIS NOS
UREET LA FACIPIS NOS
¶ Frontis Hed
¶ Frontis Txt
¶ Photo Cred
Family Circle Magazine © 2007 Meredith Corporation

Figure 1.13 This page is from the Family Circle Magazine style guide. Each design element is clearly identified with labels that indicate where style sheets should be applied and what objects come from an object library.

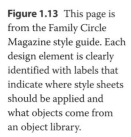

Interactive Features

InDesign offers a number of interactive features that make it possible to create forms, multimedia eBooks, and other PDF documents. If you plan on creating PDF documents that contain hyperlinks, bookmarks, buttons, or even sounds and movies, it's more productive to build them into a template beforehand (**Figure 1.14**). You can then produce a document that's intended for print media and repurpose it for an interactive PDF as well.

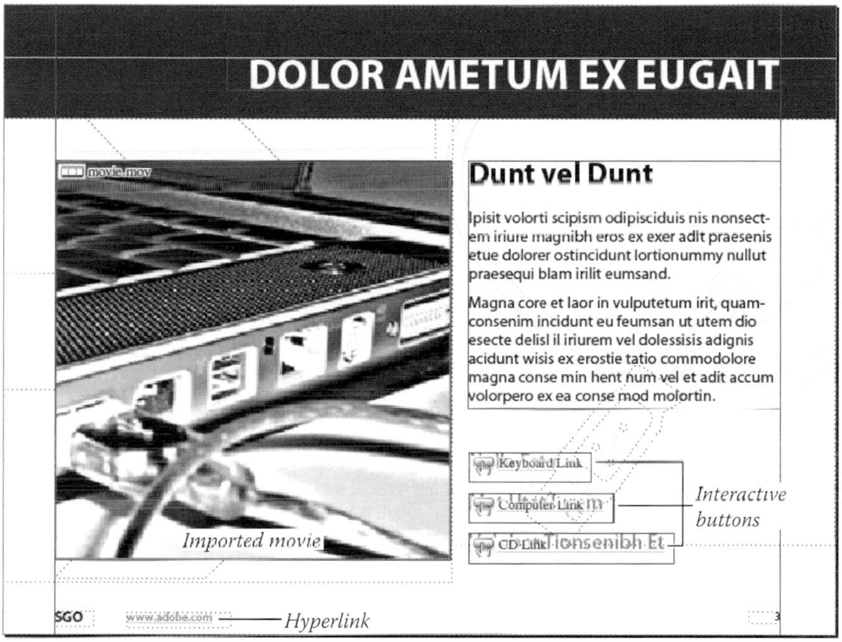
DOLOR AMETUM EX EUGAIT
movie.mov
Dunt vel Dunt
Ipisit volorti scipism odipisciduis nis nonsectem iriure magnibh eros ex exer adit praesenis etue dolorer ostincidunt lortionummy nullut praesequi blam irilit eumsand.
Magna core et laor in vulputetum irit, quamconsenim incidunt eu feumsan ut utem dio esecte delisl il iriurem vel dolessisis adignis acidunt wisis ex erostie tatio commodolore magna conse min hent num vel et adit accum volorpero ex ea conse mod molortin.
Keyboard Link
Computer Link
CD Link
Interactive buttons
Imported movie
SGO
www.adobe.com
Hyperlink

Figure 1.14 This template contains several interactive elements, including a movie, several buttons, and a hyperlink.

Data Merge

There are times when we would all like to push a button, grab a cup of coffee, and come back to our computer to find our work completed. Believe it or not, this is now a reality, and InDesign's Data Merge feature is just the ticket.

Data Merge allows you to quickly produce large volumes of work by auto-populating a template with content from a data source file—such as the names and addresses for a set of labels. To make this possible, a template is set up with data-field placeholders, which correspond to individual fields in the data source file. After the template is merged with the data source, each data-field placeholder is replaced with the incoming content and then duplicated as many times as it takes to populate every record of data.

Data Merge is great for creating large volumes of work, such as personalized letters, envelopes, and even business cards. However, it does have its limitations. In some cases, it may be more appropriate to use XML or scripting to automate a project. You will find a bonus chapter on Data Merge at www.peachpit.com/InstantInDesign.

XML

XML (eXtensible Markup Language) is a flexible data format used to distribute content to multiple destinations. XML content isn't formatted and always remains separate from its appearance in a layout. Since XML files do not depend on a specific layout, they can be formatted to match the needs of any specific destination—such as an InDesign document, PDF file, or a Web site (**Figure 1.15**). For example, an XML version of a company report may be formatted for a printed layout. The same information can be converted for onscreen viewing as a PDF, or it can be converted to HTML and placed onto a Web page.

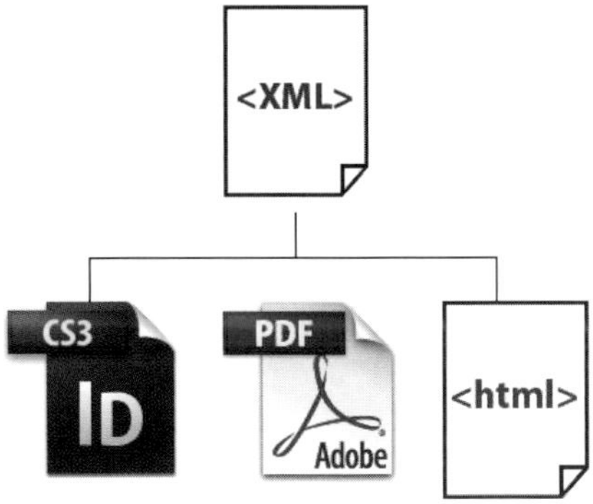
<XML>
CS3
ID
PDF
Adobe
<html>

Figure 1.15 One XML file can be presented in a variety of formats.

While XML allows data to be presented in a variety of formats, it can also be used to automate the production of pages. Setting up an automated template with XML is somewhat similar to using Data Merge. You can use XML tags to identify the type of content that an element is. If you know the order of the elements in the XML file you plan to import, you can tag placeholder frames to specify where the content should be placed and how it should be formatted. Each tagged frame corresponds to a specific element within an XML file—such as a product name and its price or names and addresses for a set of business cards (**Figure 1.16**).

A

```
<?xml version="1.0" encoding="UTF-8" standalone="yes"?>
<businesscards>
<Card>
<!-- contents of Dave McCoy  -->
      <employeeName>Dave McCoy</employeeName>
      <employeePosition>Director of Marketing</employeePosition>
      <employeeAddressln1>5034 SE 44th Avenue</employeeAddressln1>
      <employeeAddressln2>Portland, Oregon 97543</employeeAddressln2>
      <employeePhone>503-248-9876 direct</employeePhone>
      <employeeEmail>dave@metafusiontraining.com</employeeEmail>
</Card>

<Card>
<!-- contents of Gabriel Powell  -->
      <employeeName>Gabriel Powell</employeeName>
      <employeePosition>Senior Training Director</employeePosition>
      <employeeAddressln1>25 NW 23rd Place, Suite 6-122</employeeAddressln1>
      <employeeAddressln2>Portland, Oregon 97210</employeeAddressln2>
      <employeePhone>503-515-5404 direct</employeePhone>
      <employeeEmail>gabriel@metafusiontraining.com</employeeEmail>
</Card>

<Card>
<!-- contents of Jeremy Cantrell  -->
      <employeeName>Jeremy Vantrell</employeeName>
      <employeePosition>Sales Associate</employeePosition>
      <employeeAddressln1>25 NW 23rd Place, Suite 6-122</employeeAddressln1>
      <employeeAddressln2>Portland, Oregon 97210</employeeAddressln2>
      <employeePhone>503-248-9876 direct</employeePhone>
      <employeeEmail>jeremy@metafusiontraining.com</employeeEmail>
</Card>

<Card>
<!-- contents of Dale Erwing  -->
      <employeeName>Dale Erwing</employeeName>
      <employeePosition>Trainer</employeePosition>
      <employeeAddressln1>5131 Buffalo Ave. #20</employeeAddressln1>
      <employeeAddressln2>Sherman Oaks, CA 91423</employeeAddressln2>
      <employeePhone>310-795-8943 cell</employeePhone>
      <employeeEmail>dale@metafusiontraining.com</employeeEmail>
</Card>
</businesscards>
```

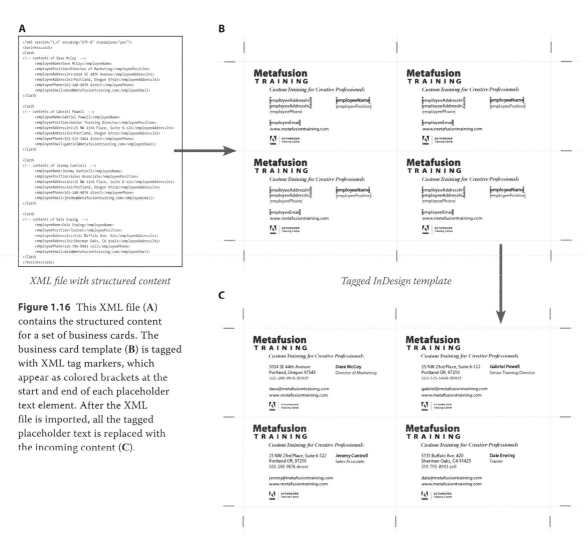

XML file with structured content

B

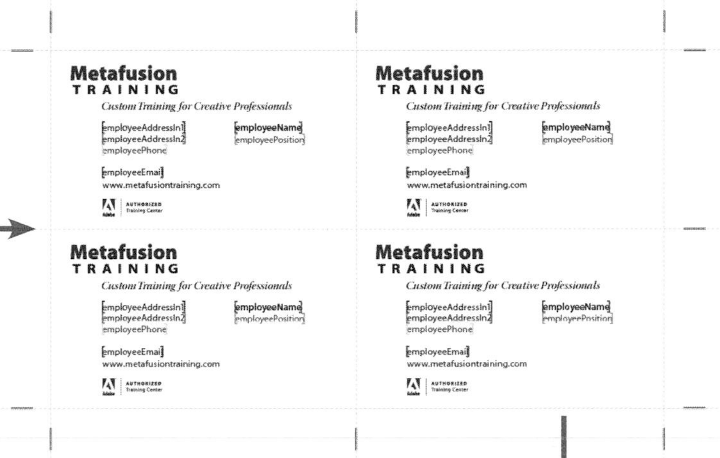
Metafusion
TRAINING
Custom Training for Creative Professionals
employeeAddressln1
employeeAddressln2
employeePhone
employeeName
employeePosition
employeeEmail
www.metafusiontraining.com
AUTHORIZED Training Center

Tagged InDesign template

C

Metafusion
TRAINING
Custom Training for Creative Professionals
5034 SE 44th Avenue
Portland, Oregon 97543
503-248-9876 direct
Dave McCoy
Director of Marketing
dave@metafusiontraining.com
www.metafusiontraining.com
25 NW 23rd Place, Suite 6-122
Portland OR, 97210
503-515-5404 direct
Gabriel Powell
Senior Training Director
gabriel@metafusiontraining.com
25 NW 23rd Place, Suite 6-122
Portland OR, 97210
503 248 9876 direct
Jeremy Cantrell
Sales Associate
jeremy@metafusiontraining.com
5131 Buffalo Ave. #20
Sherman Oaks, CA 91423
310 795 8943 cell
Dale Erwing
Trainer
dale@metafusiontraining.com

Final document

Figure 1.16 This XML file (**A**) contains the structured content for a set of business cards. The business card template (**B**) is tagged with XML tag markers, which appear as colored brackets at the start and end of each placeholder text element. After the XML file is imported, all the tagged placeholder text is replaced with the incoming content (**C**).

When you import the XML file, InDesign merges the content into the placeholder frames automatically and repeats the layout arrangement for each of the corresponding elements it finds. The incoming content also takes on the formatting that was applied to each placeholder.

It's possible to automate the production of many types of publications—from a simple price list to a set of business cards and even a large catalog. The only requirement is that you need an XML source file and a design with a predictable structure. The good news is that you do not need extensive knowledge of XML to successfully use it in InDesign.

Custom Scripts

With InDesign's scripting support, you can automate repetitive tasks, such as drawing frames, placing images, and formatting text. Scripts can perform a multitude of tasks, from applying styles to automating an entire publishing system. In fact, any action that can change a document or its contents can be scripted. Scripting also plays an integral role in XML-based workflows.

InDesign supports the use of AppleScript, JavaScript, and VBScript. It's possible to create your own scripts or run scripts that other people have created (**Figure 1.17**).

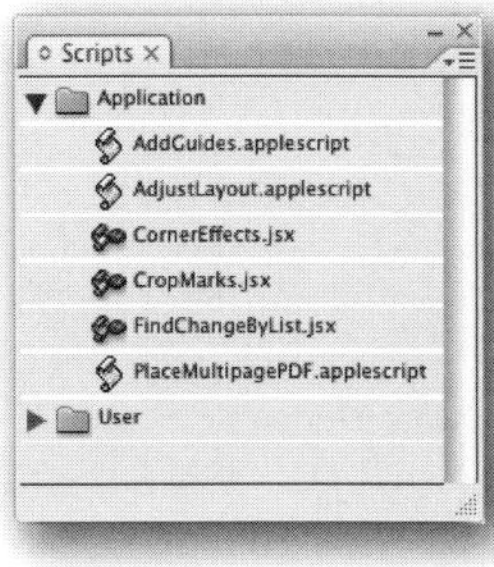
Scripts
Application
AddGuides.applescript
AdjustLayout.applescript
CornerEffects.jsx
CropMarks.jsx
FindChangeByList.jsx
PlaceMultipagePDF.applescript
User

Figure 1.17 The Scripts panel displays the scripts that are located in the Scripts folder. You can double-click a script to run it.

Scripts Folder Locations

When you create or receive a script, place it in the Scripts folder so that it shows up in the Scripts panel. Here is the location for each operating system:

- **Mac OS:** Users/[*username*]/Library/Preferences/Adobe InDesign/[*version*]/Scripts
- **Windows XP:** Documents and Settings\[*username*]\Application Data\Adobe\InDesign\[*version*]\Scripts
- **Windows Vista:** Users\[*username*]\AppData\Roaming\Adobe\InDesign\[*version*]\Scripts

2

Seven Principles of Great Template Design

GREAT TEMPLATES ARE CREATED THROUGH A CAREFULLY PLANNED COMBINATION of individual tools and technologies. Like a machine, all of the various parts work so well together that when using it, everything seems to be operating from a single intelligence.

To succeed in perfecting your page production machine, it's important to understand some of the foundational principles that support the creation of quality templates. Use the seven principles covered in this chapter to guide the decisions you make throughout the template construction process.

Know Your Tools

As graphic designers, your first instinct is to focus on the visual aspects of a project. Your training has been centered on how best to present a message, and your professional strengths lie in the creation of inventive layouts. Consequently, you often fail to concentrate on honing your production skills, which are analytic in nature and don't necessarily come easy to you. Now that you're learning how to design templates, you must embrace the full range of tools and technologies that InDesign provides.

When designing a publication intended for one-time use, the specific tools and methods you use to produce it aren't that important. As long as you create the desired results, you can get away with a poorly executed layout. However, when constructing templates, it's essential that you take a much more strategic approach to page layout and employ the most effective use of each tool available.

During the template-building process, you'll be frequently challenged and sometimes confused about the right tool or strategy to use. With a deeper understanding of the tools, including knowledge of their capabilities and limitations, you'll be able to make the most informed decisions in any given situation.

Design with a Goal in Mind

Any experienced designer will tell you there's nothing worse than a project without goals. It's like trying to paint the entire expanse of the night sky. What part of it do you paint? As creative professionals, you like lots of room to be creative, but without clearly defined limits, there's really not a problem to solve.

All successful and innovative template design is created in conjunction with a clearly defined set of objectives. No template project can begin without first defining its design and workflow requirements. After the specifications have been defined, the overall template design process will go smoothly—without wasting valuable time and money.

Consider a template that has been thrown together with little thought. No doubt there will missing elements, because there wasn't clear direction from the beginning. The wrong tool will probably be used in a particular solution, because the workflow requirements were not previously clarified. Most of all, the template will be poorly organized, harder to implement, and almost impossible to manage. You'll be left with a template that isn't fully functional and involves a lot of production time—defeating the very purpose of the template.

Speed Is a Priority

Well-built templates are built for speed. They eliminate the stress of repetitive formatting and automate routine tasks as much as possible. While constructing a template, continually ask yourself: Is there a better or faster way to create this? How can I bring this layout together in fewer steps?

Many of InDesign's tools are designed to work together. For example, by setting up a nested style, you can apply a character style in the same click that you apply a paragraph style. In addition, making a paragraph style part of an object style's definition allows you to apply the paragraph style at the same time you apply the object style. If the paragraph style also contains a nested style, you'll be combining three tools into one. What would have taken you three steps to produce you can now create with just one simple click.

As you become more familiar with InDesign's toolset, you'll discover new and better ways to reduce the number of steps it takes to produce a document. The templates you design will employ the smartest production strategies and will avoid manual labor whenever possible.

At times, you may not find a better or faster way to produce a particular layout. If so, consider modifying the design, if possible, to make it easier to create. Sometimes all it takes is changing one element to drastically speed up production.

Design for Ease of Use

The best templates pull together a variety of individual tools and technologies to create a coherent production experience. They are well thought out, organized, and highly intuitive. Any designer should be able to start a new document based on your template and begin working without having to first overcome a steep learning curve.

Always look for ways to make your template easier to use. For example, use clear, concise, and consistent naming conventions. And don't create too many style sheets, color swatches, layers, or master pages. Otherwise, the template can become unwieldy and make designers work harder to find what they need. It also helps to create a high-quality style guide that specifies exactly how to use your template.

These are just a few examples of how you can create efficient templates. Throughout this book, you'll be given countless tips on optimizing your templates for ease of use.

Employ Good Production Practices

A poorly constructed template leads to sloppy results. Consider the principle of least effort. This theory states that users will tend to utilize the most convenient method available to them. Most designers would rather use what you provide to them as a starting point instead of re-creating a layout themselves, even if it means they have to work a bit harder to produce a publication.

In other words, the way you construct the individual elements of a template determines how others will produce a publication based on it. So, it's imperative that you employ good production practices when constructing a template. Anyone using your template should be productive and be able to avoid any printing issues and other costly mistakes. This entire book is dedicated to teaching you excellent production techniques and will guide the choices you make throughout the development of your templates.

Continually Test and Explore Other Solutions

While constructing a template, incrementally test your work as you go. Although you'll be conducting a final test upon completion of the template, don't wait until the very end to examine your work. You could miss out on a valuable opportunity to improve each solution as you build it.

Testing gives you firsthand experience of what it will be like to produce a document with your template. As you test, decipher where improvements can be made and explore other options and solutions. You'll find that testing helps to transform the solutions you've come up with into better and more productive results.

Experienced designers spend a significant amount of time fine-tuning their templates, because they know their efforts will be more than repaid in time saved later, and in the final appearance of a finished publication.

Choose Between Flexibility and Rigidity

How rigid or flexible should your template be? The answer to this question depends on your specific workflow and design requirements, because every publication is different.

Flexible templates are structured to serve a variety of design choices. They don't lock you into one particular format, yet they can still save you a lot of setup time. For example, if you're creating a template for a publication that allows a lot of creative freedom, you might want to set up the template with just one or two master pages, a simple layout grid, and a few style sheets. Such a template can save layout and revision time while giving your document a consistent design and plenty of creative flexibility.

Rigid templates, on the other hand, are precisely constructed to reproduce a predictable and consistent layout, such as a catalog or price list. They contain highly structured master pages, a well-defined grid system, and an assortment of style sheets. They often even utilize custom scripts, Data Merge, or XML technology to automate production. Such templates are the most productive, because they can significantly reduce, if not completely eliminate, redundant tasks. They also require the most forethought and planning, and are certainly more difficult to construct.

In many situations, your template will lie somewhere between both extremes. It should be flexible enough to accommodate several design variations, yet rigid enough to automate redundant formatting whenever a layout follows a predictable pattern.

3

Step-by-step Approach to Designing Templates

NOW THAT THE CONCEPT OF TEMPLATES AND THE PRINCIPLES OF THEIR DESIGN have been thoroughly defined, it's time to learn the steps involved in designing a template. For your template to be successful, it must follow a clear path of development. Although this can be a rigorous process, the payoff is well worth the time and effort.

Designing a template is much like designing anything else. The project's objectives are established first. Then a preliminary mock-up layout is developed. After that, the actual template is constructed and then thoroughly tested to ensure everything functions as anticipated. Finally, the template can be implemented into a live production workflow.

This chapter walks you through each step in the template design process and forges a path toward the successful completion of any template.

Step 1: Define Your Objectives

They key to successful template design is starting with a clearly defined set of objectives. Before constructing any template, you must step back and gather as much information as possible that will influence the choices made during its construction. After you've outlined the project's objectives, the template can be optimally constructed to serve its intended purpose, and the subsequent phases in the design process should run smoothly. Even just a few hours of planning can save weeks of development time.

Three essential requirements need to be taken into consideration: design requirements, workflow requirements, and printing requirements.

Design Requirements

You need to be intimate with the publication's design for which you're constructing a template. If the design is still a work in progress, it's better to wait until it has been approved before constructing the template, or you'll be wasting valuable time and effort. The more specific the definition of the design, the more directed your efforts can be at designing a complete template.

When gathering design requirements, start with the obvious. Look at the overall page format and determine its dimensions, orientation, and arrangement (single-page or spreads). Notice how the margins and columns are set up across different layout variations. Then move on to identify the textual content and ascertain the formatting applied to each element, including the typeface, size, leading, color, word spacing, and so on. Also, identify all the graphical content, including illustrations, images, charts, and tables. Determine the formatting applied to each one and establish rules for cropping, scaling, and positioning. If the publication contains advertisements, note all the possible sizes and arrangements.

Look for other special design requirements that need to be considered. Does the publication call for a table of contents or index? Is the publication printed in multiple languages? If so, what elements of the design change from one language version to the next?

Identify any other information that influences or limits your layout choices. Does the template need to be flexible enough to allow for different design options? Or, should the template impose more structure?

Overall, you want to gain a sense of what is required to produce each element in the publication. Each publication is unique, so make sure you account for everything.

Workflow Requirements

Anything that affects the sequence of assembly is a workflow requirement. Gather any special requirements that have an effect on the way the template is constructed. Although it's not possible to predict every situation, here's a list of some common factors to consider:

- **In what order will the various design elements be produced?** The answer to this question helps you effectively organize the template, making it easier to produce the publication the template is designed for. For example, by knowing the order in which style sheets will be applied, you can optimize their organization by placing frequently used styles toward the top of the list and collecting them into style groups. The same goes for setting up master pages, object libraries, and color swatches. Name and organize them in a way that makes them easier to locate as you need them.
- **Are multiple designers producing the publication?** If so, you might need to break up the publication into separate InDesign documents and create a book file to collect the documents together and keep the page numbers, style sheets, swatches, master pages, and other items in sync. It's also necessary to create a book file when producing long documents, such as books and catalogs.
- **Are other designers using an older version of InDesign?** If so, you are restricted by the tools you use, since you'll need to utilize tools that are compatible with the older version. Tools such as InDesign CS3's new transparency effects, table and cell styles, frame fitting options, and text variables are not compatible with InDesign CS2.
- **Are there elements that must be produced with Photoshop or Illustrator?** If so, consider the use of native file formats, which have many benefits that other file formats don't have. All the layer information is preserved, so you can control the visibility of individual layers within InDesign. Transparency is preserved, so you can import a graphic without first having to flatten it. It's also easier to edit a graphic and quickly update the modified link.
- **Does the publication utilize transparency effects?** If the publication uses drop shadows, gradient feathers, or other transparency effects, you'll need to be aware of this when constructing the template to make sure the final document will be properly flattened when printing. For example, since type can interact with transparent objects in unexpected ways, it's common practice to create an extra layer for textual elements that is located above all the layers containing transparent objects and effects.

- **Is the publication printed in multiple languages?** When more than one language in a document exists, you might set up different paragraph and character styles with language-specific settings and the appropriate language dictionary for each language. Also, consider the use of layers to keep the different language content separate, which facilitates production and printing.
- **Will the publication be automated with Data Merge, XML, or another technology?** Templates that employ an automated solution have special setup requirements. So, it's important to know well in advance whether or not your publication will be automated.
- **Will the final content be repurposed for use in another form, such as on a Web site or mobile device?** If so, consider using InDesign's XML tools in your template solution. Or if you plan to export the final content directly to an XHTML document, you'll need to carefully set up your template to ensure the most optimal export results.

Printing Requirements

It's especially important to determine the publication's printing requirements, because they have a big affect on the decisions you make during the template construction process. Also, knowing this information ahead of time allows you to significantly minimize, if not totally eliminate, possible printing problems down the road. Talk with your print service provider about anything you need clarification on. To get you started, here are some common requirements to take into account:

- **Color.** Does the publication call for spot colors, process colors, or both? You don't want to use spot colors if the publication doesn't use them. Although this seems obvious, you'll be surprised how often a spot color sneaks its way into a document.

  If the publication is intended for RGB output only, such as a PDF download from a Web site, you'll want to create RGB swatches and remove CMYK swatches from the Swatches panel. It's also a good idea to specify the Document RGB color space in the template so that colors of transparent objects are properly blended. Choose Edit > Transparency Blend Space > Document RGB.

  If the publication will be printed in grayscale, your job is even easier. Just make sure that any images and graphics you'll be importing are in grayscale format so the printing process can be accelerated.

- **Color Management.** Will your template be used in a specific color-managed workflow? If so, make sure the template's color management settings are properly configured.
- **Fonts.** Determine which fonts the publication uses and make sure there are no problems with the font files, such as incomplete PostScript fonts and protected fonts, which have license restrictions and cannot be embedded in PDF or EPS files. Also, make sure the fonts are properly licensed, installed, and activated.
- **Bleed.** Do images print to the edge of the page? If so, you'll need to specify the appropriate bleed settings in your template.
- **Resolution.** Consider the medium of final distribution and determine the appropriate resolution for all the images that will be imported. Commercial printing requires a resolution within the range of 150 ppi to 300 ppi, depending on the press and screen frequency being used. Desktop printing requires a resolution within the range of 72 ppi to 150 ppi.

Step 2: Create a Mock-up Layout

Having gathered as much information as possible in terms of design, workflow, printing, and any other consideration that should be taken into account, you're prepared to create a mock-up layout.

A mock-up layout is a preliminary design that accurately represents the size, arrangement, and formatting of every graphical and textual element to be included in a publication. It also clarifies the project requirements and serves as the model from which the template is constructed.

To create a mock-up layout, build a detailed sample document that contains the entire range of elements composing the publication's design. At this point you should not be concerned with setting up the page framework, master pages, object libraries, color swatches, styles sheets, or other template elements. You'll do that in the next step. It's also not necessary to build a complete publication. Just be sure to include a sample of each page design and any possible layout variations. Do your best to make sure all elements are accounted for. While creating the mock-up, continually draw on the project's objectives and use them to shape its construction.

■ **Tip:** You can quickly generate dummy text by placing your cursor into a text frame and choosing Type > Fill With Placeholder Text. By default, the text is based on the Lorem Ipsum text that designers have been using for decades. If the Caps Lock key is held down, InDesign uses random words from an oration by Cicero.

The time and energy you spend at this stage of development is an investment that will repay you many times throughout the duration of the template construction process.

Step 3: Construct the Template

After you've clearly defined your project's objectives and created a detailed mock-up layout, you're ready to embark on the actual construction of the template. Most of what remains now is attention to detail and intelligent application of InDesign's various tools and technologies.

While constructing the template, continually remind yourself that no detail is too small to consider. Think of each aspect of the project as a decision point and an opportunity to improve the template. Don't just use the first tool you think of to create a particular element. Explore the possibilities. This is the best time to work through different ideas and strategies—before you implement the final template.

There are two approaches you can take to create a template:

- Convert the existing mock-up layout into a template. Depending on how complete the mock-up is, you might just finish building the template using the same document. However, if the mock-up you created is more of a "rough sketch," it's easier to use the second approach.
- Create a whole new document and use the mock-up layout as a model for constructing the template. The more complex the publication's design, the more likely it is you'll use this method to ensure the best results.

Decide on which method is most appropriate for your circumstances and follow the subsequent steps to construct the template. This is just an overview of the entire process. The remainder of this book is dedicated to explaining the fine details involved in each step.

1. **Set up the template's framework.** Establish the page format first, which includes the page dimensions, orientation, and arrangement. You might also need to add a bleed area and slug area. After that, create a layout grid, which is composed of margins, columns, and ruler guides. The baseline grid and document grid might also be utilized if necessary. Make sure to set up the margins, columns, and ruler guides on the master page. If your template requires more than one layout grid, be sure to create master pages for each one. See Chapter 7, "Setting Up the Framework of a Template."
2. **Set up the master pages, object libraries, and layers.** These tools work together to organize the template and make it more effective. Begin with the master page(s) by placing any recurring design elements and placeholder frames into the correct position on the layout grid. Next, create

an object library and add frequently used design elements to it. Then set up any necessary layers so that you can organize the template into logical parts. See Chapter 8, "Setting Up Master Pages, Libraries, and Layers."

3. **Create all necessary color swatches.** By creating swatches, you can globally control the color in a document, which facilitates design consistency and productivity. The type and number of swatches you create is dictated by the publication's design requirements. See Chapter 9, "Working with Color."
4. **Generate style sheets.** Use the sample content in your mock-up layout as a basis for creating all the necessary character styles, paragraph styles, object styles, cell styles, and table styles. If you're constructing the template in a different document, you can copy the sample content from the mock-up layout into the template document so you don't have to re-create the content you've already formatted. See Chapter 10, "Formatting Type and Generating Style Sheets;" Chapter 11, "Formatting Frames and Generating Object Styles;" and Chapter 12, "Formatting Tables and Generating Table and Cell Styles."
5. **Set up long document elements.** If the template you're designing will be used to construct a long document such as a book, magazine, or catalog, you might need to set up a table of contents style, generate paragraph styles that automatically format multilevel lists, or define the template's footnote options. See Chapter 13, "Adding Support for Long Documents."
6. **Finalize the template.** Once the template is constructed, it's important to clean it up and prepare it for production. This involves removing unnecessary elements, preventing potential printing problems, and specifying the template's default settings. See the section in Chapter 14, "Finalizing Your Template."

Step 4: Test the Template

This step is perhaps the most critical, because it has a direct impact on productivity and budget. By testing your template, problems are addressed ahead of time, preventing time-consuming inefficiency and costly mistakes.

To test the template, create a new document based on it and walk through a live production scenario. Keep in mind, there might always be a few unforeseen details that are overlooked, but they will be significantly minimized if you employ good testing methods. See the section in Chapter 14, "Testing Your Template," for a detailed guide to testing a template.

Step 5: Implement the Template

When your template is finalized and tested, you can package all of its elements together and put the template to use. Part of this step is automated with InDesign's package utility. Other elements must be manually collected, such as object libraries and print preset files. See the section in Chapter 14, "Implementing Your Template," for detailed information on implementing your template.

4

Getting Your Feet Wet with InDesign CS3 Templates

YOU DON'T HAVE TO BE A SEASONED DESIGNER TO CREATE HIGH-QUALITY WORK. With InDesign's sizeable collection of predesigned templates, great things are possible. They provide a convenient starting point for typical documents, because they are preset with a layout that includes layout grids, master pages, style sheets, and text and graphics placeholders. Simply open the templates and use them as a basis to build and inspire your own template design—saving countless hours of labor.

This chapter is designed to give you a complete overview of the template design process. By learning how to modify the predesigned templates that ship with InDesign, you'll learn to apply the process taught in Chapter 3, "Step-by-step Approach to Designing Templates." If you're not experienced in taking a template project from beginning to end, this is a great way to start.

Exploring the Templates that Ship with InDesign

A

CS3
ID

Phone Book.indd

B

CS3
ID

Phone Book.indt

Figure 4.1 InDesign CS3 document files use the extension .indd (**A**); InDesign CS3 template files use the extension .indt (**B**).

InDesign CS3 ships with 78 predesigned templates, which are divided into 18 categories ranging from forms, flyers, and newsletters to magazines, newspapers, and catalogs. These templates are saved in a distinct file format called an InDesign CS3 template. There are two ways to identify a template file: by looking at its file extension (.indt) or its icon (**Figure 4.1**).

Opening Templates

In general, you open templates the same way you open other documents. However, when you open a template file, InDesign opens a new untitled version of the template, not the original. This gives you a useful starting point and allows you to use templates again and again for different publications.

Here are a few ways to start a new document from a template file:

- Locate a template file and double-click its icon.
- Choose File > New > Document from Template. This takes you to Adobe Bridge and to the folder that contains the templates that ship with InDesign. Locate a template file and double-click its icon.
- You can also choose to use InDesign's welcome screen (**Figure 4.2**). If you've already closed the welcome screen or chosen not to show it at startup, you can access it again by choosing Help > Welcome Screen. From the welcome screen, choose From Template. This takes you to Adobe Bridge and to the folder that contains the templates that ship with InDesign. Locate a template file and double-click its icon.

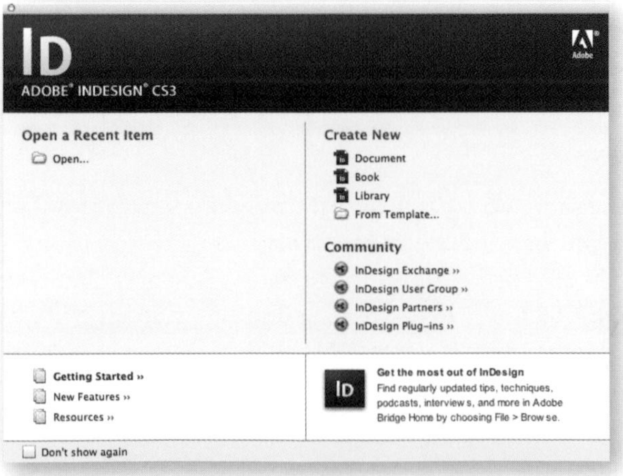
ID
ADOBE® INDESIGN® CS3
Adobe
Open a Recent Item
Open...
Create New
Document
Book
Library
From Template...
Community
InDesign Exchange »
InDesign User Group »
InDesign Partners »
InDesign Plug-ins »
Getting Started »
New Features »
Resources »
Get the most out of InDesign
Find regularly updated tips, techniques, podcasts, interviews, and more in Adobe Bridge Home by choosing File > Browse.
Don't show again

Figure 4.2 InDesign's welcome screen. From here, you can open recent documents, create new ones, learn about InDesign, and gain quick access to online resources.

Location of InDesign CS3 Templates

InDesign's predesigned templates are found in different locations depending on your operating system:

- **Windows:** C:\Program Files\Common Files\Adobe\Templates\InDesign
- **Mac OS:** /Library/Application Support/Adobe/Templates/InDesign

Editing Templates

You can make changes to an original template—without having to create a new one—by opening the original file instead of an untitled version of it. To open an original template file, choose File > Open and locate a template file. Before you click Open, select Original (Windows) or Open Original (Mac OS) (**Figure 4.3**).

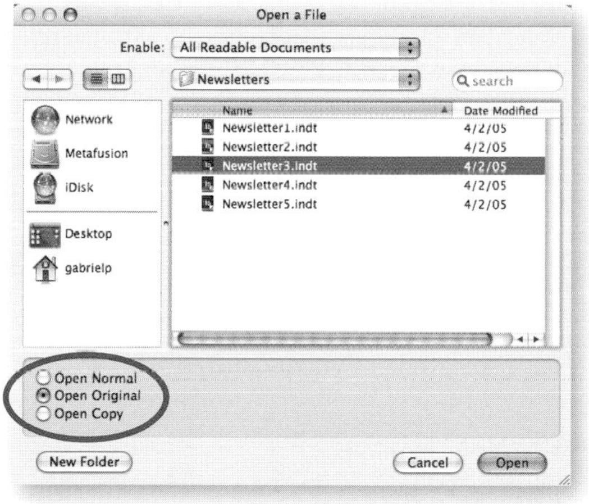
Open a File
Enable: All Readable Documents
Newsletters
search
Network
Metafusion
iDisk
Desktop
gabrielp
Name
Date Modified
Newsletter1.indt 4/2/05
Newsletter2.indt 4/2/05
Newsletter3.indt 4/2/05
Newsletter4.indt 4/2/05
Newsletter5.indt 4/2/05
Open Normal
Open Original
Open Copy
New Folder
Cancel
Open

Figure 4.3 The Open a File dialog. When opening a template file, you can choose to open it normally as an untitled version, the original file, or a copy of it.

Saving Templates

You save templates the same way you save regular documents. The only difference occurs when you save a document. To save any document into the template file format, choose File > Save As and specify a filename and location. Next, choose InDesign CS3 template for Save as Type (Windows) or Format (Mac OS) and save the document (**Figure 4.4**).

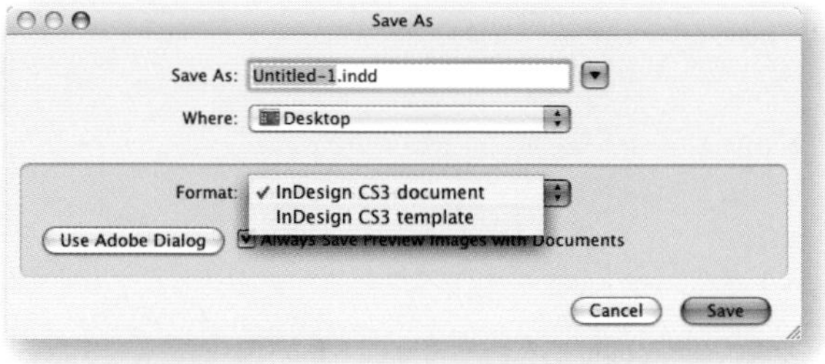
Save As
Save As: Untitled-1.indd
Where: Desktop
Format: ✓ InDesign CS3 document
InDesign CS3 template
Use Adobe Dialog
Always Save Preview Images with Documents
Cancel
Save

Figure 4.4 InDesign's Save As dialog.

When saving a template, be sure to save a preview image of it. This allows you to more easily identify the template later on when you are using Adobe Bridge to browse a collection of templates. Thumbnail previews of template files include a JPEG image of each page in the template. You can even control the size of the preview to suit your needs. For example, the Extra Large 1024x1024 option enables you to easily scan the contents of a page, making it even easier to be identified among a rather large collection of templates. Keep in mind that previews increase both file size and the time it takes to save a document.

There are two ways to save a preview image with a document:

- You can enable the option in the File Handling preferences (Preferences > File Handling). From here, you can also control the default preview size (**Figure 4.5**).
- You can enable the option in the Save As dialog. Enabling the option here also enables the option in Preferences and vice versa.

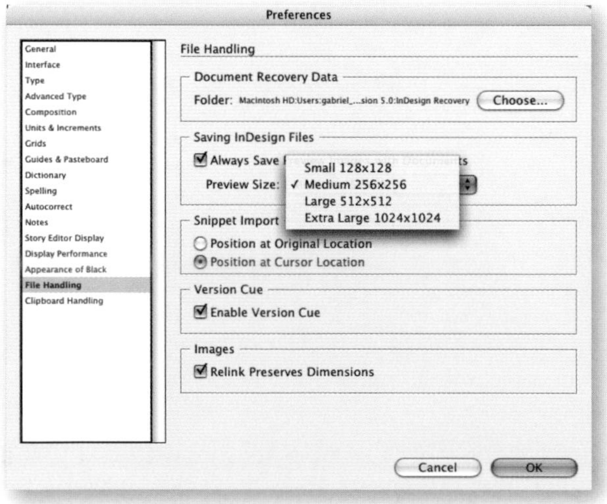
Preferences
General
Interface
Type
Advanced Type
Composition
Units & Increments
Grids
Guides & Pasteboard
Dictionary
Spelling
Autocorrect
Notes
Story Editor Display
Display Performance
Appearance of Black
File Handling
Clipboard Handling
File Handling
Document Recovery Data
Folder:
Choose...
Saving InDesign Files
Always Save
Preview Size:
Small 128x128
✓ Medium 256x256
Large 512x512
Extra Large 1024x1024
Snippet Import
Position at Original Location
Position at Cursor Location
Version Cue
Enable Version Cue
Images
Relink Preserves Dimensions
Cancel
OK

Figure 4.5 You can choose from four preview sizes when saving a preview image with a document.

Customizing Predesigned InDesign Templates

While InDesign's predesigned templates can save time, their layout is already predetermined and may not fully suit your specific design requirements. As a designer, you want to set your work apart from everyone else. It's almost always essential to personalize a predesigned template before it is ready to use. Sometimes, it's nothing more than modifying a few colors. At other times, it may require significant rework, such as exchanging fonts or revising the underlying layout grid.

The following steps will guide your template project from planning to design and on through to successful implementation. These guidelines are not hard and fast, but they serve as a basis for selecting and customizing the predesigned templates that ship with InDesign.

Step 1: Select a Template

Decide which of the predesigned InDesign templates best targets your project's goals and then open and explore its layout. If the template is suitable as is, the next step is simple—begin producing pages. However, in many cases, you'll need to move, add, subtract, and modify elements until the template meets your goals. In this case, you'll need to create a mock-up layout and then revise your chosen template based on its parameters.

EXPLORING THE TEMPLATE'S LAYOUT

When you first open one of InDesign's predesigned templates, there is always a period of discovery where you learn how the template has been built. It's critical that you take some time to explore its layout before creating a mock-up layout or revising the template.

Templates with a lot of design detail can look a bit confusing at first, but once you take a closer look, you'll find that a good deal of thought has gone into how each element is formatted and positioned. As you become familiar with the template, you'll be able to more easily add, remove, and modify its various design elements as you deem appropriate for your project.

The following steps will help you become familiar with any template:

1. **Check the template's dimensions and framework.** Select and open a template, and then choose File > Document Setup to check its dimensions. Find out if the page size and orientation will meet your design requirements. Click the More Options button to check the bleed and slug settings as well (**Figure 4.6**).

■ **Tip:** The templates that ship with InDesign vary in the measurement system they use. Many use inches, whereas others use points, or even millimeters. You can quickly switch to your favorite measurement system by right-clicking (Windows) or Control-clicking (Mac OS) each ruler and choosing the units you want from the context menu. This will change the measurement system used for the rulers, dialogs, and panels.

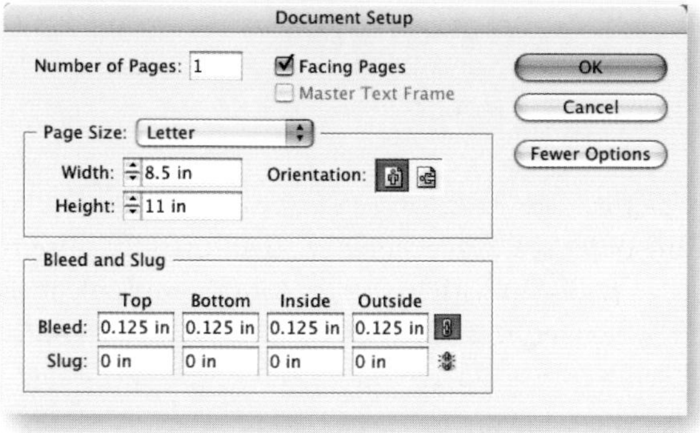
Document Setup
Number of Pages: 1
Facing Pages
Master Text Frame
OK
Cancel
Fewer Options
Page Size: Letter
Width: 8.5 in
Height: 11 in
Orientation:
Bleed and Slug
Top
Bottom
Inside
Outside
Bleed: 0.125 in 0.125 in 0.125 in 0.125 in
Slug: 0 in 0 in 0 in 0 in

Figure 4.6 The Document Setup dialog displays the page size and orientation as well as the bleed and slug specifications. If you do not see the Bleed and Slug option, click the More Options button.

● **Note:** If the page guides are not visible, make sure that you are in Normal screen mode by choosing View > Screen Mode > Normal. If you still don't see them, the guides may be hidden. Choose View > Grids & Guides > Show Guides to view the guides in the document.

Next, check the use of margins and columns. Keep in mind that InDesign lets you define separate margin and column settings on a page-by-page basis. Therefore, you'll need to navigate to each master page in the template to ensure that the settings conform to your design requirements. You can identify margin guides by their magenta color and column guides by their violet color. To verify the exact margin and column dimensions, select a master page or spread, and then choose Layout > Margins and Columns. The Margins and Columns dialog opens and displays the dimensions (**Figure 4.7**). If you have two or more pages selected, you may notice that the fields are blank where the pages don't share the same settings.

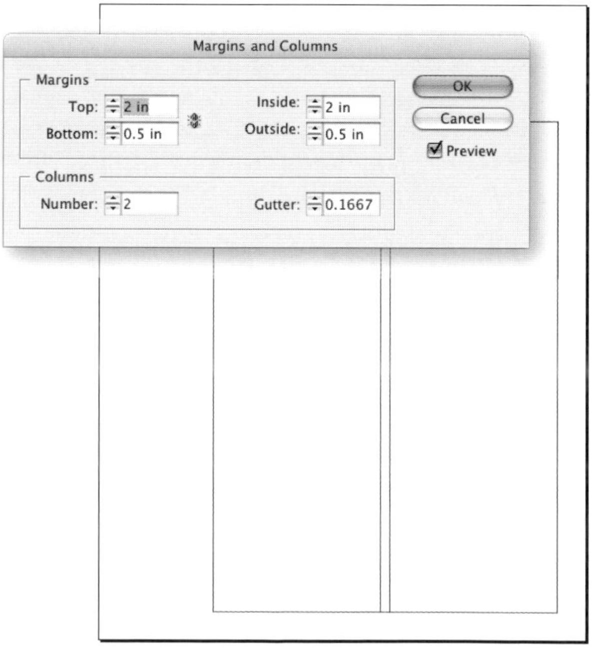
Margins and Columns
Margins
Top: 2 in
Bottom: 0.5 in
Inside: 2 in
Outside: 0.5 in
OK
Cancel
Preview
Columns
Number: 2
Gutter: 0.1667

Figure 4.7 The Margins and Columns dialog displays the margin and column specifications for the selected page—or range of pages—in the Pages panel.

It's also a good idea to find out if there are any other structural elements in use, such as horizontal and vertical ruler guides, or even a baseline grid. Determine their purpose on the page and decide whether or not they serve your design goals.

2. **Explore the master pages.** The master pages contain the layout grid as well as all the repeating objects and placeholders that form the design. A number of the templates that ship with InDesign contain multiple master pages. So, it's important to explore each master page and its elements.

   You've already checked the structural elements, so you now need to examine all the repeating objects and placeholder elements. Note the use and position of background art, logos, dividing rules, headers, footers, and any other elements on the page.

   Next, activate the Type tool and select the text within each of the placeholder text frames. Note the font, type size, leading, alignment, and other typographical attributes in use.

3. **Explore the sample pages.** Each of the templates that ships with InDesign contains at least one fully featured sample page and often even more. A sample page demonstrates the design by showing some of its possible variations. This is achieved by basing each sample page on one of the master pages and then building on that foundation by adding text and graphic placeholders to indicate the position and style of each design element. Explore each of these elements.

   Activate the Selection tool and choose Edit > Select All. This selects every frame on the active spread and shows you the size and boundaries of each frame. Note the size and position of any text and graphics frames. Considerable thought has gone into the position and size of each one. Depending on the type of document you're looking at, a sample page may consist of any number of frames. Some are made up of a single frame, whereas others contain several overlapping frames that are stacked upon each other. At first this can be quite confusing, but after taking a closer look, you'll be able to make more sense of it.

   Notice that several frames have not been included in the selection. They can easily be identified, because their bounding box did not become visible when the selection was made (**Figure 4.8**). These frames are master items and can only be modified on the master page—unless you override them. Take note of them and keep in mind which objects are coming from a master page and which objects belong to the document page.

● **Note:** If the frame edges are not visible, make sure that you are in Normal screen mode by choosing View > Screen Mode > Normal. If you still don't see them, the frame edges are currently hidden. Choose View > Show Frame Edges to view the frame edges in the document.

■ **Tip:** To click through and select individual stacked objects on a page, hold down the Command/Ctrl key while clicking where the objects are overlapping. With each click, InDesign selects the next object down in the stack. You can then use the arrow keys to move the selected object. If you don't release the mouse button upon selecting an object, you can drag it with your mouse to a new location.

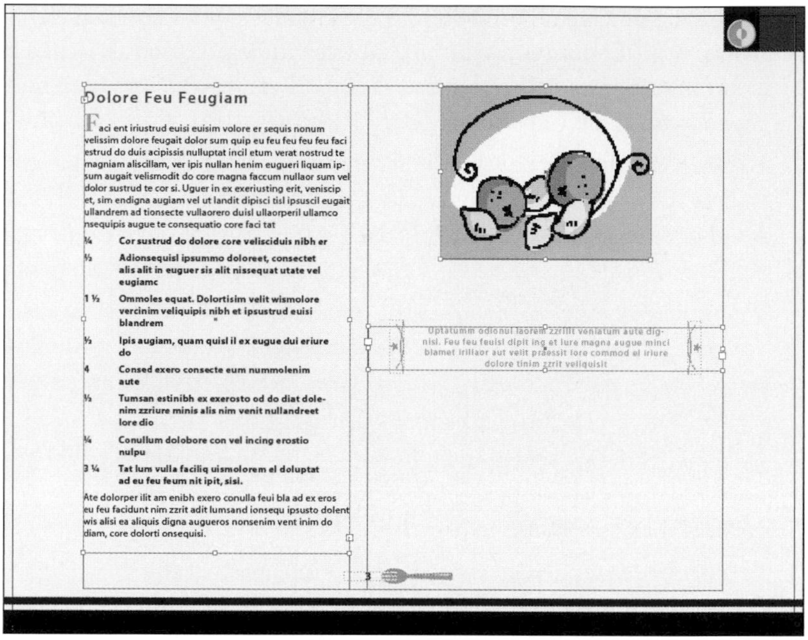
Dolore Feu Feugiam

Figure 4.8 Some frames on this page have not been included in the selection, because they are master items, which can be identified by their dotted border.

● **Note:** If you cannot select a frame and it is not a master item, then it is on another layer that has been locked. To unlock a layer, click the lock icon to the left of its name in the Layers panel.

Select each frame and note its fill color, stroke weight, transparency effects, and any other formatting in use. Then activate the Type tool and select the text within each of the placeholder text frames. Note the font, type size, leading, alignment, and all other typographical attributes in use.

4. **Examine the style sheets.** Each template that ships with InDesign includes well-defined style sheets. Since they control most of the sample page formatting, it's important to examine each style sheet and find out where and how it is being used. Then determine if it serves your design goals or if it needs to be modified.

■ **Tip:** It's important to show the hidden characters while examining text and style sheets. It helps to distinguish where paragraphs begin and end. It also reveals where spaces, tabs, and the ends of stories are located. Choose Type > Show Hidden Characters.

Begin with the paragraph and character styles. Activate the Type tool and select each typographic element, such as headlines, subheads, and the body copy. Find out if a paragraph style or character style has been applied to your selection. Keep track of the name of each style and where each is being applied. This information will serve you later when you start customizing the template.

Some paragraph styles contain nested styles. There is no immediate way of detecting when a nested style is in use. But you can make a good guess by looking for paragraphs that start with one type of formatting and end with another type of formatting. For example, a numbered list may have a sans-serif font applied to the number and a serif font applied to the main text. If you suspect a nested style is in use, open the paragraph style and choose Drop Caps and Nested Styles from the list of categories. If it contains a nested style, you'll see it in the list (**Figure 4.9**).

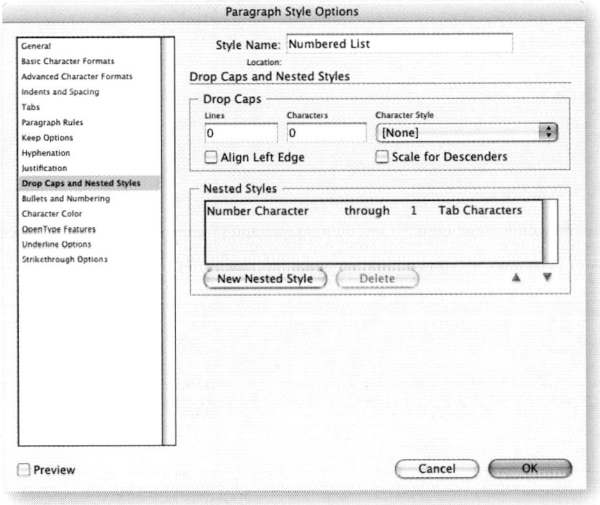
Paragraph Style Options
General
Basic Character Formats
Advanced Character Formats
Indents and Spacing
Tabs
Paragraph Rules
Keep Options
Hyphenation
Justification
Drop Caps and Nested Styles
Bullets and Numbering
Character Color
OpenType Features
Underline Options
Strikethrough Options
Style Name: Numbered List
Location:
Drop Caps and Nested Styles
Drop Caps
Lines
Characters
Character Style
0
0
[None]
Align Left Edge
Scale for Descenders
Nested Styles
Number Character
through
1
Tab Characters
New Nested Style
Delete
Preview
Cancel
OK

Figure 4.9 If a paragraph style contains a nested style, you can view it in the Paragraph Style Options dialog.

Next, find out if any object styles are in use. Look in the Object Styles panel to determine if any styles—other than the default styles—are present. If so, note the formatting they define and where they are being used within the sample pages. Only a few of the templates that ship with InDesign have object styles built into them. See template Photobook 2.indt for an example.

5. **Look for other elements in use.** After exploring a template's basic elements, look for additional elements that may be a part of it. Open the Layers panel and take note of any layers that are in use. Find out if any Table of Contents Styles have been created by choosing Layout > Table of Contents Styles. Open the Bookmarks panel, Hyperlinks panel, and States panel to see if and where any interactive elements may be in use. If you are working with one of the Data Merge templates that ship with InDesign, take note where each data-field placeholder element sits on the page (**Figure 4.10**).

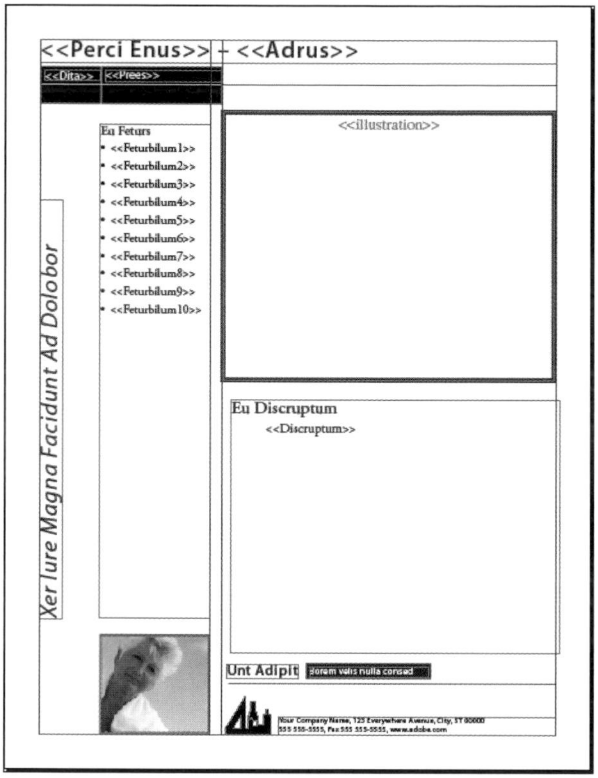
<<Perci Enus>>
<<Adrus>>
<<Dita>>
<<Prees>>
Eu Feturs
<<Feturbilum1>>
<<Feturbilum2>>
<<Feturbilum3>>
<<Feturbilum4>>
<<Feturbilum5>>
<<Feturbilum6>>
<<Feturbilum7>>
<<Feturbilum8>>
<<Feturbilum9>>
<<Feturbilum10>>
<<illustration>>
Xer Iure Magna Facidunt Ad Dolobor
Eu Discruptum
<<Discruptum>>
Unt Adipit
Lorem velis nulla consed

Figure 4.10 This template contains data-field placeholders for the various text elements on the page and one for the illustration. See Flyer DataMerge.indt within the collection of templates that ship with InDesign CS3.

Step 2: Create the Mock-up Layout

Now that you're more familiar with your chosen template, you can create a mock-up of your design. Since you are modifying a predesigned template, much of the work has already been done for you. However, this step can be more or less challenging depending on the significance of changes that need to be made. If you plan on making just a few, simply move on to the next step and revise the template wherever necessary. But if you plan on making a lot of changes, you'll need to create a mock-up layout before revising the template.

Keep in mind that you are not concerned with creating or modifying master pages, style sheets, or even swatches at this stage. You'll do that in the next step. Your goal here is to shape the sample content that represents your design. This shouldn't be too difficult since every one of the templates that ship with InDesign contain detailed sample pages, which provide a great starting point for developing your mock-up layout.

Here are some guidelines to help you transform your selected template's sample pages into a fully functional mock-up:

- **Delete all unnecessary elements.** Begin by removing any elements that you don't plan on using in your template, including placeholder frames, extra typographic elements, ruler guides, and any other objects that exist on a master page or document page that you don't need. This clears the way for new elements and makes it easier to revise the template with your own content.
- **Adjust the document dimensions.** Define the page format by making any necessary changes to the overall page size and orientation. This is also the time to specify a bleed, or even a slug area, if your intended design calls for it.
- **Adjust the document framework.** Modify the position of the margins, columns, and ruler guides that shape the framework of your intended design, and be specific. If your target design calls for a two-column grid in some cases and a five-column grid in other cases, you'll need to create a separate sample page for each layout. Also, be strategic in your use of ruler guides by positioning them where they actually serve a purpose. This makes your template clear and easy to use.
- **Define all text formatting.** Every typographic element must be clearly defined and represented in the mock-up layout. This includes all headlines, body text variations, bulleted and numbered lists, captions, folios, and so on. It's likely that the template you've selected already contains most of the required elements. Therefore, all you need to do is add any new elements to finalize the mock-up.
- **Define all frame formatting.** Every permitted graphical element and its formatting characteristics must be clearly defined and represented. This includes background art, dividing rules, text wrap requirements, color and drop shadow specifications, and so on. If your design uses tables, you'll need to represent their formatting as well.
- **Define the size and arrangement of each element.** A mock-up layout is never complete until the size and arrangement of each permitted element is clearly and accurately represented. No detail is too small to leave out.

■ **Tip:** If the left and right pages in a spread require a separate margin and column setup, select each page independently and then modify the settings.

■ **Tip:** You can easily swap a font being used throughout a document with another font by choosing Type > Find Font. You can update the style sheets as well by enabling the Redefine Style When Changing All option at the bottom of the Find Font dialog.

Step 3: Revise the Template

Having built a mock-up layout that accurately represents your design and meets your preliminary goals, you are now prepared to modify and complete your chosen template. The bulk of the work was taken care of when you created the mock-up. Your job now is to simply translate the design into a production-viable template by revising the master pages, style sheets, color swatches, and any additional elements that your template may require.

UPDATE THE MASTER PAGES

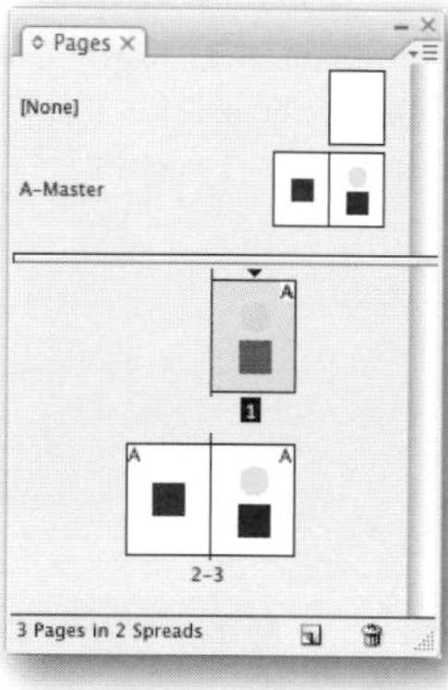
Pages
[None]
A-Master
1
2-3
3 Pages in 2 Spreads

Figure 4.11 The Pages panel provides thumbnail representations of the content for each page, allowing you to locate a page in the Pages panel instead of flipping through pages in the document window.

■ **Tip:** You can enlarge the master page icons in the Pages panel to more easily view their thumbnail previews. Choose Panel Options from the Pages panel menu and then select a larger icon size for the master pages.

Start with the master pages since they contain the template's framework, repeating objects, and placeholder elements. Study your mock-up carefully, determine which elements should be placed on the master page, and then revise the master pages. Here are two approaches you can take:

- **Copy objects to an existing master page.** If there are just a few objects that need to be added to an existing master page, simply take them from the mock-up layout. The easiest way to do this is to select the objects to be relocated and choose Edit > Cut. Then go to the master page and choose Edit > Paste in Place to paste the objects into the original X,Y position they were copied from. As objects are placed, the thumbnail representations of the master pages are updated to indicate their position. This feedback is useful for making sure that you are placing each object onto the correct master page (**Figure 4.11**).
- **Convert a mock-up spread to a master page.** If you've made significant changes to the original design or you've added a new layout option to it, you may find it easiest to just convert an existing mock-up spread to a new master page in one step. To do this, select a spread in the Pages panel and choose Save As Master from the Pages panel menu. You can also drag an entire spread from the Pages section to the Masters section. Once the new master page is created, any objects on the original spread become part of it.

  After creating the new master page, it's a good idea to edit its name, prefix, and other options before doing anything else. Select the master spread and choose Master Options for [*master spread name*] from the Pages panel menu. Choose a prefix and name. If the original mock-up spread used a master page, the newly created master will be based on the original spread's master. If you don't want to base this master on another, choose [None] for the Based on Master option (**Figure 4.12**).

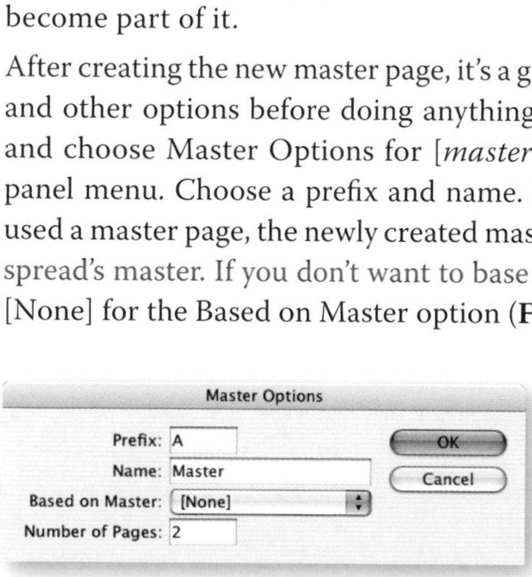
Master Options
Prefix: A
Name: Master
Based on Master: [None]
Number of Pages: 2
OK
Cancel

Figure 4.12 The Master Options dialog.

While revising the master pages, continually look for areas of improvement. Keep sight of your original design objectives and develop masters that facilitate the fast and efficient production of pages wherever possible. Here are some measures you can take to make master pages more production friendly:

- **Choose a prefix and name** that identifies the intended purpose of the master page.
- **Create a parent master and base other master pages on it** when you need master pages that require slight variations on one main design. A change to the parent master updates all of the child masters in one click, preventing you from having to edit each master page separately.
- **Delete any unused master pages** and all unnecessary master items.
- **Delete images from placeholder graphics frames,** leaving just the empty frames. This speeds up production, because you won't have to override the master frames on document pages before you can import images into them. Instead, you'll be able to position the loaded graphics icon above a master frame and click it to place the image and override the frame in a single click.
- **Apply frame fitting options to placeholder graphics frames** so that whenever new content is placed into them, the Fitting command is automatically applied. To set a fitting option, select a frame, choose Object > Fitting > Frame Fitting Options, and then specify the options.
- **Apply style sheets to master items.** Apply them to folios, chapter headings, frames with drop shadows, and so on.

● **Note:** Some options, such as Save As Master and Master Options, are not available in the Pages panel menu unless an entire spread is selected. To select a page spread, double-click the page numbers below the spread icon. To select a master spread, double-click its name.

CREATE AN OBJECT LIBRARY

If there are several elements in your design that repeat often but not consistently enough to be placed on a master page, add them to an object library. This keeps your frequently used objects organized and easy to locate when you need them.

Here are a few tips for increasing the productivity of object libraries:

- **Fill out all the item information** for each library item. This makes it easier to identify and search for an item by its name, by object type, by creation date, or by its description.
- **Change the view of an object library to List view.** This view allows more items to fit within the panel and makes it much easier to locate an item by its name and object type. To change the view, choose List View from the Object Library panel menu.

- **Place a library item at its original X,Y coordinates** by selecting it in the panel and then choosing Place Items(s) from the Object Library panel menu. This method is particularly useful when a library item needs to be positioned into the same X,Y position each time you add it to a page.

SET UP LAYERS

Each of the predesigned templates that ship with InDesign include layers to keep specific items such as artwork, text, and guides on separate layers. By using multiple layers, you can create, edit, and manage objects on each layer without affecting other objects in the layout. For example, you can use layers to display alternate design ideas or to maintain different language versions of an advertisement for the same layout.

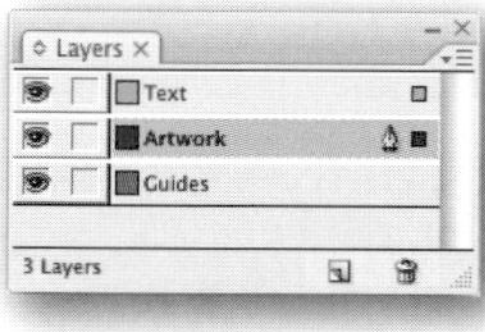
Layers
Text
Artwork
Guides
3 Layers

Figure 4.13 The layer that is currently being edited can be identified by the pen icon next to its name in the Layers panel. When an object is selected, a colored dot appears to the right side of the layer list to indicate which layer it is on.

When revising InDesign's predesigned templates, it is extremely important that you maintain constant awareness of which layer you are editing (**Figure 4.13**). Otherwise, you can unintentionally mess up their organization. Here are a few tips for working with layers:

- **Assign a color to every layer.** This makes it easier to identify the layer that each object belongs to. When you assign a color to a layer, each object on that layer displays the assigned color in its bounding box, selection handles, text wrap boundary (if a text wrap is used), frame edges, text ports, and hidden characters.
- **Move master items to higher layers.** You can use layers to specify how objects on a master page overlap objects on a document page. If you want a master item to appear in front of objects on the document page, move it to a higher layer.
- **Hide layers.** You can hide layers to prevent them from being edited or printed. Hiding layers can also be useful for hiding alternate versions of a document or to make it easier to edit parts of a document at a time.
- **Merge layers.** If you want to minimize the number of layers in your template, you can merge layers together without deleting any objects. Select two or more layers in the Layers panel and choose Merge Layers from the Layers panel menu. When layers are merged, objects from all the selected layers are moved to the target layer—as indicated by the pen icon. Only the target layer remains in the document.

● **Note:** When you merge layers that contain a mix of page objects and master items, the master items move to the back of the resulting merged layer.

DEFINE COLOR SWATCHES

Create and name color swatches for any color that is consistently used throughout your design. All permissible colors are then predefined ahead of time, allowing you to consistently apply color when producing pages.

The Swatches panel lets you create and name colors, gradients, or tints, and quickly apply them to elements in a document (**Figure 4.14**). Here are two methods for creating swatches based on the colors being used in your mock-up layout:

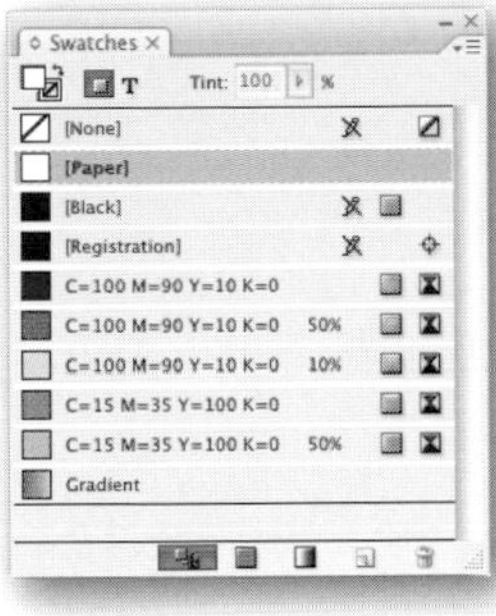

Figure 4.14 The Swatches panel.

- **Add unnamed colors to the Swatches panel.** When using the Color panel or Color picker to apply color, these colors are not automatically added to the Swatches panel and will be unnamed. If your mock-up layout contains a large number of unnamed colors, choose Add Unnamed Colors from the Swatches panel menu to quickly add them to the list.
- **Create a swatch based on the color of an object.** If you don't want every unnamed color added to the Swatches panel or if there are just a few colors that need to be added, you can manually create color swatches instead. Select the object that contains the color you want to add, and then drag the Fill box or Stroke box from the top of the Swatches panel into the list of color swatches.

After you've created all the necessary color swatches, optimize the swatch list to make it as easy to use as possible. You can enhance your template's productivity in two ways:

- **Rename the color swatches.** By default, color swatches are named according to their CMYK or RGB components, making it difficult to find a color among a large list of swatches. You can switch off this option and add your own name by double-clicking a swatch in the Swatches panel to open its options. Deselect the Name with Color Value option and name the swatch according to its intended purpose.
- **Rearrange the list of colors in the Swatches panel.** By placing frequently used colors at the top of the list in the Swatches panel, they become easier to locate when you need them. To relocate a swatch, drag it to another location within the Swatches panel. A thick line will appear, indicating where the swatch will drop when you release the mouse button.

● **Note:** If your template uses an image that contains spot colors, the colors are automatically added to the Swatches panel. You can apply these swatches to objects in your document, but you cannot rename or delete them.

UPDATE THE CHARACTER AND PARAGRAPH STYLES

Study your mock-up layout carefully and determine which styles need to be updated or if any new styles still need to be created.

Place your cursor into each text element in the mock-up layout and determine which style is applied to them. If the wrong style is currently applied, go ahead and apply the correct style. If the correct style is already applied, look for a plus sign (+) next to the style name (**Figure 4.15**). If one appears, it indicates an override, which means that some of the formatting within the selected text is not

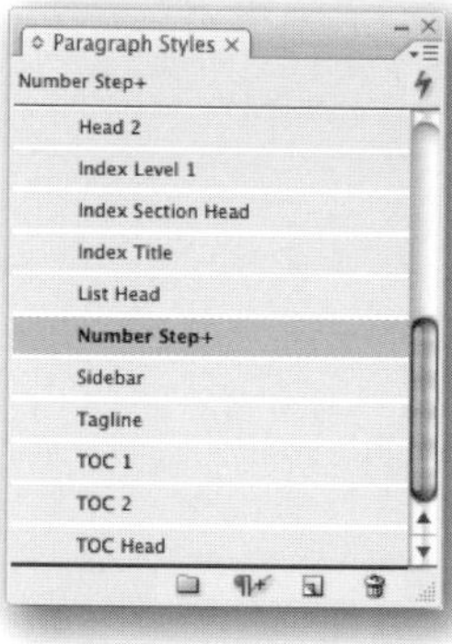
Paragraph Styles
Number Step+
Head 2
Index Level 1
Index Section Head
Index Title
List Head
Number Step+
Sidebar
Tagline
TOC 1
TOC 2
TOC Head

Figure 4.15 Some of the formatting within the selected text is not part of the Number Step style definition.

part of that style's definition. It's likely that most of the styles were overridden when you created the mock-up.

If a style has been overridden, you need to update the style with any new formatting so that your revised template contains accurate paragraph and character style definitions. Here are two approaches for updating styles:

- **Redefine a style to match the selected text.** Select the text that is formatted with the style you want to redefine, and then choose Redefine Style from the Paragraph Styles or Character Styles panel menu. As the style is updated, all the text to which it has been applied will also be updated.
- **Define a new style.** At times, you may find it easier to just delete the current style and re-create a new one based on your mock-up's current formatting. Delete the style first. Since it is being used in the document, you will be asked to replace it with another style before it can be deleted. Select [No paragraph style] when deleting a paragraph style or [None] when deleting a character style. Also, be sure to select the Preserve Formatting option to keep the formatting of text to which the style is applied (**Figure 4.16**). After the style is deleted, base the new style on the formatting of the existing sample text by selecting that text before you create the new style.

Figure 4.16 The Delete Paragraph Style dialog (**A**) and the Delete Character Style dialog (**B**). You can choose to replace a deleted style with an existing style or to remove it without replacing it.

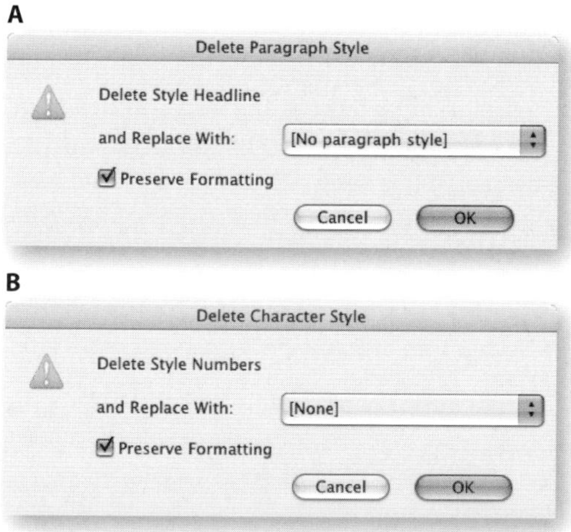
A
Delete Paragraph Style
Delete Style Headline
and Replace With:
[No paragraph style]
Preserve Formatting
Cancel
OK
B
Delete Character Style
Delete Style Numbers
and Replace With:
[None]
Preserve Formatting
Cancel
OK

While creating or redefining styles, look for ways to increase their productivity. Here are a few ways you can enhance styles:

- **Choose a name** that identifies the intended purpose of the style.
- **Add keyboard shortcuts to frequently used styles.** To add a keyboard shortcut, double-click the style name to open its options and position the insertion point in the Shortcut field. Make sure Num Lock is turned on,

and then hold down any combination of Shift, Alt, and Ctrl (Windows) or Shift, Option, and Command (Mac OS) and choose a number from the numeric keypad. You cannot use letters or nonkeypad numbers for defining style shortcuts.

- **Rearrange the list of styles** to make them easier to locate when you need them. To relocate a style, drag it to another location within the Styles panel. A thick line appears, indicating where the style will drop when you release the mouse button.
- **Organize similarly used styles into style groups** to make them easier to locate and manage. This is particularly helpful when a template contains many styles. To create a style group, select the styles to be included, and then choose New Style Group from the Styles panel menu. Choose a name that identifies its intended purpose.

SET UP NESTED STYLES

Now that you've defined all the character and paragraph styles in your template, you can boost their productive power by setting up nested styles for paragraphs that have repetitive and predictable formatting. Nested styles are especially useful for numbered lists and lead-in text. To add nested styles to a paragraph style, double-click the paragraph style, and then click Drop Caps and Nested Styles. Choose New Nested Style and specify each of its options (**Figure 4.17**). You can set up as many nested styles as necessary.

A

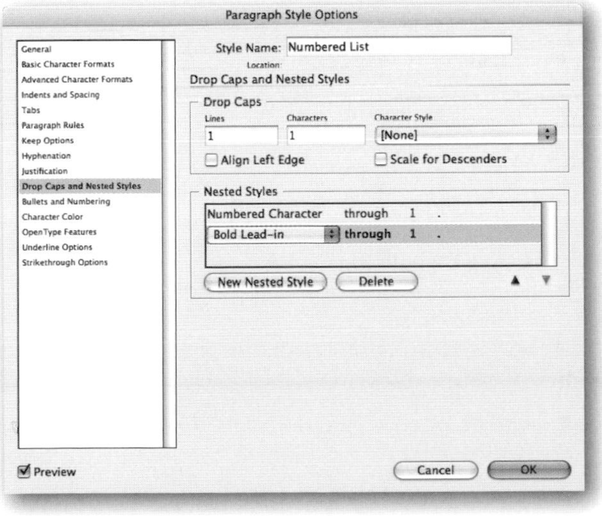
Paragraph Style Options
General
Basic Character Formats
Advanced Character Formats
Indents and Spacing
Tabs
Paragraph Rules
Keep Options
Hyphenation
Justification
Drop Caps and Nested Styles
Bullets and Numbering
Character Color
OpenType Features
Underline Options
Strikethrough Options
Style Name: Numbered List
Location:
Drop Caps and Nested Styles
Drop Caps
Lines
Characters
Character Style
1
1
[None]
Align Left Edge
Scale for Descenders
Nested Styles
Numbered Character through 1 .
Bold Lead-in through 1 .
New Nested Style
Delete
Preview
Cancel
OK

B

1. **Verate digna.** Facilla conum dio exer inci tate odipit velisim.
2. **Dolorem aut nibh.** Ip feuent la feugue consequ modiat.
3. **Ut ute consendio conse feu.** Faccum iure magnibh el inim.
4. **Nulla cor iriustrud te doluptat.** Volore veros do odipit augait nulla feuipissenim dolorem iuscilla ad do consequ.

Figure 4.17 This paragraph style contains two nested styles (**A**). As a result, Verdana Bold is applied through the number and first period and Adobe Garamond Pro Bold is applied through the lead-in text and second period (**B**).

If your template contains paragraphs that repeat a pattern of two or more types of formatting, you can take nested styles up another notch by setting them up to loop. A simple example would be to alternate bold and italic words in a paragraph (**Figure 4.18**). The repeating pattern continues infinitely even if you add or remove words in the paragraph. To loop through nested styles, do the following:

Figure 4.18 You can use looping nested styles to automatically alternate formatting throughout a paragraph.

Tatet *am* **volorero** *con* **venisl** *dolobore* **dolorer** *suscincing* **eugue** *velessequat* **loreetum** *alisi* **er** *sum* **duis** *dignis* **nullutat.** *Ut* **adignis** *nullandreet* **wisit** *nostiniam* **acilla** *conseniat* **velisim** *zzrillam,* **sit** *lam* **quam** *num* **eu** *facilla* **augiat** *ad* **mincin** *ulla* **faccum** *vero* **commolore** *dolenit* **prat** *iriliqui* **blam** *vel* **utpat.**

1. Add two or more nested styles to a paragraph style.
2. After all the nested styles have been added, create one more, choose [Repeat] from the Character Style menu, and then specify how many nested styles will be repeated. The other two options are fixed and cannot be modified.

CREATE OBJECT STYLES

Study your mock-up layout for repeating frame formatting. Look for items such as stroke weight, color, drop shadows, and text wrap. If you notice formatting that repeats often throughout the design, create object styles to significantly speed up the process of formatting frames during production (**Figure 4.19**).

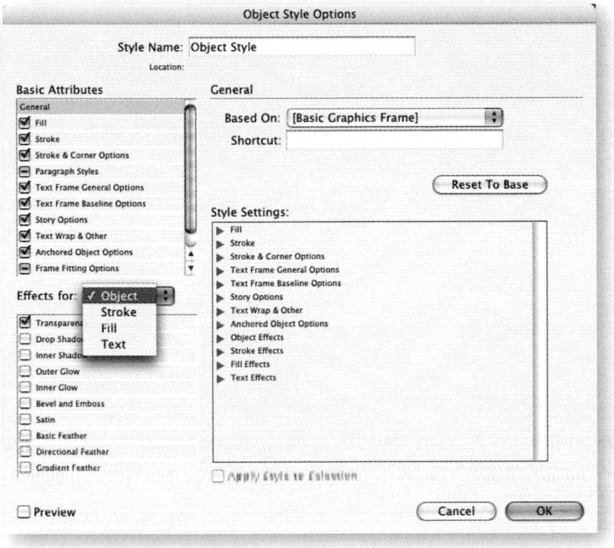
Object Style Options
Style Name: Object Style
Location:
Basic Attributes
General
Fill
Stroke
Stroke & Corner Options
Paragraph Styles
Text Frame General Options
Text Frame Baseline Options
Story Options
Text Wrap & Other
Anchored Object Options
Frame Fitting Options
Effects for: Object
Stroke
Fill
Text
Outer Glow
Inner Glow
Bevel and Emboss
Satin
Basic Feather
Directional Feather
Gradient Feather
General
Based On: [Basic Graphics Frame]
Shortcut:
Reset To Base
Style Settings:
Fill
Stroke
Stroke & Corner Options
Text Frame General Options
Text Frame Baseline Options
Story Options
Text Wrap & Other
Anchored Object Options
Object Effects
Stroke Effects
Fill Effects
Text Effects
Preview
Cancel
OK

Figure 4.19 The Object Style Options dialog. Object styles can contain many different types of formatting, making them a valuable production tool. When applying effects, choose an option from the Effects For menu to apply separate effects to an object, stroke, fill, or text.

While creating object styles, continually look for ways to improve them. Here are a few ways you can boost their productivity:

- **Name the object style** to identify its intended purpose.
- **Include the Paragraph Style category** in its definition to dramatically improve an object style's level of efficiency. When the object style is applied, the paragraph style is applied in the same click. Also, if the paragraph style includes any nested styles, they will be applied in that instance as well.
- **Add keyboard shortcuts** to frequently used object styles. To add a keyboard shortcut, double-click the style name to open its options and position the insertion point in the Shortcut field. Make sure Num Lock is turned on, and then hold down any combination of Shift, Alt, and Ctrl (Windows) or Shift, Option, and Command (Mac OS), and choose a number from the numeric keypad. You cannot use letters or nonkeypad numbers for defining style shortcuts.
- **Rearrange the list of object styles** to make them easier to locate when you need them. To relocate a style, drag it to another location within the Object Styles panel. A thick line will appear, indicating where the style will drop when you release the mouse button.
- **Organize similarly used object styles into style groups** to make them easier to locate and manage. This is particularly helpful when a template contains many object styles. To create a style group, select the object styles to be included, and then choose New Style Group from the Object Styles panel menu. Choose a name that identifies its intended purpose.

PREPARE THE TEMPLATE FOR PRODUCTION

Now that your template is finished, you need to clean it up and prepare it for production before you begin using it. While revising the template, it's likely that you generated quite a mess. This important last step in the revision process ensures that your template is clean and easy to use. When the template is ready for production, simply save it as an InDesign template file and begin the testing phase.

Here are some suggestions for preparing a template for production:

- **Eliminate sample elements.** Remove all the sample layout elements from the document. It may be best to just delete all the document pages and create new pages based on the clean master pages.
- **Override master items.** Override any master items that you will need immediate access to each time you begin a new publication. To override a master item, hold Ctrl-Shift (Windows) or Command-Shift (Mac OS), and then click the item (or drag to select multiple items). When you override a master item, its dotted bounding box becomes a solid line, indicating that it has been overridden.
- **Delete unwanted styles.** Delete any character, paragraph, and object styles you don't plan to use.
- **Set default styles.** Set the default styles for character, paragraph, and object styles. To do this, choose Edit > Deselect All. With nothing selected on the page, select the character and paragraph styles that should be the default style that is used each time the template is opened.

  There are two default object styles (**Figure 4.20**). To change the default style for text frames, choose Default Text Frame Style from the Object Styles panel menu, and then select an object style. To change the default style for unassigned frames, choose Default Graphic Frame Style from the Object Styles panel menu, and then select an object style.

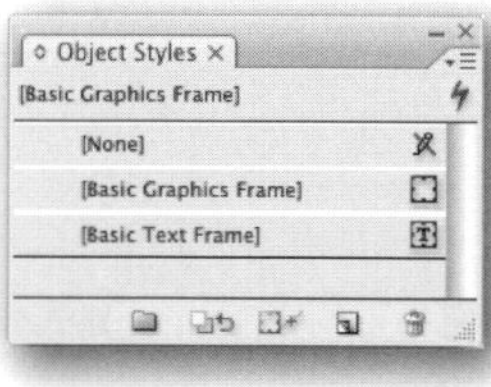
Object Styles
[Basic Graphics Frame]
[None]
[Basic Graphics Frame]
[Basic Text Frame]

Figure 4.20 Each default object style can be identified by the icon to the right of its name. The Text Frame icon marks the default style for text frames. The Graphics Frame icon marks the default style for unassigned frames.

Step 4: Test the Template

After you've revised your chosen template, simply walk through a live production scenario to test it. Use the testing principles covered in Chapter 14, "Preparing Your Template for Success," to guide you through the process and remember that no template is ever completed on your first attempt.

Step 5: Implement the Template

You're now ready to implement your template into a live production workflow. But before you do, there is still one more detail that you'll want to take care of before its final release.

To prepare your template for easier implementation, it's essential that you collect all of its supporting elements and save them, along with the template file, into one central folder. InDesign provides a handy package utility that makes it easy to do this. To package your template, choose File > Package (**Figure 4.21**).

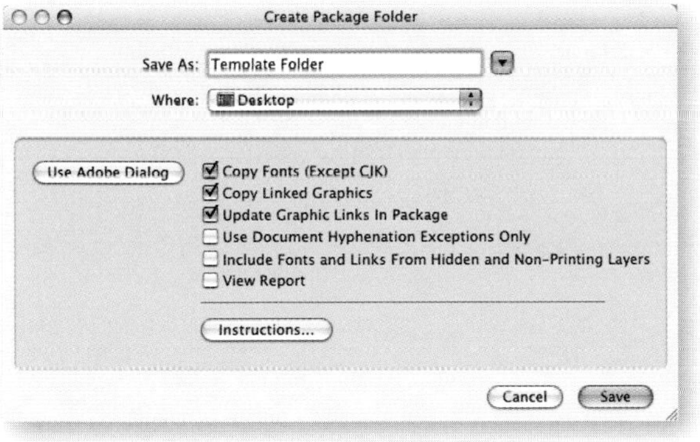
Create Package Folder
Save As:
Template Folder
Where:
Desktop
Use Adobe Dialog
Copy Fonts (Except CJK)
Copy Linked Graphics
Update Graphic Links In Package
Use Document Hyphenation Exceptions Only
Include Fonts and Links From Hidden and Non-Printing Layers
View Report
Instructions...
Cancel
Save

Figure 4.21 The Create Package Folder dialog lets you choose which elements to include in your package.

When you package a file, a folder is created that contains a copy of the InDesign document, any necessary fonts, linked graphics, and a customized report. This report includes a list of all used fonts, links, and inks required to print the document, as well as the print settings that were last saved with it (**Figure 4.22**).

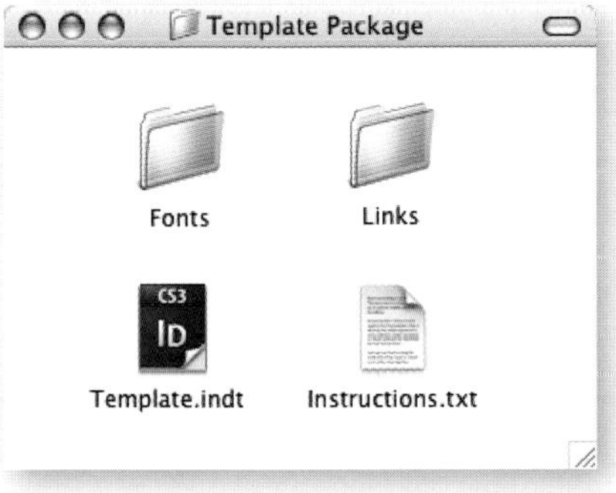
Template Package
Fonts
Links
CS3
ID
Template.indt
Instructions.txt

Figure 4.22 This folder is ready to implement into a live production workflow.

In addition to packaging any necessary fonts and linked graphics, there are a few other elements that you might consider adding to the package: object libraries, Adobe Swatch Exchange files, and any print presets. Since InDesign doesn't automatically package these elements for you, you will need to manually copy them to the package folder location.

Section 2

Setting Up InDesign to Do the Work

5

The Anatomy of a Frame

FRAMES ARE THE BASIC BUILDING BLOCKS THAT MAKE UP THE VARIOUS OBJECTS of an InDesign document. They determine the boundary, position, and dimensions for each object on a page. InDesign requires that all text, graphics, and other objects be contained within a frame. You might think of a layout as an organized collection of frames that hold all the content, from simple color-filled shapes to text and images. Although this may seem restricting at first, you will soon find that InDesign's frames are actually quite flexible.

It's important to understand the function of frames and the role they play in creating a layout. With a good understanding of frames you'll have more control over them. You'll be able to see past their limitations and will know how to set them up to most optimally serve a template. This chapter describes the composition of frames and shows you how to select and modify them using InDesign's most essential tools.

Understanding the Terminology

Let's begin with the terminology. An *object* is any printable element on a page or on the pasteboard. It may simply be a drawn path or an imported graphic, or it may be more complex, such as a group of frames. A *path* is a vector graphic, which is made up of mathematically defined lines and curves that create its geometric characteristics.

Paths are characterized by a fill and a stroke in addition to the anchor points, endpoints, and direction lines that define their shape (**Figure 5.1**). A path may be as simple as a line, circle, or rectangle, or it may become quite intricate. You can apply many types of formatting to a path, such as adding color to its fill or stroke, or adding a transparency effect to it. You can even edit the shape of a path by using drawing tools such as the Pen tool and Pencil tool.

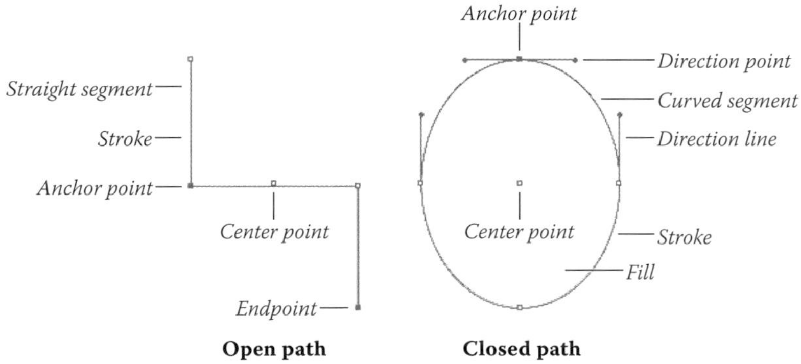
Straight segment
Stroke
Anchor point
Center point
Endpoint
Open path
Anchor point
Direction point
Curved segment
Direction line
Center point
Stroke
Fill
Closed path

Figure 5.1 Basic elements of a path.

Components of a Path

A path is made up of straight or curved segments, which are connected by anchor points. A path may be open (such as a line) or closed (such as a circle). Open paths contain endpoints at the beginning and end of the path. Direction lines determine the slope and height of a curved segment. The stroke is a path's outline and controls its formatting characteristics, such as color and line weight. The fill is the interior area of an open or closed path and controls its formatting characteristics. Each path displays a nonprinting center point, which marks the center of the path, but is not part of the actual path. It can be used to move the path and align it with other objects.

A *frame* is identical to a path except that it also serves as a container for text or graphics, or it may exist without any content. Empty frames serve as *placeholder frames*, which represent the size and position of the actual content that will eventually be imported (**Figure 5.2**). Paths and frames are essentially the same in that you can do anything to a frame that you can do to a path. The only difference is that a frame is a container version of a path. At any time, a frame can be used as a path, or vice versa.

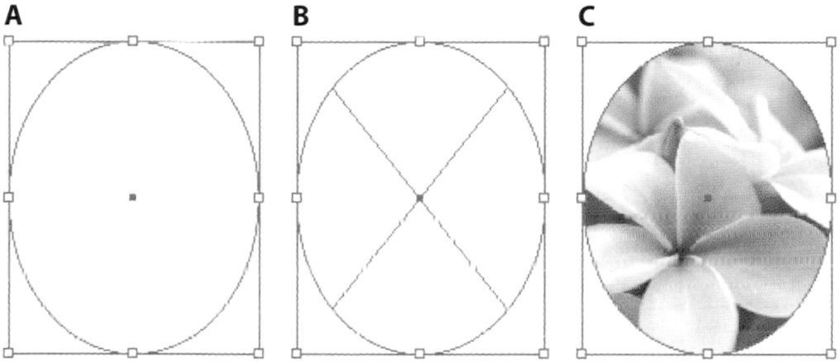
A
B
C

Figure 5.2 Paths and frames are identical except that frames function as containers for text or graphics. A frame can function as a path (**A**) or as a placeholder frame (**B**), or it may be filled with content (**C**).

Paths and frames can be combined together to form new shapes, or they may exist within other paths or frames to make them more manageable. For instance, when you want to keep a number of frames together, you can group them to treat them as one unit. Also, if you want a frame to move with a particular headline as it flows within text, you can anchor it to the headline within the text frame. This flexibility provides a wide range of design choices, making it easy to lay out a page and quickly modify it as necessary.

In addition, every object in InDesign is surrounded by a *bounding box*, which is used to perform general layout tasks, such as positioning, sizing, and duplicating objects. It is also used to track an object's horizontal and vertical dimensions as well as its X, Y position on a page. For drawn paths, the bounding box makes it easy to work with the entire object without accidentally modifying the anchor points that determine its shape. You can identify a bounding box by its rectangle shape and the eight large, hollow selection handles that exist along its perimeter. An additional point is in its center (**Figure 5.3**). The selection handles are used for resizing an object, and the center point is used for selecting and moving an object.

● **Note:** With rectangular objects, it can be difficult to tell the difference between the object's bounding box and the actual path of the object. A bounding box always displays eight large anchor points along its edge. A rectangular path always displays four small anchor points.

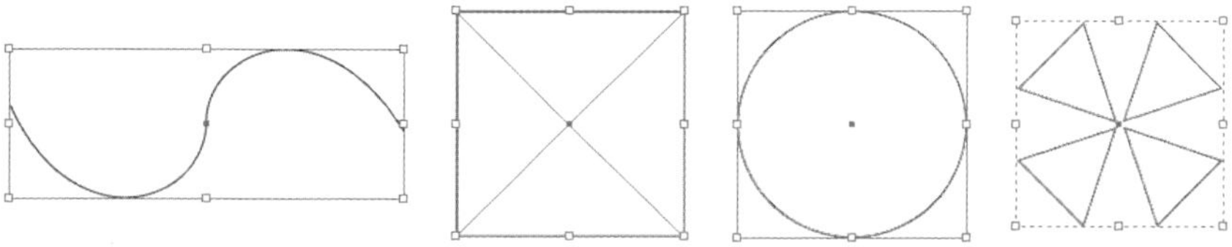

Figure 5.3 All paths, frames, and grouped objects have a bounding box. The bounding box of grouped objects appears as a dashed rectangle.

Three Types of Frames

● **Note:** Don't confuse a placeholder frame with an unassigned frame. Placeholder frames are empty text or graphic frames, whereas unassigned frames don't define any content at all—they are really just a path.

Now that you know the lingo, let's take a deeper look into the three types of frames available in InDesign. Each frame is defined by the type of content it contains. A *graphics frame* serves as a container for imported content, such as an image or logo. You can identify this frame by the nonprinting "X" within it. A *text frame* functions as a container for text. It marks the area to be occupied by text and determines how text flows through a layout. Text frames can be identified by the two large text ports on their upper-left and lower-right corners, which are used for linking text frames together. An *unassigned frame* is just a path with no defined content. Since it contains neither text nor a graphic, it is useful for borders and background colors. You can easily recognize unassigned frames, since they don't have text ports or an "X" (**Figure 5.4**). Once a frame has been created, InDesign allows you to easily convert it to one of the other frame types without having to re-create a new one.

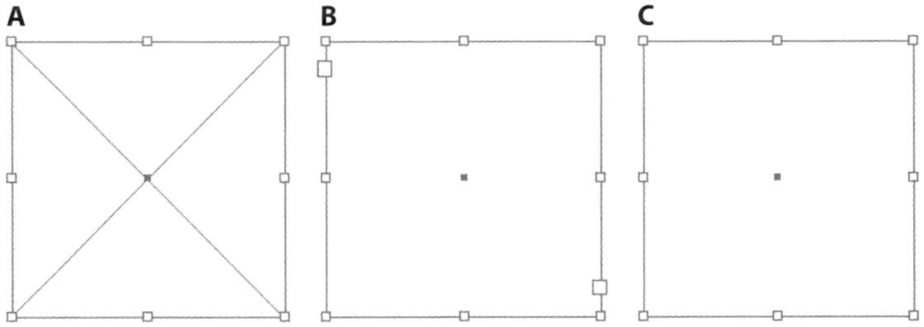
A
B
C

Figure 5.4 The three types of frames: (**A**) graphics frame, (**B**) text frame, (**C**) unassigned frame. To properly identify a frame, it must be selected.

Graphics Frame

● **Note:** If the frame edges and the "X" within graphics frames are not visible, make sure that you are in Normal screen mode by choosing View > Screen Mode > Normal. If you still don't see them, the frame edges are currently hidden. Choose View > Show Frame Edges to view the frame edges in the document.

InDesign offers a great deal of flexibility when it comes to working with graphics frames. From importing graphics to cropping and scaling, there is quite a range of available options. At first, it may take some time to get accustomed to all the possibilities.

This flexibility is due to the fact that all imported graphics consist of two connected parts. The graphics frame functions as a *container frame*, which contains *content*. The content is any imported graphic. If the graphics frame is empty, it doesn't have any content yet. To draw an empty graphics frame, use the Rectangle Frame tool, Ellipse Frame tool, or Polygon Frame tool.

It's important to understand that the content and its container frame are completely separate objects, each with its own bounding box (**Figure 5.5**). In fact, they can even be different sizes. You may have noticed this the first time you attempted to resize a graphic. As you dragged one of its handles, you expected the graphic to be resized as well, but only the container frame was resized. Simply dragging the frame of a graphic will either crop the graphic or leave empty space outside it. Although all this may seem confusing at first, you will become more comfortable with the process as your selection skills increase.

A
B

Figure 5.5 The container frame (**A**) is cropping the graphic. When the content is selected, you can see the complete boundary of the imported graphic (**B**).

SELECTING AND MODIFYING GRAPHICS FRAMES

Let's take a look at how the various parts of a graphics frame are selected and controlled. It may be difficult to discern between each part of a graphics frame at first, but once you begin selecting them, it becomes more obvious where one part ends and the other begins.

InDesign provides three essential tools for moving, scaling, cropping, and masking graphics—the Selection tool, Direct Selection tool, and Position tool (**Figure 5.6**). The tool that you use to select a graphics frame determines the kind of changes you can make to it. You can choose to use a combination of the Selection tool and Direct Selection tool, or you can use the Position tool instead. Although each method is slightly different, they both achieve the same results. After you've experimented with each method, choose the one that you feel most comfortable using. It's simply a matter of preference. Here's a detailed look at how you can use each tool when working with graphics frames:

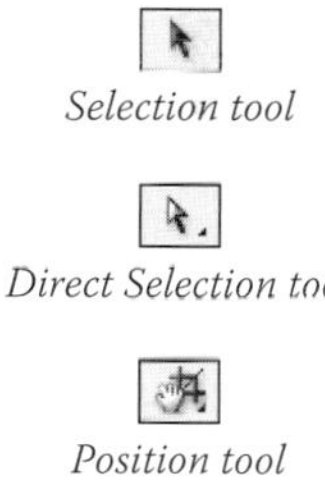
Selection tool
Direct Selection tool
Position tool

Figure 5.6 The three main tools used for working with graphics.

- **Selection tool:** Use the Selection tool to select a container frame and its content together as one unit. The bounding box of the container frame becomes visible, allowing you to crop the graphic or move it around on the page. To crop a graphic, drag one of the eight available selection handles that exist along the edge of the bounding box. To scale a graphic, hold down Ctrl (Windows) or Command (Mac OS) while simultaneously dragging one of the selection handles. The container frame and its content are scaled together. Add the Shift key to scale the graphic proportionally. To reposition a graphic, simply click and drag it to another location (**Figure 5.7**).

A
B

Figure 5.7 The container frame and its content are selected as a unit with the Selection tool (**A**). Drag the frame to reposition it. Drag a selection handle to crop the graphic (**B**).

■ **Tip:** To quickly select a container frame's content while the Selection tool is active, double-click a graphic to switch to the Direct Selection tool, and then click one more time to select the content. To switch back to the Selection tool and simultaneously select the container frame, double-click the graphic again.

- **Direct Selection tool:** Use the Direct Selection tool to select either the edge of a container frame or the content within it. When the content is selected, you see its bounding box. It will always be a different color from the container frame's bounding box, making it easier to identify. If you position the Direct Selection tool above a graphic, it automatically changes to the Hand tool. Use it to drag and reposition the graphic within the container frame. If you hold down the mouse button for a moment before you drag it, you'll see a dynamic preview of the graphic. Any part of the graphic that exists beyond the edge of its container frame will be ghosted back to help you visualize what is being cropped out. To scale content independently of its container frame, drag any one of its selection handles (**Figure 5.8**). To scale the content proportionally, hold the Shift key while you resize it.

A
B
C

Figure 5.8 The content is selected with the Direct Selection tool (**A**). Hold down the mouse button before you drag it to see a dynamic preview of the entire graphic (**B**). Drag a selection handle to resize the graphic within the container frame (**C**).

To select the edge of a container frame, select the perimeter of the viewable graphic with the Direct Selection tool. You will see the anchor points that define its shape. Select and move them when you want to reshape the container frame. You can also use the Pen tool in conjunction with the Direct Selection tool to create an irregular shape out of it. The graphic will become masked wherever the path overlaps it. If the graphic has a clipping path active, you can modify it with the Direct Selection tool as well (**Figure 5.9**). In fact, you can select and modify any path—such as lines, custom drawn paths, and frame edges—with the Direct Selection tool (**Figure 5.10**).

A
B

Figure 5.9 The edge of the container frame is selected with the Direct Selection tool (**A**). If a clipping path is active, use the Direct Selection tool to select and edit its shape (**B**).

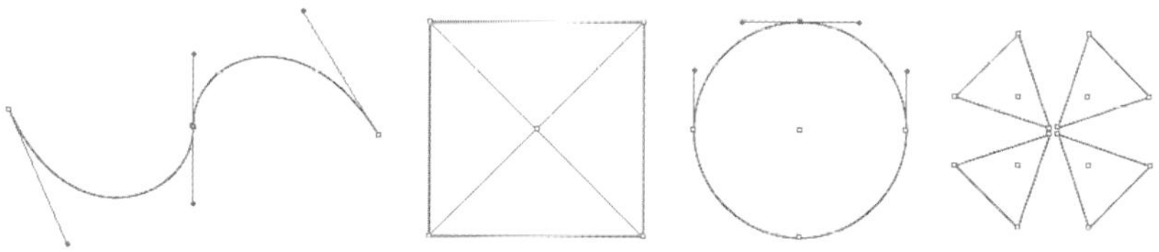

Figure 5.10 Use the Direct Selection tool to select and modify any path. See Figure 5.3 to see the same objects selected with the Selection tool.

- **Position tool:** The Position tool allows you to resize and crop a graphic, move a graphic within a container frame, and move a container frame and its content to a new location. To locate the Position tool, click and hold the Direct Selection tool to display a menu where the tool can be found. When the menu appears, select the tool (**Figure 5.11**).

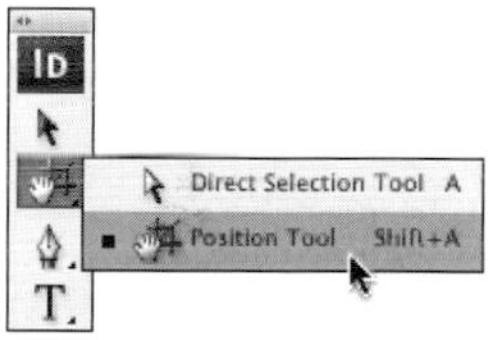
Direct Selection Tool A
Position Tool Shift+A

Figure 5.11 Selecting the Position tool from the toolbox.

The Position tool is quite dynamic, automatically changing as you place it over different parts of a graphic. When it's placed directly over a graphic, it changes to the Hand tool to indicate that you can drag the graphic within the container frame (**Figure 5.12**). If you hold down the mouse button for a moment before you drag it, you'll see a dynamic preview of the graphic.

When it is placed over the edge of the container frame, it changes to the Selection tool to indicate that you can select it (**Figure 5.13**). Once selected, you can crop the graphic by dragging one of the selection handles toward or away from the graphic. To resize a graphic, hold down Ctrl (Windows) or Command (Mac OS) while simultaneously dragging one of the selection handles. The container frame and its content are scaled together. Add the Shift key to scale the frame and graphic proportionally. To reposition a graphic, select and drag the center point of its container frame to a new location.

■ **Tip:** You can more easily reposition a graphic by holding down Ctrl (Windows) or Command (Mac OS) to temporarily switch to the Selection tool. With the Selection Tool active, select anywhere within the graphic and drag it to a new location.

Figure 5.12 Place the Position tool directly over a graphic to automatically access the Hand tool.

Figure 5.13 Place the Position tool directly over the edge of a container frame to select it.

Text Frame

All editable text in InDesign must reside within a text frame. Like graphics frames, text frames can be moved, resized, and reshaped. They can also be linked together to allow text to flow from one frame into another within a document.

Text frames are composed of two basic parts—a bounding box and a frame. A bounding box surrounds the frame and is used to move, resize, and duplicate it. All the text exists within the text frame. To create an empty text frame, activate the Type tool and then drag to define the width and height of the new frame. The tool you use to select a text frame determines the kind of changes you can make to it.

SELECTING AND MODIFYING TEXT FRAMES

Figure 5.14 The Type tool.

Let's take a look at how each part of a text frame is selected and controlled. Just as the Selection tool and Direct Selection tool are used for working with graphics frames, they are used for text frames as well. The Type tool is used to select, edit, and format text within a frame (**Figure 5.14**). Here's a look at how you can use each tool when working with text frames:

■ **Tip:** To quickly fit a text frame to its content, select the frame and double-click any one of the selection handles with the Selection tool.

- **Selection tool:** Use the Selection tool for general layout tasks such as moving and sizing a text frame. When you select a text frame with the Selection tool, its bounding box becomes visible. Drag it to another location to relocate the text frame. To resize a text frame, drag one of the eight available selection handles. To scale a text frame and its content together, hold down Ctrl (Windows) or Command (Mac OS) while simultaneously dragging one of the selection handles. To scale the text proportionally, hold down the Shift key as well.

There is a considerable difference between scaling and resizing text frames. When you resize a text frame, the text within it remains the same size and simply reflows as the frame's size increases or decreases (**Figure 5.15**). When you scale a text frame, the text within it is also scaled with the frame as its size increases or decreases (**Figure 5.16**).

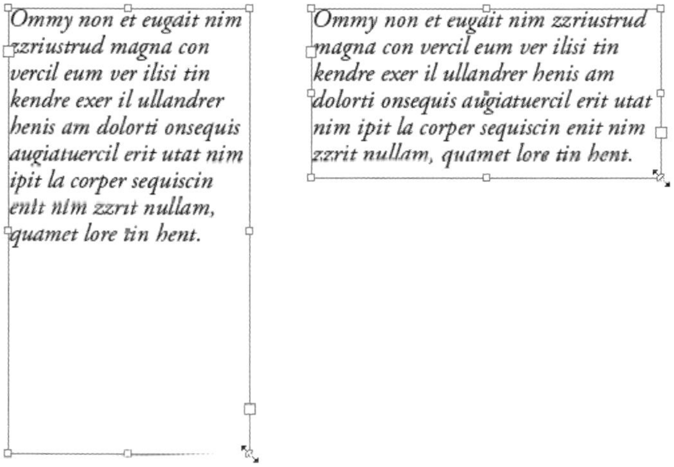
Ommy non et eugait nim
zzriustrud magna con
vercil eum ver ilisi tin
kendre exer il ullandrer
henis am dolorti onsequis
augiatuercil erit utat nim
ipit la corper sequiscin
enit nim zzrit nullam,
quamet lore tin hent.
Ommy non et eugait nim zzriustrud
magna con vercil eum ver ilisi tin
kendre exer il ullandrer henis am
dolorti onsequis augiatuercil erit utat
nim ipit la corper sequiscin enit nim
zzrit nullam, quamet lore tin hent.

Figure 5.15 As a frame is resized, the text within it remains the same size and reflows to conform to the new frame dimensions.

De vogels vliegen.
De vogels vliegen.

Figure 5.16 As a frame is scaled, the text within it is scaled along with the frame.

- **Direct Selection tool:** Use the Direct Selection tool to select the edge of a text frame and alter its shape. Once the frame is selected, you will see the anchor points that define its shape. Select and move them when you want to reshape the frame. You can also use the Pen tool in conjunction with the Direct Selection tool to create an arbitrary shape. Once a text frame is reshaped, the text reflows within its new shape (**Figure 5.17**).

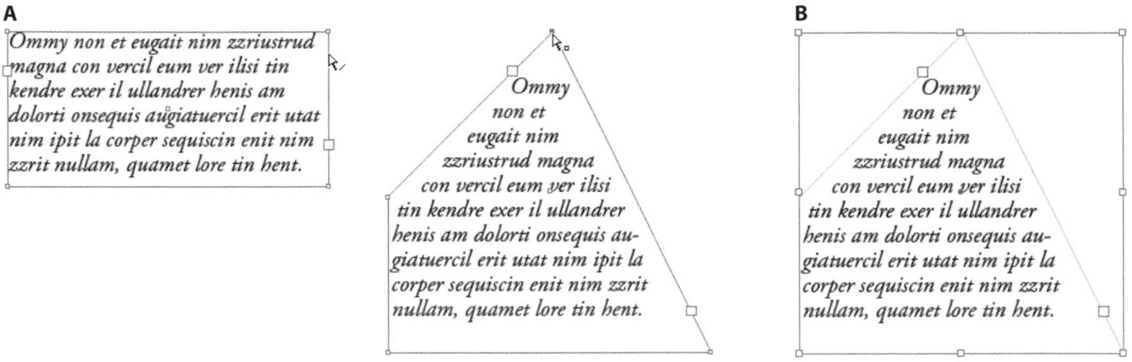
A
Ommy non et eugait nim zzriustrud magna con vercil eum ver ilisi tin kendre exer il ullandrer henis am dolorti onsequis augiatuercil erit utat nim ipit la corper sequiscin enit nim zzrit nullam, quamet lore tin hent.
Ommy non et eugait nim zzriustrud magna con vercil eum ver ilisi tin kendre exer il ullandrer henis am dolorti onsequis au-giatuercil erit utat nim ipit la corper sequiscin enit nim zzrit nullam, quamet lore tin hent.
B
Ommy non et eugait nim zzriustrud magna con vercil eum ver ilisi tin kendre exer il ullandrer henis am dolorti onsequis au-giatuercil erit utat nim ipit la corper sequiscin enit nim zzrit nullam, quamet lore tin hent.

Figure 5.17 Selecting a text frame with the Direct Selection tool allows you to modify the path that defines its shape (**A**). Note that although the shape of the text frame has been modified, its bounding box remains the same (**B**).

■ **Tip:** Press the Escape key to exit a type frame and activate the Selection tool. The frame's bounding box is automatically selected. Using this procedure makes it easy to quickly switch to another tool using a keyboard shortcut.

- **Type tool:** Use the Type tool to enter, edit, or format text within a frame. If you want to move or resize a text frame without switching from the Type tool to the Selection tool, hold down Ctrl (Windows) or Command (Mac OS) and then move or resize it. When you release the key, the Type tool is still active.

TYPE ON A PATH

In addition to placing text directly within a frame, you can flow it along the edge of any path, from straight lines and curves to rectangles and circles. Once you've placed some text on a path, you can slide it along the path, flip it over to the opposite side of the path, and even apply special effects to the characters. Like other text frames, paths with type have an in port and an out port to allow text to flow to and from them.

■ **Tip:** It's possible to place text within a text frame and flow type along its path at the same time.

Paths with type are composed of several components that allow you to control the text as well as the path. As with all paths and frames, a bounding box surrounds the path. The text flows along the edge of the path. A start bracket and end bracket appear in front of and behind the text to allow you to adjust its start and end position. A center bracket appears in the middle of the text to allow you to slide the type along the path or flip it to the other side (**Figure 5.18**).

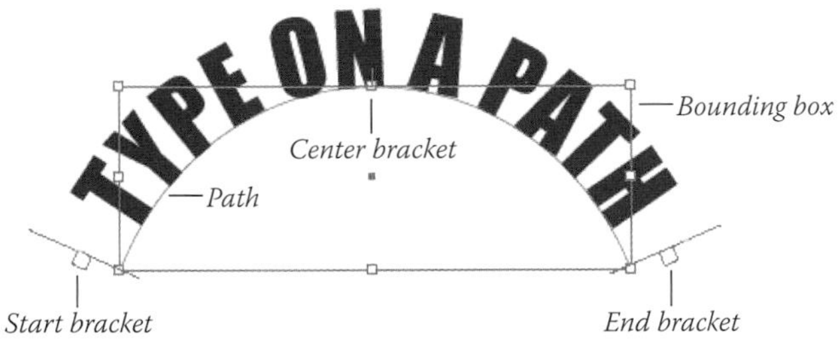
TYPE ON A PATH
Bounding box
Center bracket
Path
Start bracket
End bracket

Figure 5.18 Paths with type on them have several parts that allow you to control the text as well as the path.

To place type on a path, use the Type on a Path tool (click and hold the Type tool to display a menu containing the Type on a Path tool). Position the tool on the path until a small plus sign appears next to it. When you click the insertion point on a closed path, the starting point of the text is established. On open paths, the starting point of the text is determined by the paragraph's alignment.

You can change the starting position of the text by selecting the path with the Selection tool or Direct Selection tool and then dragging the start bracket to the left or right accordingly. Drag the end bracket when you want to change the end position of the text. To slide text along a path or flip it to the other side, drag the center bracket to the left, right, up, or down accordingly. If you want to modify the path, select it with the Direct Selection tool. Naturally, you can use the Pen tool as well to continue editing the path.

Unassigned Frame

Unassigned frames are essentially closed paths with no defined content. They are useful for borders, background colors, and so on. You create an unassigned frame when you draw a frame with the Rectangle tool, Ellipse tool, or Polygon tool. You can also create one by drawing a custom path with the Pen tool or Pencil tool.

Like text frames, unassigned frames are composed of two basic parts—a bounding box and a frame. A bounding box surrounds the frame and is used to move, resize, and duplicate it. The frame has no content, but you can control the formatting characteristics of its fill and stroke, and also apply transparency effects to it. The tool you use to select an unassigned frame determines the kind of changes you can make to it.

SELECTING AND MODIFYING UNASSIGNED FRAMES

Unassigned frames are selected and modified in the same manner that all frames are. The Selection tool and Direct Selection tool are the ones you need, but you can also use other tools, such as the Pen tool, Pencil tool, and Scissors tool.

Here's a look at the essential tools:

- **Selection tool:** Use the Selection tool for moving and sizing an unassigned frame. Once selected, the frame's bounding box becomes visible. Drag it to another location to move it. To resize it, drag one of the eight selection handles. To resize it proportionally, hold down the Shift key as you resize it.

  Unassigned frames can be difficult to select if their fill doesn't have a color applied to it. You won't be able to select them by clicking within the frame. You have to either select the edge of the frame or drag a marquee over the frame to select it.

- **Direct Selection tool:** Use the Direct Selection tool to select the edge of the frame. Once selected, the anchor points that define its shape appear. Select and move them to reshape the frame. You can use the Pen tool and other path modification tools to further customize the frame's shape.

Redefining a Frame's Content

InDesign is very flexible when it comes to redefining a frame's purpose. In fact, it's not completely necessary to build frames specifically for text or graphics. InDesign provides several ways to redefine a frame's content:

- To convert a path or text frame to a graphics placeholder frame, select a path or an empty text frame and then choose Object > Content > Graphic.
- To convert a path or graphics frame to a text placeholder frame, select a path or an empty graphics frame and then choose Object > Content > Text.
- To convert a text or graphics frame to an unassigned frame (path only), select an empty frame and then choose Object > Content > Unassigned.
- A path or text frame is automatically converted to a graphics frame when you select it with the Selection tool and replace its contents with an imported or pasted graphic.
- An empty graphics frame is automatically converted to a text frame when you select it with the Type tool. This feature can be disabled by choosing Preferences > Type and then deselecting the Type Tool Converts Frames to Text Frames option.

● **Note:** When a frame contains text or graphics, you cannot redefine it using the Content menu (Object > Content).

Now that the composition of frames has been thoroughly defined, you are well on your way to mastering InDesign. Knowledge of frames and how they function is a key ingredient to successful template design. As you become more efficient at selecting and modifying the different types of frames, you will be able to design and produce a template with much more efficiency than ever before.

6

Frames in Action

NOW THAT YOU UNDERSTAND THE COMPOSITION OF FRAMES AND HOW TO select and modify them, let's take a deeper look into their layout and design capabilities. Most designers likely spend more time working with frames than any other activity. By taking full advantage of the opportunities that frames provide, you can simplify your work and ensure a consistent and straightforward template.

In this chapter, you'll first explore techniques for measuring, positioning, and transforming frames. Then you'll discover several ways to combine frames to make them easier to manage. These methods are easy to use and will pay you many times over for the time you invest in learning them.

Understanding the Rulers

Before you can be truly efficient moving and transforming frames, it's vital that you understand how to work with InDesign's rulers. They allow you to make onscreen measurements and aid in the process of moving and transforming frames on the page.

InDesign provides two rulers: one is located on the top and the other is on the left side of the document window (**Figure 6.1**). The *horizontal ruler* (x-axis) governs frame width, horizontal scaling, X location, and other horizontal measurements—such as tabs and indents. The *vertical ruler* (y-axis) governs frame height, vertical scaling, Y location, and other vertical measurements. By default, the rulers begin measuring from the top-left corner of each spread in a document.

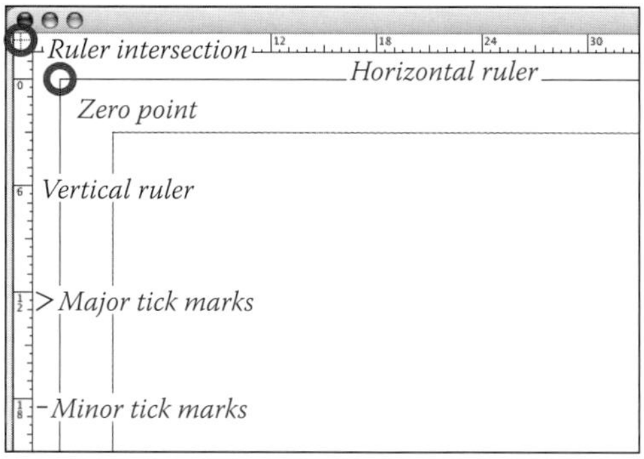
Ruler intersection
Horizontal ruler
Zero point
Vertical ruler
Major tick marks
Minor tick marks

Figure 6.1 The horizontal and vertical rulers. Each ruler displays the major and minor tick increments of the current measurement system.

● **Note:** If you don't see the rulers, choose View > Show Rulers. If one or both of the rulers are covered by a panel, relocate the panel to another location. It's important to see the full length of each ruler.

Each ruler contains several tick marks that display the major and minor increments of the current measurement system. So, if your current unit of measure is set for inches, a major ruler increment appears every inch and minor increments appear on each major fraction of an inch. As you increase the magnification of the page, more and more ruler detail is displayed, allowing you to make extremely precise measurements (**Figure 6.2**).

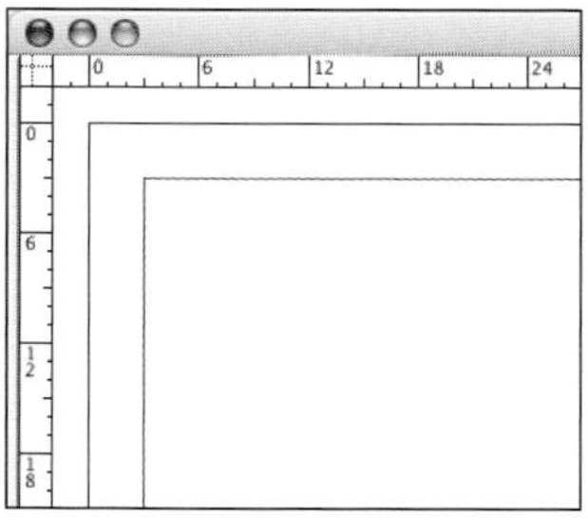
0
6
12
18
24

75% magnification level

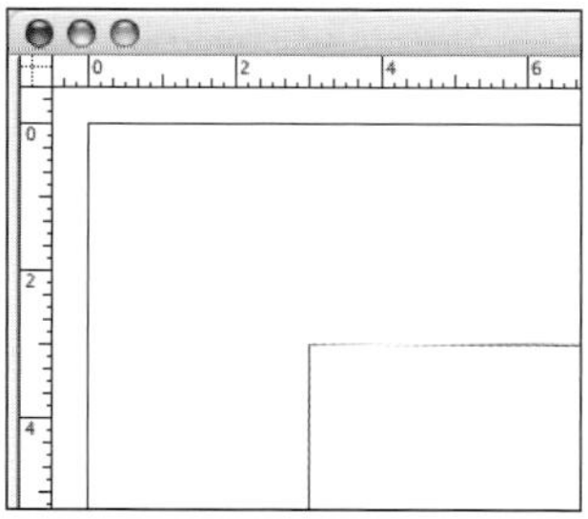
0
2
4
6

300% magnification level

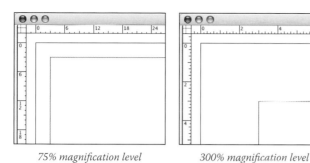

Figure 6.2 As the magnification of the page increases, more ruler detail is displayed.

Changing the Measurement System

InDesign's default measurement system is picas. However, if you feel more comfortable with another system, you can change it. You can even set up different systems for the horizontal and vertical rulers if necessary. When you change the measurement system, InDesign's rulers, panels, and dialogs are updated to reflect the new units of measure (**Figure 6.3**).

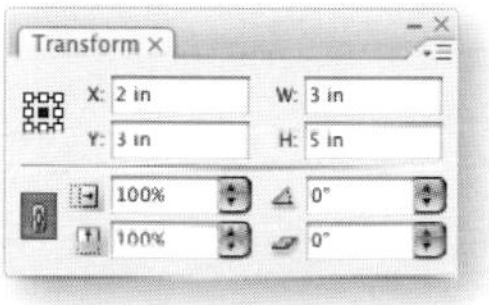
Transform
X: 2 in
W: 3 in
Y: 3 in
H: 5 in
100%
0°

Transform panel

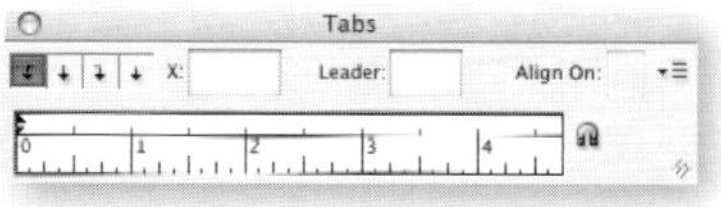
Tabs
X:
Leader:
Align On:

Tabs panel

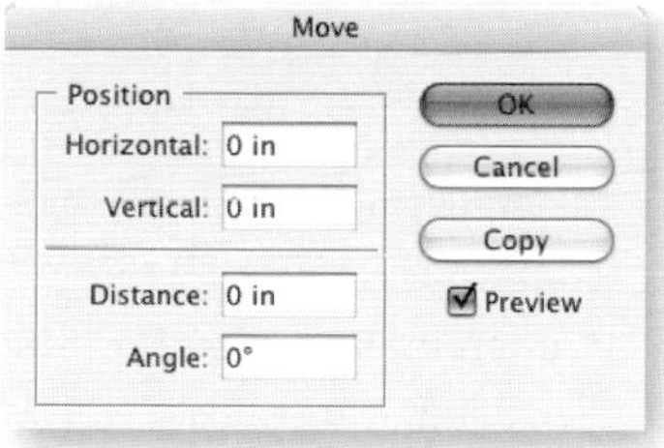
Move
Position
Horizontal: 0 in
Vertical: 0 in
Distance: 0 in
Angle: 0°
OK
Cancel
Copy
Preview

Move dialog box

Figure 6.3 InDesign's panels and dialogs reflect the current measurement system.

You can change the measurement system in two ways:

- Choose Edit > Preferences > Units & Increments (Windows) or InDesign > Preferences > Units & Increments (Mac OS). Choose the desired system for Horizontal and Vertical.
- Right-click (Windows) or Control-click (Mac OS) a ruler and choose the desired system from the context menu. By right-clicking or Control-clicking at the intersection of the horizontal and vertical rulers, you can change the system for both rulers at the same time.

● **Note:** Changing the measurement system doesn't actually move guides or objects. Therefore, when the ruler tick marks change, they most likely won't line up with objects aligned to the old tick marks.

The measurement system you choose depends on the type of work you are currently doing. You might choose to work in inches when defining a document's overall dimensions and when placing ruler guides on a page. You might then switch to points or picas to more easily work with smaller objects.

Overriding Measurement Units Quickly

InDesign allows you to specify a unit of measure other than the one displayed in its panels and dialogs. For example, if your current measurement system is in points, but you want a 6x6 inch frame, highlight the existing width and height values and enter **6in**. InDesign converts it to points for you. The following chart specifies the abbreviations to use when overriding the default units of measure.

Units	Abbreviation	Example
Points	pt	6pt
Picas	p	12p
Picas and Points	p (between values)	12p6
Inches	i, in, inch, "	8.25in
Millimeters	mm	10mm
Centimeters	cm	40cm
Ciceros	c	5c
Agates	ag	5ag
Percentage	%	25%

Working with the Zero Point

■ **Tip:** You can lock the zero point to prevent it from being relocated. To lock or unlock the zero point, right-click (Windows) or Control-click (Mac OS) the zero point of the rulers and then choose Lock Zero Point or Unlock Zero Point from the context menu.

The *zero point* is the place at which the zeros on the horizontal and vertical rulers intersect (Figure 6.1). The rulers begin measuring from wherever it is located. By default, the zero point is located at the top-left corner of each spread in a document. You can change its location by moving it, which is useful for taking measurements from different positions in a layout.

To relocate the zero point, drag from the intersection of the horizontal and vertical rulers to the position on the layout where you want to measure from (**Figure 6.4**). To reset the zero point to its default location, double-click the intersection of the horizontal and vertical rulers.

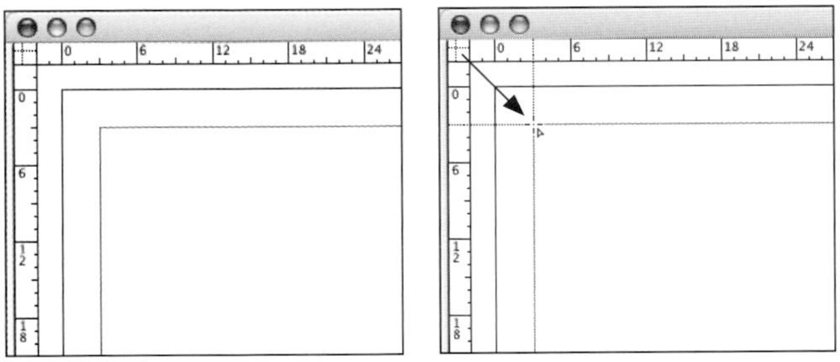

Figure 6.4 Drag the intersection of the horizontal and vertical rulers to establish a new zero point.

When you relocate the zero point, it appears in the same relative location in each spread of the document. For example, if you move it to the left margin on the left page, it appears in that same location in each spread throughout the document, allowing you to consistently measure and position frames from spread to spread.

● **Note:** It's critical that you constantly observe where the zero point is located if you want to accurately measure and position frames in a document.

CHANGING THE HORIZONTAL RULER ORIGIN

By default, the horizontal ruler starts at the left edge of the page and measures across the entire spread. When you want to measure across individual pages or from the spine outward, you can modify the horizontal ruler origin.

You can change the horizontal ruler origin in two ways:

- Choose Edit > Preferences > Units & Increments (Windows) or InDesign > Preferences > Units & Increments (Mac OS). Choose one of the three options in the Origin menu—Spread, Page, or Spine.
- Right-click (Windows) or Control-click (Mac OS) the horizontal ruler and choose Ruler Per Page, Ruler Per Spread, or Ruler Per Spine from the context menu (**Figure 6.5**).

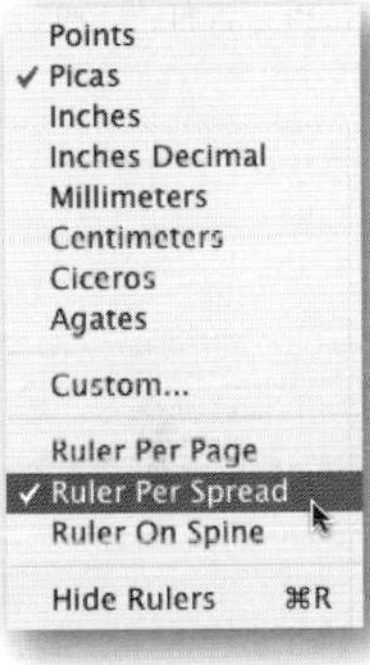
Points
✓ Picas
Inches
Inches Decimal
Millimeters
Centimeters
Ciceros
Agates
Custom...
Ruler Per Page
✓ Ruler Per Spread
Ruler On Spine
Hide Rulers ⌘R

Figure 6.5 The context menu in the horizontal ruler allows you to quickly switch between the three ruler origin options.

Choose Ruler Per Page when you want the rulers to start at zero from the left edge of each page in a spread. This allows you to more easily measure and position frames on a page-by-page basis.

Use the Ruler Per Spread option when you want the rulers to start at zero from the left edge of the spread and continue measuring across the entire spread. This makes it easier to measure and position frames on a spread-by-spread basis.

● **Note:** If you set the horizontal ruler origin at the spine, the origin becomes locked. You will not be able to relocate the ruler origin by dragging from the intersection of the rulers until you choose another origin option.

The Ruler On Spine option is useful when you are working with multipage spreads and want to set the ruler origin at the top-left corner of the leftmost page as well as at the binding spine. The horizontal ruler measures from the leftmost page to the binding spine and from the binding spine to the rightmost page. For example, if a spread is composed of four pages, the horizontal ruler measures from the leftmost page across the second page to the binding spine. It starts over again at the binding spine and continues measuring across the fourth page (**Figure 6.6**).

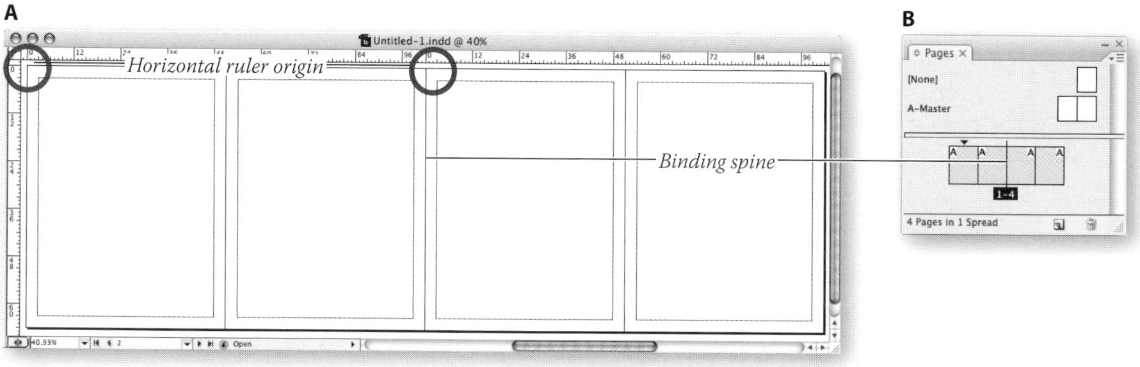
A
B
Untitled-1.indd @ 40%
Horizontal ruler origin
Binding spine
Pages
[None]
A-Master
1-4
4 Pages in 1 Spread

Figure 6.6 The Ruler On Spine option was chosen for this four-page spread (**A**). The position of the binding spine is indicated in the Pages panel (**B**).

Measuring, Positioning, and Transforming Frames

When creating templates, it's especially important that you carefully consider the size and position of every repeating object and placeholder frame on the page. By using the numbers—instead of arrows or preset menus—to move and transform frames, you'll increase your productivity and make it easier for someone else to more precisely produce pages with your template.

Here's a look at InDesign's most essential tools for working with frames. With a good understanding of how to use them, you can more skillfully and systematically arrange frames in a template.

The Transform and Control Panels

The Transform and Control panels share the same functions for moving and transforming frames (**Figure 6.7**). But the Control panel is context-sensitive and displays additional commands depending on the active tool or selection. For instance, when the Type tool is active, it displays character and paragraph related functions. When the Selection tool or Direct Selection tool is active, it displays transform related functions.

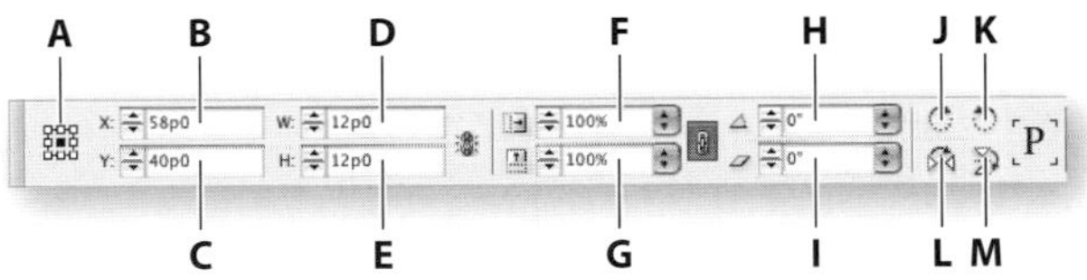
A B D F H J K
X: 58p0
Y: 40p0
W: 12p0
H: 12p0
100%
100%
0°
0°
C E G I L M

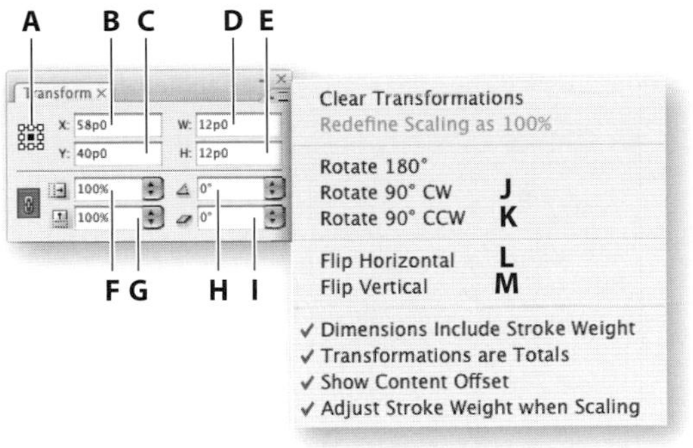
A B C D E
Transform
X: 58p0
Y: 40p0
W: 12p0
H: 12p0
100%
100%
0°
0°
F G H I
Clear Transformations
Redefine Scaling as 100%
Rotate 180°
Rotate 90° CW J
Rotate 90° CCW K
Flip Horizontal L
Flip Vertical M
✓ Dimensions Include Stroke Weight
✓ Transformations are Totals
✓ Show Content Offset
✓ Adjust Stroke Weight when Scaling

Figure 6.7 The Transform and Control panels. A few of the commands in the Transform panel menu are also available as buttons in the Control panel. Reference point locator (**A**), Horizontal X location (**B**), Vertical Y location (**C**), Width (**D**), Height (**E**), Scale X Percentage (**F**), Scale Y Percentage (**G**), Rotation angle (**H**), Shear X angle (**I**), Rotate 90° clockwise (**J**), Rotate 90° counterclockwise (**K**), Flip horizontal (**L**), and Flip vertical (**M**).

Both panels provide two essential functions for working with frames. First, they display precise information about a frame's size, position, rotation angle, and so on. Second, they allow you to numerically move and transform frames.

When a frame is selected, its size and position information is shown in the current measurement system and is relative to the position of the zero point and the chosen reference point of the frame. Its angle information is relative to an imaginary horizontal line that has an angle of 0°.

When you want to move or transform a frame, there are several ways to change a field's value. You can choose a preset value from one of the pop-up menus or click the arrow buttons in the Control panel to increase or decrease the value in increments. You can also specify a value by manually typing it in, allowing you to apply transformations more quickly.

■ **Tip:** After entering a value into one of the fields in the Transform or Control panel, hold the Shift key and press Enter/Return. The setting is applied to the selected object, but the field remains selected so you can continue typing a new value without having to click into the field again.

Pay Attention to What's Selected

Remember to carefully observe which tool you're using to select a frame before you begin transforming it. Use the Selection tool to select a frame when you want to move or transform both the frame and its content. Use the Direct Selection tool to move or transform only part of a path, just an image and not its container frame, or an individual frame within a group. To transform a frame without transforming its content, direct-select the frame and select all the anchor points first. If multiple frames are selected, the information displayed in the Transform and Control panels represents all the selected frames as a unit.

SETTING THE REFERENCE POINT

Both the Transform and Control panels have a small icon called the *reference point locator* (Figure 6.7). It is useful when performing a multitude of tasks—from measuring a frame's position to resizing, rotating, distributing, and aligning frames. In fact, all transformations originate from an object's reference point.

To specify the transformation origin for a selected frame, click any one of the nine points on the reference point locator. When using the Rotate, Scale, and Shear tools, you can specify a custom transformation origin instead of using one of the nine predetermined reference points (**Figure 6.8**).

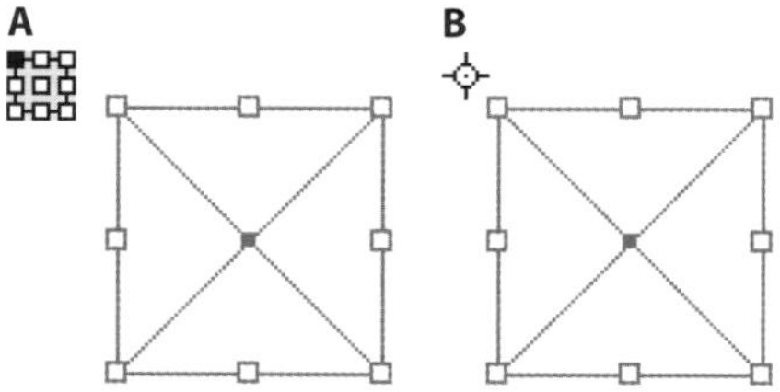
A
B

Figure 6.8 Each reference point directly corresponds to the nine selection handles on a frame's bounding box (**A**). If a custom transformation origin has been specified, it is indicated by a small nonprinting target icon (**B**).

Measuring the Position of Frames

To make onscreen measurements, you need to establish a point of origin and a point of reference. The location of the zero point determines the point of origin, whereas a selected frame's reference point determines the point of reference. The X and Y values displayed in the Transform and Control panels refer to the selected reference point on a frame's bounding box relative to the location of the zero point.

So, if you want to find out how far the top-left corner of a frame is from the top left margin of the page, you need to move the zero point to the margin and then specify the top-left reference point in the reference point locator.

The X and Y position of selected frames can be measured from three places:

- The position of a frame in relation to the zero point of the document. Select a frame or multiple frames with the Selection tool to view their position on the page or spread (**Figure 6.9**).

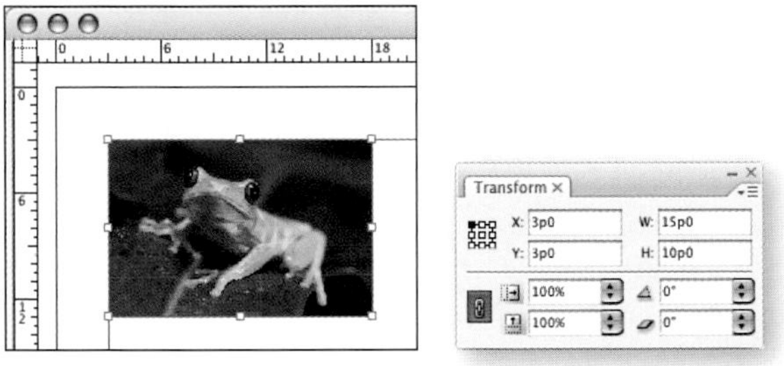
Transform
X: 3p0
Y: 3p0
W: 15p0
H: 10p0
100%
100%

Figure 6.9 The container frame's position is displayed relative to the zero point of the document. In this case, InDesign measures from the top-left corner of the page to the top-left corner of the image.

- The position of a graphic in relation to the zero point of its container frame. Select a graphic with the Direct Selection tool to view its position within the container frame (**Figure 6.10**).

● **Note:** The zero point of a container frame is always its top-left corner.

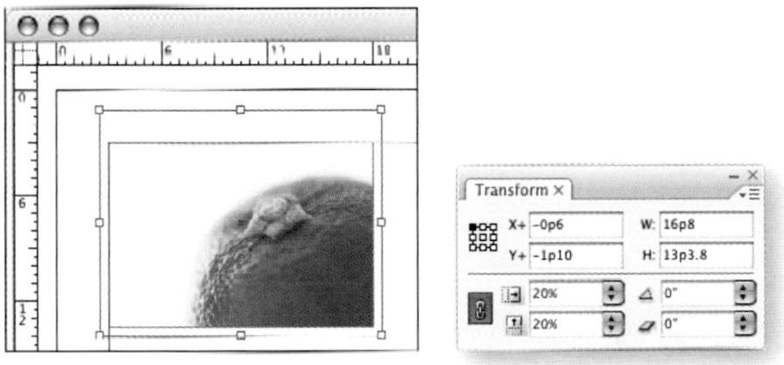
Transform
X+ -0p6
Y+ -1p10
W: 16p8
H: 13p3.8
20%
20%

Figure 6.10 The graphic's position is displayed relative to the zero point of its container frame. In this case, InDesign measures from the top-left corner of the container frame to the top-left corner of its content.

- The position of a graphic in relation to the zero point of the document. Turn off Show Content Offset from either the Transform or Control panel menus and then select the graphic with the Direct Selection tool to view its position on the page or spread (**Figure 6.11**).

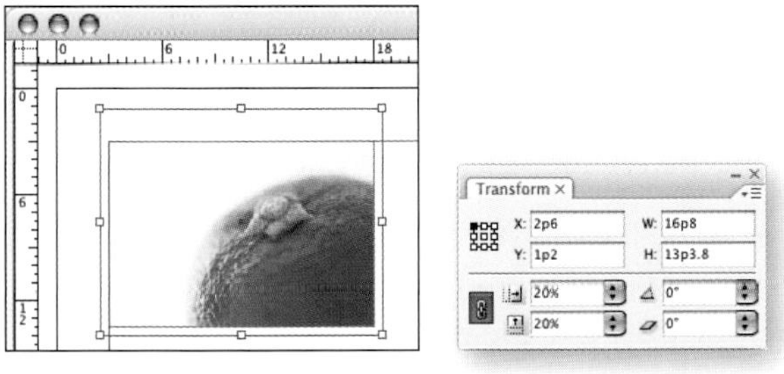
Transform
X: 2p6
Y: 1p2
W: 16p8
H: 13p3.8
20%
20%

Figure 6.11 The graphic's position is displayed relative to the zero point of the document. Since the Show Content Offset command has been turned off, InDesign measures from the top-left corner of the page to the top-left corner of the graphic within the container frame.

Show Content Offset Command

The Show Content Offset command determines the position of a graphic that is selected with the Direct Selection tool. Turn it off to view its position in relation to the zero point of the document. Turn it on to view its position in relation to the zero point of its container frame. When it's on, the X/Y icons in the Transform and Control panels change to X+/Y+. By default, it is turned on.

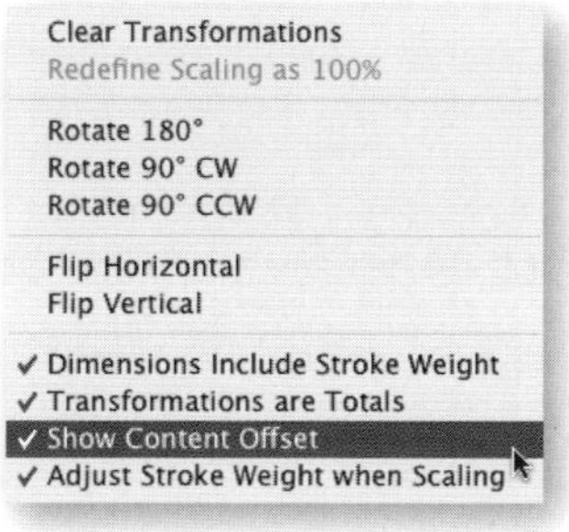
Clear Transformations
Redefine Scaling as 100%
Rotate 180°
Rotate 90° CW
Rotate 90° CCW
Flip Horizontal
Flip Vertical
✓ Dimensions Include Stroke Weight
✓ Transformations are Totals
✓ Show Content Offset
✓ Adjust Stroke Weight when Scaling

THE MEASURE TOOL

Figure 6.12 The Measure

Another way to take measurements is to use the Measure tool (**Figure 6.12**). It can calculate the distance between any two points in the document window. When you take a measurement, its distance is displayed in the Info panel (**Figure 6.13**). All measurements are displayed in the units of measure currently set for the document. Once you've taken a measurement, the line remains visible until you switch to another tool or take another measurement.

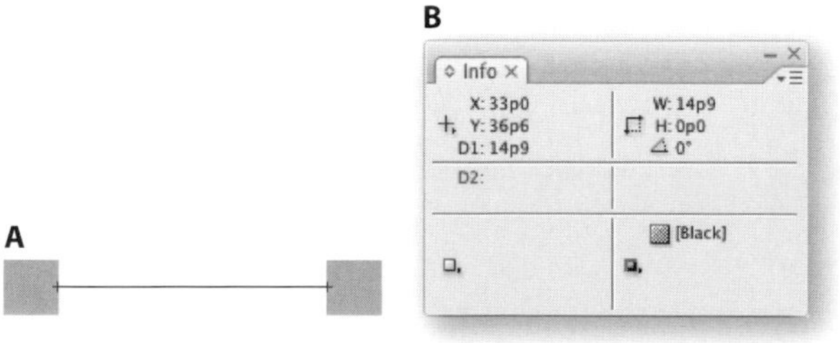
B
Info
X: 33p0
Y: 36p6
D1: 14p9
W: 14p9
H: 0p0
0°
D2:
[Black]
A

Figure 6.13 The distance of the measure line (**A**) is displayed as D1 in the Info panel (**B**). If a second measure line exists, it shows up as D2.

To select the Measure tool, click and hold the Eyedropper tool to display it. Click the point you want to measure from and drag to the point you want to measure to. Hold the Shift key as you drag to measure in a straight line.

To create a second line of measurement, position the tool over either end point of the measure line and hold Alt (Windows) or Option (Mac OS) as you drag a second line.

When you take a measurement, the Info panel displays the length of the first line as D1 and the length of the second line as D2. The resulting angle of the two measure lines is also displayed next to the angle icon.

The Measure tool is great for taking quick measurements on the page, but you may find that it takes more effort to make precise measurements compared to using the zero point and the X, Y information provided in the Transform and Control panels.

Numerically Position Frames

InDesign is quite flexible and provides several ways to move and position frames on a page. It's possible to drag them or use the arrow keys on your keyboard to nudge them to a specific location. However, when creating a template for fast and efficient page layout, it's important to position repeating objects and placeholder frames at specific X, Y locations. This makes the document's design more consistent and easier to repeat. You can use both the Transform and Control panels to numerically position frames on the page. You can also choose to use the Move dialog.

Note: Be sure to round off the X and Y position values of placeholder frames and repeating objects. This creates consistency within a template and facilitates production.

USING THE TRANSFORM OR CONTROL PANEL

Perhaps the most efficient way to position a frame on the page is by changing the values of the X and Y location fields in the Transform or Control panel. Simply enter the horizontal and vertical distances that you want the object to move. Positive values move a frame down and to the right, and negative values move a frame up and to the left.

Imagine that you want to place a frame three inches down and three inches across from the zero point, and you're using the top-left reference point. You would select the frame and type **3in** into the Y field and **3in** into the X field. The top-left corner of the frame would then be relocated to that position.

Tip: If you want to quickly duplicate a frame and its position onto other pages within a document, copy the frame and choose Edit > Paste in Place to paste it into the same X, Y location you copied it from.

Tip: You can type fractions instead of decimals into panels and dialogs. So, to get 1/2 inch, type ***1/2in*** instead of .5in.

USING THE MOVE DIALOG

You can use the Move dialog to specify an exact location for a frame or move it a precise distance or angle (**Figure 6.14**). One of the advantages of using this method is the ability to preview the effect before you apply it. You can also move a copy of the frame instead of the original by clicking Copy instead of OK. To quickly bring up the Move dialog, double-click the Selection tool or Direct Selection tool.

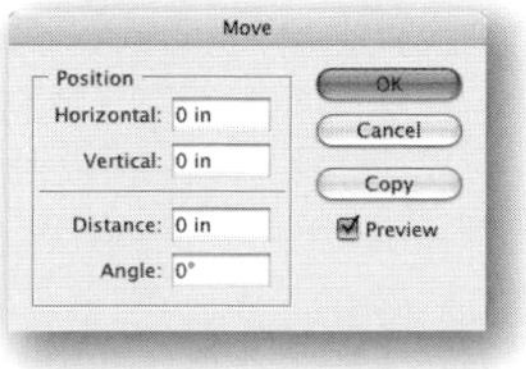

Move
Position
Horizontal: 0 in
Vertical: 0 in
Distance: 0 in
Angle: 0°
OK
Cancel
Copy
Preview

Figure 6.14 The Move dialog.

Aligning and Distributing Frames

There is no better tool for aligning and distributing frames than the Align panel. It provides the easiest and most efficient way to horizontally or vertically align and distribute frames along the selection, margins, page, or spread.

The Align panel is broken down into three sections—Align Objects, Distribute Objects, and Distribute Spacing (**Figure 6.15**). Be sure to choose Show Options from the panel menu to view all the options.

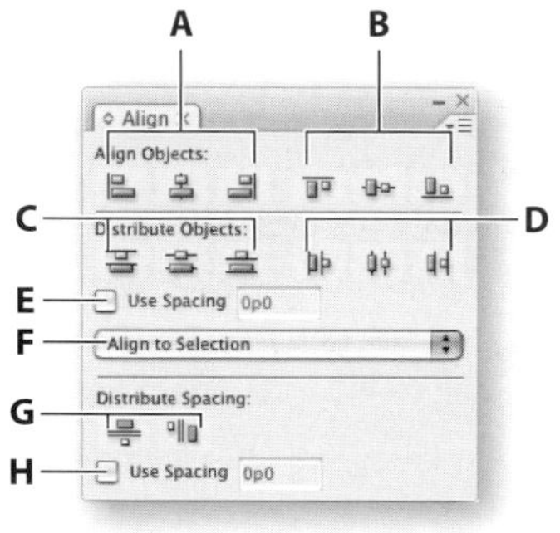
A
B
Align
Align Objects:
C
Distribute Objects:
D
E
Use Spacing
0p0
F
Align to Selection
Distribute Spacing:
G
H
Use Spacing
0p0

Figure 6.15 The Align panel. Vertical alignment buttons (**A**), Horizontal alignment buttons (**B**), Vertical distribution buttons (**C**), Horizontal distribution buttons (**D**), Distribute objects precisely option (**E**), Alignment location options (**F**), Distribute spacing buttons (**G**), and Distribute spacing precisely option (**H**).

To align two or more frames, select them and choose one of the six icons in the top section of the panel. To distribute frames, InDesign requires that you select three or more frames. Choose from one of the six icons in the second section of the panel to place equal spacing between each selected frame. The two outermost frames will stay in place while the other frames move equally between them. If you turn on the Use Spacing option and enter a value into the Use Spacing field before you select a distribution option, the selected frames will be distributed at your specified value along their horizontal or vertical axes.

The pop-up menu at the bottom of the Distribute Objects section allows you to specify whether you want to align or distribute objects based on the selection, margins, page, or spread.

The simplest and most intuitive way to distribute equal spacing between frames—especially those of different sizes—is to select three or more frames and choose one of the Distribute Spacing options. This method places equal spacing between the bounding boxes of the selected frames. If you turn on the Use Spacing option and enter a value into the Use Spacing field, the selected frames will be distributed equally at your specified value along their horizontal or vertical axes.

Numerically Resize Frames

When you know the exact size you want a frame to be, you can enter the Width and Height values (W: and H: fields) into the Transform or Control panel. You can enlarge a selected frame equally around all sides by setting the reference point to the center point and then entering new Width and Height values.

When you want to scale a frame to specific percentages, you can enter the values into the Scale X Percentage and Scale Y Percentage fields. To maintain the original proportions of the frame, make sure the Constrain Proportions For Scaling icon is selected before scaling it (**Figure 6.16**).

After scaling a frame, the container frame's scaling values are reset to 100%. To view how much an image has actually been scaled, you'll have to direct-select the content. This behavior is due to the fact that the Apply To Content preference is selected in General preferences (**Figure 6.17**). If you prefer to see the scaling values of the container frame remain as specified, select the Adjust Scaling Percentage option instead. This way if you scale an image, both the container frame and its content display the same scaling values in the Transform and Control panels.

■ **Tip:** You can type a specific distance, such as ***1in*** or ***6p***, in the Scale X Percentage and Scale Y Percentage fields.

Figure 6.16 The Constrain Proportions For Scaling icon is located in both the Transform

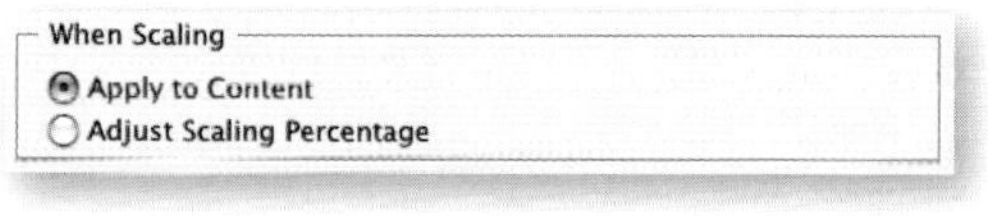
When Scaling
Apply to Content
Adjust Scaling Percentage

Figure 6.17 InDesign's scaling options are located in General Preferences. Choose Edit > Preferences > General (Windows) or InDesign > Preferences > General (Mac OS).

USING THE SCALE DIALOG

You can use the Scale dialog to numerically scale a frame (**Figure 6.18**). One of the advantages of using this method is the ability to preview the effect before you apply it. You can also scale a copy of the frame instead of the original by clicking Copy instead of OK. To quickly open the Scale dialog box, select an object in the layout and double-click the Scale tool.

● **Note:** When multiple frames are selected, the scaling value will always display as 100%. If a group is selected, the scaling value will display for the entire group. You can select individual frames to see the applied scaling value.

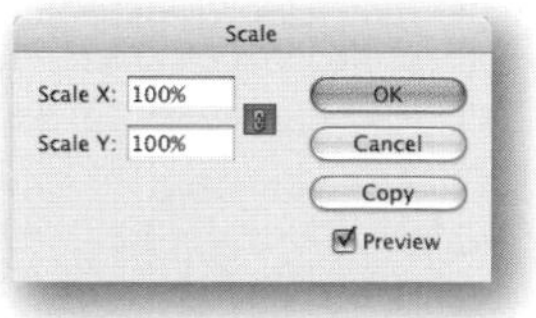
Scale
Scale X: 100%
Scale Y: 100%
OK
Cancel
Copy
Preview

Figure 6.18 The Scale dialog.

Stroke Weight in Measurements

A frame's stroke weight plays an integral role in its size and position. By default, stroke weight is included in the dimensions of frames. So when you select a frame, the Width/Height and X/Y values in the Transform and Control panels represent the outer edge of the frame's stroke. When you want the panel measurements to represent the size and position of a frame without its stroke weight, deselect Dimensions Include Stroke Weight from either the Transform or Control panel menu.

When scaling a frame, you can choose whether or not to include the frame's stroke weight. Select Adjust Stroke Weight When Scaling from either the Transform or Control panel menu to disable or enable the option. By default, the option is enabled.

Transforming Frames

There are several ways—both interactive and numeric—to rotate, skew (shear), and flip frames in InDesign. Each method will achieve similar results, so it's up to you to decide which approach to use to transform a frame. Just keep in mind that your goal is to make a template and its elements effortless to reproduce. For example, if you use the Rotate tool to turn a frame, refer back to the Control panel to round off the rotation value. By using transformation values that are simple to remember, anyone can pick up your template and re-create it with ease.

USING THE TRANSFORM OR CONTROL PANEL

Both the Transform and Control panels allow you to numerically rotate and skew frames. To rotate a frame, enter an angle into the Rotation Angle field or choose one of the preset values from the pop-up menu.

To horizontally skew a frame, enter an angle into the Shear X Angle field or use one of the preset values from the pop-up menu. For a vertical skew, enter the same angle in both the Shear X Angle field and the Rotation field.

■ **Tip:** In the Transform and Control panels, you can duplicate the selected frame and apply the transformation to the duplicate (instead of the original). Enter the value and press Alt-Enter (Windows) or Option-Return (Mac OS).

To flip a frame, use the Flip commands from the Transform panel menu or the Flip Horizontal and Flip Vertical buttons in the Control panel. The flip/rotate indicator in the middle of the Control panel let's you know how and when a frame is flipped (**Figure 6.19**). It's also possible to numerically flip a frame by typing negative values into the Scale X Percentage or Scale Y Percentage fields.

USING THE TRANSFORMATION TOOLS

InDesign supplies a few tools for manually transforming frames. To rotate a frame, use the Rotate tool (**Figure 6.20**). Set the reference point in the reference point locator or drag the target icon anywhere on the page. Then position the Rotate tool away from the reference point and drag the frame in the direction you want it rotated.

You can use the Shear tool to skew a frame (**Figure 6.21**), but it's much easier to numerically skew a frame using the Control panel or the Shear dialog. You can use the Shear tool, but the results will be unpredictable.

To flip a frame, you can use the Selection tool to pull one side of a frame's bounding box past the opposite side. However, it's much easier to use the Control panel.

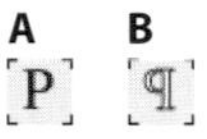
A
B
P
¶

Figure 6.19 The flip/rotate indicator appears solid black if a selected frame is not flipped (**A**). If a frame is flipped, the indicator appears white with a black outline (**B**). The position of the indicator also changes to show how the frame is currently flipped.

Figure 6.20 The Rotate tool.

Figure 6.21 The Shear tool.

USING THE DIALOGS

Another method you can use for rotating and skewing a frame is to use a dialog. The Rotate dialog lets you rotate a frame and preview the rotation before you apply it (**Figure 6.22**). To quickly access the dialog, select a frame and double-click the Rotate tool.

The Shear dialog lets you make precise skewing transformations (**Figure 6.23**). It's especially useful for previewing the transformation before you apply it. Select a frame and double-click the Shear tool to access the dialog.

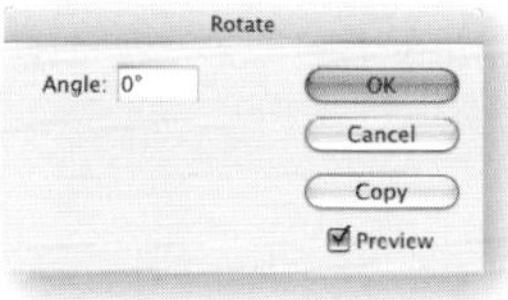
Rotate
Angle: 0°
OK
Cancel
Copy
Preview

Figure 6.22 The Rotate dialog.

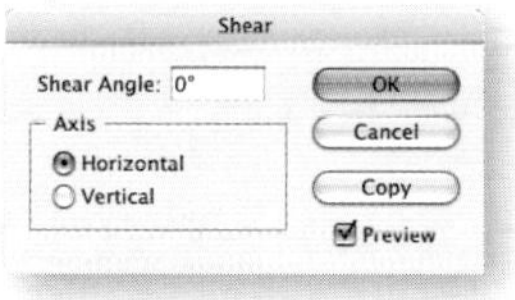
Shear
Shear Angle: 0°
Axis
Horizontal
Vertical
OK
Cancel
Copy
Preview

Figure 6.23 The Shear dialog.

■ **Tip:** To open dialogs, Alt-click (Windows) or Option-click (Mac OS) as you click a Control panel icon. For instance, when a frame is selected, hold down Alt or Option and click the Rotation Angle icon to open the Rotate dialog.

CLEARING TRANSFORMATIONS

If you want to simultaneously clear all the transformations you've applied to a frame, select the frame and choose Clear Transformations from the Transform or Control panel menu.

Calculating Values in Panels and Dialogs

You can perform basic math in any numerical field within InDesign's panels and dialogs. InDesign uses the current measurement system to calculate values, but you can specify values in another measurement system as well. Here are two ways to enter mathematical expressions in a numerical field:

- You can use the current value as part of a mathematical expression. Click after the current value and then type a mathematical expression using a single operator, such as + (plus), - (minus), x (multiplication), / (division), or % (percent). For example, if you want to move a selected frame two inches to the right, you can simply type **+2in** after the current X value in the Transform or Control panel.
- You can replace the entire current value with a mathematical expression. Select the current value and replace it with a mathematical expression using one of the operators mentioned above. For example, if you want to place a frame directly in the horizontal middle of a letter-size page, you don't have to visually drag the frame to its new position. Instead, you can select the frame, specify the center reference point, and then type **8.5/2in** into the X field in the Transform or Control panel.

Grouping, Nesting, Anchoring, and Stacking

Now that you understand how to measure frames, position them on a page, and transform their shapes, let's focus on some of the ways frames can be organized and combined when creating a template layout.

Grouping Frames

Figure 6.24 When you create a group, a dashed line appears around the group's bounding box.

Grouping allows you to combine several frames, so you can work with them as a single unit—a group (**Figure 6.24**). You can then move or transform the frames without affecting their individual positions or attributes. For instance, you might group a collection of text and graphics frames on a master page to make it possible to override them in one click when you need to modify them on a document page later on.

To group frames together, first select the frames that you want to include and then choose Object > Group. To ungroup them, select the group and choose Object > Ungroup. It's also possible to group several groups together, creating subgroups. However, try to minimize the amount of subgroups that you create. Otherwise, the groups and subgroups can become quite complex and make it difficult to work with the individual frames. By minimizing subgroups, the template remains clean and more straightforward to the designer who will be using it.

● **Note:** Grouping objects can change their stacking order in relation to other ungrouped objects on a page.

SELECTING FRAMES WITHIN A GROUP

Instead of ungrouping a group to edit an individual frame, you can use the Direct Selection tool to select and modify the frame without disturbing the other members of the group. Here are some tips for selecting frames within a group:

- To select a frame within a group, select it with the Direct Selection tool. To select a frame and all of its anchor points, hold Alt (Windows) or Option (Mac OS) as you select it, or click on its center point. Note that if you are selecting a frame that contains a graphic, you must click on the frame's edge to select the frame instead of its content.
- To select more than one frame within a group, hold the Shift key as you use the Direct Selection tool to select multiple frames. To select all the objects in a group or subgroup, hold Alt (Windows) or Option (Mac OS) as you double-click an object. Triple-click to select an entire group that contains multiple subgroups.
- To select a frame's bounding box within a group, use the Direct Selection tool to select the frame and then switch to the Selection tool. The bounding box of the frame will become available. It's also possible to double-click on a graphics frame or unassigned frame with the Direct Selection tool to simultaneously select its bounding box and switch to the Selection tool.

Nesting and Anchoring Objects

When a graphics frame or path contains an object, the contained object is said to be *nested*. When a text frame contains an object, the contained object is considered *anchored*. It's possible to place paths inside frames, frames inside frames, and groups inside frames.

Nesting and anchoring objects can give you a lot of freedom in combining objects and can really speed up production time. For example, you can anchor a graphic into a text frame so that if the text flows, the graphic moves along with it. If you're working with a long document that contains a lot of text, it's vital that you anchor graphics frames whenever possible. Then you won't have to go back and reposition each and every graphic if the text reflows.

To place an object into a frame, do one of the following:

- To nest an object into a graphics frame or unassigned frame, select the object with the Selection Tool and copy (or cut) the object. Then select the frame you want to paste the object into and choose Edit > Paste Into. If the nested object is bigger than its container frame, it will be masked. To paste multiple objects inside a frame, group them first.
- To anchor an object into a text frame, select and copy the object. Then position the text cursor where you want the object to appear and choose Edit > Paste. You can anchor as many objects into a text frame as necessary. Drag an anchored object up or down with the Selection tool to reposition it within the text. To further customize the position of an anchored object, choose Object > Anchored Object > Options.

SELECTING NESTED AND ANCHORED OBJECTS

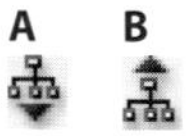
A
B

Figure 6.25 The Select Content button (**A**) is useful for selecting nested objects and the content of a graphics frame. Use the Select Container button (**B**) to switch back to the container frame if its content is currently selected.

To select a nested object, use the Direct Selection tool. If you are selecting a nested graphics frame that contains an image, you must click on the frame's edge to select the frame instead of its content. You can also select the container frame and then use the Select Content button in the Control panel to select its nested object (**Figure 6.25**).

When an object is anchored within a text frame, use the Selection tool or Direct Selection tool to move it or edit its shape. Use the Type tool to select the object as if it were a text character. You can even kern the object to add more white space between it and its adjacent letter.

Stacking Order

● **Note:** By default the rotate, scale, and shear values for nested objects are displayed relative to the pasteboard. To display transformation values for nested objects relative to the container frame, deselect Transformations Are Totals from the Transform or Control panel.

Whenever you create or import objects, they are stacked in the order in which they were created or imported. InDesign lets you select through overlapping objects and arrange their stacking order. Don't confuse stacking order with layers. Arranging objects is not the same as using the Layers panel to arrange separate layers.

To select objects within a stack, do one of the following:

- Hold Ctrl (Windows) or Command (Mac OS) as you continually click through the stack until you select the object you want. Once you select an object, continue holding the mouse button to drag the object to another location.

- Click the Previous Object and Next Object buttons in the Control panel repeatedly until you select the object you want (**Figure 6.26**). Ctrl-click (Windows) or Command-click (Mac OS) either button to select the first or last object in a stack.

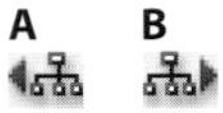
A
B

Figure 6.26 The Previous Object button (**A**) and the Next Object button (**B**).

To arrange a selected object within a stack, do the following:

- To move a selected object to the front or back, choose Object > Arrange > Bring to Front or Object > Arrange > Send to Back.
- To move a selected object forward or backward within the stack, choose Object > Arrange > Bring Forward or Object > Arrange > Send Backward. It pays off to learn the keyboard shortcuts for each of these commands.

7

Setting Up the Framework of a Template

THE FIRST STEP IN CREATING A TEMPLATE IS TO SET UP ITS FOUNDATIONAL framework—page dimensions, margins, columns, and any additional grid structure. Once the framework is in place, all the other template elements can be assembled. A well-designed framework enhances the organization of a template and ensures a smooth and efficient production workflow.

It's worth mentioning that attention to detail at this stage of development is critical. As when building a house, you don't want to have to go back and rework its foundation after you've already built the walls and put a roof on it. The time you spend developing and fine-tuning a template's framework will repay you a thousandfold.

This chapter shows you how to set up a template's page format and construct a layout grid. It is, however, impossible to predict every possible design solution. Therefore, you are provided with principles and guidelines instead of specific solutions. Eventually, practice will develop into experience, and you'll be able to provide the best solutions for your own particular projects.

Study the Mock-up Layout

Before carrying out any detailed work on a template's framework, you need to first study your mock-up layout and think carefully about the scope and scale of your project. This helps you understand the information that will influence or limit the choices you make in its construction. For projects such as posters, small brochures, and booklets, you may only need a bare skeleton of margins, columns, and ruler guides to aid in the alignment of the few objects on the page. For larger projects such as books, magazines, and catalogs, a much more intricate framework is necessary. Once you understand the design objectives and the range of content that your template must include, you are ready to translate the mock-up into a production-viable template.

Setting Up the Page

Your first task is to set up the page format—its dimensions, orientation, and arrangement (single page or spread). Additional structure can be added to the page by establishing a bleed area and slug area.

The choices you make are dictated by the type of document you're producing. If you're creating a newsletter template, you'll probably choose a standard page size, such as US letter or A4, and set up the pages to face each other in a spread format. When creating a brochure template, you'll likely set up a single-page document that is horizontally oriented with a bleed area around all four sides. In more creative situations, you might even specify a custom page size.

● **Note:** The page size you specify should be the final trim size of the publication you will produce. It's common practice to design to the full trim size of a page, bleed over its edges, and let the printer choose the oversize to print on.

InDesign provides two ways to define the page structure:

- Choose File > New > Document to create a new document. In the New Document dialog, choose from one of the preset page sizes or specify a custom width and height for your document (**Figure 7.1**). If your template requires a single-page setup, deselect the Facing Pages option. Otherwise, keep it selected if you plan on working with spreads, as in the case of books, magazines, and catalogs. Choose a page orientation by clicking either the Portrait or Landscape button.

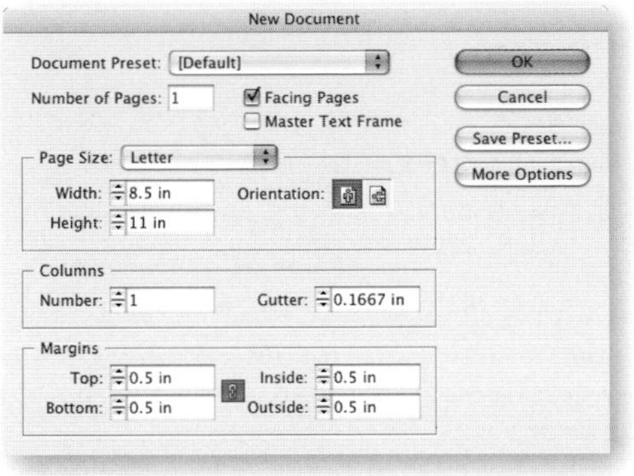
New Document
Document Preset: [Default]
Number of Pages: 1
Facing Pages
Master Text Frame
OK
Cancel
Save Preset...
More Options
Page Size: Letter
Width: 8.5 in
Height: 11 in
Orientation:
Columns
Number: 1
Gutter: 0.1667 in
Margins
Top: 0.5 in
Bottom: 0.5 in
Inside: 0.5 in
Outside: 0.5 in

Figure 7.1 The New Document dialog.

- If you're modifying a document that has already been created, you can change the structure of the page by choosing File > Document Setup. The Document Setup dialog provides all the same options as the New Document dialog except for the Margins and Columns sections and the list of document presets (**Figure 7.2**).

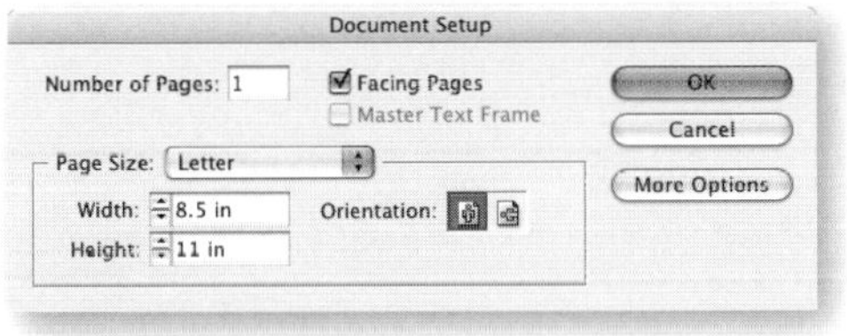
Document Setup
Number of Pages: 1
Facing Pages
Master Text Frame
OK
Cancel
More Options
Page Size: Letter
Width: 8.5 in
Height: 11 in
Orientation:

Figure 7.2 The Document Setup dialog.

Bleed and Slug Area

If you plan on printing images to the edge of the page, you need to add a bleed area around its perimeter. A measurement of 1/8in (3mm) is typically used to allow for any deviations when the paper is trimmed to its final size. Larger documents, such as banners and big posters, require up to a 1/4in (6mm) bleed. Bleed guides are created around the perimeter of the defined page size when you specify a bleed.

Specify a slug area when you need to designate a location for production information, printing instructions, or any other information. For instance, you might make a place for the job number and designer's name to more easily track a project. Also, if the publication you're creating a template for will be passed through an editorial review process, you might create an approval chart to track the progress of every page as it flows between the hands of each editor (**Figure 7.3**). As with the bleed, slug guides are created outside the perimeter of the defined page size. If your template has a bleed area as well, don't forget to specify slug values that exist beyond the bleed guides.

● **Note:** The bleed and slug settings are applied to the entire document, not to individual pages. It's not possible to set up custom bleed and slug areas on a page-by-page basis unless you use ruler guides.

Job #	ART-1010	Version	Sign-off Here:	
Date	08/12/07	Comp. ( )	Kathi	
Designer	Gabriel Powell	First ( )	Bruce	
Filename	Example.indd	Second ( )	Lonny	
Location	server1	Final ( )	Steve	

Figure 7.3 Example slug.

● **Note:** When printing, you can choose whether or not to include the bleed and slug areas you've defined. It's especially useful to include them when outputting in-house proofs. Your service provider will also print the bleed area and perhaps the slug area too, if it contains instructions pertinent to the job.

To specify a bleed and/or slug area, do one of the following:

- In the New Document dialog, click the More Options button (**Figure 7.4**). The Bleed and Slug section appears allowing you to enter bleed and slug dimensions. To make the bleed or slug areas extend evenly on all four sides, click the chain icon (**Figure 7.5**). Otherwise, the values can be different on each side of the page, if necessary.

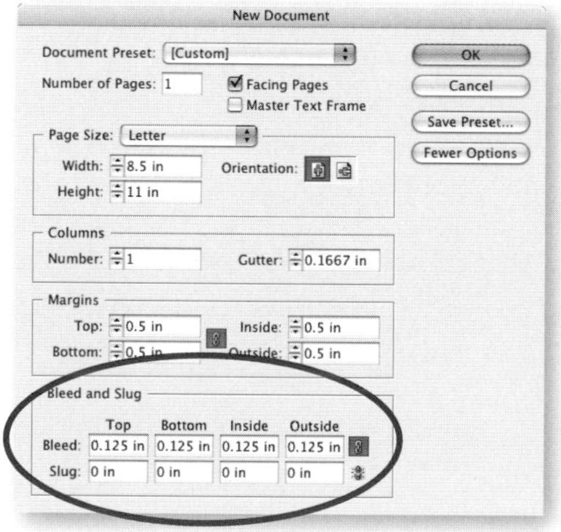
New Document
Document Preset: [Custom]
Number of Pages: 1
Facing Pages
Master Text Frame
OK
Cancel
Save Preset...
Fewer Options
Page Size: Letter
Width: 8.5 in
Height: 11 in
Orientation:
Columns
Number: 1
Gutter: 0.1667 in
Margins
Top: 0.5 in
Bottom: 0.5 in
Inside: 0.5 in
Outside: 0.5 in
Bleed and Slug
Top
Bottom
Inside
Outside
Bleed: 0.125 in 0.125 in 0.125 in 0.125 in
Slug: 0 in 0 in 0 in 0 in

Figure 7.4 The Bleed and Slug section is displayed when you click the More Options button.

Figure 7.5 Click the chain icon to make all the values equal. This icon exists in a number of InDesign's panels and dialogs.

- If you're working on a preexisting document, open the Document Setup dialog and click the More Options button to reveal the Bleed and Slug section.

Third-party Slug Plug-ins

Several plug-ins have been created by third-parties that expand the slug capabilities of InDesign. They make it easier to create slugs and automatically update the slug information as updates are made to the document. Information such as font and image usage, version status, job number, and other information about a document's contents and status can be managed by one of the following plug-ins:

- **Slug Cubed** (www.tripletriangle.com)
- **Slugger ID** (www.gluon.com)
- **Stamp It** (www.knowbody.dk)

■ **Tip:** InDesign includes several predefined text variables that are useful for setting up a slug: Creation Date, Modification Date, Output Date, and File Name. To insert one of these variables, choose Type > Text Variables > Insert Variable, and then choose the variable you want to insert.

Constructing a Layout Grid

Once the page format is set up, you need to create a layout grid for your template. A layout grid serves as a construction plan that indicates where the different elements of a document will be placed. It takes the guesswork out of page layout and speeds up production. It also gives the designer freedom to introduce design variations without forsaking readability or consistency. In large workflows, a well-defined layout grid allows multiple designers to collaborate more effectively on projects.

An underlying framework helps readers find information in the same place each time they turn a page. When headings, page numbers, sidebars, pull-quotes, and other repeating elements are in the same location, the readability of a document significantly increases.

Layout grids come in many shapes and sizes, and there are different approaches for using them—from a simple one-column grid that determines the type area and folio position for a novel, to more complex grid systems, such as those used in magazines and newspapers.

The Composition of a Layout Grid

A layout grid is composed of horizontal and vertical lines that determine margins, columns, and the space between elements on a page. As the lines converge and intersect, a structure of *grid units* is formed. These units are the

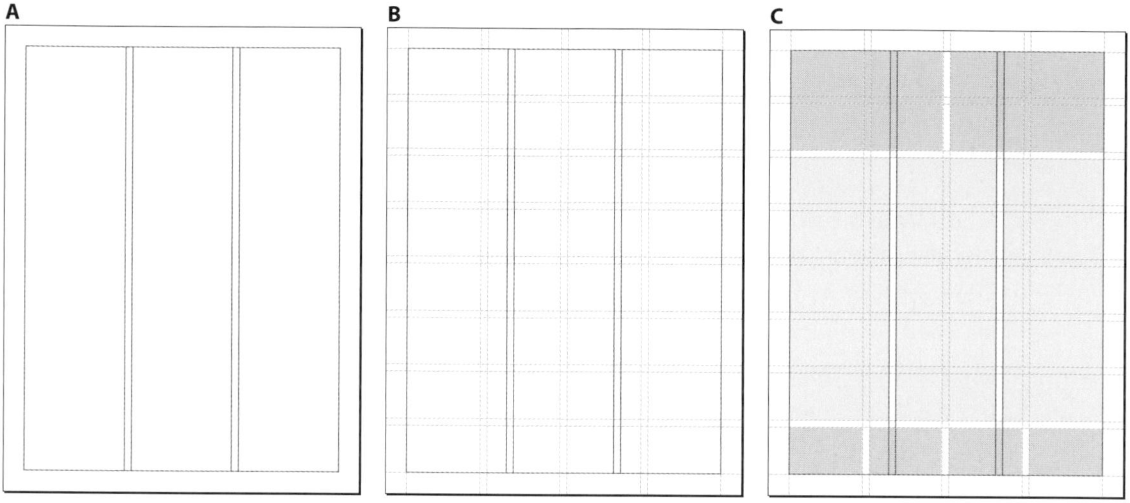
A
B
C

Figure 7.6 In a simple three-column setup, three grid units are separated by gutter space (**A**). More grid units can be created by placing ruler guides on the page (**B**). Use the layout grid to size and align elements on the page (**C**).

● **Note:** Page elements do not have to be confined to individual grid units. They determine the placement of text and graphics but not necessarily their size. One graphic may fill one, two, three, or even more units. The way grid units are used depends on the parameters of a document's design.

primary locations in a template where you arrange text and graphics (**Figure 7.6**). The more grid units a template has, the more flexible and multifunctional it becomes.

Individual grid units can range in size and proportion depending on where and how often the horizontal and vertical lines intersect. Some units have *white space* on one or two of their sides, and others can be completely surrounded by it. This space is crucial in preventing text and graphics from running into each other. Grid lines don't appear on the printed publication, but their influence may be evident in the uniformity and organization of elements from one page to the next.

Planning a Layout Grid

The construction of a layout grid is, in theory, relatively simple. Once the page dimensions are specified, margins, columns, ruler guides, and a baseline grid can be established.

However, designing a proper grid system can be demanding work, requiring a significant amount of attention, experience, and foreknowledge. If you are new to the art of template design, you should plan on spending a considerable amount of time developing the most suitable configuration.

Here are some guidelines for planning a layout grid:

- **Design with a purpose.** There are no right or wrong layout grids. The grid you choose should be uniquely designed to represent the content and design objectives of your mock-up layout. Some are quite flexible, giving the designer room for creativity. Other grids limit design choices in exchange for higher productivity and design consistency. For example, large catalogs and directories are better served with a highly structured grid system.
- **Keep it simple.** The most optimal layout grid communicates how a document should be produced and offers designers flexibility, whenever possible, without overwhelming them with too many possibilities.
- **Suit to fit.** If either the text or graphics refuse to fit the structure of the layout grid, the grid is not working. Do not force the material. It's better to redesign it. Grids should fit the assortment of elements rather than forcing them to fit.
- **Multiple layout grids.** It's possible for a single publication to contain more than one layout grid. A text-heavy page may use a simple setup, whereas complex layouts might require a more intricate setup. It's quite common for different sections in long documents, such as catalogs, to each use a different grid structure. There's no limit—aside from common sense—to the number of layout grids that can be in a template.

WHERE TO BEGIN?

Start by studying the mock-up layout and gather the information that will affect the construction of the template's grid system. Here are some factors that should be taken into account as you study your design:

- **Repetition of elements.** Look for repeating elements. This is the most important factor to consider when designing a layout grid, because it is structured around repetition. How are the various elements arranged on the page? Are they organized in a uniform structure, or are they randomly positioned? The answers to these questions help you to determine how flexible or structured your grid needs to be.
- **Page format.** Is the publication a single or multiple page design? Is it horizontally or vertically oriented? Does it allow images to bleed off the page or not? Knowing this information helps to determine the arrangement of margins and columns.
- **Page count.** If you know the page count and have an idea of how much material must fit into the specified number of pages, consider shaping the margins and columns to accommodate all the text and graphics.

- **Content type.** Is the publication text heavy, graphics heavy, or is there a balance of both elements? The variety and amount of content in a publication has a direct influence on the structure of the grid. For instance, multiple columns and a baseline grid are suitable for text-heavy documents.
- **Text detail.** Find out how much text there is and how it is broken down. Is there one long article, a lot of short articles, or a mix of both? Does the design call for visual elements—such as charts, graphics, and pull-quotes—within the text area? Are there section heads, folios, footnotes, or endnotes?
- **Graphic detail.** Study the photos and illustrations to find out if there are similarities or not in their size and proportions. Are there a lot of rectangular graphics or more irregularly shaped graphics? Are they predominantly horizontal or vertical, or is there a mix of both? Can the graphics be cropped and scaled, or is the designer not permitted to modify them?
- **Miscellaneous elements.** Does the design call for captions, sidebars, or text wraps? Do you need to allocate space for advertisements? Do you need to account for any visual white space? Are there any other elements that need to be considered?
- **Additional language translations.** If the publication will be printed in several languages, consider constructing a grid that accommodates the expansion of each translation. For example, when English text is translated into Spanish, the translation can occupy between 20–30 percent more physical space on a page than the English text.

Your Grid Construction Toolkit

InDesign has a collection of tools that work together to help you set up a layout grid. Here's a look at each tool and its function in a grid system.

MARGINS

Margins are an essential component of any layout grid. Unfortunately, their importance is often overlooked. It's easy to fall back on InDesign's default margins, but by doing so you are missing out on huge opportunities. For one, margins have an impact on the reader's first impression of a page, since they are seen at first glance. They also speed up productivity by making it easier to position text and graphics. Therefore, margins should always be specified with a particular purpose in mind rather than arbitrarily.

The main purpose of margins is to frame the content of a page. What remains after defining them is the *type area*—also referred to as the print area

(**Figure 7.7**). Although it may eventually be divided into columns, it's useful for now to imagine the type area as a solid block to make it easier to judge proportions.

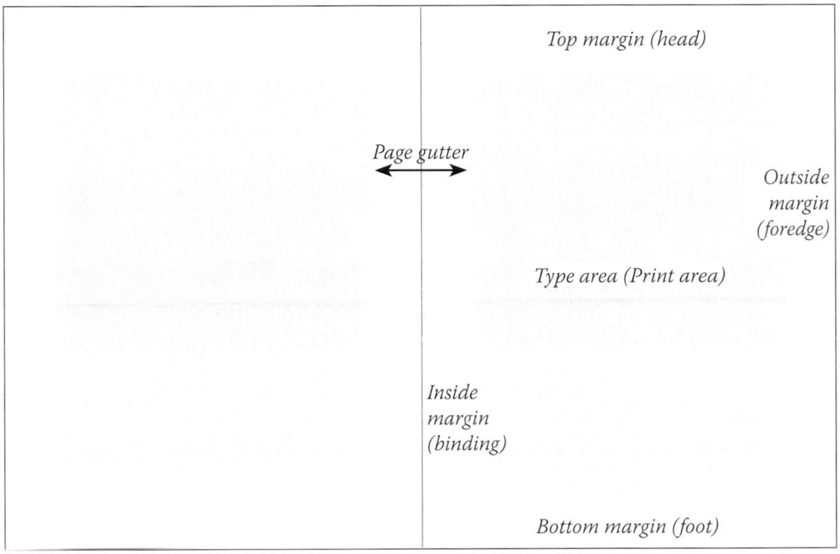
Top margin (head)
Page gutter
Outside margin (foredge)
Type area (Print area)
Inside margin (binding)
Bottom margin (foot)

Figure 7.7 The anatomy of margins. Page size minus margins equals type area.

The type area can be utilized in different ways. It can be used as an indefinite region that loosely defines where text and graphic elements should be arranged. This method typically works best with variable designs. On the other hand, it might function as a fixed layout zone that dictates where specific content must be placed. In this case, a clear boundary is established between the type area and the margin space.

It's also possible to use a combination of both methods where the type area defines a layout zone for certain content, but some design elements are allowed to break its boundaries.

InDesign provides two ways to define margins:

- **In a new document.** When starting a new document, you can enter measurements in the New Document dialog to specify the distance between the margin guides and the edge of each page. If Facing Pages is selected, the Left and Right margin option names change to Inside and Outside. To make the margins even on all four sides, click the chain icon. Otherwise, the values can be different on each side of the page if the chain icon is disabled.
- **In a preexisting document.** If you want to edit the position of margin guides in a preexisting document, choose Layout > Margins and Columns

Tip: You can change margin and column settings for individual pages and spreads. When you change the settings on a master page, you affect the setting for all pages to which the master is applied. Changing the settings on regular pages affects only those pages selected in the Pages panel.

Note: By default, margin guides are magenta and the column guides are violet. Since column guides appear in front of margin guides, the left and right margins will appear violet if the column guides are overlapping the margin guides.

and then make the necessary adjustments (**Figure 7.8**). Before you make any changes, be sure to first select the page or pages you want to modify in the Pages panel. To preview the changes before you apply them, select the Preview option.

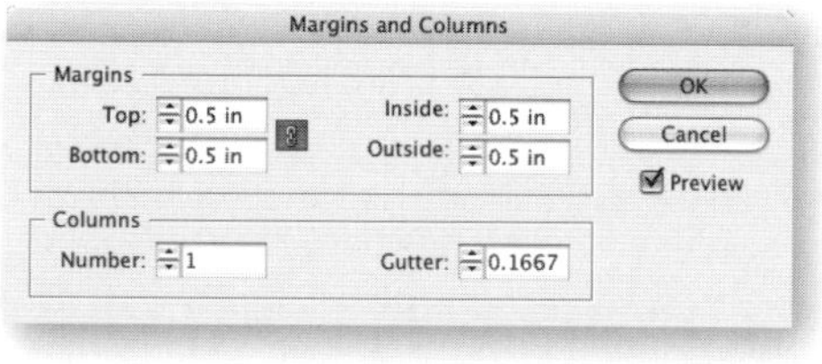
Margins and Columns
Margins
Top: 0.5 in
Bottom: 0.5 in
Inside: 0.5 in
Outside: 0.5 in
OK
Cancel
Preview
Columns
Number: 1
Gutter: 0.1667

Figure 7.8 The Margins and Columns dialog.

When choosing margins, set them up to suit the particular template you're creating. A series of illustrations and guidelines in **Figure 7.9** will help you create the most optimal margins.

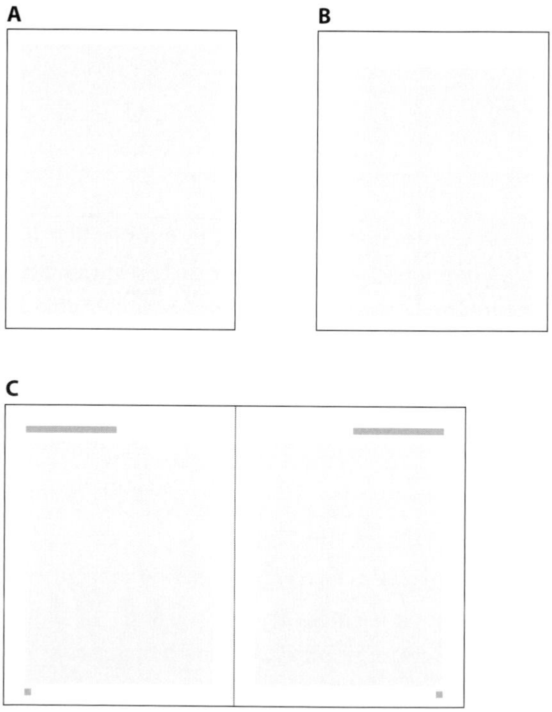
A
B
C

Figure 7.9 This collection of layouts demonstrates basic principles for setting up margins. The yellow block in each figure represents the type area. You can apply these principles to any type of publication whether it's a book, magazine, newspaper, or even an advertisement, brochure, or set of business cards.

(**A**) Generic margins are useful for layouts with a variable design, such as posters, ads, flyers, and newspaper pages containing multiple articles. This setup gives you the most flexibility in design options but reduces the possibility for high-speed production.

(**B**) When you are certain the type area has to be confined to a particular region within the page, identify it with margins. Even with variable designs, it helps tremendously to at least specify the area where the bulk of the layout will occur.

(**C**) Position the margins away from static elements on the perimeter of the page. This prompts the designer to place text and other variable content within the type area away from folios, headings, rules, and any other elements whose position is fixed on the page.

D

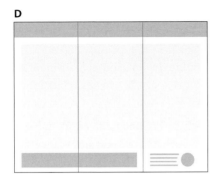

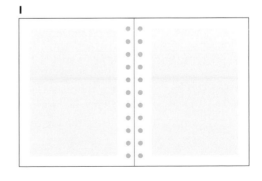

(**D**) The margins in this brochure clearly define the type area, keeping it away from the static elements on the outside edges of the page.

(**E & F**) Set up the margins to create two distinct layout zones: the type area and the margin space. This arrangement is useful for keeping elements like images, ads, captions, and section heads within the margin space while the main content is maintained within the type area.

(**G**) When elements like headlines, images, large charts, and diagrams are repeatedly positioned on the page, you can build the margins around them. This defines their position and separates them from the type area. This figure illustrates a repeating section opener in a book or other long document.

(**H**) Margins don't have to be absolute. They can be used as a design aid, where a specific type area is defined, but certain elements like pull-quotes, images, and captions are allowed to break the type area.

(**I**) When determining the inside margins, be sure to account for any binding requirements and the thickness of the document. In thick books, the inside margins must be adjusted to allow for curvature when the book is open.

E

Section

F

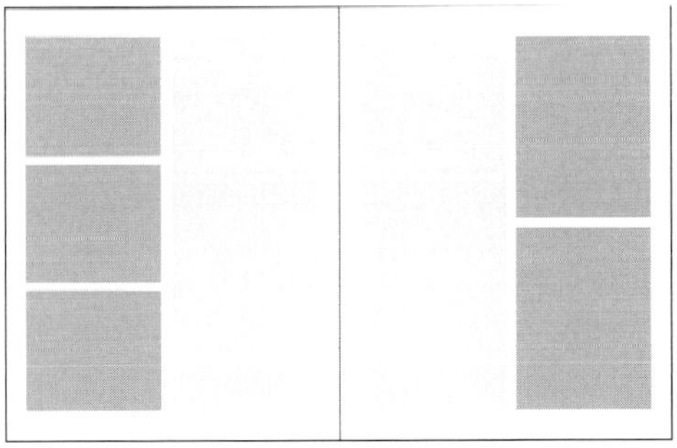

G

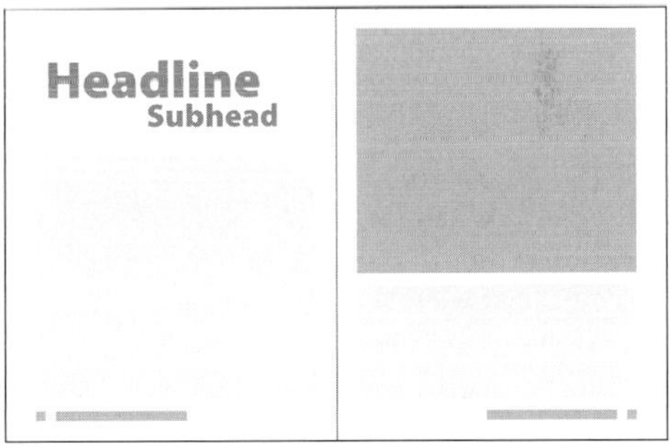
Headline
Subhead

H

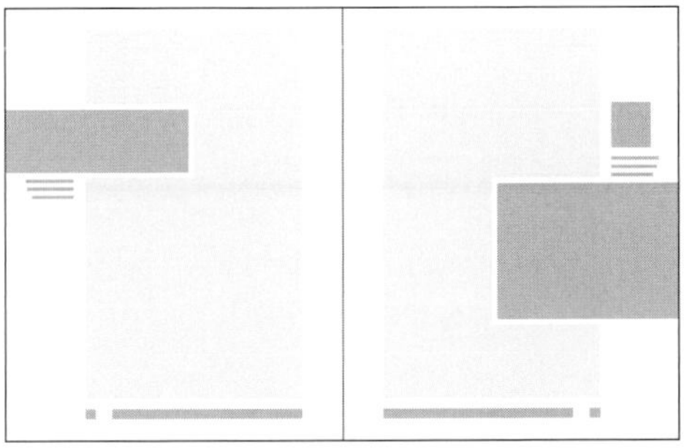

I

COLUMNS

The general purpose of columns is to direct the flow of text and determine its position on the page. They are also used to guide the horizontal placement of graphics and other design elements. The gutter space between each column prevents objects from colliding on the page.

You can set up columns as soon as the margins have been determined. Note that there is always at least one column on a page. Before you add additional columns, you have a single-unit grid. When you divide the type area into several columns, multiple grid units are established. The number of columns you choose depends on your objectives and the kind of layout you're developing a template for.

Like the type area, columns can be utilized in several different ways. Fewer columns limit the number of design options and can be used to dictate the arrangement of text and graphics. As more columns are created, additional grid units become available to work with. This increases your design options and makes for a more flexible template. Five-columns provide more flexibility than a three-column layout. Seven-columns are even more flexible than a five-column layout, and so on.

● **Note:** If vertical ruler guides were used to create column guides, you cannot use the automatic text flow feature. InDesign creates text frames according to the position of the margin and column guides, but not ruler guides.

One of the most important functions of columns in InDesign is to assist in automating text flow. If you set up a template's margins and columns to specifically define the type area, you can use InDesign's automatic text flow feature to automate the production of multiple-page documents. When using this feature, InDesign automatically generates text frames that adhere to the margin and column guides on the page (**Figure 7.10**). Additional pages are also created until all the text has been placed into the document.

InDesign provides three ways to set up columns:

- **In a new document.** When starting a new document, you can specify the number of columns to be created in the New Document dialog. Enter a value into the Gutter field to specify the width of the space between columns. Gutter width can be adjusted for more white space between columns or when a rule runs between them.
- **In a preexisting document.** If you want to edit the column arrangement in a preexisting document, open the Margins and Columns dialog and make the necessary adjustments. Before you make any changes, be sure to first select the page or pages you want to modify in the Pages panel. To preview the changes before you apply them, select the Preview option.

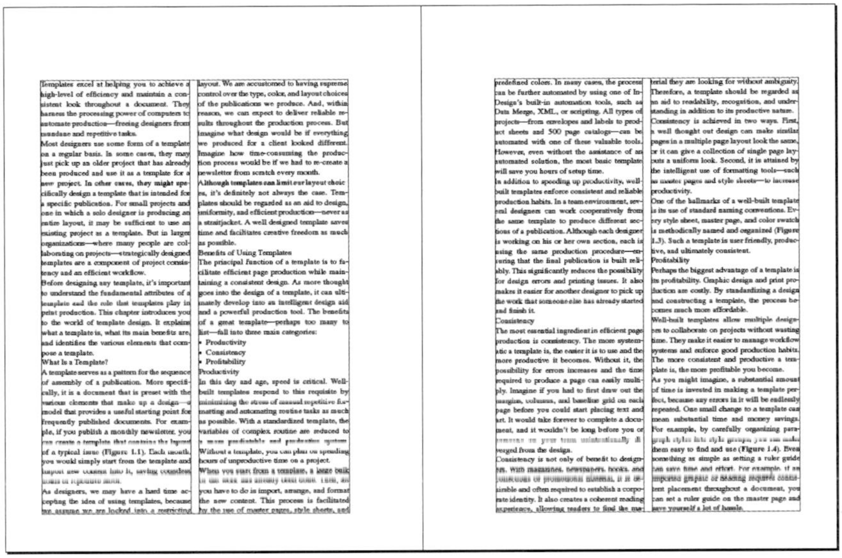

Figure 7.10 InDesign's automatic text flow feature was used to create text frames based on the margin and column setup of this spread.

- **In individual text frames.** Individual text frames can contain columns. This allows you to set up columns within a frame that are independent from those on the page. You can also control the tops and bottoms of all the columns at once by resizing the frame. However, if you want the columns to start or end at different positions on the page, you'll have to create separate frames.

  To create columns within a text frame, select one or more text frames and choose Object > Text Frame Options (**Figure 7.11**). Specify the number of columns and a gutter space. You can also specify an exact width for each column. Select Fixed Column Width to maintain the column width when you resize the frame. If this option is selected, resizing the frame can change the number of columns, but their width will stay the same.

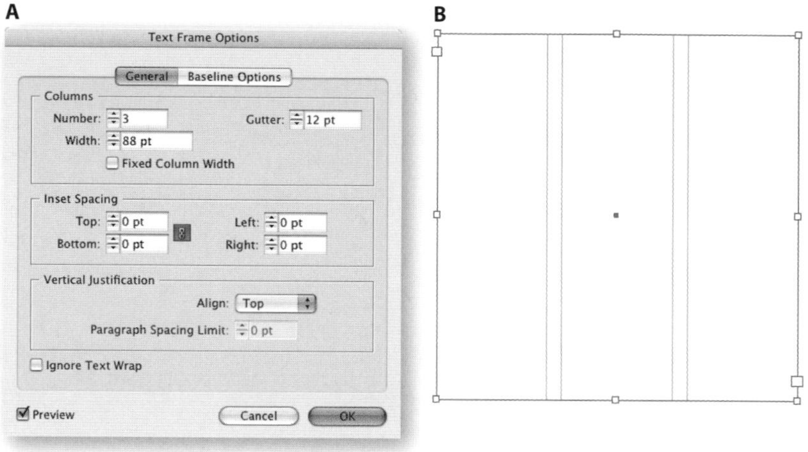
A
Text Frame Options
General
Baseline Options
Columns
Number: 3
Gutter: 12 pt
Width: 88 pt
Fixed Column Width
Inset Spacing
Top: 0 pt
Bottom: 0 pt
Left: 0 pt
Right: 0 pt
Vertical Justification
Align: Top
Paragraph Spacing Limit: 0 pt
Ignore Text Wrap
Preview
Cancel
OK
B

Figure 7.11 The Columns section within the Text Frame Options dialog (**A**) is used to create columns within a text frame (**B**).

Columns are always created in equal proportions within the boundary of the margins. If your mock-up design calls for unequal column widths, you can manually drag the column guides to a new position and the gutter space will be automatically maintained. To adjust column guides, you'll first have to unlock them. Choose View > Grids & Guides > Lock Column Guides to deselect it. Using the Selection tool, drag a column guide to a new position on the page. You can't drag it past an adjacent column guide or beyond the edge of the page.

Figure 7.12 provides a series of illustrations and guidelines that will help you set up the most optimal column arrangements.

RULER GUIDES

After margins and columns have been established, you might want to add additional structure to your layout grid by establishing ruler guides. Although they are often misused and tend to accumulate unnecessarily on a page, ruler guides actually play a vital role in constructing the framework of a template.

Their most important function is to form visible guidelines and boundaries that aid in the consistent placement of design elements. Depending on your design objectives, you may set up just a few or perhaps several guides.

Horizontal guides are used for the vertical alignment of objects, whereas vertical guides are used for horizontal alignment. If columns already exist, you may only need a few vertical guides to define intercolumn spacing. Horizontal guides are often used to form rows down a page.

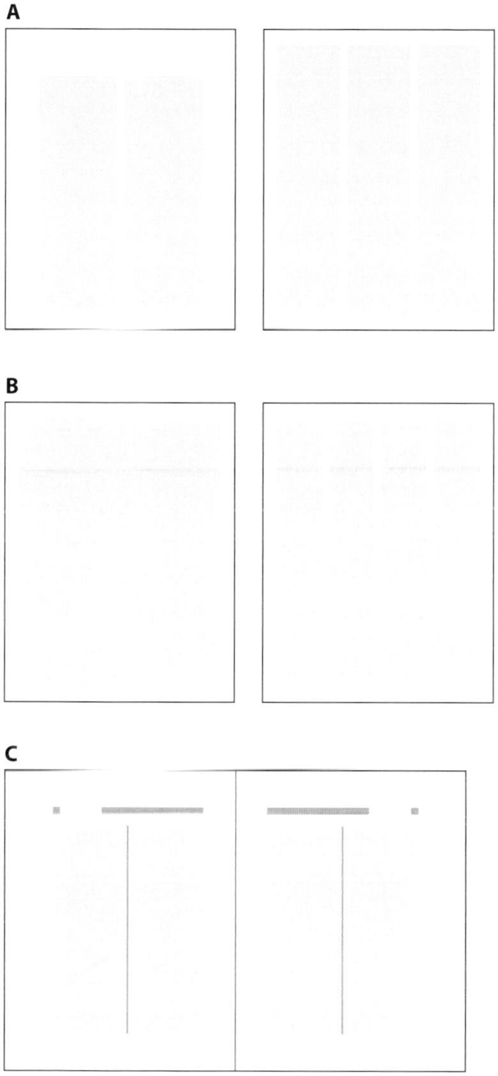

Figure 7.12 This collection of layouts demonstrates basic principles for setting up columns.

(**A**) Column width and height is often based on the font, type size, line length, leading, and the amount of text in a document. As a rough guide, try for 40–70 characters (including spaces) per line. Wide columns accommodate larger type sizes, whereas narrow columns accommodate smaller sizes. Text-heavy documents often require multiple columns that are both tall and narrow.

(**B**) The number of columns you choose depends on the layout you're creating a template for. A single-unit grid might be used to specify space for a full-page ad or photo. More columns may be added to establish a multiple-unit grid that accommodates text-heavy pages or permits creative freedom.

(**C**) Templates with fewer columns are suitable for dictating the exact placement of text and graphics. This setup benefits any project with a repetitive design, such as catalogs and text-heavy documents.

(**D**) Templates with more columns provide additional options for placing and sizing text and images. Magazines, newsletters, and brochures with a lot of design elements usually benefit from a template with four or more columns. You can see in both of these figures that a lot of opportunities for varying a design are possible with multicolumn grids.

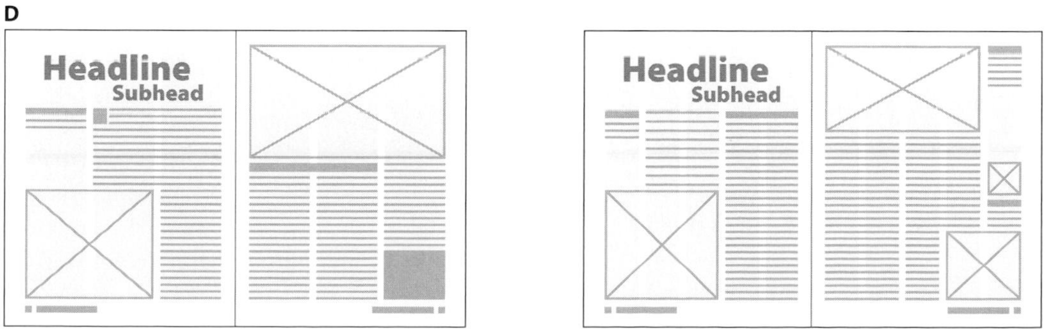
D
Headline
Subhead
Headline
Subhead

The unique advantage of ruler guides is their flexibility. You can freely position as many of them as necessary on a page or spread. As more guides are created, more grid units are formed. As a result, more design options become available. However, too many options can destroy the underlying unity that the grid provides and also slow down the production process.

InDesign provides two ways to create ruler guides:

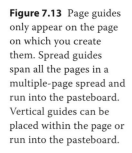

■ **Tip:** To create horizontal and vertical guides at the same time, press Ctrl (Windows) or Command (Mac OS) as you drag from the ruler intersection to the desired location.

- **Use the rulers.** You can click inside the horizontal or vertical ruler and drag a guide to the desired location. To create a page guide, drop the guide onto a page. To create a spread guide, drop the guide onto the pasteboard (**Figure 7.13**). If necessary, you can convert a previously created spread guide to a page guide by dragging it onto a page, and vice versa.

  You can also double-click on the horizontal or vertical ruler to create a spread guide. If you hold the Shift key when you place the guide, it will be placed at the location of the nearest ruler tick mark. So you don't have to be so precise where you double-click.

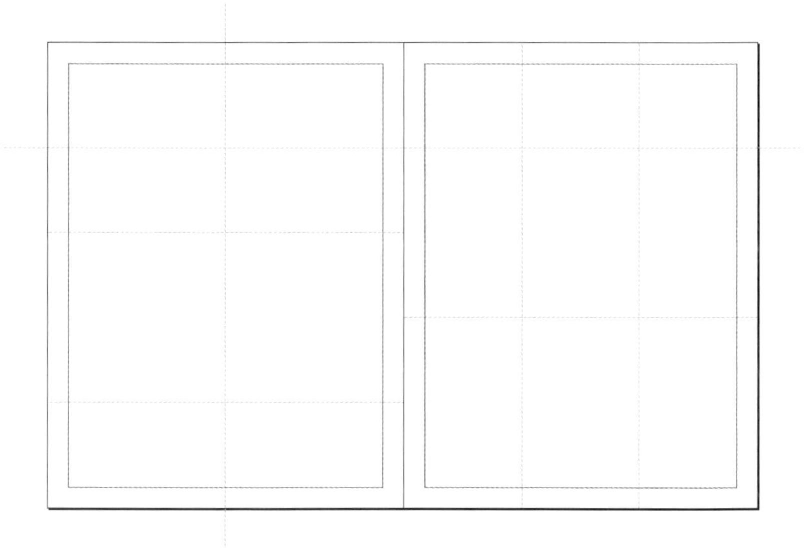

Figure 7.13 Page guides only appear on the page on which you create them. Spread guides span all the pages in a multiple-page spread and run into the pasteboard. Vertical guides can be placed within the page or run into the pasteboard.

- **Use Create Guides dialog.** When you want to quickly set up multiple ruler guides or divide a page with guides, you can use the Create Guides dialog. It offers a powerful range of options for setting up vertical columns and horizontal rows. It can even be used to construct an entire grid structure, complete with margins, columns, rows, and gutter space. To get started, choose Layout > Create Guides (**Figure 7.14**).

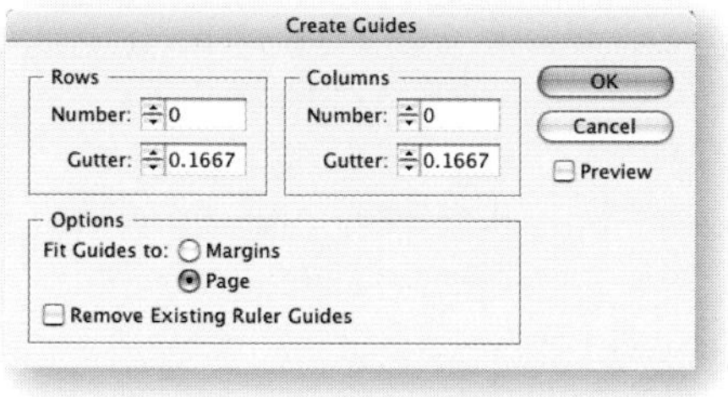
Create Guides
Rows
Number: 0
Gutter: 0.1667
Columns
Number: 0
Gutter: 0.1667
OK
Cancel
Preview
Options
Fit Guides to: Margins
Page
Remove Existing Ruler Guides

Figure 7.14 The Create Guides dialog.

Type a value into the Number fields to specify the number of rows or columns you want to set up. For Gutter, type a value to specify the desired spacing between rows or columns. The Fit Guides To option lets you choose whether the guides will be spaced evenly within the margins or the page edges. If you select Remove Existing Ruler Guides, any existing guides, except those on locked or hidden layers, will be deleted from the document. By selecting Preview, you can see the guides on the page before clicking OK.

■ **Tip:** You can set the current magnification as the view threshold for a new guide by pressing Alt (Windows) or Option (Mac OS) as you drag it to the page.

● **Note:** Columns created with the Create Guides dialog are not the same as those created with the Margins and Columns command. Ruler guides cannot control text flow when a text file is placed. To create columns appropriate for automatic text flow, you must use the Margins and Columns command.

At first glance, ruler guides may appear quite basic. You simply drag a ruler guide onto a page and start using it. However, InDesign offers a few ways to make them even more useful.

Selecting guides. To select a single guide, click on it with the Selection tool or Direct Selection tool. To select multiple guides, hold the Shift key as you click the guides you want to include in the selection. You can also drag over multiple guides, as long as you don't include other objects in the selection. If you do, the objects will be selected instead. InDesign prevents you from selecting both ruler guides and objects in the same selection.

■ **Tip:** To select all of the guides on the selected page or spread at once, press Ctrl-Alt-G (Windows) or Command-Option-G (Mac OS). This only selects the ruler guides, even if other objects exist on the page.

Ruler Guides dialog. This unassuming dialog contains two important options: View Threshold and Color (**Figure 7.15**). Choose Layout > Ruler Guides to see the options. The View Threshold option determines the magnification below which a guide is hidden and above which it is displayed. For example, if you don't want to see a guide until you've zoomed in at 100%, set its view threshold at 100%. The guide remains hidden until the page is magnified at 100% or higher.

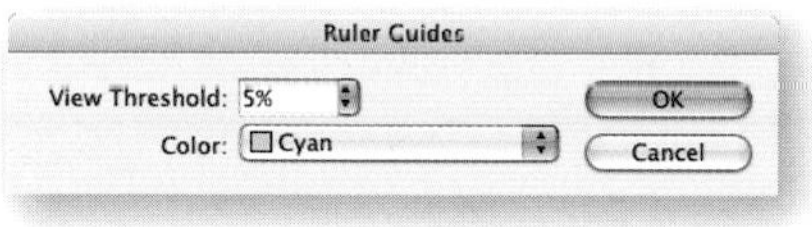
Ruler Guides
View Threshold: 5%
Color: Cyan
OK
Cancel

Figure 7.15 The Ruler Guides dialog.

The Color option allows you to change the color of a selected guide. A guide is displayed using this color when it is not selected. You can select multiple

● **Note:** If you can't select a ruler guide, it might be locked, on a master page, or on a locked layer.

■ **Tip:** You can change the default color and threshold value for all the guides you create in a document by changing the options in the Ruler Guides dialog without any guides selected.

ruler guides to change the options for all of them at one time. It's a good idea to change the color of guides when you want to convey where different kinds of objects should be placed on the page.

Locking guides. Guides can be locked in place by choosing View > Grids & Guides > Lock Guides. This locks all the guides in the current document. You can also lock individual guides by selecting them and choosing Object > Lock Position. Although you can still select the guide, you won't be able to move it. A third option is to lock the layer a guide is on.

Deleting guides. Too many guides can clutter a layout. To delete them, select one or more guides and then press the Delete key.

Moving guides. Guides can be relocated in several ways. You can drag them, use the arrow keys to nudge them, or enter a new position into the X/Y fields on the Transform or Control panel. For example, select a horizontal guide and type **11/2** into the Y field to place the guide halfway down an 11 inch page.

You can use the Align panel to distribute equal spacing between guides. Select multiple guides and click either the Distribute Vertical Centers or Distribute Horizontal Centers button. To use a specific spacing, select Use Spacing in the Distribute Objects section and type a value into the field. The pop-up menu just below allows you to specify whether you want to distribute the selected guides based on the selection, margins, page, or spread. The same buttons and options can be found in the Control panel.

If you want to move guides to another page or document, copy (or cut) and paste them. The guides will appear in the same position if you're pasting them onto a page that is the same size and orientation that the original guides came from.

Figure 7.16 shows a few illustrations and guidelines that explain different ways to utilize guides.

● **Note:** There is only one baseline grid per document that appears on every spread. It can't be adjusted for individual pages and spreads, nor assigned to a master page or layer. However, individual text frames can have their own baseline grid.

BASELINE GRID

The baseline grid is an invaluable tool for managing text alignment. It allows you to control the vertical position of text and balance columns across pages. The grid looks like ruled notebook paper and appears on every spread in a document. When the Align to Baseline Grid command is activated, each line of text in a selected paragraph is forced to align to the baseline grid (**Figure 7.17**).

To view the baseline grid, choose View > Grids & Guides > Show Baseline Grid. You can modify the starting point of the grid, its color, and the spacing between grid lines by choosing Edit > Preferences > Grids (Windows) or InDesign > Preferences > Grids (Mac OS) (**Figure 7.18**).

A

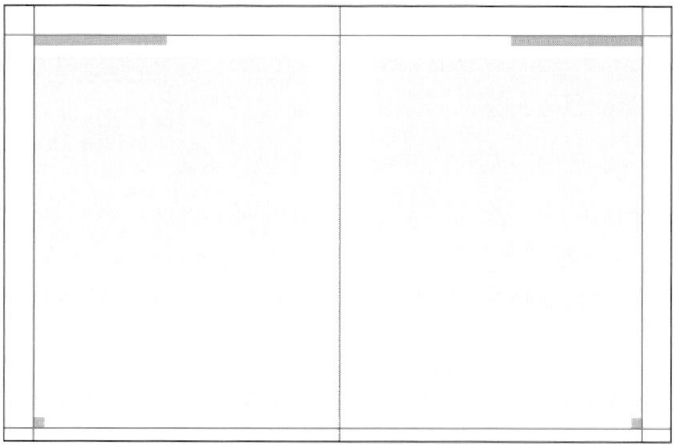

Figure 7.16 This collection of layouts demonstrates basic principles for using ruler guides. (**A**) Use ruler guides to specify the exact placement of repeating elements, such as page numbers and headings that exist outside of the type area. (**B**) Create additional ruler guides to establish more grid units and white space. Use horizontal guides to form rows that specify the vertical placement of objects. Use vertical guides to form optional column structure. Text and graphics can then snap neatly into the grid intersections. (**C**) Ruler guides are multifunctional. In this brochure, they are used to specify the fold marks and page boundaries for repeating elements. The color of the fold mark guides has been changed to set them apart from the rest of the grid structure. (**D**) For graphic-heavy projects like posters, you can use ruler guides in place of margins and columns to create an entire multi-unit grid system upon which text and graphics can be creatively scaled and arranged.

B

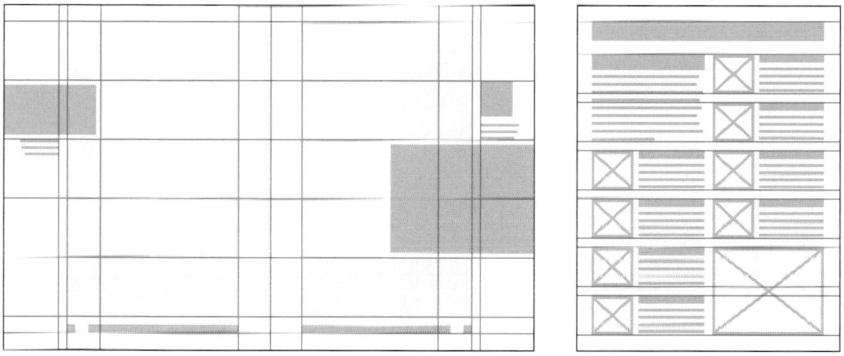

C

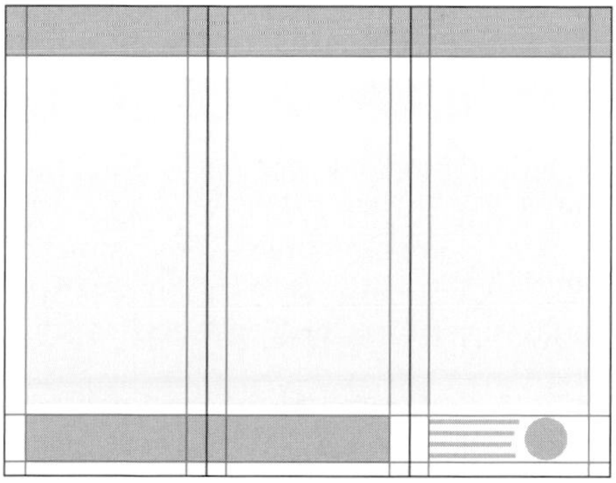

D

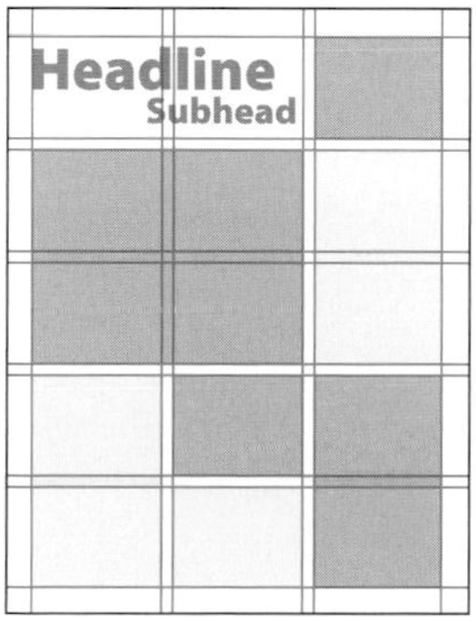
Headline
Subhead

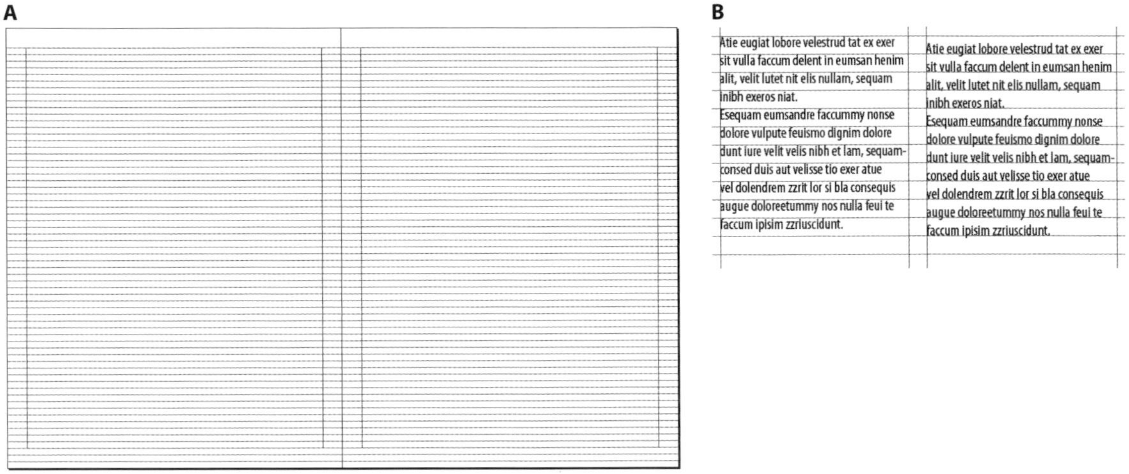
A
B
Atie eugiat lobore velestrud tat ex exer sit vulla faccum delent in eumsan henim alit, velit lutet nit elis nullam, sequam inibh exeros niat.
Esequam eumsandre faccummy nonse dolore vulpute feuismo dignim dolore dunt iure velit velis nibh et lam, sequam-consed duis aut velisse tio exer atue vel dolendrem zzrit lor si bla consequis augue doloreetummy nos nulla feui te faccum ipisim zzriuscidunt.
Atie eugiat lobore velestrud tat ex exer sit vulla faccum delent in eumsan henim alit, velit lutet nit elis nullam, sequam inibh exeros niat.
Esequam eumsandre faccummy nonse dolore vulpute feuismo dignim dolore dunt iure velit velis nibh et lam, sequam-consed duis aut velisse tio exer atue vel dolendrem zzrit lor si bla consequis augue doloreetummy nos nulla feui te faccum ipisim zzriuscidunt.

Figure 7.17 The default baseline grid (**A**). The text in the right column is aligned to the baseline grid (**B**).

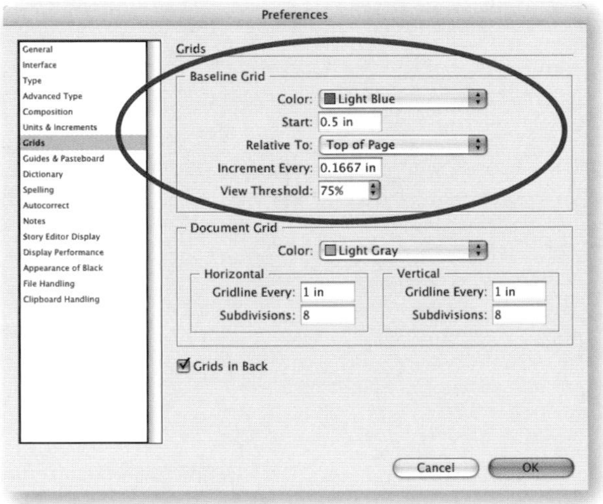
Preferences
General
Interface
Type
Advanced Type
Composition
Units & Increments
Grids
Guides & Pasteboard
Dictionary
Spelling
Autocorrect
Notes
Story Editor Display
Display Performance
Appearance of Black
File Handling
Clipboard Handling
Grids
Baseline Grid
Color: Light Blue
Start: 0.5 in
Relative To: Top of Page
Increment Every: 0.1667 in
View Threshold: 75%
Document Grid
Color: Light Gray
Horizontal
Gridline Every: 1 in
Subdivisions: 8
Vertical
Gridline Every: 1 in
Subdivisions: 8
Grids in Back
Cancel
OK

Figure 7.18 The Baseline Grid section of Grids Preferences.

■ **Tip:** You can use the baseline grid to scale and align graphics to leading increments. If you want to snap objects to the baseline grid, choose View > Grids & Guides > Snap to Guides.

■ **Tip:** It's useful to set up the vertical ruler to display custom ruler increments that match the value in the Increment Every field. Then the ruler's major tick marks line up with the baseline grid.

Color. Select a color for the baseline grid from the Color menu. It's a good idea to choose a color that's distinct from any other guides in your template.

Start & Relative To. Choose from one of the options in the Relative To menu to determine where the grid should start from. The Top Margin option displays the baseline grid within the type area rather than across the entire page, reducing page clutter. To determine how far from the top of the page or margin the grid should start, specify a value in the Start field. A value of 0 is usually a good place to begin unless you have a good reason for starting the text farther down the page.

Increment Every. To control the spacing between grid lines, specify a value in the Increment Every field. It's best to type a value that is equal to or a multiple of the leading of your body text. The lines of text then snap perfectly to the baseline grid. If a paragraph's leading value is larger than the Increment Every value, the text will skip one or more grid lines, depending on how much larger the value is. For instance, if a paragraph with a leading value of 14 is aligned to a 12-point grid, it's effective leading rounds up to 24 points, causing the text to align to every other grid line. You can also force lines of text to the next available leading increment by adding space before or after paragraphs, which is useful for adding additional space after headlines.

View Threshold. This option determines the magnification below which the baseline grid is hidden and above which it is displayed. It will remain hidden until the page is magnified at the specified value or higher.

After you've set up the baseline grid, you can force text to align to it. There are two ways to do this: locally or as part of a paragraph style's definition. To locally align one or more selected paragraphs, click the Align to Baseline Grid button in either the Paragraph panel or Control panel. To turn it off and allow the paragraph's leading value to determine the line spacing, click the Do Not Align to Baseline Grid button (**Figure 7.19**). To turn the option on as part of a paragraph style's definition, go to the Indents and Spacing section of any paragraph style and choose All Lines from the Align to Grid menu. Choose None to turn it off (**Figure 7.20**).

● **Note:** It's best not to use auto leading when aligning text to the baseline grid. It's more user friendly if you specify an easier leading value to work with, such as 12.

■ **Tip:** Use a higher View Threshold value, such as 125%, to allow you to view an entire spread without the grid lines in your way. When you are ready to see them, just zoom in past 125%.

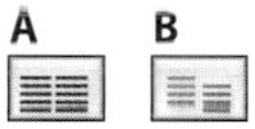
A
B

Figure 7.19 The Align to Baseline Grid button (**A**) and the Do Not Align to Baseline Grid button (**B**).

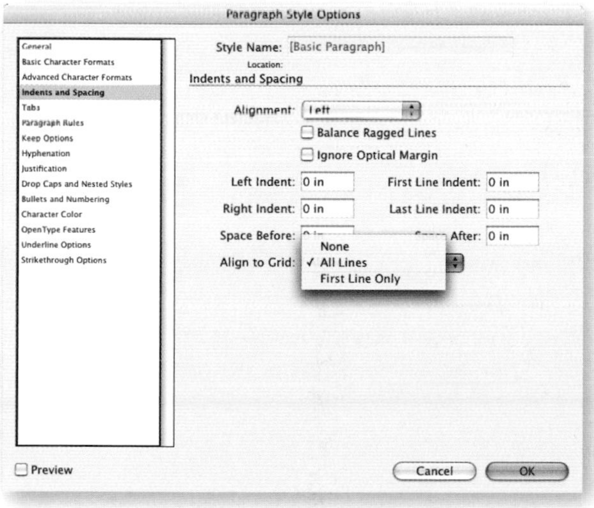
Paragraph Style Options
General
Basic Character Formats
Advanced Character Formats
Indents and Spacing
Tabs
Paragraph Rules
Keep Options
Hyphenation
Justification
Drop Caps and Nested Styles
Bullets and Numbering
Character Color
OpenType Features
Underline Options
Strikethrough Options
Style Name: [Basic Paragraph]
Location:
Indents and Spacing
Alignment: Left
Balance Ragged Lines
Ignore Optical Margin
Left Indent: 0 in
First Line Indent: 0 in
Right Indent: 0 in
Last Line Indent: 0 in
Space Before:
After: 0 in
Align to Grid:
None
✓ All Lines
First Line Only
Preview
Cancel
OK

Figure 7.20 The Indents and Spacing section of the Paragraph Style Options dialog.

Of course, you don't always want to give the baseline grid power over the text elements in your template. Feel free to break away from it whenever necessary, such as when your template uses a variety of type and leading sizes. There are alternative methods to manage the alignment of text. One way is to create a paragraph style that is not aligned to the baseline grid so it can go anywhere and have any leading.

Another option is to align just the first line of text to the baseline grid. This is useful for keeping the first line of a paragraph aligned to the body text in adjacent columns, even though its size and leading values prevent the rest of the paragraph from adhering to the grid (**Figure 7.21**). To apply this option to a selected paragraph, click the Align to Baseline Grid button, and then choose Only Align First Line to Grid from either the Paragraph or Control panel menu. You can also choose First Line Only from the Align to Grid menu in the Indents and Spacing section of a paragraph style.

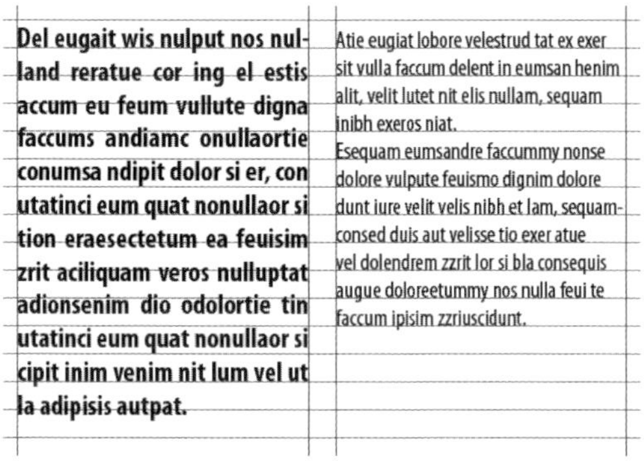
Del eugait wis nulput nos nul-
land reratue cor ing el estis
accum eu feum vullute digna
faccums andiamc onullaortie
conumsa ndipit dolor si er, con
utatinci eum quat nonullaor si
tion eraesectetum ea feuisim
zrit aciliquam veros nulluptat
adionsenim dio odolortie tin
utatinci eum quat nonullaor si
cipit inim venim nit lum vel ut
la adipisis autpat.
Atie eugiat lobore velestrud tat ex exer
sit vulla faccum delent in eumsan henim
alit, velit lutet nit elis nullam, sequam
inibh exeros niat.
Esequam eumsandre faccummy nonse
dolore vulpute feuismo dignim dolore
dunt iure velit velis nibh et lam, sequam-
consed duis aut velisse tio exer atue
vel dolendrem zzrit lor si bla consequis
augue doloreetummy nos nulla feui te
faccum ipisim zzriuscidunt.

Figure 7.21 The intro paragraph on the left uses the First Line Only option. The body text on the right is set to All Lines.

■ Tip: You can rotate a frame that has a baseline grid and the text will continue to align to the grid. On the other hand, text that is aligned to the document baseline grid will no longer snap to the grid if the text is rotated.

A third option is to use a separate baseline grid for individual text frames, such as captions or sidebar notes that are sized differently than your body copy. Frame grids function independently from the document baseline grid. To apply a baseline grid to a text frame, choose Object > Text Frame Options, click the Baseline Options tab, and then select Use Custom Baseline Grid (**Figure 7.22**). The options that follow are basically the same settings used to modify the document baseline grid. However, frame grid options deserve additional explanation because of the different uses for some of the options.

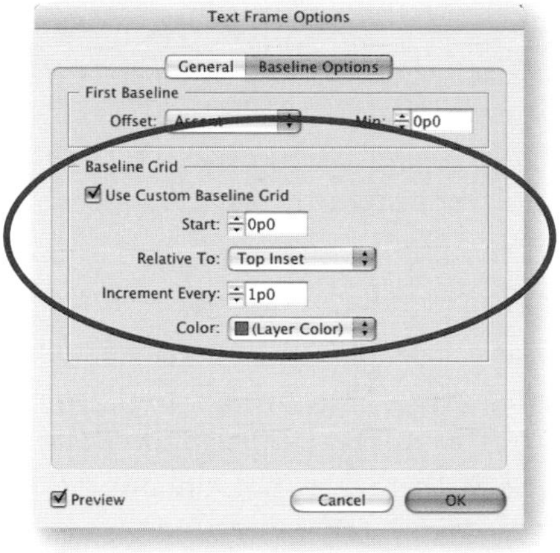
Text Frame Options
General
Baseline Options
First Baseline
Offset:
Min:
0p0
Baseline Grid
Use Custom Baseline Grid
Start:
0p0
Relative To:
Top Inset
Increment Every:
1p0
Color:
(Layer Color)
Preview
Cancel
OK

Figure 7.22 The Baseline Grid section of the Text Frame Options dialog.

Relative To. Choose from one of the options in the Relative To menu to determine where the grid should start from:

- The Top of Page and Top Margin options measure the frame grid from outside the frame itself. Both options, in effect, give you an additional baseline grid to work with on the page. If you move a text frame up or down, the position of the first baseline changes relative to the top of the page or margin, and the text inside the frame won't move until an entire new line of type can fit into the frame and snap to the next available grid line. These options are useful for keeping multiple text frames on a spread aligned to one baseline grid while other text continues aligning to the document baseline grid.
- The Top of Frame and Top Inset options measure the frame grid from within the frame. This allows you to keep text aligned to a baseline grid that operates independently of any other baseline grid. You can move a text frame anywhere on the page and the text inside will not change. Use the Top Inset option if you've applied inset spacing to the top of a text frame and you don't want to see grid lines in that space.

Start. Type a value to offset the grid from the location chosen in the Relative To menu.

Increment Every. Type a value to determine the spacing between grid lines. Type a value that is equal to or a multiple of the leading of your body text, just as you did for the document baseline grid.

Color. Select a color to use for the grid lines. This helps to distinguish the frame grid from the document's baseline grid.

DOCUMENT GRID

Another option for setting up a layout grid is to use InDesign's document grid feature. It allows you to precisely align objects—both horizontally and vertically—without having to create ruler guides, margins, or columns. It typically works great for image-heavy projects, where all you need is a grid structure that accommodates creative freedom. But when it comes to text-heavy projects, the document grid will never replace the function of margins and columns.

To view the document grid, choose View > Grids & Guides > Show Document Grid. At first, it looks like a large piece of graph paper that overlays the entire pasteboard (**Figure 7.23**). While you might find this distracting, the document grid is actually quite useful once you learn how to customize it.

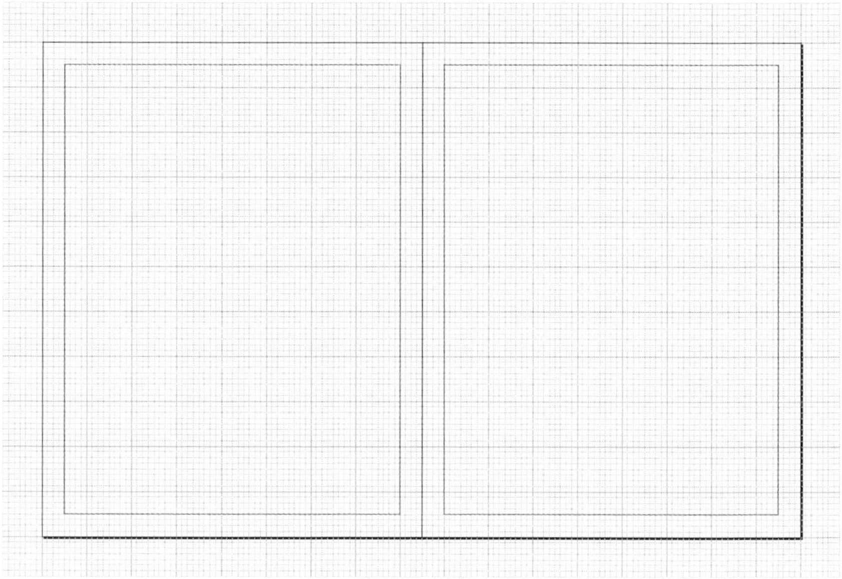

Figure 7.23 The document grid appears on every spread in a document and covers the entire pasteboard. It can't be adjusted for individual pages and spreads, nor assigned to a master page or layer.

To modify the document grid, choose Edit > Preferences > Grids (Windows) or InDesign > Preferences > Grids (Mac OS) (**Figure 7.24**). In the Document Grid section, specify a value in both Gridline Every fields to adjust the frequency of the horizontal and vertical gridlines. This determines the size of each square in the grid. Specify a value in both Subdivisions fields to determine the number of horizontal and vertical subdivisions within each grid square. The more grid units you create, the more creative freedom the grid provides.

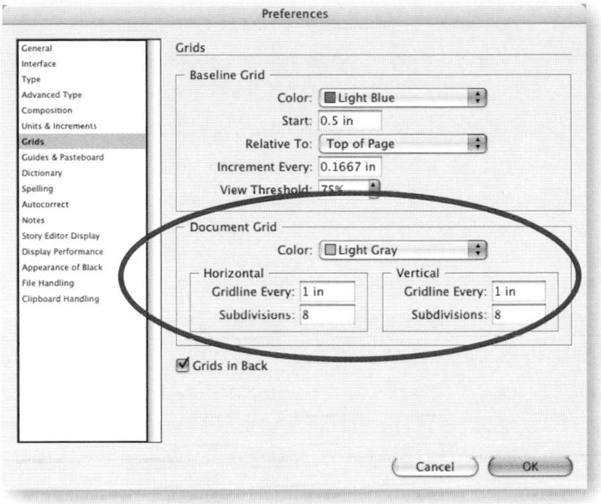
Preferences
General
Interface
Type
Advanced Type
Composition
Units & Increments
Grids
Guides & Pasteboard
Dictionary
Spelling
Autocorrect
Notes
Story Editor Display
Display Performance
Appearance of Black
File Handling
Clipboard Handling
Grids
Baseline Grid
Color: Light Blue
Start: 0.5 in
Relative To: Top of Page
Increment Every: 0.1667 in
Document Grid
Color: Light Gray
Horizontal
Gridline Every: 1 in
Subdivisions: 8
Vertical
Gridline Every: 1 in
Subdivisions: 8
Grids in Back
Cancel
OK

Figure 7.24 The Document Grid section of Grids Preferences.

Use the Color menu to specify a color for the grid. The Grids in Back option lets you choose whether you want the document and baseline grids in front or behind all other objects in a document.

Once you've set up the document grid, you can choose to start it at a different place on the page by relocating the zero point. If you want to be able to snap objects to the gridlines, choose View > Grids & Guides > Snap to Document Grid.

Guides and Pasteboard Preferences

When constructing a layout grid, you can choose to use different colors for margin and column guides, or even the bleed and slug guides. For instance, you might decide to change the color of the column guides from violet to a less prominent color to make it easier to see the layout when the guides are showing. You can even change the preview background color to make it easier to distinguish between the pasteboard and your layout when Preview mode is on. Black works well for making your design stand out.

To customize the color of guides and the preview background, choose Edit > Preferences > Guides & Pasteboard (Windows) or InDesign > Preferences > Guides & Pasteboard (Mac OS) (**Figure 7.25**). Under the Color section, choose the desired color from each of the menus. Choose the Custom option from the bottom of a menu to specify a custom color.

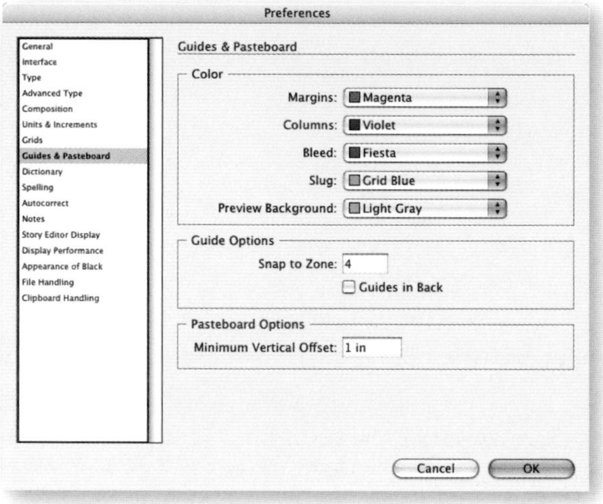
Preferences
General
Interface
Type
Advanced Type
Composition
Units & Increments
Grids
Guides & Pasteboard
Dictionary
Spelling
Autocorrect
Notes
Story Editor Display
Display Performance
Appearance of Black
File Handling
Clipboard Handling
Guides & Pasteboard
Color
Margins: Magenta
Columns: Violet
Bleed: Fiesta
Slug: Grid Blue
Preview Background: Light Gray
Guide Options
Snap to Zone: 4
Guides in Back
Pasteboard Options
Minimum Vertical Offset: 1 in
Cancel
OK

Figure 7.25 Guides & Pasteboard Preferences.

● **Note:** Make sure that Snap to Guides is turned on if you want objects to snap to guides as you draw, move, or resize them. Choose View > Grids & Guides > Snap to Guides.

The Snap to Zone preference determines how close an object needs to be before it snaps to a guide. Specify a value in pixels. The guides on the page must be visible for snapping to occur; however, objects continue snapping to the baseline and document grids even when the grids are hidden.

The Guides in Back option allows you to control whether the guides are displayed in front or behind the objects on the page. Keep in mind that sending the guides to the back of your layout can make it quite difficult to arrange objects. It's best to leave them in front and then hide them to get them temporarily out of the way.

Enter a value for Minimum Vertical Offset to specify how far the pasteboard extends out from the page or spread. It's particularly useful to increase the value if you prefer more space above and below each spread in your template.

Showing and Hiding the Layout Grid

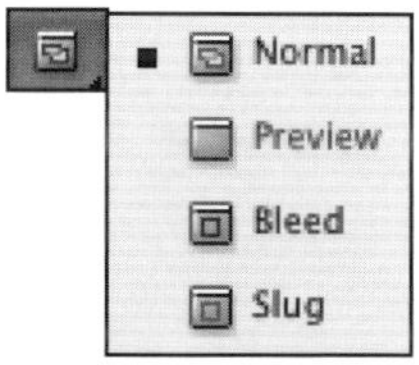
Normal
Preview
Bleed
Slug

Figure 7.26 Use the Mode buttons to quickly switch between view modes.

There may be times when you want to switch off the distracting grids and guides to make it easier to see the layout as if it were printed. InDesign offers several ways to do this.

But the fastest way to switch off the grids and guides, including all nonprinting objects, is to use the Mode buttons at the bottom of the toolbox (**Figure 7.26**). To switch from one view mode to another, click and hold the mode button until the options become available, and then choose the desired mode. If you prefer menus over buttons, you can choose the same commands from the Screen Mode menu (View > Screen). Each mode serves a specific purpose:

- **Normal mode** is the default view mode. When it is active, all the grids and guides are visible, including all nonprinting objects. The pasteboard is white.
- **Preview mode** switches off all the grids, guides, and nonprinting objects. The pasteboard is set to the preview background color defined in Preferences. Anything extending beyond the edge of the page is no longer visible.
- **Bleed mode** is similar to Preview mode. It switches off the grids, guides, and nonprinting objects, and the pasteboard is set to the preview background color. The difference is that any printing elements within the bleed area remain visible. Anything extending beyond the edge of the bleed area is hidden.
- **Slug mode** is similar to Preview mode and Bleed mode. It switches off the grids, guides, and nonprinting objects, and the pasteboard is set to the preview background color. The difference is that any printing elements within the bleed and slug areas remain visible. Anything extending beyond the edge of the slug area is hidden.

■ **Tip:** Use the keyboard shortcut W to switch between Normal mode and the mode that was last used. This doesn't work if your Type tool is active within a text frame.

The only disadvantage to using the view modes is that you must choose between showing or hiding all the grids and guides at once. So, if you want to turn off the guides without hiding the baseline grid, for instance, you'll have to use the View menu instead. Choose View > Grids & Guides to find the commands for independently showing or hiding the guides, baseline grid, or document grid.

■ **Tip:** You can place ruler guides on a separate layer that can later be turned off to hide just the guides on that layer without having to turn off all the guides at the same time.

Printing the Layout Grid

There may be times when you want to output a document with its underlying grid structure intact. This is useful for checking proofs. Or you might need to supply sample pages that detail a project's design parameters to a group of editors and proofreaders. You might also want to output a hard copy of your template along with its visible grid structure.

InDesign lets you print visible guides and the baseline grid—not hidden or on a hidden layer—when exporting a PDF file or printing to any printer. To include them when outputting a document, select the Print Visible Guides and Baseline Grids option in the General area of the Print dialog. When exporting a PDF, choose the Visible Guides and Grids option in the General area of the Export Adobe PDF dialog. You can control which guides and grids are visible in the View menu.

● **Note:** InDesign will not print the document grid, even if it is visible.

Taking Advantage of Layout Adjustment

No template is ever completed on your first attempt. You'll likely make small changes or even major overhauls as you design and evaluate new possibilities. You might alter just the margins or the number of columns. At other times, you may have to change the template's page size or even its orientation. In either case, you could spend a significant amount of time and effort reorganizing objects to fit the new layout.

Fortunately, InDesign's Layout Adjustment feature can save the day by doing much of that work for you. If you make a change using the Document Setup or Margins and Columns commands when Layout Adjustment is enabled, text and graphics frames are moved and resized based on the new relative position of page edges, margins, column guides, and ruler guides.

● **Note:** Layout Adjustment affects columns within text frames differently than it does page columns. If a text frame is resized during a layout adjustment, the columns within it change depending on the Fixed Column Width option in the Text Frame Options dialog. If the option is selected, columns are added or removed as necessary. If the option is not selected, columns are resized proportionally.

For example, if you want to convert a two-column layout to three columns, enable Layout Adjustment and then adjust the number of columns. InDesign adds a new column guide, creates a text frame for it, and then resizes and repositions the three frames to adhere to the new column guides. If an image was arranged within one of the columns, it may also be resized relative to the new column width.

The results are more predictable when a layout is tightly based on a well-defined grid structure, where objects are snapped to margin, column, and ruler guides. But when objects don't adhere to guides or when a layout is cluttered with unnecessary guides, the results can be disastrous.

Setting Options for Layout Adjustment

The various rules that determine the behavior of a layout adjustment are found in the Layout Adjustment dialog (**Figure 7.27**). Keep in mind that modifying these options does not change anything right away. Layout Adjustment is triggered when you make changes to page size and orientation, margins and columns, or when a new master page is applied.

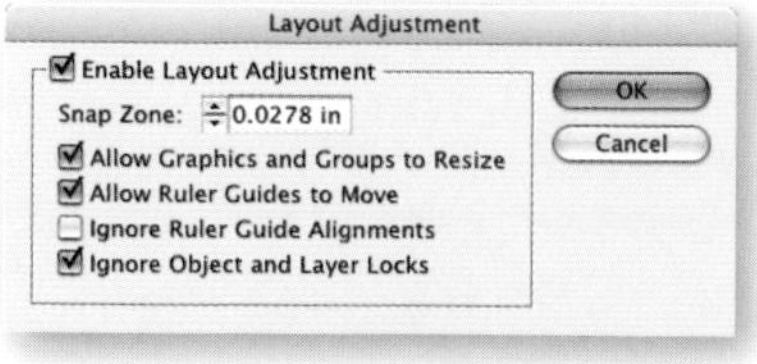
Layout Adjustment
Enable Layout Adjustment
Snap Zone: 0.0278 in
Allow Graphics and Groups to Resize
Allow Ruler Guides to Move
Ignore Ruler Guide Alignments
Ignore Object and Layer Locks
OK
Cancel

Figure 7.27 The Layout Adjustment dialog.

To allow a layout to be automatically adjusted, choose Layout > Layout Adjustment and select the Enable Layout Adjustment option. You can fine-tune its behavior using these options:

- **Snap Zone.** When an object is closer than this value to a guide, it is considered aligned to the guide and can be moved or resized during a layout adjustment.
- **Allow Graphics and Groups To Resize.** This option allows graphics and groups to be scaled during a layout adjustment. If deselected, graphics and groups can be moved but not resized.
- **Allow Ruler Guides to Move.** If you want ruler guides to be repositioned relative to the new page size, margin, or column settings, keep this option on.
- **Ignore Ruler Guide Alignments.** When this option is selected, objects won't be adjusted to stay aligned to ruler guides when their position changes. It's a good idea to turn on this option if the position of ruler guides haven't been well planned.
- **Ignore Object and Layer Locks.** When this option is selected, individually locked objects and objects on a locked layer are allowed to be repositioned during a layout adjustment.

● **Note:** Layout Adjustment is not triggered by making changes to the document grid, the baseline grid, or by dragging ruler guides or column guides.

8

Setting Up Master Pages, Libraries, and Layers

WITH THE FOUNDATIONAL FRAMEWORK IN PLACE, THE NEXT STEP IS TO SET UP master pages, object libraries, and layers. Each of these tools serves a specific function yet work together to enhance the organization of a template and facilitate productivity.

Master pages commonly contain a layout grid, any recurring design elements, and placeholder frames. By using master pages, you can create a consistent layout throughout the pages in a publication. You can also automate layout changes, since any modification you make to a master page is automatically reflected on all the pages that have that master page applied.

Object libraries are a perfect counterpart to master pages. They allow you to store frequently used elements that recur throughout a publication but not consistently enough to be placed on a master page. Layers help you organize a template's elements into logical segments, making it easier to create and edit specific areas of a publication without affecting other areas.

Setting Up Master Pages

Begin by studying your mock-up layout and determine which design elements repeat frequently and consistently enough to be placed on a master page. Here are a few guidelines to follow as you set up master pages:

- **Don't place rarely used items.** Elements that recur infrequently should not be placed on a master page. Otherwise, you'll create more cleanup work for yourself later on. It's best to place occasionally used design elements into an object library instead of on a master page, giving you convenient access to them as you need them.
- **Create additional master pages as necessary.** You might have to make more than one master page if your mock-up calls for different layout grids or several design alternatives. For instance, magazines typically have a master page for each editorial section and others for different types of advertisement layouts.
- **Keep the number of master pages to a minimum.** Set up master pages for just the layouts that appear regularly. Don't overbloat a template with master pages that are hardly ever used. This makes a template confusing and difficult to use. Your goal is to reduce the amount of labor involved in the production process, not create more work.

● **Note:** If you check the Master Text Frame option in the New Document dialog, an empty text frame is created that adheres to the margin guides and matches the specified column settings. If your template requires more variation, leave this option deselected.

Creating Master Pages

The first time you create a new document, it has one default master page (A-Master), which takes on the margin and column settings you defined in the New Document dialog.

To create a new master page from scratch, choose New Master from the Pages panel menu. In the New Master dialog, specify the following settings (**Figure 8.1**):

Figure 8.1 The New Master dialog.

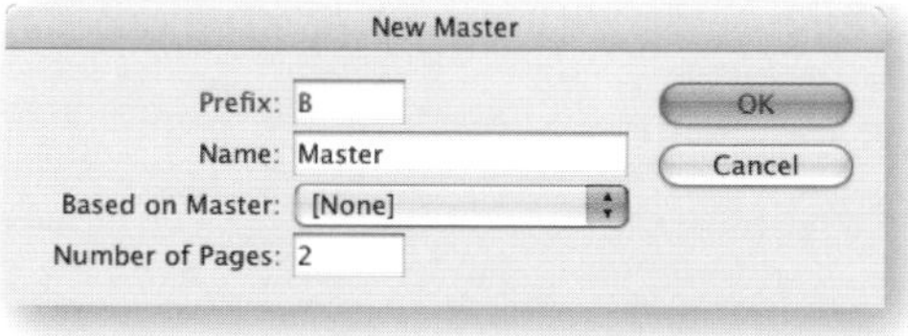
New Master
Prefix: B
Name: Master
Based on Master: [None]
Number of Pages: 2
OK
Cancel

- **Prefix.** The prefix identifies the master page that is applied to each page in the Pages panel. You can type up to four characters, which appear in front of the hyphen in the master page's name. Choose a prefix that associates the master page with its intended purpose. For instance, you might use TOC to identify a master page as the table of contents layout.

- **Name.** Type a name that identifies the purpose of the master page. It's a good idea to use a naming convention that is simple and recognizable.
- **Based on Master.** Choose an existing master page on which you would like to base this master page, or choose None. By basing one master page on another, you can create a variation of a main master page, which is called the *parent master*. Any master pages based on the parent master are called *child masters*.

  For example, you might create a parent master that contains the basic grid structure and any objects common to every page in a publication and then base all the other master pages on it. A change to the basic layout requires modifying just the parent master instead of editing each master page (**Figure 8.2**). This is a powerful way to maintain design consistency and ease of editability.

● **Note:** When a master page is based on another, the prefix of its parent master appears at the top of each of its page icons in the Pages panel.

A

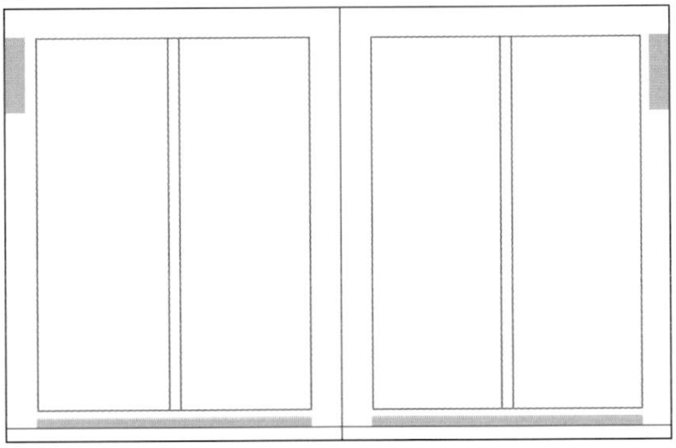

A-Base Master

B

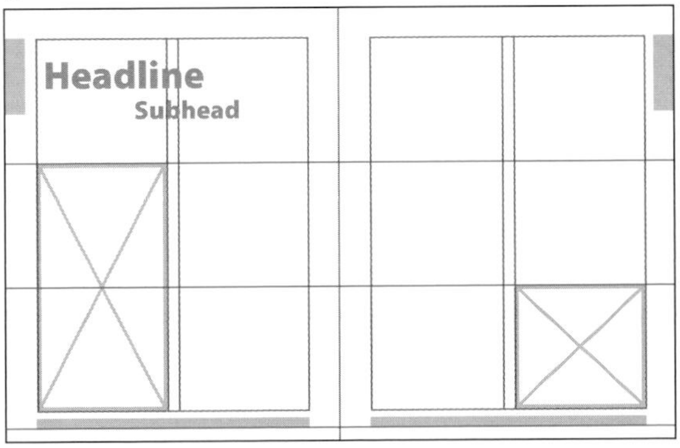
Headline
Subhead

B-Section Layout (Based on A)

C

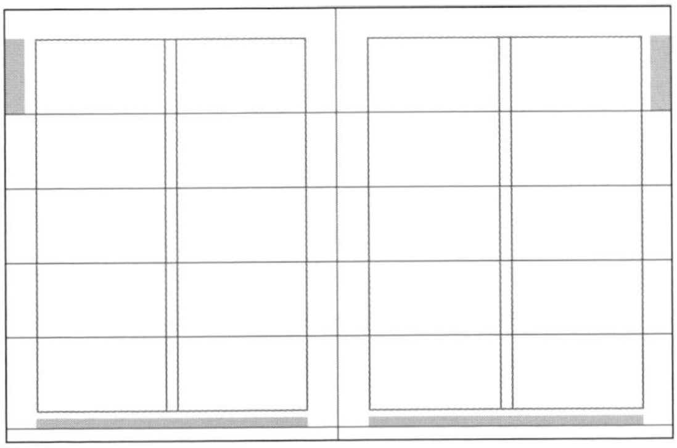

C-All Layout (Based on A)

Figure 8.2 This master page setup shows two master pages (B, C) based on one parent master (A). Each child master inherits the master items and grid structure from the parent master, yet they contain their own master items and grid structure as well.

Use this option with a definite purpose. Basing master pages on other master pages works well when a publication uses common elements throughout its pages. But when a design is less consistent and predictable, this solution can work against you.

- **Number of Pages.** Specify a value for the number of pages you want in the master spread. You can choose up to ten pages.

CONVERT A PAGE SPREAD TO A MASTER PAGE

Another way to create a new master page is to convert an existing page spread in your mock-up layout to a master page. Simply drag a spread from the Pages section of the Pages panel to the Masters section. You can also select a spread and choose Save as Master from the Pages panel menu. If the page spread you are converting currently has a master page applied to it—which is most likely the case—the new master page will be based on the same master page. If you don't want the new master page to be based on another, select it, choose Master Options for [*master spread name*] from the Pages panel menu, and then choose None from the Based on Master menu.

COPY AN EXISTING MASTER PAGE

If you want to use an existing master page as a starting point for creating a new one, you can duplicate a master page within the same document or copy a master page from another InDesign document.

■ **Tip:** To copy just a few objects from one master page to another and maintain their *X*, *Y* position, select the objects and choose Edit > Copy. Then go to the other master page and choose Edit > Paste in Place.

To duplicate an existing master page, drag its name to the New Page button at the bottom of the Pages panel. You can also select a master spread and choose Duplicate Master Spread [*spread name*] from the Pages panel menu.

To copy a master page from another document, open the document containing the master page you want to copy, and then drag the name of the master page to the destination document's window. To quickly arrange the open document windows next to each other, choose Window > Arrange > Tile Horizontally or Window > Arrange > Tile Vertically.

Constructing the Layout of a Master Page

● **Note:** You can't see the dotted border on master items if the frame edges are hidden or if the document is currently in Preview mode.

After you've created a master page, you can work on its layout by double-clicking its name or one of its page icons in the Pages panel. Anything you place on a master page is called a *master item*, which globally appears on each document page with that master applied. Master items are surrounded by a dotted border, allowing you to distinguish them from other objects on document pages (**Figure 8.3**).

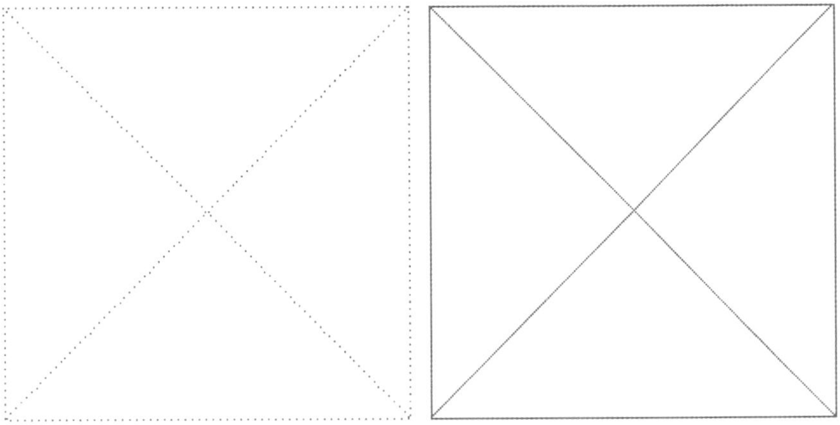

Figure 8.3 The frame with the dotted bounding box on the left is a master item. The frame with the solid line on the right is not connected to a master page.

Several types of objects are commonly placed on a master page: the layout grid, repeating design elements, and placeholder frames. As a general guideline, establish the layout grid first, and then set up the repeating elements and any necessary placeholder frames.

SETTING UP PLACEHOLDER GRAPHICS FRAMES

Graphics placeholders are empty frames used to indicate the position, size, and scaling of graphical elements and images. They regulate a design by forcing the designer to adhere to the limitations they impose. When producing pages, the designer imports content into each placeholder and makes any necessary adjustments to it.

Depending on the type of template you're creating, the number of graphics placeholders will vary. Layouts with a rigid design will likely need several of them. But for a layout that requires a lot of flexibility, it's better not to use them at all. Instead, rely on the grid structure for image placement (**Figure 8.4**).

Here are some strategies for setting up placeholder graphics frames:

- **Use the Rectangle Frame tool.** Use this tool to draw placeholder graphics frames. Since they contain a visual X when they are empty, their purpose in the template is clearly identified. You might also apply a light color, such as 20% black, to the frame to help further identify it.

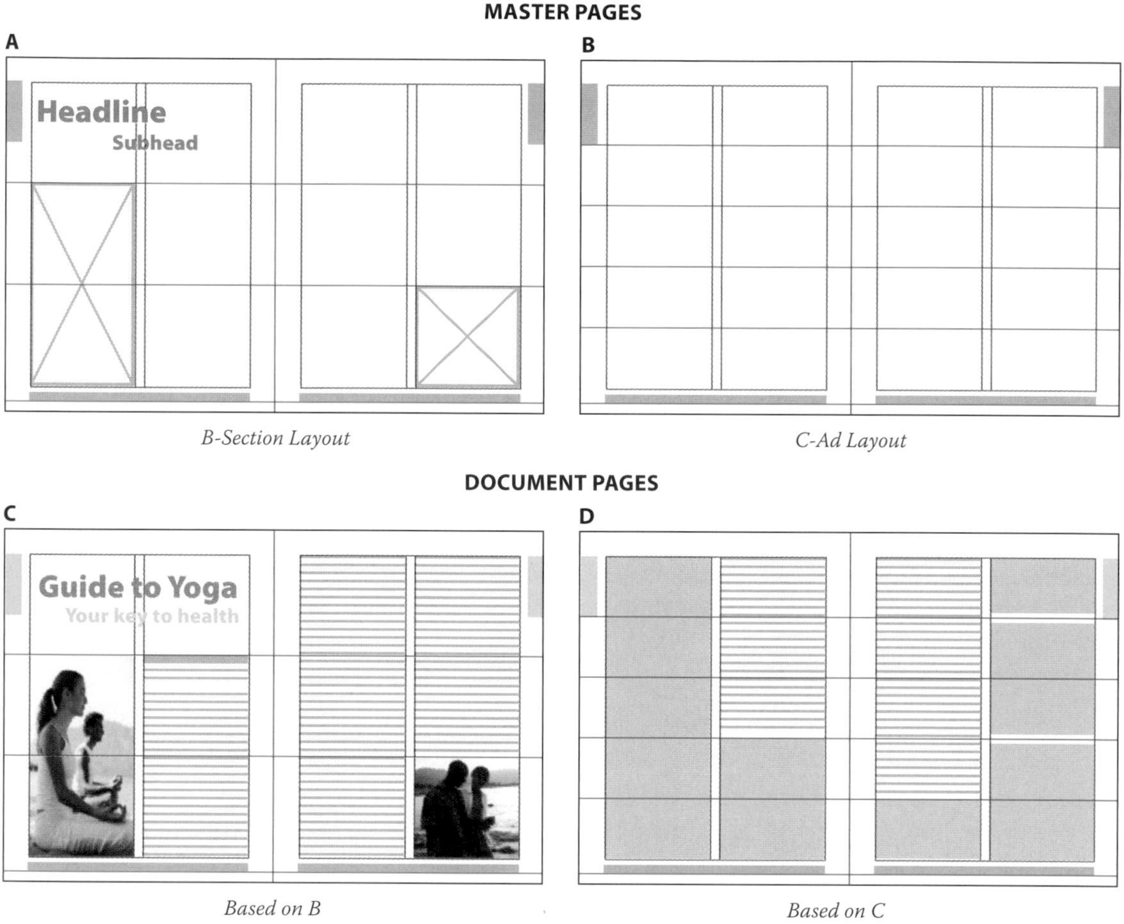
MASTER PAGES
A
Headline
Subhead
B
B-Section Layout
C-Ad Layout
DOCUMENT PAGES
C
Guide to Yoga
Your key to health
D
Based on B
Based on C

Figure 8.4 The *B-Section Layout* master page contains a placeholder text frame for the headline and subhead, and two placeholder graphics frames to specify the mandatory location of two images. The *C-Ad Layout* master page doesn't contain placeholder frames. Instead, it relies on its grid structure to guide the placement of text and advertisements.

- **Set Frame Fitting Options.** You can associate fitting options to a placeholder graphics frame so that when new content is placed into the frame, the fitting options are automatically applied. Select one or more empty frames, choose Object > Fitting > Frame Fitting Options, and then specify a crop amount, reference point, and fitting action (**Figure 8.5**).

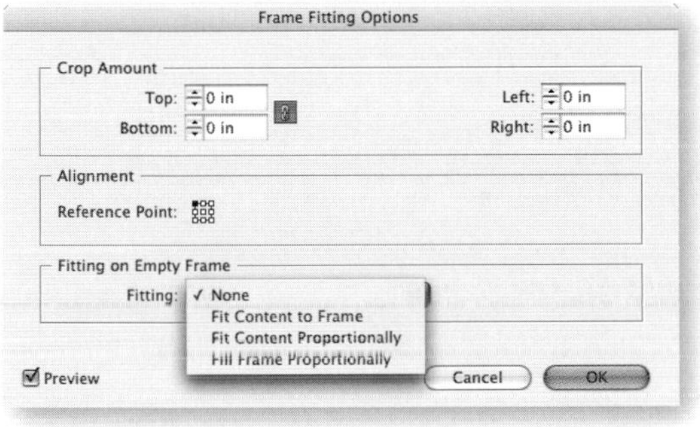
Frame Fitting Options
Crop Amount
Top: 0 in
Bottom: 0 in
Left: 0 in
Right: 0 in
Alignment
Reference Point:
Fitting on Empty Frame
Fitting: ✓ None
Fit Content to Frame
Fit Content Proportionally
Fill Frame Proportionally
Preview
Cancel
OK

Figure 8.5 The Frame Fitting Options dialog.

Begin by specifying a Reference Point. This determines what happens to the image when the cropping and fitting options are applied. For example, if you select the top-left reference point and choose Fit Content Proportionally, the image will be cropped on either the right or bottom side—away from the reference point—if it must be cropped to fit into the container frame.

For Crop Amount, specify the position of the image's bounding box in relation to the container frame. Positive values crop the image, whereas negative values add space between the image's bounding box and the container frame. From the Fitting menu, choose an action that determines how you want the image to fit within the placeholder graphics frame when it is placed.

● **Note:** The fitting action is applied once content is placed into an empty frame. It is not automatically reapplied when you later resize the frame.

- **Apply object styles.** By applying object styles to placeholder graphics frames, you will be able to globally control their formatting later on. A considerable number of settings can be controlled with one object style, including frame fitting options, text wrap, stroke and fill color, transparency effects, and more.
- **Snap to guides.** If you eventually plan to use the Layout Adjustment feature, snap each placeholder graphics frame to margin, column, or ruler guides. Each graphic will then automatically adjust to fit the new layout when you change the margins, columns, or page size.

SETTING UP PLACEHOLDER TEXT FRAMES

Text placeholders serve two major functions: to control the placement of text on the page and to display typographic specifications for repeating text elements, such as page numbers, chapter and section headings, running headers and footers, and any other element that repeats consistently throughout a publication.

Here are some strategies for setting up placeholder text frames:

■ **Tip:** To quickly resize a text frame to fit its content, double-click one of the frame's handles. Double-clicking the top or bottom handle resizes the frame's height while maintaining its width. Double-clicking the left or right handle resizes the frame's width while maintaining its height. Double-click a corner handle to resize both the height and width of the frame at the same time.

- **Use sample text.** By using sample text, the formatting and purpose of a text placeholder is clearly communicated. It also indicates the amount of text that can fit within a frame, which is useful for chapter numbers, running headers and footers, large headlines, and so on. However, avoid using too much sample text. Otherwise, you'll have to delete superfluous text each time you apply a master page.
- **Optimize text frame size.** Consider how much text will eventually appear within each text frame and make them large enough to hold all the text. If a placeholder frame is too small, placing too much text into it causes overset. On the other hand, unnecessarily large frames can overlap other frames on the page, making it difficult to make selections. By optimizing the size of each text frame, you minimize the amount of cleanup work that must be done during production (**Figure 8.6**).

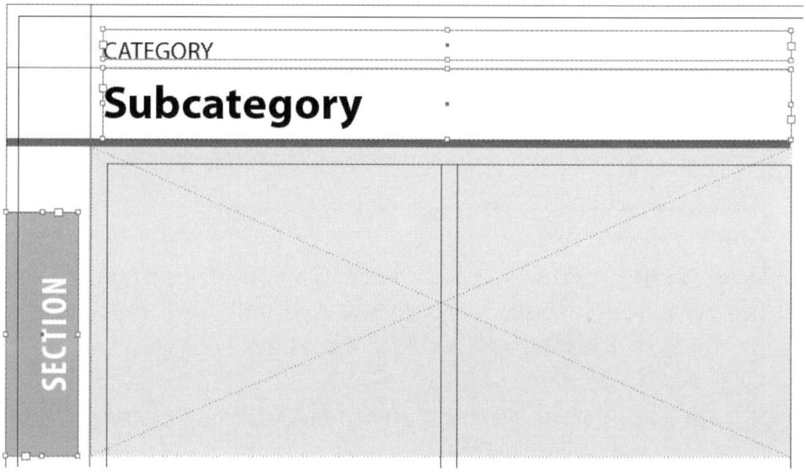
CATEGORY
Subcategory
SECTION

Figure 8.6 The size of each placeholder text frame is optimized to its content. To further optimize each frame, the category placeholder is bottom aligned to its frame, the subcategory is center aligned, and the section marker is bottom aligned with a bottom inset spacing applied.

- **Use empty text frames.** Although text placeholders commonly contain sample text, markers, and text variables, they can also be empty. Empty frames are useful for imposing limitations on the amount of text that a frame can contain and for determining the exact location of text on the page.

It is especially necessary to create empty text placeholders when ruler guides form the layout grid instead of actual margin and column guides or when you need to create text locations that don't strictly adhere to the layout grid (**Figure 8.7**). When the type area is consistent, such as in a book, it's more efficient to rely on margins and columns instead of creating master text frames.

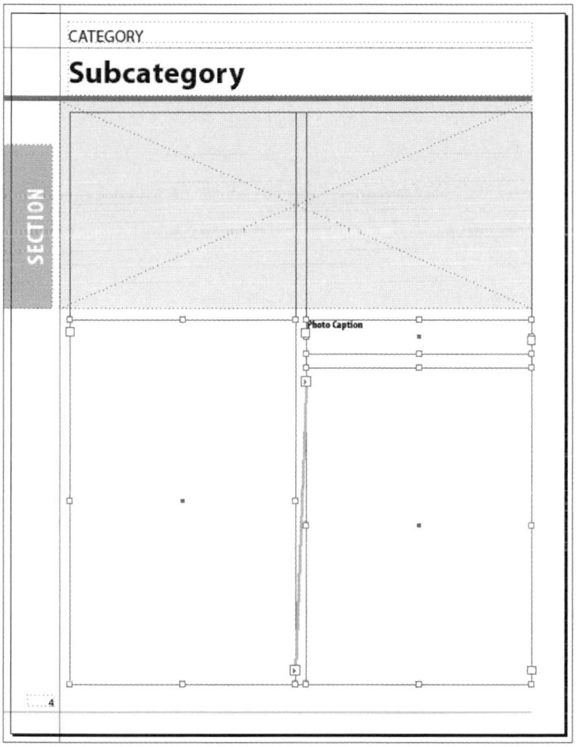
CATEGORY
Subcategory
SECTION
Photo Caption
4

Figure 8.7 This layout calls for a large photo with a caption below it. A placeholder was set up for the caption and two empty text frames were created to control the position of the body text.

- **Thread empty frames together.** You can thread empty text frames together on a master spread so that when you place text while holding the Shift key, it automatically flows within the preestablished frames and additional pages are created until all the text is placed. However, if you plan on letting InDesign generate frames for you when you place text, don't create master text frames. Instead, clearly define the type area with margins and columns.
- **Apply style sheets.** By applying paragraph and character styles to placeholder text on the master pages, the styles will automatically be applied to each textual element as you create pages.

■ **Tip:** You can apply a paragraph style to an empty frame so that the text you place into it later on will take on that style.

● **Note:** The Next Page Number and Previous Page Number markers are used for maintaining the jump lines of stories that continue to other pages.

- **Use page number and section markers.** You can insert page number and section markers to specify the formatting and position of page numbers and section headings. As you add, remove, and rearrange pages, the markers automatically update, preventing you from having to manually renumber pages or update section headings. Using markers also ensures that the page numbers and section headings on each page are always correct.

  To insert a page number marker, choose Type > Insert Special Character > Markers > Auto Page Number. On a master page, the page number marker displays the master page prefix. On a document page, it displays the page number (**Figure 8.8**).

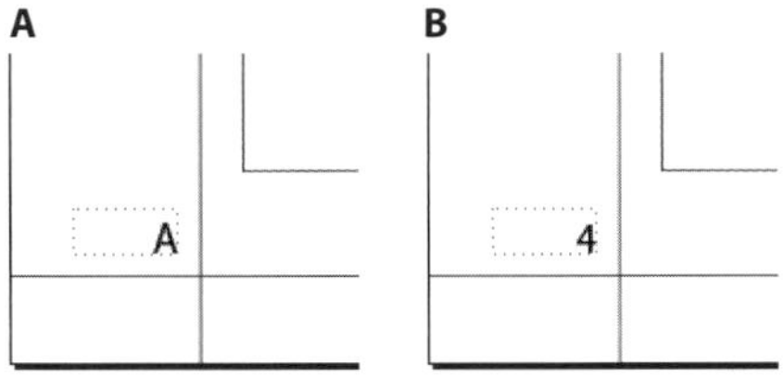
A
B
A
4

Figure 8.8 The page number marker on A-Master (**A**) and on page 4 (**B**).

■ **Tip:** Arabic numerals (1, 2, 3) are used to number pages by default. You can also use Roman (i, ii, iii) or alphanumeric (a, b, c) numbering by choosing Layout > Numbering & Section Options and then selecting a numbering style from the Style menu.

  To insert a section marker, choose Type > Insert Special Character > Markers > Section Marker. On a master page, the section marker displays the word *Section*. On a document page, nothing is displayed until the section marker is defined (**Figure 8.9**). To define the section marker, select the first page in a section, choose Layout > Numbering & Section Options, and then type the name of the section into the Section Marker field. Each section marker that appears within that section of the document will be replaced with the defined section marker (**Figure 8.10**).

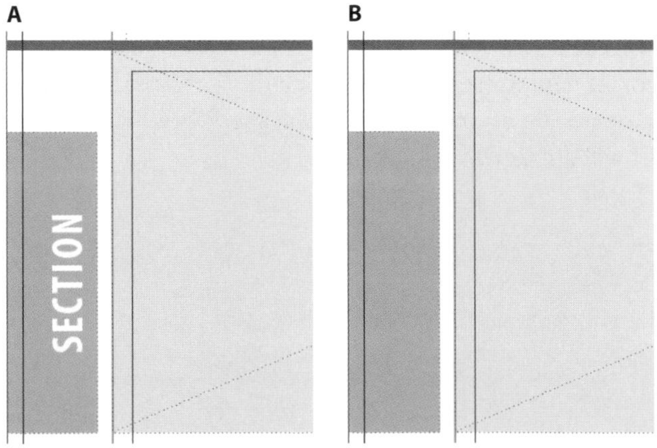
A
B
SECTION

Figure 8.9 The section marker on a master page (**A**) and on a document page before the section marker has been defined (**B**).

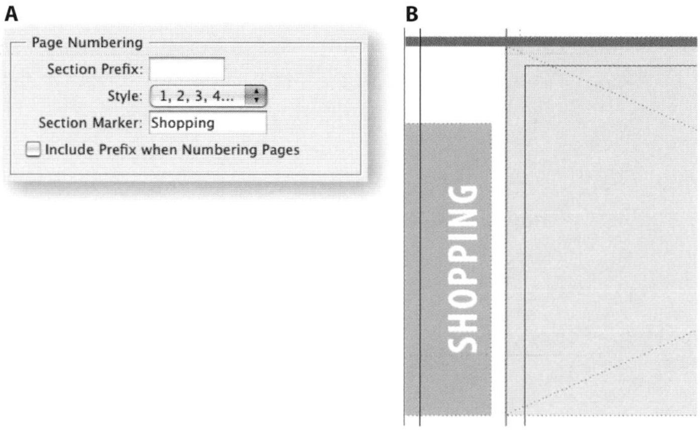
A
Page Numbering
Section Prefix:
Style: 1, 2, 3, 4...
Section Marker: Shopping
Include Prefix when Numbering Pages
B
SHOPPING

Figure 8.10 The Page Numbering section of the Numbering & Section Options dialog (**A**). The text in the Section Marker field replaces the section marker on the document page (**B**).

SETTING UP TEXT VARIABLES

A text variable is a type of placeholder text that automatically updates according to its defined context. For example, you can insert a text variable for Modification Date so the current date is automatically inserted each time you open and modify a document. InDesign includes several predefined text variables that you can use as is: Chapter Number, Creation Date, File Name, Last Page Number, Modification Date, Output Date, Running Header. You can also modify their format or create your own.

To insert a text variable, choose Type > Text Variables > Insert Variable, and then choose the variable you want to insert. You can place variables before or after other characters in a text frame or within their own frame. Text variables appear as if you typed them and take on the formatting you apply to them.

Each text variable is surrounded by a box using the color of the layer it's on (**Figure 8.11**). The box automatically expands and retracts to fit the text it contains. Once the box reaches the end of the text frame, it stops expanding and its enclosed text becomes compressed. Also, variable text does not break to form new lines. So, make sure you create a text frame large enough to include all the information that it will eventually contain.

● **Note:** Text variables can be placed on master pages and document pages. Place them on a master page when you want them to globally appear throughout the document. Place them on a document page to create a singe instance.

■ **Tip:** As you add, remove, and rearrange pages, some text variables may not immediately update with new information until you force the screen to redraw by holding the Shift key and pressing F5.

July 23, 2007 10:21 PM#

Figure 8.11 To view the box that surrounds each variable instance, choose Type > Show Hidden Characters.

■ **Tip:** You can import text variables that you've already created. Choose Type > Text Variables > Define, click Load, and then locate the document that contains the variables you want to import.

To create or edit a text variable, choose Type > Text Variables > Define, and then click New or select an existing variable and click Edit (**Figure 8.12**). Type a name for the variable that clearly identifies its purpose, such as "First Product on Page" or "Running Title." From the Type menu, choose a variable type, and then specify its options (**Figure 8.13**). InDesign provides a variety of variable types to choose from and depending on which one you select, different options are available.

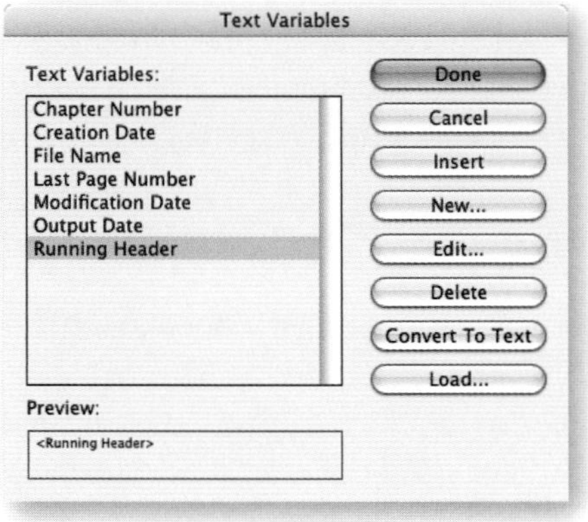
Text Variables
Text Variables:
Chapter Number
Creation Date
File Name
Last Page Number
Modification Date
Output Date
Running Header
Done
Cancel
Insert
New...
Edit...
Delete
Convert To Text
Load...
Preview:
<Running Header>

Figure 8.12 The Text Variables dialog manages the text variables in your template. The Preview area at the bottom shows what the selected variable looks like.

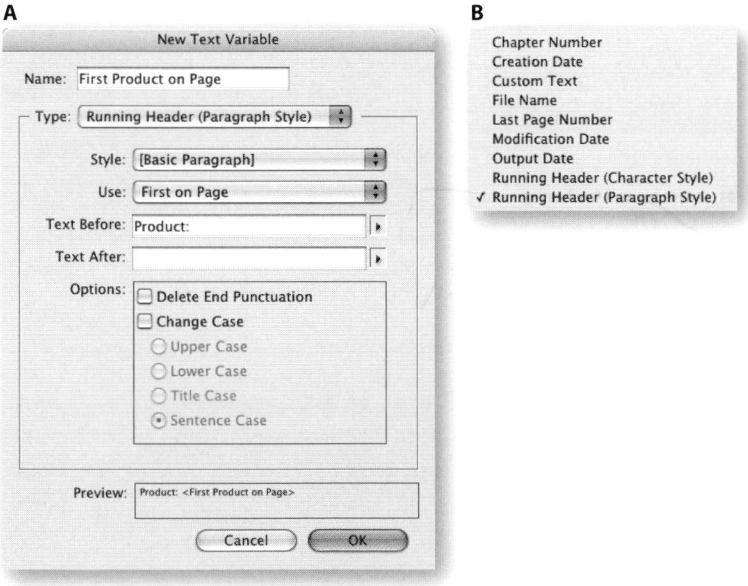
A
New Text Variable
Name: First Product on Page
Type: Running Header (Paragraph Style)
Style: [Basic Paragraph]
Use: First on Page
Text Before: Product:
Text After:
Options:
Delete End Punctuation
Change Case
Upper Case
Lower Case
Title Case
Sentence Case
Preview: Product: <First Product on Page>
Cancel
OK
B
Chapter Number
Creation Date
Custom Text
File Name
Last Page Number
Modification Date
Output Date
Running Header (Character Style)
✓ Running Header (Paragraph Style)

Figure 8.13 This text variable uses the Running Header (Paragraph Style) type (**A**). Nine variable types are available in the dialog's Type menu (**B**).

Here's a list of each variable type and a description of the options each provides:

- **Text Before and Text After fields.** Each variable type (except Custom Text) has a Text Before and Text After field, which allows you to specify text that will be added before or after the variable. For instance, you can add the word "Chapter" before the Chapter Number variable to create a "Chapter 1" effect. To insert special characters, click the triangle to the right of each field.
- **Chapter Number.** A variable created with the Chapter Number type inserts the document's chapter number. Insert optional text before or after the variable and choose a numbering style for it from the Style menu (**Figure 8.14**).

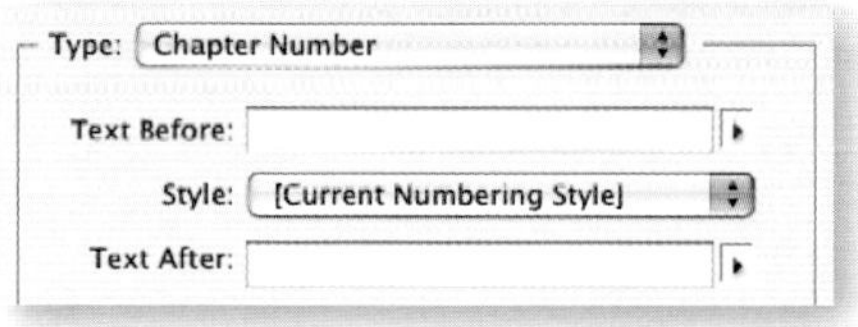

Type: Chapter Number
Text Before:
Style: [Current Numbering Style]
Text After:

Figure 8.14 The Chapter Number options.

● **Note:** If you choose a numbering style other than *[Current Numbering Style]*, it will override the style specified in Numbering & Section Options.

The chapter number variable functions much like the page number and section markers. Simply insert the variable, choose Layout > Numbering & Section Options, and then type a number into the Chapter Number field. If the document is part of a book file, you can choose to continue numbering from the previous document in the book or use the same number as the previous document (**Figure 8.15**).

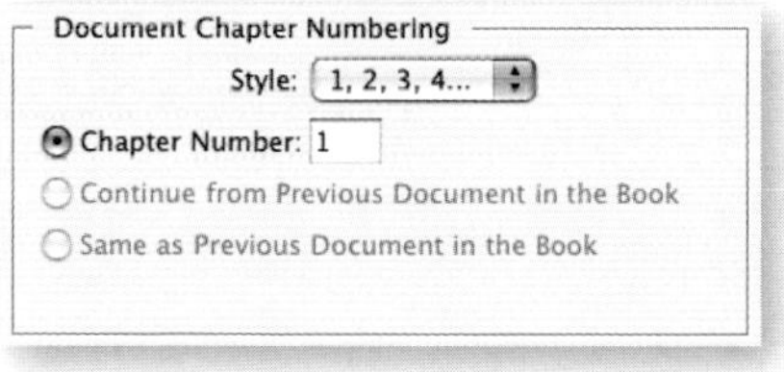

Document Chapter Numbering
Style: 1, 2, 3, 4...
Chapter Number: 1
Continue from Previous Document in the Book
Same as Previous Document in the Book

Figure 8.15 The Document Chapter Numbering section of the Numbering & Section Options dialog.

● **Note:** A single document can have only one chapter number assigned to it. As a result, the chapter number variable is commonly used in documents that are part of a book file. If you prefer to divide one document into chapters, create sections and use the section marker to label chapter numbers instead.

- **Creation Date, Modification Date, and Output Date.** Each of these variable types has the same options but function differently (**Figure 8.16**). Creation Date inserts the date or time the document is first saved. Modification Date inserts the date or time the document was last saved. Output Date inserts the date or time you start a print job, export to PDF, or package the document.

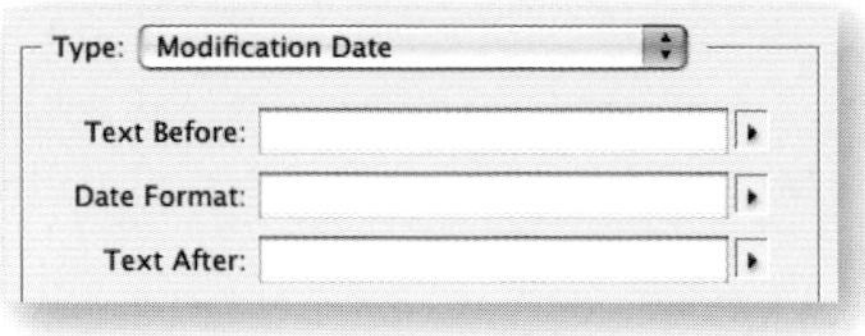
Type: Modification Date
Text Before:
Date Format:
Text After:

Figure 8.16 The Modification Date options. The same options are available for Creation Date and Output Date.

Insert optional text before or after the date and set up the date format. You can type the date format into the Date Format field or choose format options by clicking the triangle to the right of the field. For example, the date format, "MM/dd/yy" displays as 06/12/88 and "h:mm a" displays as "10:35 AM."

Date Formats

Abbreviation	Description	Example
d	Day number, no leading zero	5
dd	Day number, leading zero	05
E	Weekday name, abbreviated	Tue
EEEE	Full weekday name	Tuesday
M	Month number, no leading zero	9
MM	Month number, leading zero	09
MMM	Abbreviated month name	Sep
MMMM	Full month name	September
yy or YY	Year number, last two digits	07
y or YYYY	Full year number	2007
G or GGGG	Era, abbreviated or expanded	AD or Anno Domini
h	Hour, no leading zero	6
hh	Hour, leading zero	06
H	Hour, no leading zero, 24-hour format	18
HH	Hour, leading zero, 24-hour format	18
m	Minute, no leading zero	3
mm	Minute leading zero	03
s	Second, no leading zero	5
ss	Second, leading zero	05
a	AM or PM, two characters	AM
z or zzzz	Time zone, abbreviated or expanded	PST or Pacific Standard Time

- **Custom Text.** You use this variable type for inserting any combination of text and special characters (**Figure 8.17**). It is especially useful for placeholder text or any information that needs to be quickly updated later on. For example, if you're creating a template that has a project code appearing in multiple locations, you can create a custom text variable for the project code. Every time you start a new project, simply update the text variable with the real code and every variable instance throughout the document will automatically update.

■ **Tip:** The Creation Date, Modification Date, and Output Date variable types are useful for setting up text variables in the slug area.

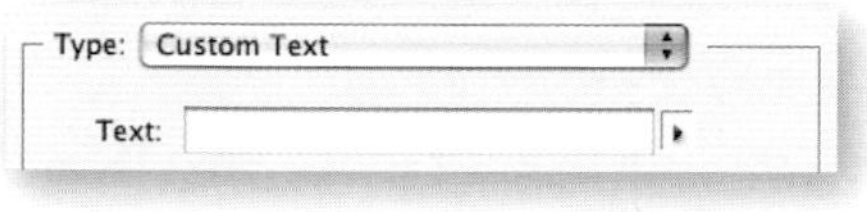
Type: Custom Text
Text:

Figure 8.17 The Custom Text options. To insert special characters, click the triangle to the right of the Text field.

- **File Name.** This variable type inserts the name of the current file and is updated whenever you save the file. It's particularly useful in the slug area, so that after you've printed the document, it's easy to track down the electronic version. To include the full folder path with the file name, select the Include Entire Folder Path option. You can also include the file name extension by selecting Include File Extension (**Figure 8.18**).

● **Note:** The path or extension appears once the document is saved.

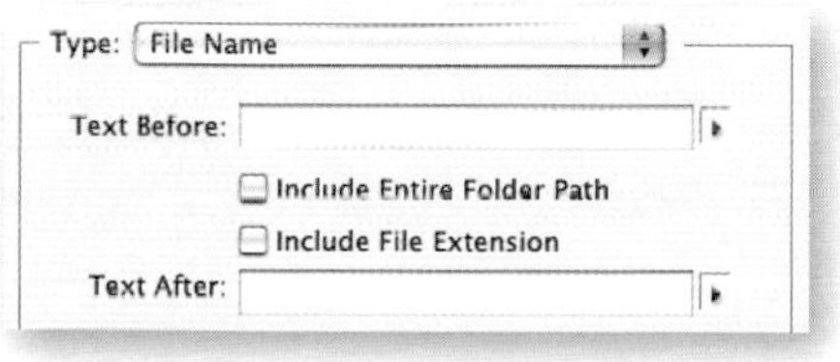
Type: File Name
Text Before:
Include Entire Folder Path
Include File Extension
Text After:

Figure 8.18 The File Name options.

- **Last Page Number.** This variable type inserts the preceding page number. It's commonly used for setting up a "Page 2 of 6" numbering format. In this case, "Page" and "of" are typed into a frame. The number 2 is generated by the page number marker, and the number 6 is generated by the Last Page Number variable. Specify a numbering style from the Style menu and choose an option from the Scope menu to determine whether the last page number in the section or the document is used (**Figure 8.19**).

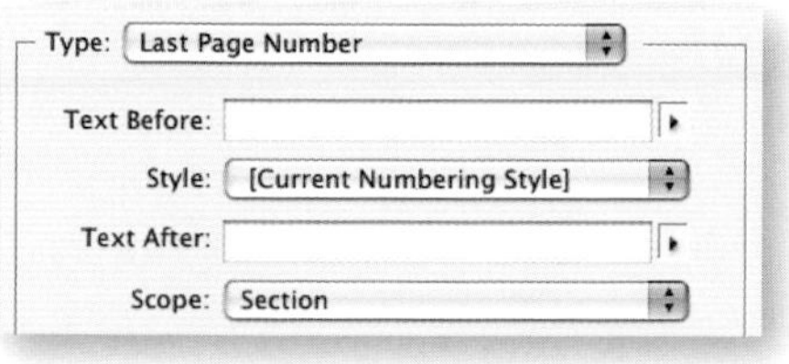
Type: Last Page Number
Text Before:
Style: [Current Numbering Style]
Text After:
Scope: Section

Figure 8.19 The Last Page Number options.

● **Note:** On a master page, Running Header variables display the name of the variable enclosed in greater-than and less-than delimiters, such as *<Running Header>*.

- **Running Header (Paragraph Style).** This variable type inserts either the first or last occurrence of text on the page to which a specified paragraph style is applied. For example, if you're creating a catalog, you can set up running header variables at the top of each page—one that displays the first use of the specified paragraph style on the left-facing page and another that displays the last use of that paragraph style on the right-facing page (**Figure 8.20**).

A

CATEGORY#
Product: <First Product on Page>#
SECTION#

B

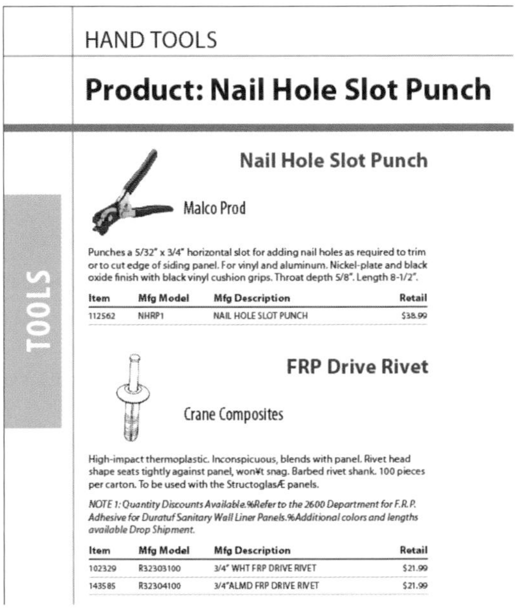
HAND TOOLS
Product: Nail Hole Slot Punch
TOOLS
Nail Hole Slot Punch
Malco Prod
Punches a 5/32" x 3/4" horizontal slot for adding nail holes as required to trim or to cut edge of siding panel. For vinyl and aluminum. Nickel-plate and black oxide finish with black vinyl cushion grips. Throat depth 5/8". Length 8-1/2".
Item Mfg Model Mfg Description Retail
112562 NHRP1 NAIL HOLE SLOT PUNCH $38.99
FRP Drive Rivet
Crane Composites
High-impact thermoplastic. Inconspicuous, blends with panel. Rivet head shape seats tightly against panel, won¥t snag. Barbed rivet shank. 100 pieces per carton. To be used with the StructoglasÆ panels.
Item Mfg Model Mfg Description Retail
102329 R32303100 3/4" WHT FRP DRIVE RIVET $21.99
143585 R32304100 3/4"ALMD FRP DRIVE RIVET $21.99

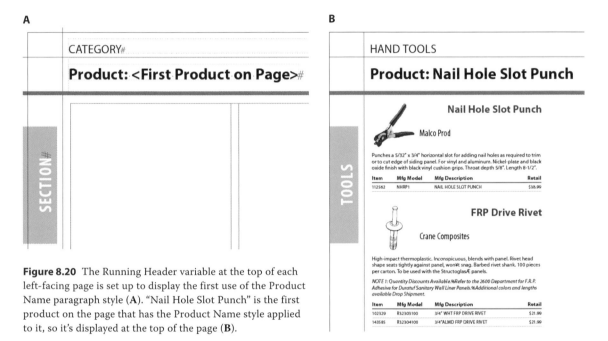

Figure 8.20 The Running Header variable at the top of each left-facing page is set up to display the first use of the Product Name paragraph style (**A**). "Nail Hole Slot Punch" is the first product on the page that has the Product Name style applied to it, so it's displayed at the top of the page (**B**).

● **Note:** If no occurrence of the specified style is found on a page, the previous occurrence of the applied style is used. If there isn't a previous occurrence in the document, the variable is empty.

When setting up a Running Header variable, first find out which paragraph style is applied to the text you want displayed in the header, and then choose that paragraph style from the Style menu (**Figure 8.21**). Next, choose an option from the Use menu to determine whether the first or last occurrence of the specified paragraph style on the page is displayed.

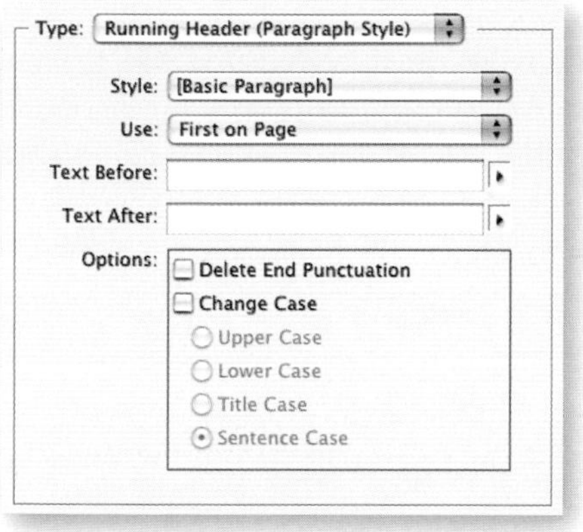
Type: Running Header (Paragraph Style)
Style: [Basic Paragraph]
Use: First on Page
Text Before:
Text After:
Options:
Delete End Punctuation
Change Case
Upper Case
Lower Case
Title Case
Sentence Case

Figure 8.21 The Running Header (Paragraph Style) options.

■ **Tip:** You can convert a text variable to regular text by selecting the variable and choosing Type > Text Variables > Convert Variable To Text.

Select the Delete End Punctuation option if you want the variable to show the text without end punctuation, such as periods, exclamation marks, and question marks. You can also change the case of the displayed text by selecting the Change Case option and then choosing one of its suboptions: Upper Case, Lower Case, Title Case, or Sentence Case.

- **Running Header (Character Style).** This variable type functions exactly like the Running Header (Paragraph Style) variable except that it inserts the first or last occurrence of text on the page to which a specified character style is applied. The Style menu displays the list of character styles in the document instead of paragraph styles, and all the other options are the same.

Working with Master Items

When you apply a master page to a document page, all the master items automatically appear in the same position on the document page. In the same manner, when you base one master page on another, the child master picks up all the objects from its parent master (**Figure 8.22**). This provides a good starting point from which you can create a layout or construct a new master page.

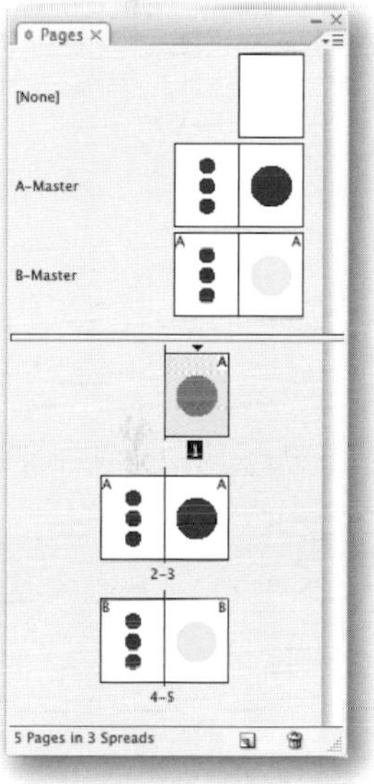
Pages
[None]
A-Master
B-Master
2-3
4-5
5 Pages in 3 Spreads

Figure 8.22 You can identify which master page is applied to document pages and other master pages, because its prefix appears at the top corner of each page it's applied to in the Pages panel.

OVERRIDING MASTER ITEMS

Master items cannot be modified on a document page or child master unless the master item is first overridden. To override a master item, press Ctrl-Shift (Windows) or Command-Shift (Mac OS), and then click the item or drag to select multiple items. To override all the master items on a selected spread, choose Override All Master Page Items from the Pages panel menu.

● **Note:** When you override a frame that is threaded to other frames, all the frames in that thread are overridden, even if they are on a different page in a spread.

● **Note:** Overriding a master item always breaks the connection to the local frame's content. Even if you don't customize any attributes, the text or graphic within the local frame is no longer connected to the master item.

When you override a master item, a local copy of it is made on the page, and its dotted border becomes a solid line. However, its connection with the master page is not broken. This allows you to selectively customize the attributes of the local copy. For example, you can change its stroke and fill color. Then, if you change the stroke or fill color of that object on the master page, those changes will not update the local copy. However, changes to other attributes, such as size, rotation, and transparency will continue to update the local copy because they have not been overridden.

If you want to remove an override to make an object match the master page, select it and choose Remove Selected Local Overrides from the Pages panel menu. To remove all overrides from a selected spread, deselect all objects and choose Remove All Local Overrides from the Pages panel menu. The local copy of the master item is removed and it cannot be selected, as indicated by its dotted border.

DETACHING MASTER ITEMS

When you don't want any connection between an object and its original master page, you can detach it. A detached object no longer updates with the master page, because its connection is broken. To detach a master item, you must first override it and then choose Detach Selection from Master from the Pages panel menu.

TIPS FOR WORKING WITH MASTER ITEMS

Here are some tips that will help you construct master pages and work with them more successfully:

● **Note:** If you prevent a threaded text frame from being overridden, all text frames in that thread have the same setting applied.

- **Prevent master items from being overridden.** To prevent one or more master items from being overridden, select them and deselect Allow Master Item Overrides On Selection from the Pages panel menu. The master item won't display a frame edge when viewed on a document page. This is helpful when you want to prevent certain elements, such as repeating background art, from being modified on a document page.
- **Lock master items.** You can lock a master item to prevent it from being accidentally moved on a document page when it is overridden. You are still able to modify its content and attributes, but you won't be able to move its position and consequently prevent the local copy from moving when the master item is relocated. To lock an object, select it and choose Object > Lock Position. When you want to unlock the object, choose Object > Unlock Position.

- **No need to override placeholder frames.** You don't have to override placeholder text or graphics frames to place content into them. With no frame selected, use the Place command to import the content, and then click the loaded Place icon on a master frame. The frame will be overridden and accept the content.
- **Text wraps still apply.** You don't have to override a master item with a text wrap applied to it for text to wrap around it.
- **Hide master items.** If you want to temporarily hide all the master items on a document page, choose Hide Master Items from the Pages panel menu. This makes it easy to work with just the local objects on the page or quickly find out which objects are master items.
- **Set up multiple views of one document.** You can set up multiple views of a document so that you can edit a master page in one window and see the results instantly updating on the document page in another window (**Figure 8.23**). Choose Window > Arrange > New Window, and then choose Window > Arrange > Tile Horizontally or Tile Vertically. Set one window to view a master page and another to view a document page.

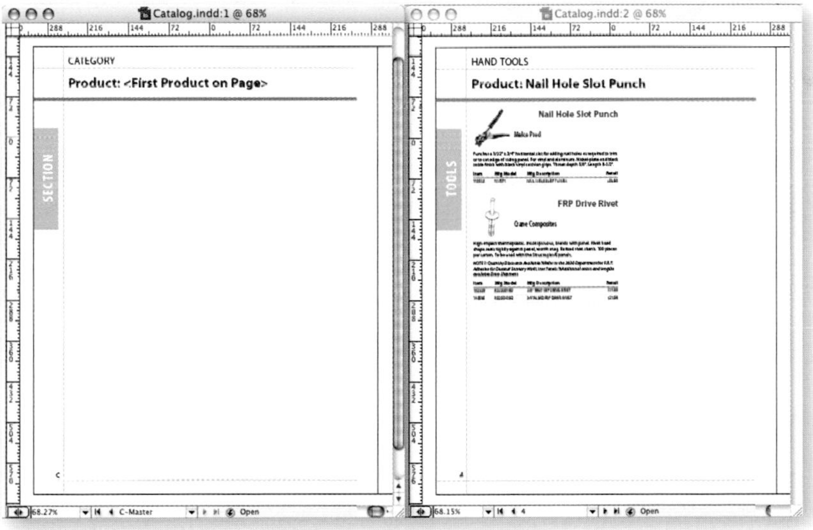
Catalog.indd:1 @ 68%
CATEGORY
Product: <First Product on Page>
SECTION
C-Master
Open
Catalog.indd:2 @ 68%
HAND TOOLS
Product: Nail Hole Slot Punch
Nail Hole Slot Punch
FRP Drive Rivet
TOOLS
Open

Figure 8.23 The window on the left displays the master page and the other displays the document page. The title of each window is followed by a colon and then by a number, indicating that it's another view of the same document.

- **Optimize the Pages panel.** You can make several modifications to the Pages panel to make it easier to use. Resize the panel to make room for more pages. Drag the divider line—which separates the master pages from the document pages—up or down to fit more pages in the top or bottom of the panel.

You can also adjust the size of the page thumbnails and view the pages horizontally instead of vertically. Choose Panel Options from the Pages panel menu. Specify a thumbnail size from the Icon Size menu. Uncheck the Show Vertically option to view the pages horizontally. These options can be customized for both document pages and master pages (**Figure 8.24**). Larger thumbnails make it easier to locate a particular page without having to click every page to find it. View pages horizontally to fit more pages into the panel and reduce the amount of scrolling necessary to navigate through a document.

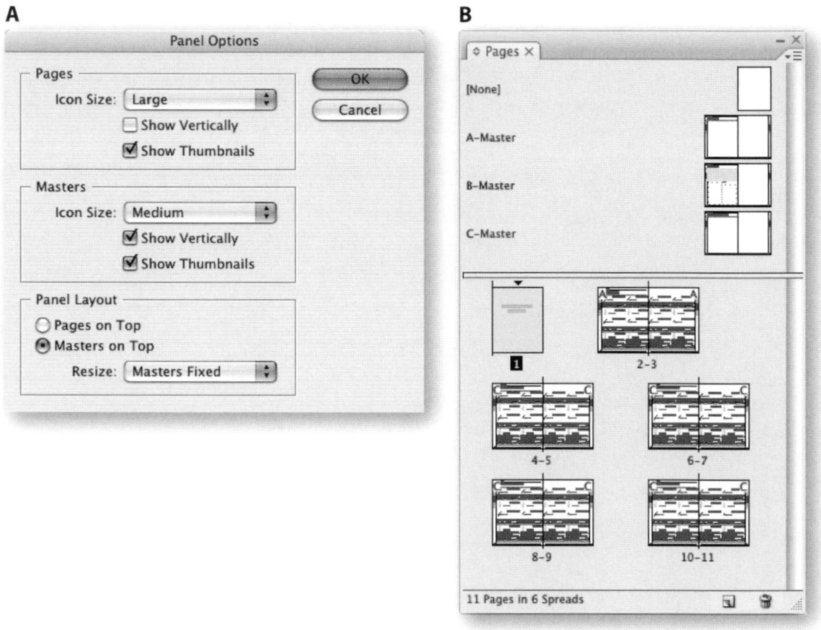
A
B
Panel Options
Pages
Icon Size:
Large
Show Vertically
Show Thumbnails
OK
Cancel
Masters
Icon Size:
Medium
Show Vertically
Show Thumbnails
Panel Layout
Pages on Top
Masters on Top
Resize:
Masters Fixed
Pages
[None]
A-Master
B-Master
C-Master
1
2-3
4-5
6-7
8-9
10-11
11 Pages in 6 Spreads

Figure 8.24 The Panel Options dialog (**A**). The Pages panel reflects the changes made in Panel Options (**B**).

Setting Up Object Libraries

Object libraries provide a central repository for frequently used graphics, text, and entire page layouts. They help you keep your design elements organized and easy to locate when you need them. You can add many types of objects to a library, including logos, background art, grouped objects, ruler guides, and more.

You can also create as many object libraries as you need for a project. One library might contain a collection of placeholder design elements, such as custom drawn shapes, predesigned tables, and anything else that serves as a starting point for a design. Another library could contain layout alternatives that aren't used often enough to set up master pages for.

Creating an Object Library

To create an object library, choose File > New > Library and specify a name and location for the library. The library appears as a panel within InDesign and also exists as an actual file on disk. It's a good idea to save the library in the same location as the template it will accompany. Also, keep in mind that the name you specify becomes the name of the library's panel tab.

To add an object to the library, drag one or more selected objects to the Object Library panel. If you add multiple objects at a time, they become one library item—whether they're grouped or not. You can add an entire page, including ruler guides, by choosing Add Items on Page [*number*] from the Object Library panel menu.

■ **Tip:** You can organize several objects on a page, such as a collection of logos, and then add them all at once to a library as separate items. Choose Add Items on Page *[number]* as Separate Objects from the Object Library panel menu.

When you add an object to a library, any text, image, and positional attributes are preserved. Text retains its formatting and any applied paragraph or character styles. Graphics retain their link information, formatting, and any applied object styles. Similarly, tables maintain any applied table and cell styles. If the original object was organized onto several layers, its layer information is also maintained.

To place a library item onto a page, drag it from the Object Library panel to any location on the page. To place an item at its original X, Y position, select it and choose Place Items(s) from the Object Library panel menu. There is no limit to the number of times a library item can be added to a document.

When you place a library item, all of its attributes are copied with it. Any swatches are added to the Swatches panel. Paragraph styles, character styles, object styles, table styles, and cell styles are brought into the document as well. If the Paste Remembers Layers option has been selected from the Layers panel menu, the object's layer information will be maintained and additional layers will be added to the document if they don't already exist.

● **Note:** When adding library items to a document, styled content that uses the same styles as those already in the destination document use the destination document's styles instead. Styles with different names are added to the document.

Organizing an Object Library

After adding an object to a library, it's important to identify it to make it easier to locate when you need to use it. At first, a new library item is given the name, *unassigned*. You'll want to change its name, define what type of object it is, and give it a description. To edit a library item's information, double-click it (**Figure 8.25**). Change the Item Name, Object Type, and Description options as necessary.

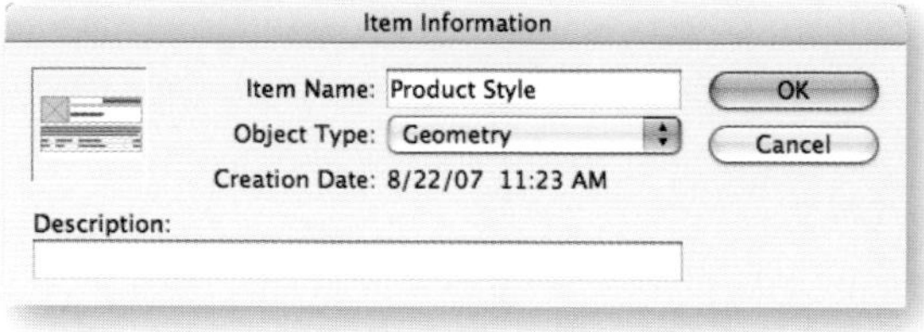
Item Information
Item Name: Product Style
Object Type: Geometry
Creation Date: 8/22/07 11:23 AM
Description:
OK
Cancel

Figure 8.25 The Item Information dialog.

■ **Tip:** Hold down Alt (Windows) or Option (Mac OS) as you add an object to a library to instantly display the Item Information dialog.

You can view library items as thumbnails or as a text list. To change how they are displayed, choose List View, Thumbnail View, or Large Thumbnail View from the Object Library panel menu (**Figure 8.26**). You can also sort library items by choosing Sort Items from the Object Library panel menu and choosing one of the sort methods: Name, Newest, Oldest, or Type.

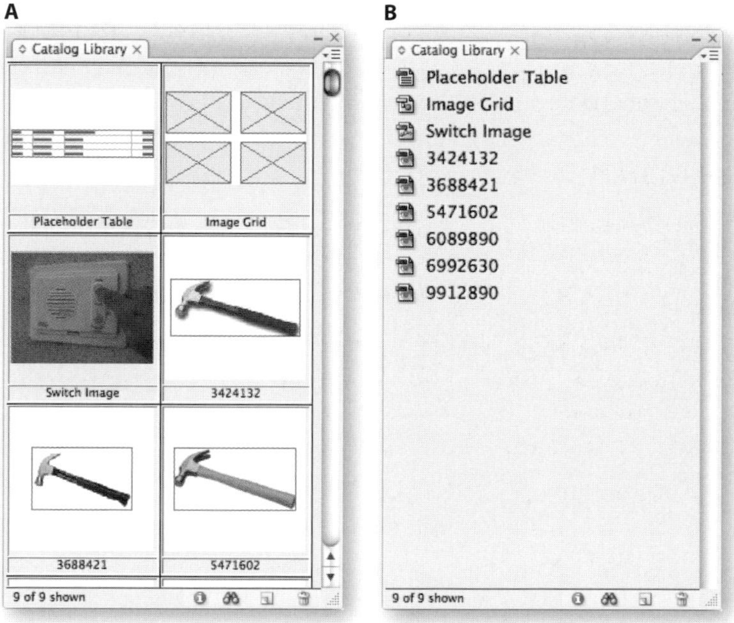
A
Catalog Library
Placeholder Table
Image Grid
Switch Image
3424132
3688421
5471602
9 of 9 shown
B
Catalog Library
Placeholder Table
Image Grid
Switch Image
3424132
3688421
5471602
6089890
6992630
9912890
9 of 9 shown

Figure 8.26 Thumbnail view lets you see a preview of each library item (**A**). List view makes it possible to see more items in the library at a time (**B**). The icon to the left of each item's name identifies what type of object it is.

When you want to find a particular library item, you can search for it by Item Name, Creation Date, Object Type, or Description. Choose Show Subset from the Object Library panel menu to filter the displayed items (**Figure 8.27**). To search all objects in the library, select Search Entire Library. To refine a previous search, select Search Currently Shown Items. In the Parameters section, choose a search category from the first menu. From the second menu, specify what must be included or excluded from the search. For example, you can include all items that contain the word "logo" in their names and exclude all items that are labeled as a Text object type.

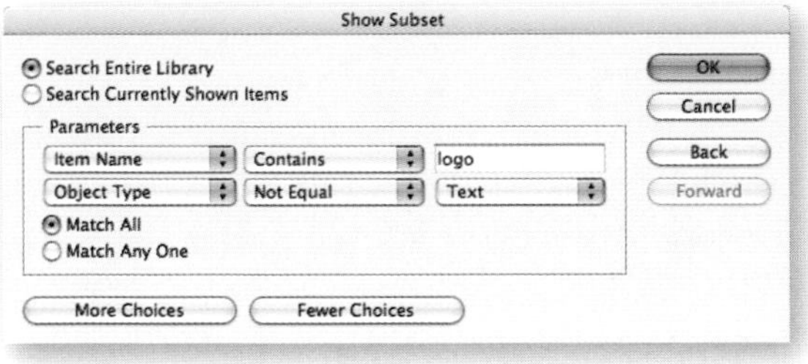
Show Subset
Search Entire Library
Search Currently Shown Items
Parameters
Item Name
Contains
logo
Object Type
Not Equal
Text
Match All
Match Any One
More Choices
Fewer Choices
OK
Cancel
Back
Forward

Figure 8.27 The Show Subset dialog.

Next, type a word, a date, or choose an option from the menu that you want to search for within the search category you specified. To add search criteria, narrowing down the search, click More Choices. Click Fewer Choices to remove search criteria. If more than one search criteria exist, select Match All to show only those objects that match all search criteria, or select Match Any One. When you conduct a search, all objects except for the results of your search are hidden from view. To show all the objects again, choose Show All from the Object Library panel menu.

■ **Tip:** The bottom-left corner of the Object Library panel displays how many items the library contains and how many are showing. This is an easy way to find out if a subset of the library is currently showing.

Managing Library Items

It's a good idea to keep all your library items in one or more InDesign documents. This preserves the original objects, making them easier to update and manage. You'll also always have a backup of each object.

When you need to modify a library item, make the necessary changes to the original object and select it. Then select the object you want to replace in the Object Library panel. With both objects selected at the same time, choose Update Library Item from the Object Library panel menu.

If you want to copy an item from one library to another, open both libraries at the same time, and then drag the item to the other library. To move an item, instead of copy it, hold down Alt (Windows) or Option (Mac OS) as you drag the item to the other library.

Setting Up Layers

Layers are an invaluable part of a template's construction. By default, every InDesign document contains at least one layer. Although there are many uses for layers, here is a list of uses that particularly benefit templates:

● **Note:** Master items on a higher layer appear in front of all objects on lower layers, but they always appear behind all objects assigned to the same layer on document pages.

- **Maintain a separate layer for master items.** Create a layer for master items and keep that layer above other layers. All the master items will always be in front of the objects on lower layers. This is the only way to keep master items in front of other objects on document pages without having to override master items first.

- **Template instructions.** Create a layer for template usage instructions and sample pages. Keep the layer hidden so the information is there when you need it, but is kept out of view and won't ever print.
- **Manage ruler guides.** Place ruler guides on separate layers when you need to manage them separately from other objects or layout grids.
- **Multilingual publications.** If you are creating a template for a multilingual publication, set up a base layer for the basic design and separate layers for each language version. This facilitates production and keeps the publication in one document.
- **Manage type and transparency.** If your design uses a lot of transparency effects, set up a layer for transparent objects and another for type. Keep the type layer above the layer with transparency. This ensures that type won't interact with transparency in unexpected ways and consequently become rasterized or converted to outlines when the document is printed.

Creating Layers

To create a new layer, click the New Layer button at the bottom of the Layers panel. A new layer will be created at the top of the list. Double-click a layer to name it and specify its options as follows (**Figure 8.28**):

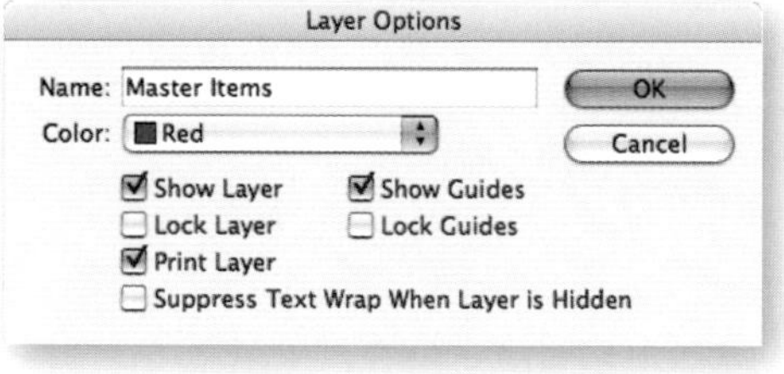
Layer Options
Name: Master Items
Color: Red
OK
Cancel
Show Layer
Show Guides
Lock Layer
Lock Guides
Print Layer
Suppress Text Wrap When Layer is Hidden

Figure 8.28 The Layer Options dialog.

■ **Tip:** You can create a new layer above a the selected layer by holding down Ctrl (Windows) or Command (Mac OS) as you click the New Layer button.

- **Name.** Give the layer a name that clearly identifies its purpose.
- **Color.** Choose a color that identifies the layer and all the objects that belong to it. Each object's bounding box displays the color of the layer it's on, so try using colors that make it easier to distinguish between the layers of different objects on the page.
- **Show Layer.** Using this option is the same as using the eye icon in the Layers panel. Select it to make a layer visible. Deselect it to hide all the objects on that layer and prevent them from printing.

- **Lock Layer.** This option is the same as making the lock icon visible in the Layers panel. If you want to prevent changes to all the objects on a layer, select this option. You might create a layer for master items that can't be altered and keep that layer locked.
- **Show Guides.** This option allows you to make the guides on individual layers visible or invisible. For instance, you might set up an alternative layout grid on a separate layer and turn it on as you need it.
- **Lock Guides.** Select this option to prevent changes to the ruler guides on a layer.
- **Print Layer.** Select this option to make a layer printable or deselect it to make the layer nonprintable. Later, when printing or exporting to PDF, you can choose whether or not to print hidden and nonprinting layers. This option is useful for layers that contain production notes and template instructions.
- **Suppress Text Wrap When Layer Is Hidden.** If the layer contains objects with a text wrap applied to them, select this option to allow text on other layers to flow normally—instead of being affected by the text wrap—when the layer is hidden.

■ **Tip:** Instead of making an entire layer nonprintable, you can choose to prevent individual objects from printing by selecting the Nonprinting option in the Attributes panel.

Working with Layers

Anytime you create or place a new object, it is placed on the target layer. To target a layer, click it in the Layers panel. The targeted layer displays a pen icon next to its name (**Figure 8.29**). If the targeted layer is hidden or locked, you cannot create or place new objects on that layer.

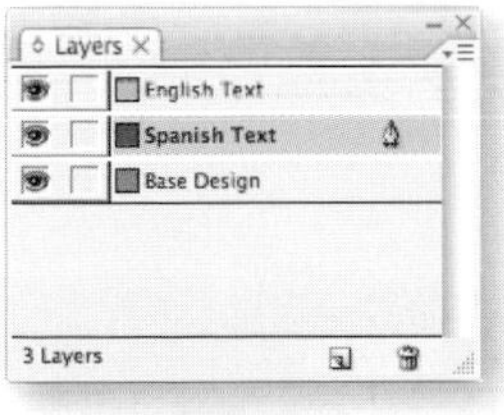
Layers
English Text
Spanish Text
Base Design
3 Layers

Figure 8.29 The Layers panel. The targeted layer is highlighted and displays a pen icon to the right of its name.

InDesign lets you select any object regardless of what layer it's on. When you select an object, a colored dot appears in the Layers panel next to the name of the layer it belongs to (**Figure 8.30**). You can move objects to another layer by selecting the objects and then dragging the colored dot to the other layer. To copy selected objects to another layer, hold down Alt (Windows) or Option (Mac OS) as you drag the colored dot to the other layer.

■ **Tip:** You can select all the objects on a layer by holding down Alt (Windows) or Option (Mac OS) as you click a layer in the Layers panel.

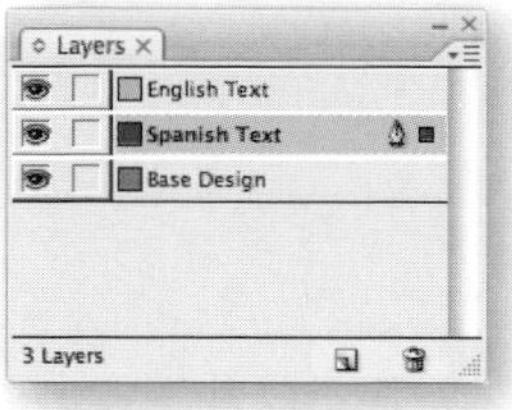
Layers
English Text
Spanish Text
Base Design
3 Layers

Figure 8.30 The red dot on the Spanish Text layer indicates that one or more objects on the layer are currently selected.

To rearrange the stacking order of layers, simply drag a layer up and down in the list of layers. You can also select more than one layer and drag them all at the same time. When you change the order of a layer, all of its objects are moved with it, but they still maintain their own stacking order within that layer.

To make it easier to edit parts of a document without accidentally changing other objects, you can hide and lock layers. To hide a layer, click the eye icon at the far left of the layer's name. You can hide all the layers except for the selected layer by choosing Hide Others from the Layers panel menu. To show a layer, click the square to show the eye icon (**Figure 8.31**). You can lock all the layers except for the selected layer by choosing Lock Others from the Layers panel menu. When you hide a layer, all of its objects are hidden, making it easier to edit other objects on the page.

Layers
English Text
Spanish Text
Base Design
3 Layers

Figure 8.31 The Spanish Text layer in this multilingual publication is hidden to keep it out of view while the English Text layer is being edited. The Base Design layer is locked to prevent accidental changes to it.

To lock a layer, click the square at the immediate left of the layer's name. The lock icon appears, indicating the layer is locked (Figure 8.31). To unlock a layer, click the lock icon to remove it from the square. All the objects on the locked layer are still visible, but you cannot select them. However, some attributes can be edited indirectly, such as when you edit a swatch or paragraph style.

If you plan on pasting cut or copied objects from one page to another or from one document to another, activate the Paste Remembers Layers command to ensure that objects retain their layer assignments when pasted. If the command is not active, the pasted objects are pasted together on the target layer. To activate the command, select Paste Remembers Layers from the Layers panel menu.

9

Working with Color

THERE ARE FEW ASPECTS OF DESIGN THAT HAVE SUCH A SIGNIFICANT IMPACT AS color. Whether it's a logo, a folio, or some simple lines and shapes, color plays an important role in your publications. However, inconsistent color reveals sloppy design and production skills. Ensure consistent design, save time, and build a stronger brand by using the powerful color capabilities of InDesign as you build your templates.

In this chapter you'll learn how to create, customize, and manage a variety of color options. There isn't enough space to review color theory and help you pick pleasing color combinations, but you'll learn how to work efficiently with the colors you choose for your fills, strokes, text, and tables.

Creating Color Swatches

The purpose of creating color swatches is to globally control the color in your document. Color swatches make it possible to quickly modify color without having to locate and adjust each object separately. Any change you make to a color swatch affects all the objects, such as text, frames, and tables, to which it has been applied. Needless to say, color swatches can save you a lot of time and really help ensure consistency.

As is typical for an Adobe application, there's more than one way to work with color in InDesign. By using the Color panel, you'll find a familiar way to mix colors with multiple color sliders. If you click the panel menu, you'll see that you can even mix colors in a variety of color modes: CMYK, RGB, and Lab (**Figure 9.1**).

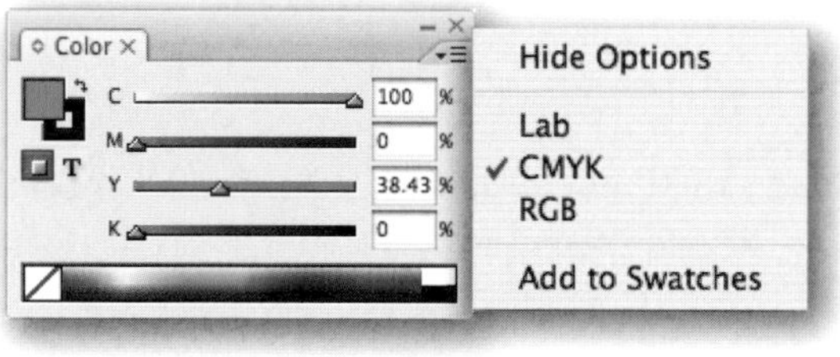
Color
C
M
Y
K
100
0
38.43
0
T
Hide Options
Lab
✓ CMYK
RGB
Add to Swatches

Figure 9.1 You can mix colors in the Color panel, but the Swatches panel is the most efficient place to create swatches.

Preparing Templates for Colored Paper

You might have noticed a few swatches at the top of the Swatches panel that cannot be removed: [None], [Paper], [Black], and [Registration]. Generally speaking, default settings in Adobe applications that cannot be edited or deleted are wrapped in bracket characters. One notable exception to this rule is the [Paper] swatch.

While you can't remove the [Paper] swatch, you can edit it for an interesting effect. If you plan on printing your design on colored paper, double-click the [Paper] swatch and change the swatch to an approximation of the color of paper you'll be using. This isn't a reliable way to perform color management, but it's an easy way to preview the effect of printing on colored paper. Note that the paper color affects how your document previews in InDesign, but the color won't actually be printed (**Figure 9.2**).

If you're using a custom [Paper] swatch color and you want an object in your template to appear to have no color, don't apply the [Paper] swatch. Instead, use the [None] swatch when you want no color.

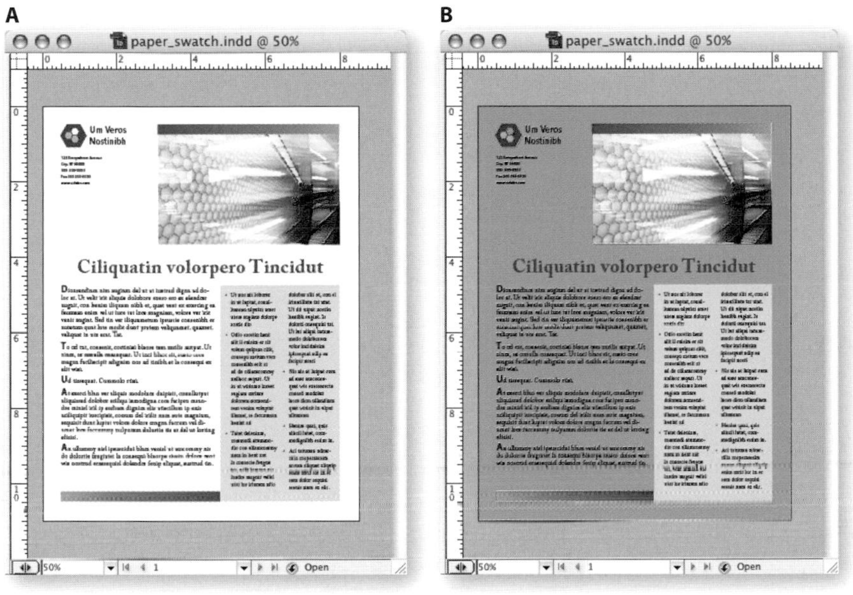
A
paper_swatch.indd @ 50%
Um Veros Nostinibh
Ciliquatin volorpero Tincidut
B
paper_swatch.indd @ 50%
Um Veros Nostinibh
Ciliquatin volorpero Tincidut

Figure 9.2 Here's an example of a template with the default [Paper] swatch (**A**) and with a custom [Paper] swatch (**B**).

While there's technically nothing wrong with mixing colors in the Color panel, it can be tempting to mix and use colors without first defining them as reusable color swatches. The problem with not defining color swatches before you apply color to your design is that it's much harder to apply consistent color, not to mention how difficult it is to change colors after the fact.

With that warning in mind, use the Swatches panel to mix colors and create swatches for your templates. You could simply click the New Swatch button at the bottom of the Swatches panel, but you'll save some time by choosing New Color Swatch from the panel menu (**Figure 9.3**). By choosing this command from the panel menu, you'll be able to name your swatches immediately, and you can create several swatches all in one process.

● **Note:** You can also create a new color swatch by mixing color in the Color panel and then clicking the New Swatch button in the Swatches panel. If you use this method, be sure to double-click the swatch definition and give it a recognizable name before you're done.

You have several decisions to make in the New Color Swatch dialog, so let's start at the top and work downward:

1. By default, new color swatches are named according to their color values. Some experienced designers might find this useful, but I recommend deselecting the "Name with Color Value" check box and giving the swatch a name based on its use or function (**Figure 9.4**). It's especially important for a template that might be used by other people to change the names of color swatches so that content contributors who might not have as much design experience as you can understand the purpose of the various swatches. For example, if you define a blue swatch that will be used for alternating

row colors in a table, considering naming the swatch something like "Blue Table Row." If for some reason you want to revert back to the color values, you can always select the "Name with Color Value" check box again.

Swatches
Tint:
[None]
[Paper]
[Black]
[Registration]
C=100 M=0 Y=0 K=0
C=0 M=100 Y=0 K=0
C=0 M=0 Y=100 K=0
C=15 M=100 Y=100 K=0
C=75 M=5 Y=100 K=0
C=100 M=90 Y=10 K=0
New Color Swatch...
New Tint Swatch...
New Gradient Swatch...
New Mixed Ink Swatch...
New Mixed Ink Group...
Duplicate Swatch
Delete Swatch...
Swatch Options...
Load Swatches...
Save Swatches...
Select All Unused
Add Unnamed Colors
✓ Name
Small Name
Small Swatch
Large Swatch
Merge Swatches
Ink Manager...
Hide Options

Figure 9.3 Create new color swatches with the Swatches panel.

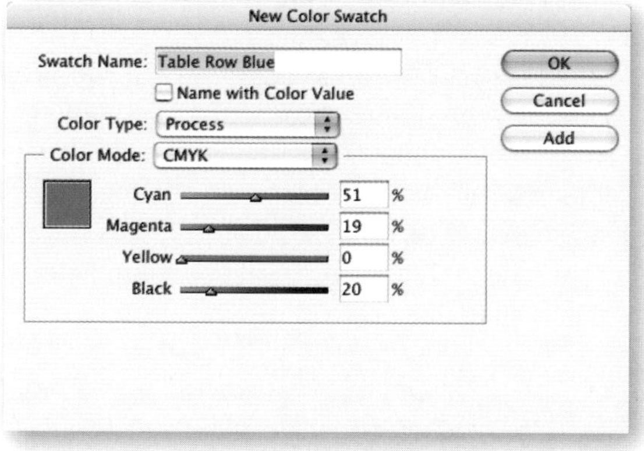
New Color Swatch
Swatch Name: Table Row Blue
Name with Color Value
Color Type: Process
Color Mode: CMYK
Cyan 51 %
Magenta 19 %
Yellow 0 %
Black 20 %
OK
Cancel
Add

Figure 9.4 Consider naming your color swatches based on their use in the template.

2. The default Color Type value is Process, which is a mix of Cyan (C), Magenta (M), Yellow (Y), and Black (K), the standard four printing inks used in professional color printing. You can also choose Spot and I'll discuss that color type later in this chapter. For most color swatches you'll leave this value set to Process.
3. The third choice you need to make in the New Color Swatch dialog is the Color Mode. The default value is CMYK, which is the best choice for design projects destined for professional color printing. If you're creating templates

for onscreen documents, you might want to change the Color Mode to RGB, and some color gurus will prefer to mix their colors in the Lab Color Mode. You'll also notice a variety of other choices such as various Pantone libraries, which I'll discuss later in the "Spot Color Swatches" section.

4. With the first three decisions made, you can finally start mixing your color values with the color sliders to create exactly the color you want to use. After you create a color, click the Add button to add it to your list of swatches. You can continue to mix and add multiple new color swatches using the previous three steps without leaving the New Color Swatch dialog. When you're done creating all your swatches, click OK.

■ **Tip:** You can also create a new swatch based on your mock-up layout by selecting an object, such as a colored frame, and dragging the fill or stroke icon from the Tools panel or the Swatches panel into the swatches list.

Tint Swatches

A common way to give the impression that your publications use more colors than they actually do is to use varying tints of the same colors. For example, you might create a color swatch and use it at 100 percent, but then use the same color at 75% and 50% for lighter renditions. You could of course just adjust the tint percentage on a case-by-case basis, but if you decide for some reason that all the 50% tints need to be reduced to 20% tints, that will be a lot of work to fix.

Instead of managing these tints manually, you can use tint swatches to control your color variations. To create a tint swatch, select an existing swatch in the Swatches panel and then choose a tint value (from 0% to 100%) with the Tint slider at the top of the Swatches panel. When you've selected the appropriate tint value, just click the New Swatch button at the bottom of the Swatches panel (**Figure 9.5**). Your new tint swatch is created with the same name as the base swatch, but the tint value is listed next to the swatch name.

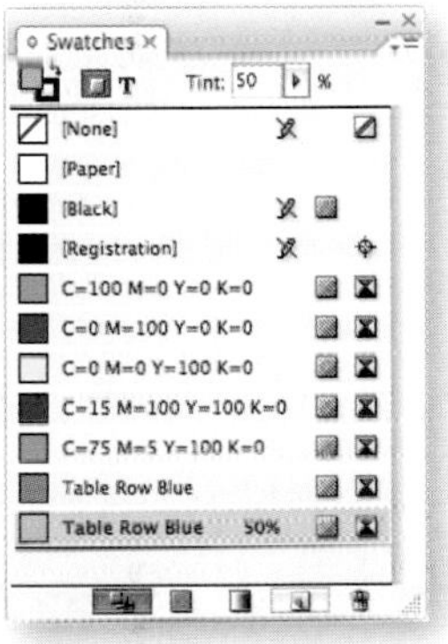
Swatches
Tint: 50 %
[None]
[Paper]
[Black]
[Registration]
C=100 M=0 Y=0 K=0
C=0 M=100 Y=0 K=0
C=0 M=0 Y=100 K=0
C=15 M=100 Y=100 K=0
C=75 M=5 Y=100 K=0
Table Row Blue
Table Row Blue 50%

Figure 9.5 Tint swatches can be based on process and spot swatches but cannot be based on gradient swatches, mixed ink swatches, or mixed ink groups, which we'll discuss later in this chapter.

Gradient Swatches

The swatch types discussed in the previous sections are solid colors, but gradient swatches are unique in that they allow you to create a gradual blend between two or more colors. Create a new gradient swatch by choosing New Gradient Swatch from the Swatches panel menu and following these steps:

1. Give your new gradient swatch a recognizable name.
2. Choose Linear or Radial for the gradient type.
3. Select and edit the color stops along the bottom of the gradient ramp. You can mix colors for the gradient stops using the Lab, CMYK, or RGB color spaces by choosing an option from the Stop Color menu, and you can also choose from your existing color swatches.

■ **Tip:** If you change the base swatch, all tint swatches related to that swatch are automatically changed.

■ **Tip:** If you select an object on the page prior to creating the gradient swatch, you can get a preview of how it will look once applied by enabling the Preview option in the Gradient Options dialog.

4. To add a new color stop, just click in any empty space on the bottom of the gradient ramp. To remove a color stop, click and hold on the stop and drag down with your cursor until the stop disappears. Remember that you must have at least two stops to create the gradient effect.
5. To change how quickly the colors in a gradient transition from one color to another, select a small diamond icon on the top of the Gradient Ramp and slide it to the left or right (**Figure 9.6**).

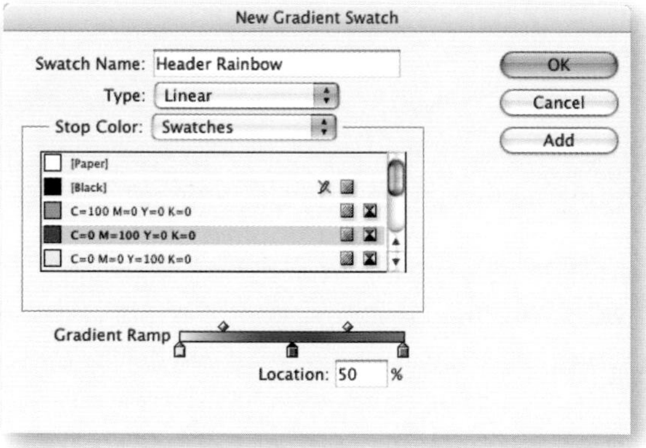
New Gradient Swatch
Swatch Name: Header Rainbow
Type: Linear
Stop Color: Swatches
[Paper]
[Black]
C=100 M=0 Y=0 K=0
C=0 M=100 Y=0 K=0
C=0 M=0 Y=100 K=0
Gradient Ramp
Location: 50 %
OK
Cancel
Add

Figure 9.6 Gradient swatches can add visual interest to your templates as long as you don't go overboard.

● **Note:** Check with your print service provider before you create a gradient that blends from a four-color process swatch to a spot color swatch. This can be a challenging effect to reproduce on the printed page.

6. Click the Add button to add the gradient swatch and mix more gradients. Click OK when you're done.

Spot Color Swatches

Process colors are composed of varying combinations of the standard CMYK inks used in the printing process. Printed materials that only use combinations of these four standard inks are referred to as four-color jobs but can reproduce a stunning variety of color, including full-color photography.

There are additional inks used for printing, called spot colors, which are printed using premixed inks from a vendor such as Pantone. You might have a two-color newsletter template that just uses black and one spot color for a logo or a five-color job that uses the four process colors and one additional spot color. I've seen as many as 28 different inks used in a single print job, but using that many inks is very rare and quite expensive.

Common print jobs include two-color, four-color, or four-color plus one or two spot colors. Your printing specifications and budget should dictate whether you create spot color swatches. Always discuss the details of your printing requirements with your print service provider before committing to special inks in a template.

Create a spot color swatch like you would a normal swatch, but in the New Color Swatch dialog, choose a swatch library such as one of the Pantone libraries from the Color Mode menu. Now you can choose the specific spot color, such as a logo or brand color, from the list of available spot colors (**Figure 9.7**).

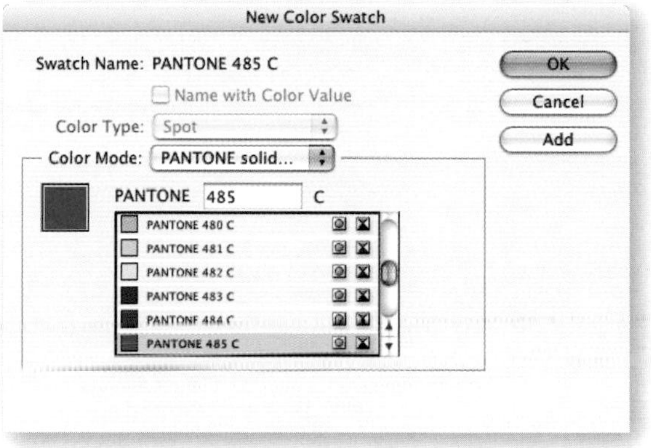
New Color Swatch
Swatch Name: PANTONE 485 C
Name with Color Value
Color Type: Spot
Color Mode: PANTONE solid...
PANTONE 485 C
PANTONE 480 C
PANTONE 481 C
PANTONE 482 C
PANTONE 483 C
PANTONE 484 C
PANTONE 485 C
OK
Cancel
Add

Figure 9.7 Spot color swatches may be needed to achieve a specific color that cannot be reproduced with four-color process printing technology.

Mixed Ink Swatches

Mixed inks are a creative way to give your publications the effect of having used more colors than were actually printed. Your budget might limit you to a two-color printing process, but being forced to choose from just two colors, say black and one spot color, doesn't mean your designs have to look like 80s clip art. Mixed inks can give the impression that your low-budget print job was created with more plates and a bigger budget.

To create a mixed ink swatch, follow these steps:

1. Create at least one spot color swatch.
2. Choose New Mixed Ink Swatch from the Swatches panel menu.
3. Give your new swatch a meaningful name, based on its function.
4. Select at least two swatches, including at least one spot color swatch, by clicking in the column to the left of the swatch names. The four-process swatches (CMYK) and any existing spot color swatches are available for mixing, but custom process swatches, tints, and gradients are not included (**Figure 9.8**).
5. Use the percentage sliders to the right of each active swatch to adjust how the inks combine to create the new swatch. Click Add to add the color to your swatches panel, or OK when you're done.

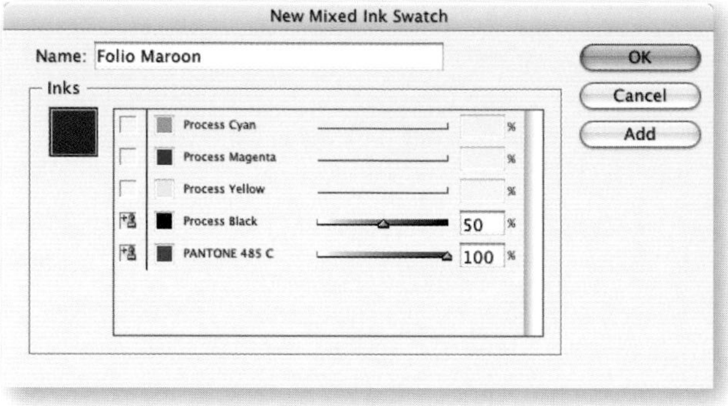
New Mixed Ink Swatch
Name: Folio Maroon
OK
Cancel
Add
Inks
Process Cyan
Process Magenta
Process Yellow
Process Black
50 %
PANTONE 485 C
100 %

Figure 9.8 Mix multiple inks for the effect of a broader color palette in your templates.

● **Note:** If the New Mixed Ink Swatch command is grayed out in the Swatches panel menu, it means you don't have any spot color swatches in your file. Create a spot color swatch before proceeding.

Part of the beauty of mixed ink swatches is that they retain their link to the original swatches. For example, you might create a mixed ink swatch of black and an orange spot color for an autumn publication template. When winter comes around, you can change the spot color to red, and when spring comes around, you can change it again to green. This affords you a delicate balance between flexibility and control at the same time in a template.

Mixed Ink Groups

Mixed ink swatches are great, but if you need to create several different combinations of the same inks, it's a very tedious process. That's where mixed ink groups come in. They follow the same principles as individual mixed ink swatches but with an added component of time-saving automation.

To create a mixed ink group, follow these steps:

1. Create at least one spot color swatch.
2. Choose New Mixed Ink Group from the Swatches panel menu.
3. Give your new swatch group a useful base name. Note that swatches in the group will use the name you assign followed by a suffix and serial number, as in Foliage Swatch 1, Foliage Swatch 2, and so on.
4. Select at least two swatches, including at least one spot color swatch, by clicking in the column to the left of the swatch names. The four-process swatches (CMYK) and any existing spot color swatches are available for mixing, but custom process swatches, tints, and gradients are not included.
5. Adjust the Initial, Repeat, and Increment values to vary how the inks make new combinations. For example, choose two inks, set their initial value to 0%, their repeat value to 3, and the increment value to 25% to create 16 unique mixed ink swatches that represent the matrix of options. This process can be a bit confusing at first, so click the Preview Swatches button and decide if you're getting the color combinations you desire (**Figure 9.9**).

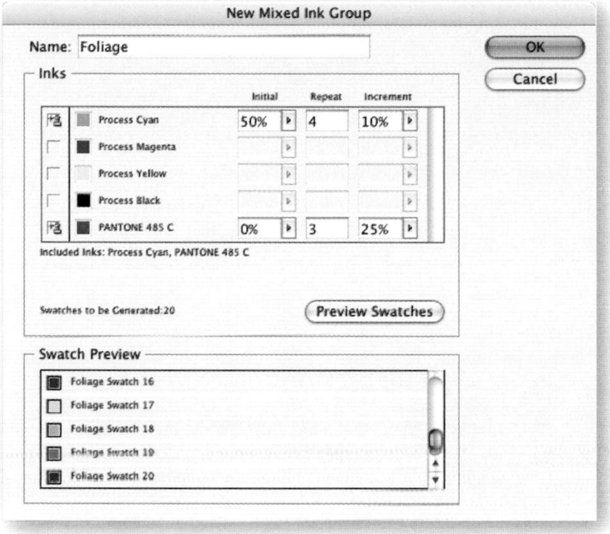
New Mixed Ink Group
Name: Foliage
OK
Cancel
Inks
Initial
Repeat
Increment
Process Cyan
50%
4
10%
Process Magenta
Process Yellow
Process Black
PANTONE 485 C
0%
3
25%
Included Inks: Process Cyan, PANTONE 485 C
Swatches to be Generated:20
Preview Swatches
Swatch Preview
Foliage Swatch 16
Foliage Swatch 17
Foliage Swatch 18
Foliage Swatch 20

Figure 9.9 Mixed ink groups are an easy way to "fake" lots of color in a document with as few as two inks.

6. Click OK when you're done to add the new mixed ink group and all the resulting mixed ink swatches.

A mixed ink group is really a dynamically linked set of mixed ink swatches. This means you can easily change the group in a variety of ways:

- Change the definition of a spot color swatch that is used in the mixed ink group.
- Double-click the mixed ink group in the Swatches panel to open the Mixed Ink Group Options dialog and change which swatches are included in the group (**Figure 9.10**). Note that mixed ink groups can be difficult to identify when the Swatches panel is not in list mode. In the Small Swatch and Large Swatch views, a mixed ink group is indicated by a solid black triangle in the lower-right corner, and the mixed ink swatches that are a part of the group are indicated by a small black and white triangle.
- Double-click an individual swatch that is part of the mixed ink group and adjust the percentages of the various inks.

The first two changes instantly affect all the swatches in the group, whereas the last change affects just the one swatch you happen to edit. It's incredible to think of how much time you can save by updating the color scheme of multiple swatches and refreshing the look of an entire template with just a few quick changes to a mixed ink group.

Swatches
Tint: 50 %
PANTONE 485 C
Folio Maroon
Foliage
Foliage Swatch 1
Foliage Swatch 2
Foliage Swatch 3
Foliage Swatch 4
Foliage Swatch 5
Foliage Swatch 6
Foliage Swatch 7
Foliage Swatch 8
Foliage Swatch 9

Figure 9.10 You can easily change all the swatches in a mixed ink group with just a few clicks.

Loading Swatches

So far I've discussed several ways to create a variety of swatch types, but that doesn't mean all swatches have to be created directly inside your template. It's easy to load color swatches from another InDesign document into your template. Simply choose Load Swatches from the Swatches panel menu, select another InDesign document or template, and click Open (**Figure 9.11**).

Swatches
Tint: 50 %
[None]
[Paper]
[Black]
[Registration]
C=100 M=0 Y=0 K=0
C=0 M=100 Y=0 K=0
C=0 M=0 Y=100 K=0
Table Row Blue
Table Row Blue 50%
Header Rainbow
PANTONE 485 C
New Color Swatch...
New Tint Swatch...
New Gradient Swatch...
New Mixed Ink Swatch...
New Mixed Ink Group...
Duplicate Swatch
Delete Swatch...
Swatch Options...
Load Swatches...
Save Swatches...
Select All Unused
Add Unnamed Colors
✓ Name
Small Name
Small Swatch
Large Swatch
Merge Swatches
Ink Manager...
Hide Options

Figure 9.11 Load swatches from another InDesign document to save time and ensure consistency.

The Load Swatches command automatically loads all the unique swatches from the other document into your template. This makes it easy to use the same set of swatches, such as corporate brand colors, without going through the tedious process of re-creating the same swatches for each new template.

■ **Tip:** If you create color swatches with an InDesign document open, the swatches will be added to that file. However, if you create swatches with no documents open, the swatches are saved in the application preferences so that any new document you create will use those base swatches. This is helpful to understand because if you never use the red, green, and blue swatches, you can close all documents, delete those unused swatches, and all new templates you create will omit those swatches. On the other hand, if there's a swatch, such as a Pantone spot color, that you'll use frequently, you should define that swatch first with no document

Sharing Swatches

You might be an InDesign user, but that doesn't mean all your design ideas will start as InDesign mock-ups. In some cases you'll start sketching something in Photoshop or drafting a logo in Illustrator. In those situations, it can be very convenient to share a set of color swatches between multiple Adobe applications, not just between your InDesign files.

Back in the CS2 days, Adobe introduced the Adobe Swatch Exchange (ASE) swatch format as a way to share swatches between multiple Adobe applications. That means Adobe InDesign, Illustrator, and Photoshop all have the ability to save selected swatches to this new interchange format, which can in turn be loaded into an InDesign template. To use the ASE swatch format, follow these steps:

1. In Photoshop choose Save Swatches for Exchange from the Swatches panel menu. In Illustrator, choose Save Swatch Library as ASE from the Swatches panel menu (**Figure 9.12**).

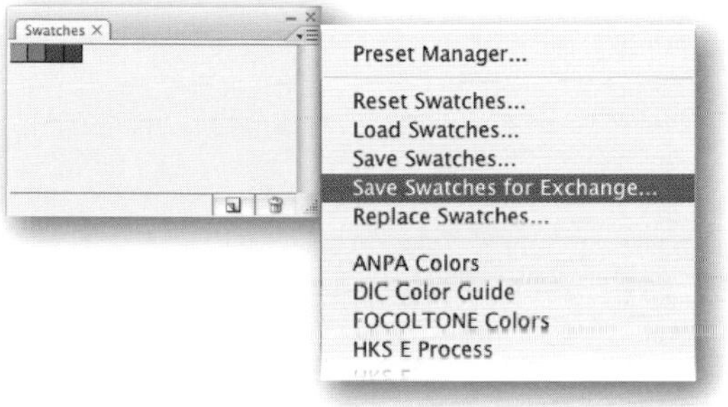
Swatches
Preset Manager...
Reset Swatches...
Load Swatches...
Save Swatches...
Save Swatches for Exchange...
Replace Swatches...
ANPA Colors
DIC Color Guide
FOCOLTONE Colors
HKS E Process

Figure 9.12 Save swatches from other Adobe applications for reuse in your InDesign templates.

2. Save the .ase file in a convenient location, such as your desktop.
3. To import the .ase file into InDesign, choose Load Swatches from the Swatches panel menu and then select the .ase file created in the previous step. All the saved swatches are added to your InDesign template.

● **Note:** Only solid color swatches are supported in the ASE format. This means gradient and pattern swatches from Illustrator cannot be exchanged with other applications.

Organizing Swatches

After you've gone through the process of creating the swatches you need for your template, you'll want to tidy things up for the sake of everybody who will use your template. For example, leaving lots of swatches in the template that will never be used can be confusing for another designer. You could choose Select All Unused from the Swatches panel menu and delete the unused swatches, but just because a swatch isn't used in a template doesn't mean you won't be using it in the final design.

DELETING UNUSED SWATCHES

It's best to examine your swatches one at a time to determine if you really need them. If you don't need a swatch, select it in the Swatches panel and click the Delete button at the bottom of the panel. If you attempt to delete a swatch that is in use, InDesign warns you that the swatch needs to be remapped (**Figure 9.13**). Consider that a friendly warning; in most cases you'll click Cancel and keep the swatch after all.

■ **Tip:** If you've consistently named your swatches based on their use, it should be easy to identify swatches with default names such as C=15, M=100, Y=100, and K=0 as unused and delete them from the Swatches panel.

Delete Swatch
Remove Swatch and Replace with:
Defined Swatch:
[Black]
Unnamed Swatch
Cancel
OK

Figure 9.13 Deleting a used swatch reveals this helpful warning dialog.

Cooler Color with Kuler

Create pleasing combinations of color swatches based on color harmony rules with the free Web-based service at http://kuler.adobe.com. This Flash-driven color community site allows you to mix colors, store your favorites, and share them with others. You can download your swatches as well as those created by other designers in the .ase format for easy use in your InDesign templates.

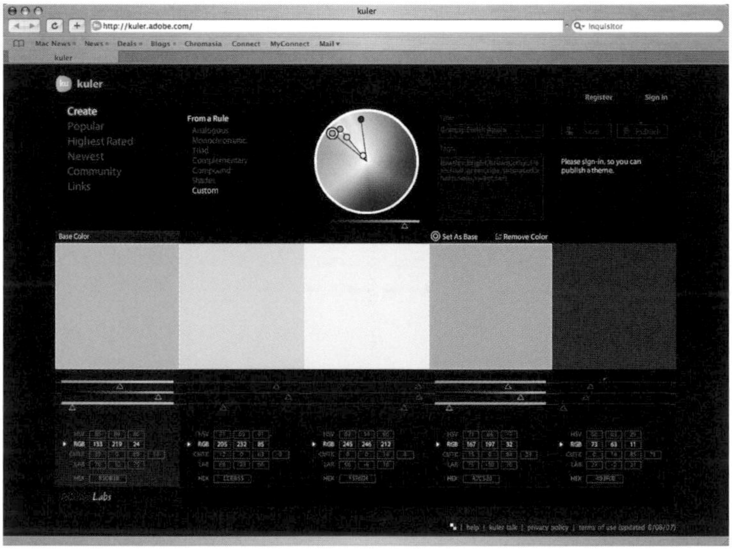
kuler
http://kuler.adobe.com/
kuler
Create
Popular
Highest Rated
Newest
Community
Links
From a Rule
Custom
Register
Sign In
Please sign-in, so you can publish a theme.
Base Color
Set As Base
Remove Color
Labs

FINDING UNNAMED SWATCHES

While leaving a bunch of unused swatches in a template makes it unnecessarily difficult for other designers to wade through your disorganization, using lots of unnamed swatches in a document is also a bad habit. If you followed the directions earlier in this chapter for creating color swatches, your template should be clean and orderly, but you know how easy it is to skip those important steps.

To ensure that all the colors in your mock-up layout are accounted for, choose Add Unnamed Swatches from the Swatches panel menu (**Figure 9.14**). This command forces InDesign to inventory every frame, text, and table in your entire layout. Unnamed swatches are added to the bottom of the Swatches panel and named according to their color values. At this point you should double-click each new swatch to edit its name in the Swatch Options dialog.

CHANGING THE SWATCH ORDER

At this point you should have all your colors accounted for and have deleted those you don't need. That means it's a great time to organize the swatches that will be a part of your template. Consider organizing your swatches according to hue, page, section, or type (solid, spot, gradient, tint, etc.). Whichever system you choose, consider how other designers will use your template and try to accommodate their most frequent tasks.

To change the order of swatches in the Swatches panel, just click and hold a swatch and then drag it to a new location in the list. If you want to move several swatches at once, you can select contiguous swatches by holding the Shift key and clicking in the Swatches panel or select noncontiguous swatches by pressing Ctrl/Command when you click. With multiple swatches selected, you can drag them anywhere in the list (**Figure 9.15**).

■ **Tip:** Many designers mistakenly use the [Registration] swatch (a combination of 100% Cyan, 100% Magenta, 100% Yellow, and 100% Black that helps printers align the multiple plates of a printing job) when they should be using [Black]. While you can't delete any swatch listed in brackets, you can move them. Consider moving the [Registration] swatch to the very bottom of the list in the Swatches panel so you're not tempted to use it unless you actually need it.

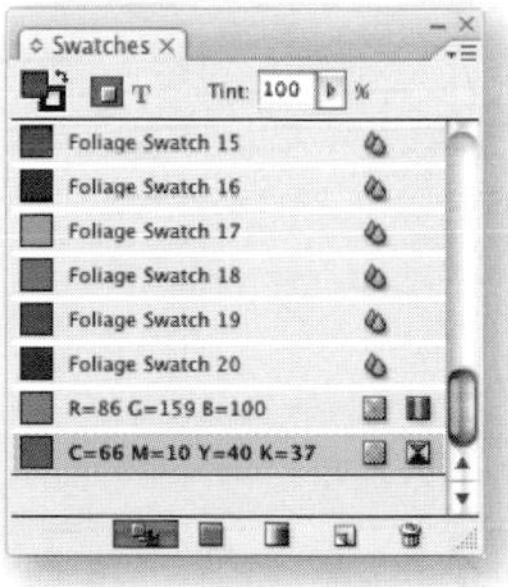
Swatches
Tint: 100 %
Foliage Swatch 15
Foliage Swatch 16
Foliage Swatch 17
Foliage Swatch 18
Foliage Swatch 19
Foliage Swatch 20
R=86 G=159 B=100
C=66 M=10 Y=40 K=37

Figure 9.14 Make sure all the colors you used in your mock-up layout are identified as named swatches.

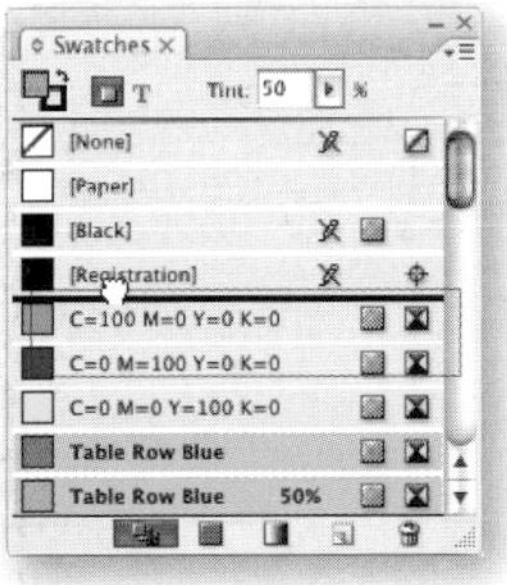
Swatches
Tint: 50 %
[None]
[Paper]
[Black]
[Registration]
C=100 M=0 Y=0 K=0
C=0 M=100 Y=0 K=0
C=0 M=0 Y=100 K=0
Table Row Blue
Table Row Blue 50%

Figure 9.15 Change the order of your swatches to make your production workflow more efficient.

CHANGING THE SWATCHES PANEL VIEW

By now you have created, named, and organized all of your swatches. One of the last options you might want to adjust is how the swatches are viewed in the Swatches panel. The default setting is the Name view. You can also choose Small Name, Small Swatch, or Large Swatch from the Swatches panel menu.

For better or worse, the view options for the Swatches panel are an application setting and are not file specific. So, while you can control the order of the swatches in your templates, you can't enforce how the swatches are viewed. Feel free to suggest how users of your templates should change their Swatches panel view settings, but know that ultimately it's up to the individual.

FILTERING THE SWATCHES PANEL

Swatches
Tint: 50 %
[None]
Header Rainbow

Figure 9.16 Filter your swatches with the buttons at the bottom of the Swatches panel.

When working with swatches in your template, it can sometimes be helpful to filter your swatches based on their type. To view only solid color swatches, click the Show Color Swatches button at the bottom of the Swatches panel. If you'd rather see just your gradient swatches, click the Show Gradient Swatches button (**Figure 9.16**). When you're ready to see all of the swatches again, click the Show All Swatches button.

NAVIGATING THE SWATCHES PANEL

One of my favorite tips for working with color swatches in InDesign is to force the focus of your keyboard and cursor on the Swatches panel. If you press Ctrl-Alt (Windows)/Command-Option (Mac OS) and click in the Swatches panel, you'll notice a thick black stroke appears around the inside perimeter of the Swatches panel (**Figure 9.17**).

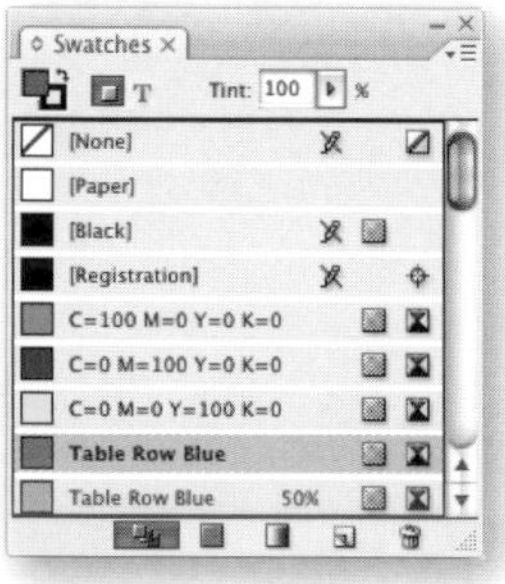
Swatches
Tint: 100 %
[None]
[Paper]
[Black]
[Registration]
C=100 M=0 Y=0 K=0
C=0 M=100 Y=0 K=0
C=0 M=0 Y=100 K=0
Table Row Blue
Table Row Blue 50%

Figure 9.17 Force focus on the Swatches panel so you can navigate the panel with keyboard shortcuts and experiment with different swatches.

This black stroke is a visual indicator that InDesign's attention ("focus" in user interface parlance) is now on the Swatches panel instead of the document. The benefit of this sneaky little detail is that if you have a really long list of swatches, you can start typing the first few letters of your desired swatch name and InDesign will select that swatch for you. It's just one more good reason to name your swatches based on their function instead of using the default color values naming convention.

Another practical use of this cool production trick is if you want to experiment with different colors. Select an object before you force focus on the Swatches panel. You can then use the arrow keys to navigate up and down the list of your swatches, changing the color of the selected object at the same time. It's an easy way to quickly experiment with several color options.

CONFIGURING COLOR MANAGEMENT

I certainly can't cover the vast subject of color management in a single section, but I'd be remiss if I didn't try to steer you in the right direction. As much as I'd like to give you all sorts of advice about how to establish a color managed workflow, my best advice is to encourage you to talk with your print service provider or color management consultant.

Based on the suggestions you receive from your print service provider, you'll choose Edit > Color Settings and make any required adjustments. Your print service provider might even supply you with a custom color-settings file that you can load directly from the Color Settings dialog (**Figure 9.18**).

● **Note:** For more information about establishing a color managed workflow, read <italic>Real World Color Management, Second Edition<italic> from Peachpit Press.

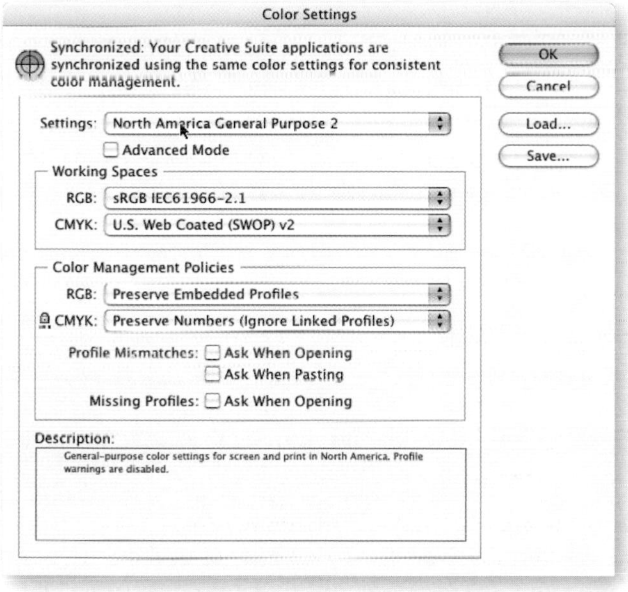
Color Settings
Synchronized: Your Creative Suite applications are synchronized using the same color settings for consistent color management.
OK
Cancel
Load...
Save...
Settings: North America General Purpose 2
Advanced Mode
Working Spaces
RGB: sRGB IEC61966-2.1
CMYK: U.S. Web Coated (SWOP) v2
Color Management Policies
RGB: Preserve Embedded Profiles
CMYK: Preserve Numbers (Ignore Linked Profiles)
Profile Mismatches: Ask When Opening
Ask When Pasting
Missing Profiles: Ask When Opening
Description:
General-purpose color settings for screen and print in North America. Profile warnings are disabled.

Figure 9.18 Consult with your print service provider and adjust your InDesign color settings accordingly.

If your account manager at your service bureau gives you a long, blank stare when you ask about color management, you're probably safe leaving the settings in their default configuration of "North American General Purpose 2." You might also consider finding a new print vendor!

Lastly, if you use other Adobe applications other than InDesign, you should synchronize the color settings across multiple applications using Adobe Bridge. Just follow these easy steps:

1. Select File > Browse in Adobe InDesign to launch Adobe Bridge.
2. Choose Edit > Creative Suite Color Settings.

3. Select the color settings configuration you want to use across InDesign, Photoshop, Illustrator, and Acrobat and then click Apply (**Figure 9.19**).

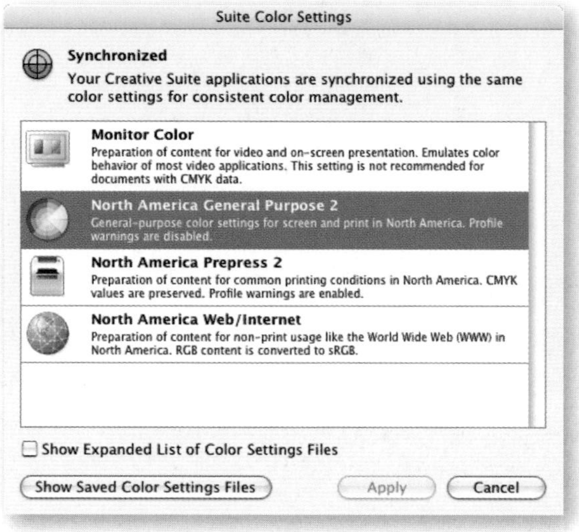
Suite Color Settings
Synchronized
Your Creative Suite applications are synchronized using the same color settings for consistent color management.
Monitor Color
Preparation of content for video and on-screen presentation. Emulates color behavior of most video applications. This setting is not recommended for documents with CMYK data.
North America General Purpose 2
General-purpose color settings for screen and print in North America. Profile warnings are disabled.
North America Prepress 2
Preparation of content for common printing conditions in North America. CMYK values are preserved. Profile warnings are enabled.
North America Web/Internet
Preparation of content for non-print usage like the World Wide Web (WWW) in North America. RGB content is converted to sRGB.
Show Expanded List of Color Settings Files
Show Saved Color Settings Files
Apply
Cancel

Figure 9.19 Use Adobe Bridge to synchronize color settings for multiple applications with a single click.

This simple configuration doesn't magically calibrate all of your monitors, printers, and scanners for soft proofing, but at least your images will look consistent between the various Adobe applications.

10

Formatting Type and Generating Style Sheets

FORMATTING TYPE CAN BE AN ENJOYABLE AND CREATIVE PROCESS, BUT CAN also become a production nightmare when you are suddenly faced with having to meet an impossible deadline, which is often the case. If you've ever meticulously selected and manually formatted all the text in a document, you know just what I mean.

When constructing templates, it's especially important that you utilize tools that reduce as much manual formatting as possible. Fortunately, InDesign provides an assortment of tools that can accelerate, if not completely automate, the process of formatting text.

This chapter provides detailed information about InDesign's most essential typographic tools and teaches you how to generate style sheets based on the sample text in a mock-up layout.

Essential Character Formatting

■ **Tip:** Choose Show Options from the Character panel menu to display all the available formatting controls.

■ **Tip:** The most efficient way to format text is to use keyboard shortcuts. For a detailed list of all the shortcuts, choose Edit > Keyboard Shortcuts and click the Show Set button.

Character-level formatting is applied to individually selected characters or a range of selected text. To access InDesign's character formatting controls, you can use either the Character panel or Control panel (**Figure 10.1**). To access the controls in the Control panel, activate the Type tool and click the Character Formatting Controls button at the top-left side of the panel.

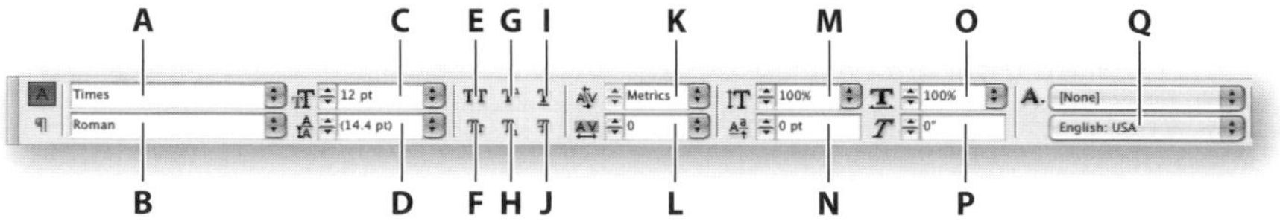
A
C
E G I
K
M
O
Q
Times
Roman
12 pt
(14.4 pt)
Metrics
0
100%
0 pt
100%
0°
[None]
English: USA
B
D
F H J
L
N
P

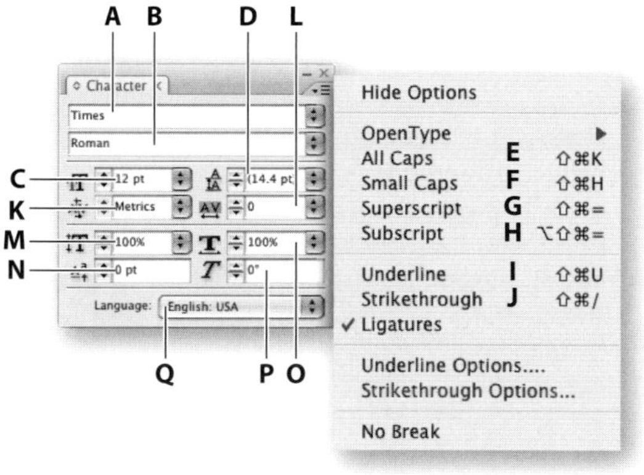
A B D L
Character
Times
Roman
C
K
M
N
12 pt
(14.4 pt)
Metrics
0
100%
100%
0 pt
0°
Language: English: USA
Q P O
Hide Options
OpenType
All Caps E ⇧⌘K
Small Caps F ⇧⌘H
Superscript G ⇧⌘=
Subscript H ⌥⇧⌘=
Underline I ⇧⌘U
Strikethrough J ⇧⌘/
✓ Ligatures
Underline Options....
Strikethrough Options...
No Break

Figure 10.1 The Character and Control panels. A few of the options in the Character panel menu are also available as buttons in the Control panel. Font Family menu (**A**), Type Style menu (**B**), Font Size (**C**), Leading (**D**), All Caps (**E**), Small Caps (**F**), Superscript (**G**), Subscript (**H**), Underline (**I**), Strikethrough (**J**), Kerning (**K**), Tracking (**L**), Vertical Scale (**M**), Baseline Shift (**N**), Horizontal Scale (**O**), Skew (**P**), Language menu (**Q**).

Selecting a Typeface and Type Style

A *typeface* (also called a font family) is a collection of fonts that share common characteristics and are designed to be used together, such as Times New Roman. A *type style* is an alternative version of a font within a typeface, such as regular, bold, semibold, italic, and so on. The actual names vary from typeface to typeface.

When you switch from one typeface to another, InDesign tries to match the type style with one of the available styles in the new typeface. For instance, Times Bold automatically changes to Helvetica Bold when you switch from Times to Helvetica. Times Italic will even change to Helvetica Oblique.

Although the appropriate type style is often applied as expected, it's certainly not always the case. For instance, Garamond Premier Pro Medium Subhead will find no equivalent type style if you were to switch to Adobe Garamond Pro. In that case, Regular would be selected instead. Whenever the type style names differ between typefaces, the results can be unpredictable when you switch to another typeface. Pay particular attention to this when editing paragraph styles. If you switch typefaces, you can cause a missing font issue if an applied character style is using a type style not available in the new typeface (**Figure 10.2**).

> Unt lor iure minisi tem dunt autem at. Nim dit, vulputat la conulpute dio dolor illam illuptat. Ip eugiam acincidunt lore dolobore con nonse zzrillam incilla vendrem nim am, quamet, quiscinit, core conse velisl iusci er sequat. Adiamconse tie molor senis nulluptat la consequate facilit utat lobore min velit prat alit acilit dolortis nonse minibh.

Figure 10.2
The paragraph style applied to this paragraph was updated to use a different typeface, but the character style is still using a variation of Italic that's not available in the new typeface. Each applied instance is highlighted to indicate the selected type style is not available.

Kerning and Tracking

The difference between kerning and tracking is often confused. *Kerning* controls the space between specific pairs of letters, whereas *tracking* controls how tight or loose a selected range of text is. You can first kern individual pairs of letters and then tighten or loosen an entire line of text without affecting the relative kerning of the letter pairs.

AUTOMATIC KERNING OPTIONS

InDesign offers two types of automatic kerning to choose from: Metrics Kerning and Optical Kerning. By default, InDesign uses Metrics Kerning, which utilizes the kern pairs built into most fonts. Kern pairs determine the spacing between specific letter pairs, such as LA, P., To, Ty, We, Yo, and so on. Some fonts contain more kern pairs than others. When a font contains minimal kern pairs or none at all, you will have to manually kern some letter pairs yourself. That is, unless you use Optical Kerning.

Optical Kerning adjusts the spacing between adjoining characters based on their shape—ignoring any built-in kern pairs. This option is especially useful when combining multiple typefaces in the same line. Since each font may use different kerning information, they might not look correct next to each other when using the Metrics Kerning option. By using Optical Kerning, you can automatically achieve more consistent and visually correct spacing between characters (**Figure 10.3**).

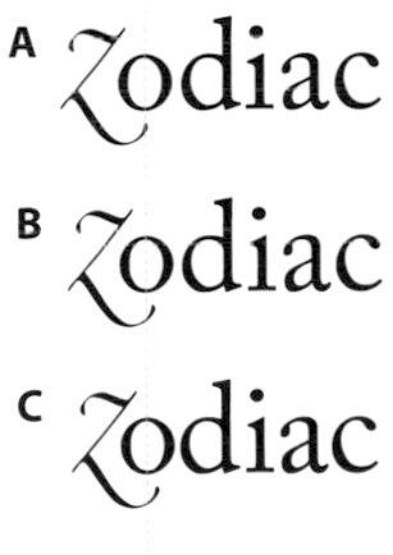
A Zodiac
B Zodiac
C Zodiac

Figure 10.3
Use the blue guide as a reference to see how each kerning option affects the space between the letter Z and o. Metrics Kerning (**A**), Optical Kerning (**B**), Optical Kerning with additional tracking (**C**).

To switch between kerning options, select the text you want to kern and choose either Metrics or Optical from the Kerning menu in the Character panel or Control panel. Metrics and Optical Kerning values appear in parenthesis.

Leading

Leading is the space between lines of type. It's measured from the baseline of one line of text to the baseline of the line above it. With InDesign, leading can either be applied as a character attribute or a paragraph attribute. As a character attribute, you can apply more than one leading value within the same paragraph, which is useful for creating type effects. As a paragraph attribute, the leading value applies to the entire paragraph (**Figure 10.4**).

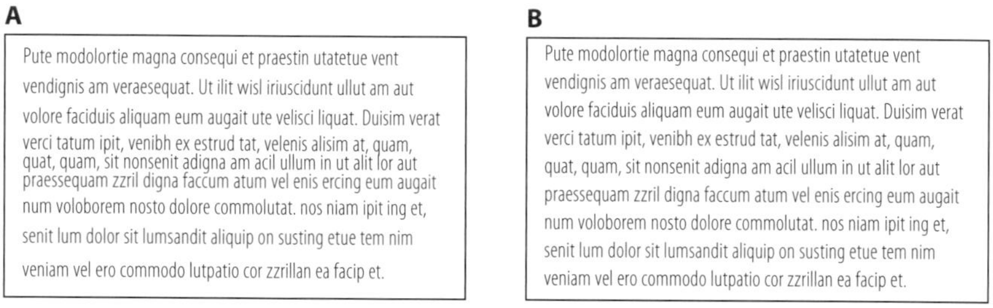
A
Pute modolortie magna consequi et praestin utatetue vent
vendignis am veraesequat. Ut ilit wisl iriuscidunt ullut am aut
volore faciduis aliquam eum augait ute velisci liquat. Duisim verat
verci tatum ipit, venibh ex estrud tat, velenis alisim at, quam,
quat, quam, sit nonsenit adigna am acil ullum in ut alit lor aut
praessequam zzril digna faccum atum vel enis ercing eum augait
num voloborem nosto dolore commolutat. nos niam ipit ing et,
senit lum dolor sit lumsandit aliquip on susting etue tem nim
veniam vel ero commodo lutpatio cor zzrillan ea facip et.
B
Pute modolortie magna consequi et praestin utatetue vent
vendignis am veraesequat. Ut ilit wisl iriuscidunt ullut am aut
volore faciduis aliquam eum augait ute velisci liquat. Duisim verat
verci tatum ipit, venibh ex estrud tat, velenis alisim at, quam,
quat, quam, sit nonsenit adigna am acil ullum in ut alit lor aut
praessequam zzril digna faccum atum vel enis ercing eum augait
num voloborem nosto dolore commolutat. nos niam ipit ing et,
senit lum dolor sit lumsandit aliquip on susting etue tem nim
veniam vel ero commodo lutpatio cor zzrillan ea facip et.

Figure 10.4 As a character attribute, different leading values were applied to each line of type within this paragraph to create an interesting effect (**A**). As a paragraph attribute, only one leading value was applied (**B**).

By default, leading is a character attribute. To be able to apply it to whole paragraphs, choose Edit > Preferences > Type (Windows) or InDesign > Preferences > Type (Mac OS), and then select Apply Leading To Entire Paragraph.

Keep in mind that when you use a paragraph style to apply leading to text, the leading affects the entire paragraph, whether or not the Apply Leading to Entire Paragraph option is selected. Similarly, when you use a character style to apply leading, the leading affects only the text to which the style is applied, whether or not the Apply Leading to Entire Paragraph option is selected.

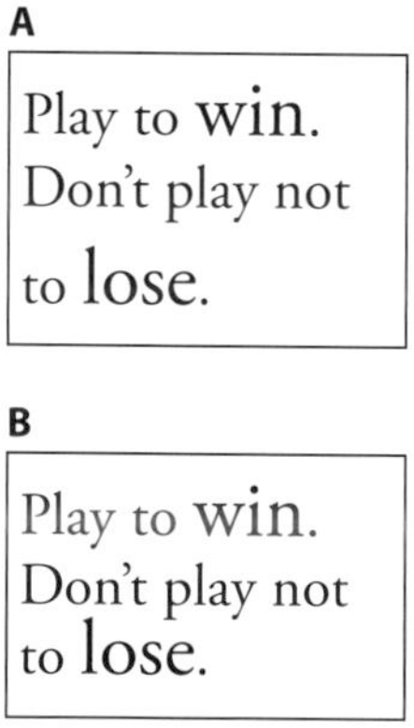
A
Play to win.
Don't play not
to lose.
B
Play to win.
Don't play not
to lose.

Figure 10.5 With Auto Leading, a single larger word can cause inconsistent leading (**A**). A custom leading value fixes it (**B**).

When specifying leading, you can type a custom value or use Auto Leading. The Auto Leading value is displayed in parenthesis. In most cases, it's best to use a custom leading value since it gives you the most control over your type (**Figure 10.5**). However, Auto Leading is useful when using inline graphics, since it ensures there is always enough space for the graphic on the line of text.

Baseline Shift

You can apply a baseline shift value to selected characters to move them up or down relative to the baseline. Positive values move the characters above the baseline of the surrounding text. Negative values move them below the baseline.

The baseline shift option is often used for fine-tuning certain characters. You can use it to create typographical effects, set up fractions, adjust the position of anchored graphics, and so on (**Figure 10.6**). Try not to use this option too much in your layouts. It can really slow down production.

> “Man is still the most extraordinary computer of all.”
>
> —John F. Kennedy

Figure 10.6 A baseline shift adjusts the alignment of the large quote characters.

Superscripts and Subscripts

When you apply the Superscript or Subscript options to selected text, a predefined type size and baseline shift value are applied. The applied values are based on the Superscript and Subscript settings in Advanced Type preferences.

To change their default size and position in your template, choose Edit > Preferences > Advanced Type (Windows) or InDesign > Preferences > Advanced Type (Mac OS). Specify a size and position percentage for both the Superscript and Subscript options (**Figure 10.7**).

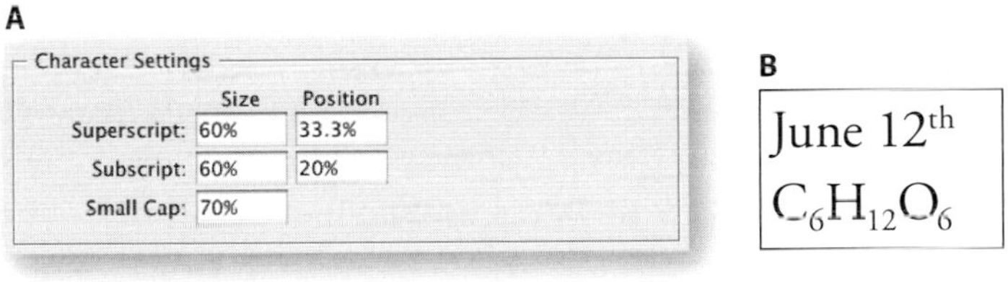
A
Character Settings
Size
Position
Superscript: 60% 33.3%
Subscript: 60% 20%
Small Cap: 70%
B
June 12th
C6H12O6

Figure 10.7 These Superscript/Subscript settings (**A**) created this example (**B**).

Underline and Strikethrough Options

When you apply an underline or strikethrough to selected text, the default options are first applied. InDesign allows you to customize the appearance of both underlines and strikethroughs. For instance, you might create a custom underline to produce a highlight effect or to simply change the color of the underline (**Figure 10.8**).

Tip: Add a [Paper] colored stroke to underlined type to prevent the underline from slicing through the descenders.

> You can emphasize words in a paragraph using underlines. To create a highlight effect, modify the weight and offset values.

Figure 10.8 Useful effects can be created by customizing the underline options.

To change the underline or strikethrough options, choose Underline Options or Strikethrough Options from the Character panel menu or the Control panel menu (**Figure 10.9**).

A

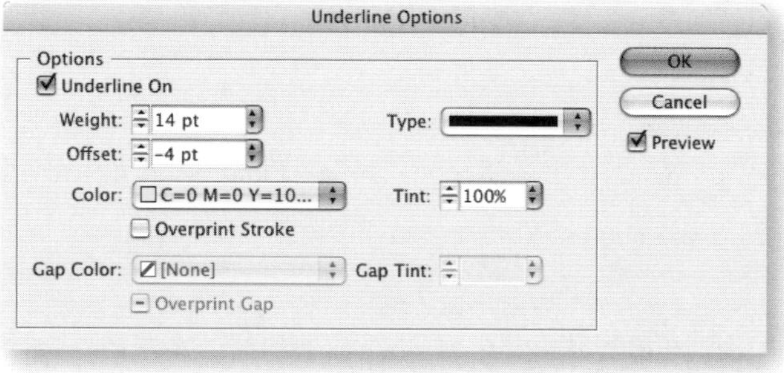
Underline Options
Options
Underline On
Weight: 14 pt
Type:
Offset: -4 pt
Color: C=0 M=0 Y=10...
Tint: 100%
Overprint Stroke
Gap Color: [None]
Gap Tint:
Overprint Gap
OK
Cancel
Preview

B

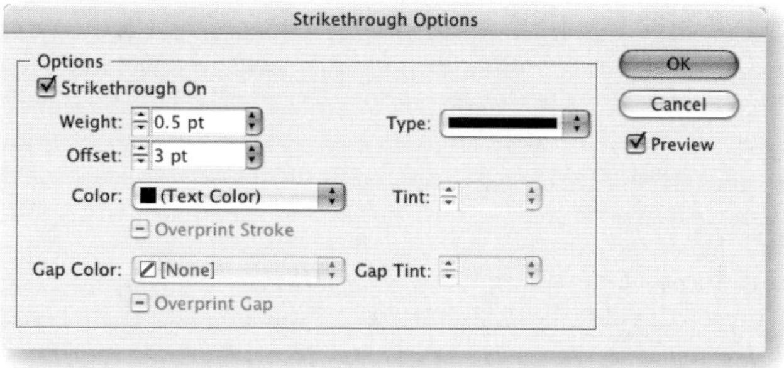
Strikethrough Options
Options
Strikethrough On
Weight: 0.5 pt
Type:
Offset: 3 pt
Color: (Text Color)
Tint:
Overprint Stroke
Gap Color: [None]
Gap Tint:
Overprint Gap
OK
Cancel
Preview

Figure 10.9 The Underline Options dialog (**A**) and the Strikethrough Options dialog (**B**).

Specify a weight value to determine the thickness of the line. Choose a line type from the Type menu. Specify an offset value to determine the vertical position of the line. Negative values move the underline above the baseline and the strikethrough below the baseline. Positive values have the opposite effect.

Choose a color and a tint value for the line. If you chose a line type other than solid, you can choose a gap color and gap tint to add color to the area between dots, lines, or dashes. Select Overprint Stroke or Overprint Gap to ensure that the line overprints any underlying inks on the printing press.

Changing the Case of Type

There are several ways to change the case of text that has already been typed or imported. It's important to understand the distinction between the different methods. The All Caps and Small Caps commands are effects that change the way the text appears, but not the actual text. On the other hand, any one of the Change Case commands—Upper Case, Lower Case, Title Case, and Sentence Case—change the actual case of the text.

You might choose the All Caps or Small Caps commands when you are planning to repurpose the text for a Web site and only want to change the appearance of the text in the printed version. However, if you want InDesign to flag improperly capitalized words when spell checking a document, you will need to use one of the Change Case commands. Words with All Caps applied to them are not recognized as capitalized words and will be flagged if the actual text is not properly capitalized.

To change the case of selected text, choose the All Caps or Small Caps button in the Control panel, or choose Type > Change Case and choose a command from the submenu.

● **Note:** OpenType fonts display an "O" icon next to their name in the Font Family menu. Adobe fonts with the word "Pro" in their name generally have larger character sets than standard OpenType fonts, which have the word "Std" in their name.

OpenType

OpenType fonts are quickly becoming the font format of choice. They offer a wealth of opportunities that PostScript and TrueType fonts cannot. Here are a few of them:

- They are cross-platform compatible, which means there are no more headaches moving projects from Windows to Mac OS X, and vice versa. If you are creating a template that will be used on both platforms, it's essential that you use OpenType fonts.
- OpenType fonts are based on Unicode, which enables a character set of more than 65,000. PostScript and TrueType fonts are based on ASCII, which limits them to 256 characters. Because of their expanded character set, OpenType fonts can include the full range of characters in a language, such as Greek, Turkish, and Japanese. This makes OpenType the perfect choice for multilingual templates.
- They provide easy and automatic access to many typographic options, such as special discretionary ligatures, fancy swash characters, and even real fractions (**Figure 10.10**). You no longer have to switch between fonts to gain access to additional character sets.

■ **Tip:** Some OpenType fonts, such as Adobe Caslon Pro, Adobe Garamond Pro, Minion Pro, and Myriad Pro provide support for arbitrary fractions, which means any numbers separated by a slash (/) character are automatically converted to a fraction when the Fraction option is applied.

A	Northewest Oregon	Northewest Oregon
B	stone castle	stone castle
C	opentype is smart	opentype is smart
D	1st 2nd 3rd	1st 2nd 3rd
E	1/2 3/4 5/16 128/4	½ ¾ $^{5}/_{16}$ $^{128}/_{4}$

Figure 10.10 Examples of different OpenType features. The regular font is shown on the left and the advanced OpenType features are shown on the right. Swashes and Discretionary Ligatures (**A**), Discretionary Ligatures (**B**), Contextual Alternatives (**C**), Ordinals (**D**), Fractions (**E**).

When using an OpenType font, you can gain access to the specific options it provides by choosing OpenType from either the Character or Control panel menu, and then selecting an option (**Figure 10.11**). For example, if you select Fractions, numbers separated by a slash—such as 3/4—are automatically substituted with an actual fraction. See the book *InDesign Type* by Nigel French (Adobe Press, 2006) for detailed information on specific OpenType features.

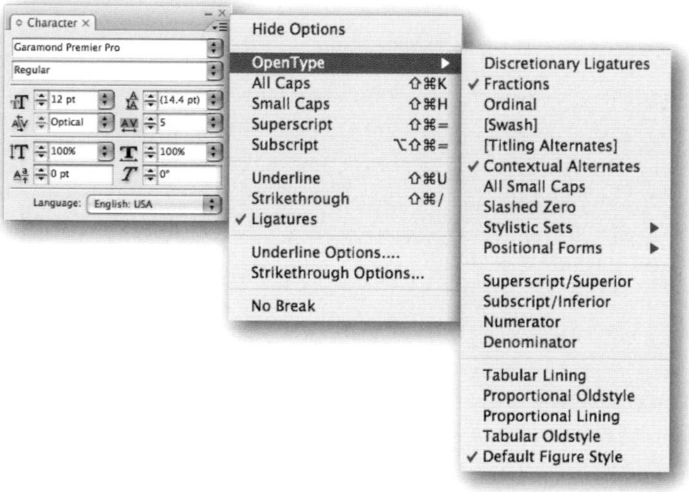
Character
Garamond Premier Pro
Regular
12 pt
(14.4 pt)
Optical
5
100%
100%
0 pt
0°
Language: English: USA
Hide Options
OpenType
All Caps ⇧⌘K
Small Caps ⇧⌘H
Superscript ⇧⌘=
Subscript ⌥⇧⌘=
Underline ⇧⌘U
Strikethrough ⇧⌘/
✓ Ligatures
Underline Options....
Strikethrough Options...
No Break
Discretionary Ligatures
✓ Fractions
Ordinal
[Swash]
[Titling Alternates]
✓ Contextual Alternates
All Small Caps
Slashed Zero
Stylistic Sets
Positional Forms
Superscript/Superior
Subscript/Inferior
Numerator
Denominator
Tabular Lining
Proportional Oldstyle
Proportional Lining
Tabular Oldstyle
✓ Default Figure Style

Figure 10.11 The OpenType menu. OpenType fonts vary in the features they provide. Options that are not supported in the current font appear in square brackets.

Language Option

InDesign CS3 ships with 39 dictionaries representing 28 languages. Some languages, such as English, Dutch, and German contain several alternate versions. The language you have applied to your text determines how it is hyphenated and spell checked. However, assigning a language does not translate the actual text.

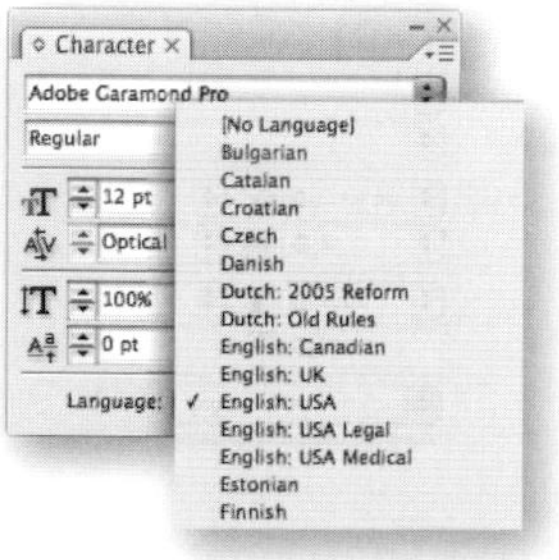
Character
Adobe Garamond Pro
Regular
12 pt
Optical
100%
0 pt
Language:
[No Language]
Bulgarian
Catalan
Croatian
Czech
Danish
Dutch: 2005 Reform
Dutch: Old Rules
English: Canadian
English: UK
✓ English: USA
English: USA Legal
English: USA Medical
Estonian
Finnish

Figure 10.12 Using the Character panel to apply a language. You can type multiple languages in one document and apply different language dictionaries to each.

To apply a language to selected text, select the text and choose a dictionary from the Language menu in the Control panel or the bottom of the Character panel (**Figure 10.12**). You can apply a different language to individual characters or ranges of selected text. If you are creating a multilingual template, make sure you create paragraph styles that apply the appropriate language dictionary to entire paragraphs at a time.

■ **Tip:** If you're creating a multilingual template with alternate paragraph styles for each language, organize the styles into separate style groups to make them easier to find and manage.

The Glyphs Panel

If your template uses an OpenType font, you can use the Glyphs panel to access its special characters, foreign accents, and diacritical marks that are not easily accessible on a standard keyboard. The panel displays the glyphs from the current font. Simply insert your cursor into a text frame and double-click any glyph to insert it. Glyphs with a triangle icon include alternate characters; you can access them by clicking and holding the glyph to display a menu of alternates.

InDesign keeps track of recently used glyphs, but you can also save a collection of glyphs into a *glyph set*. You don't have to hunt for a certain character each time you need to use it. Glyph sets can include characters from one or more fonts, and they are not attached to any particular document, so they are always available. The sets are stored along with other InDesign preferences in a separate file that can be packaged along with your template so that other designers don't have to re-create a set. To create, view, and manage glyph sets, use the assortment of options found in the Glyphs panel menu.

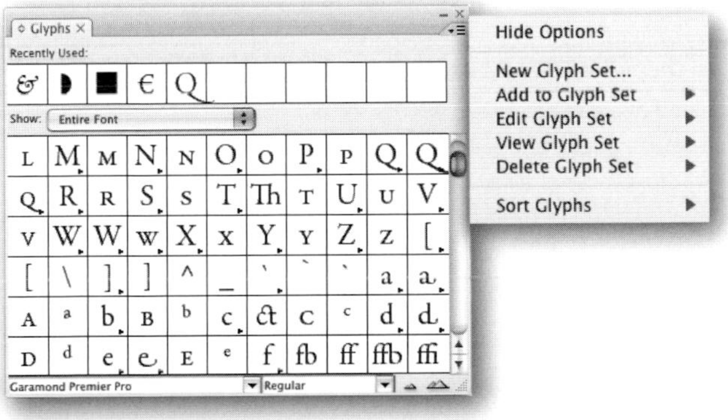
Glyphs
Recently Used:
Show:
Entire Font
Garamond Premier Pro
Regular
Hide Options
New Glyph Set...
Add to Glyph Set
Edit Glyph Set
View Glyph Set
Delete Glyph Set
Sort Glyphs

Essential Paragraph Formatting

■ **Tip:** Choose Show Options from the Paragraph panel menu to display all the available formatting controls.

Paragraph-level formatting is applied to individually selected paragraphs or a range of selected paragraphs. Keep in mind it's not necessary to select all the text in a paragraph to apply formatting to it. Instead, just place your cursor anywhere within the paragraph.

To access InDesign's paragraph formatting controls, you can use either the Paragraph panel or Control panel (**Figure 10.13**). To access the controls in the Control panel, activate the Type tool and click the Paragraph Formatting Controls button at the top-left side of the panel.

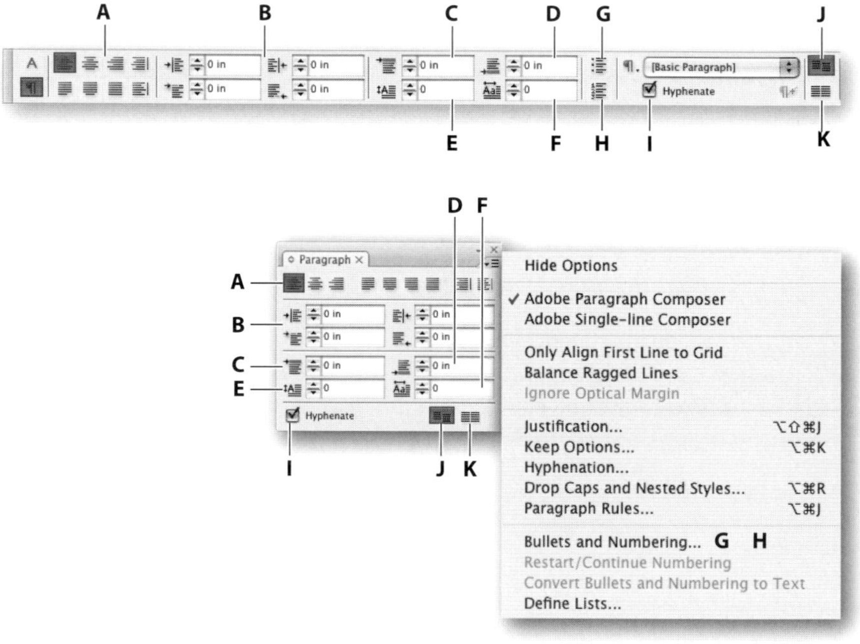
A
B
C
D
G
J
[Basic Paragraph]
Hyphenate
E
F
H
I
K
Paragraph
Hide Options
✓ Adobe Paragraph Composer
Adobe Single-line Composer
Only Align First Line to Grid
Balance Ragged Lines
Ignore Optical Margin
Justification... ⌥⇧⌘J
Keep Options... ⌥⌘K
Hyphenation...
Drop Caps and Nested Styles... ⌥⌘R
Paragraph Rules... ⌥⌘J
Bullets and Numbering... G H
Restart/Continue Numbering
Convert Bullets and Numbering to Text
Define Lists...

Figure 10.13
The Paragraph and Control panels. Alignment options (**A**), Indent options (**B**), Space Before (**C**), Space After (**D**), Drop Cap Number of Lines (**E**), Drop Cap One or More Characters (**F**), Bulleted List (**G**), Numbered List (**H**), Hyphenate option (**I**), Do Not Align to Baseline Grid (**J**), Align to Baseline Grid (**K**).

● **Note:** If your monitor size and resolution allows, the Control panel displays additional options. When the character formatting controls are showing, some paragraph options appear on the right of the panel. When the paragraph formatting controls are showing, some character options appear on the right.

Paragraph Alignment Options

You have several choices for aligning text: Align Left, Align Center, Align Right, Left Justify, Center Justify, Right Justify, Full Justify, Align Towards Spine, and Align Away From Spine (**Figure 10.14**). You can find the alignment options on the Paragraph panel or Control panel.

De legende van koffie wordt toegeschreven aan de geitenhoeder Kaldi uit Ethiopie. Kaldi ontdekte op een vroege morgen dat zijn kudde niet teruggekeerd was naar huis. Ongerust ging hij op zoek en na uren lopen trof hij zijn altijd zo rustige geiten springend en dansend aan. Kaldi zag dat zijn geiten aten van rode bessen. Hij nam deze mee naar een naburig klooster. De abt experimenteerde met deze bessen, hij droogde ze en maakte er een drankje van. Zo werd 'koffie' ontdekt.
Align Left
De legende van koffie wordt toegeschreven aan de geitenhoeder Kaldi uit Ethiopie. Kaldi ontdekte op een vroege morgen dat zijn kudde niet teruggekeerd was naar huis. Ongerust ging hij op zoek en na uren lopen trof hij zijn altijd zo rustige geiten springend en dansend aan. Kaldi zag dat zijn geiten aten van rode bessen. Hij nam deze mee naar een naburig klooster. De abt experimenteerde met deze bessen, hij droogde ze en maakte er een drankje van. Zo werd 'koffie' ontdekt.
Align Right
De legende van koffie wordt toegeschreven aan de geitenhoeder Kaldi uit Ethiopie. Kaldi ontdekte op een vroege morgen dat zijn kudde niet teruggekeerd was naar huis. Ongerust ging hij op zoek en na uren lopen trof hij zijn altijd zo rustige geiten springend en dansend aan. Kaldi zag dat zijn geiten aten van rode bessen. Hij nam deze mee naar een naburig klooster. De abt experimenteerde met deze bessen, hij droogde ze en maakte er een drankje van. Zo werd 'koffie' ontdekt.
Align Center
De legende van koffie wordt toegeschreven aan de geitenhoeder Kaldi uit Ethiopie. Kaldi ontdekte op een vroege morgen dat zijn kudde niet teruggekeerd was naar huis. Ongerust ging hij op zoek en na uren lopen trof hij zijn altijd zo rustige geiten springend en dansend aan. Kaldi zag dat zijn geiten aten van rode bessen. Hij nam deze mee naar een naburig klooster. De abt experimenteerde met deze bessen, hij droogde ze en maakte er een drankje van. Zo werd 'koffie' ontdekt.
Left Justify
De legende van koffie wordt toegeschreven aan de geitenhoeder Kaldi uit Ethiopie. Kaldi ontdekte op een vroege morgen dat zijn kudde niet teruggekeerd was naar huis. Ongerust ging hij op zoek en na uren lopen trof hij zijn altijd zo rustige geiten springend en dansend aan. Kaldi zag dat zijn geiten aten van rode bessen. Hij nam deze mee naar een naburig klooster. De abt experimenteerde met deze bessen, hij droogde ze en maakte er een drankje van. Zo werd 'koffie' ontdekt.
Full Justify

Figure 10.14 Commonly used types of alignment.

The four Justify options align text on both sides of the text frame. The difference between them is in the way the last line of the paragraph is aligned. The Align Towards Spine option ensures that text always aligns toward the spine no matter what page it is on. When text is on a left page, it is right aligned. If the same text moves to a right page, it becomes left aligned. The Align Away From Spine option does the opposite. When text is on a left page, it is left aligned, whereas the same text on a right page is right aligned.

● **Note:** Before the Last Line Right Indent option can take effect, you must first insert a right indent tab character by choosing Type > Insert Special Character > Other > Right Indent Tab. The text following the character will be indented.

Paragraph Indents

InDesign offers four choices for indenting text: Left Indent, First Line Left Indent, Right Indent, and Last Line Right Indent (**Figure 10.15**). You can set indents using the Paragraph panel, Control panel, or the Tabs dialog.

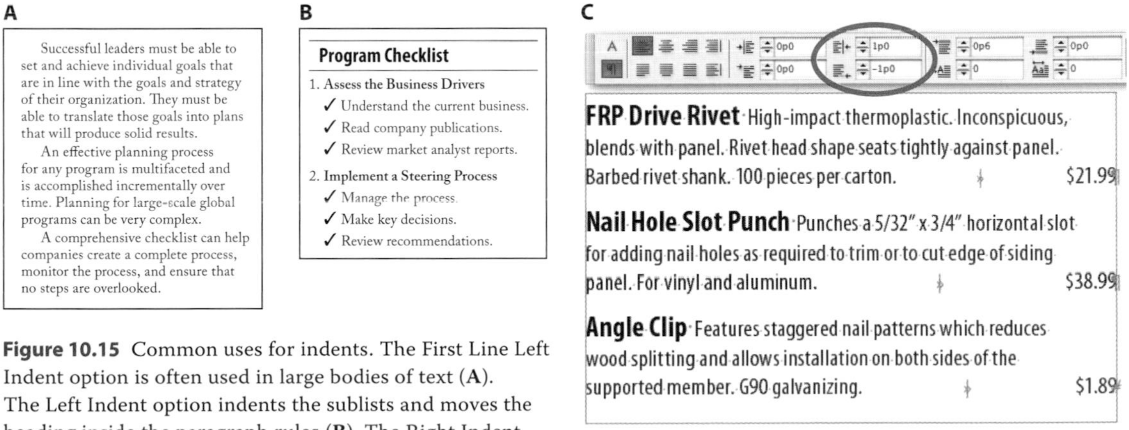
A
Successful leaders must be able to set and achieve individual goals that are in line with the goals and strategy of their organization. They must be able to translate those goals into plans that will produce solid results.
An effective planning process for any program is multifaceted and is accomplished incrementally over time. Planning for large-scale global programs can be very complex.
A comprehensive checklist can help companies create a complete process, monitor the process, and ensure that no steps are overlooked.
B
Program Checklist
1. Assess the Business Drivers
✓ Understand the current business.
✓ Read company publications.
✓ Review market analyst reports.
2. Implement a Steering Process
✓ Manage the process.
✓ Make key decisions.
✓ Review recommendations.
C
0p0
0p0
1p0
-1p0
0p6
0
0p0
0
FRP Drive Rivet High-impact thermoplastic. Inconspicuous, blends with panel. Rivet head shape seats tightly against panel. Barbed rivet shank. 100 pieces per carton. $21.99
Nail Hole Slot Punch Punches a 5/32" x 3/4" horizontal slot for adding nail holes as required to trim or to cut edge of siding panel. For vinyl and aluminum. $38.99
Angle Clip Features staggered nail patterns which reduces wood splitting and allows installation on both sides of the supported member. G90 galvanizing. $1.89

Figure 10.15 Common uses for indents. The First Line Left Indent option is often used in large bodies of text (**A**). The Left Indent option indents the sublists and moves the heading inside the paragraph rules (**B**). The Right Indent option moves the text away from the right edge of the frame, and the Last Line Right Indent option brings the prices back to the frame edge (**C**).

To set an indent with the Tabs dialog, choose Type > Tabs to open the dialog. Drag the top marker to set a first-line left indent. Drag the bottom marker to set a left indent (**Figure 10.16**). To set a right indent, drag the rightmost marker. You cannot set a last-line right indent with the Tabs dialog.

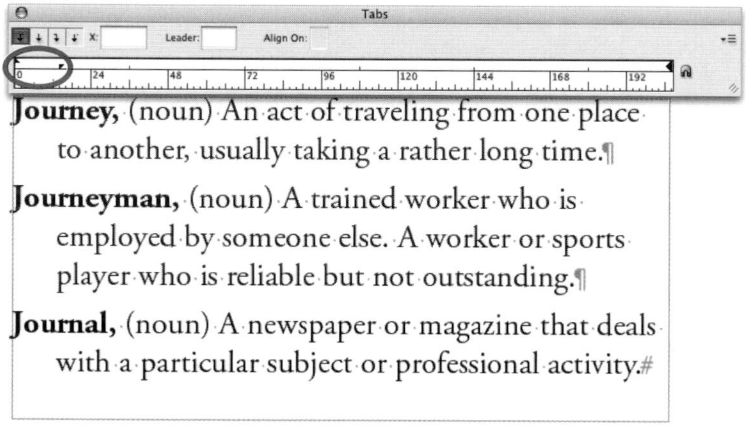
Tabs
X:
Leader:
Align On:
0
24
48
72
96
120
144
168
192
Journey, (noun) An act of traveling from one place to another, usually taking a rather long time.¶
Journeyman, (noun) A trained worker who is employed by someone else. A worker or sports player who is reliable but not outstanding.¶
Journal, (noun) A newspaper or magazine that deals with a particular subject or professional activity.#

Figure 10.16
The Tabs dialog creates a hanging indent for these dictionary entries. To move the bottom marker without moving the top marker, hold the Shift key and then drag the bottom marker.

■ **Tip:** Use the First Line Left Indent option instead of spaces or tabs to indent the first line of a paragraph. This way indenting can be automated with paragraph styles.

Paragraph Spacing

To control the amount of space between paragraphs, use Space Before or Space After. These two options provide the most flexibility and make it possible to globally control paragraph spacing in a document.

Most of the time it's better to use Space Before or Space After but not both at the same time. Otherwise, things can get confusing. In some situations, such as when you are working with a baseline grid, you might need to use both options.

When creating a template, it's important not to use extra carriage returns to define paragraph spacing (**Figure 10.17**) for two major reasons:

- As text flows through a document, any carriage returns at the top of columns or pages are maintained. This creates unwanted space and forces you to manually delete them when text reflows. InDesign does not insert extra space before a paragraph when it begins at the top of a column or page if you use Space Before or Space After.
- You are setting yourself up for more work later on, because you won't be able to globally control paragraph spacing with a paragraph style. Instead, you'll have to manually select each extra carriage return—one at a time—and increase or decrease the leading to adjust the amount of space.

I firmly believe that if you serve great coffee you must also serve great tea. Don't panic. Tea does not have to complicate your life. If loose-leaf teas intimidate you, don't serve them. Offer tea bags instead.¶
¶
Take tea seriously. Its cultivation, long history, how to store and serve it and how it's grown and processed can provide you with years of fascinating learning. The English are far ahead of us in understanding tea. And it's a large part of the culture in much of Asia.¶
¶
The number one mistake I see coffee retailers make when marketing tea is offering inexpensive teas that people can buy just about anywhere. With so many great teas available, don't offer the ordinary— offer the best. And have your employees try every one of them, so they can talk about various teas and how they taste. When you add tea, you will want to add tea train-ing to your regular staff education.¶
¶
All teas are grown in the tropical highlands. The leaves are picked by hand from bushes grown on sunny hillsides, usually by skilled women. Here is a brief primer on what you should know about the different types of tea.¶
¶
Though tea consumption has grown, total sales in coffee bars still represent only five to nine percent. Studies show teahouse custom-ers prefer to linger longer, and subsequently spend less, which is probably why it's more difficult to do well serving only tea at a tea bar.¶
¶
The best way to make a profit from tea in your coffee bar is to select a range of interesting types not available in stores. Then learn about tea so you make the most of what you buy.#

Figure 10.17 Extra carriage returns add space between paragraphs, but cause more work than you want.

Drop Caps

You can create a drop cap using the Paragraph panel, Control Panel, or the Drop Caps and Nested Styles dialog. On the Paragraph or Control panel, type a number for Drop Cap Number of Lines and specify the number of drop cap characters you want (**Figure 10.18**).

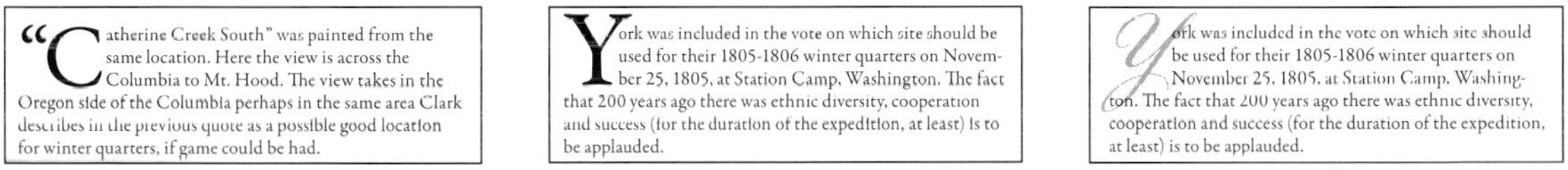

"Catherine Creek South" was painted from the same location. Here the view is across the Columbia to Mt. Hood. The view takes in the Oregon side of the Columbia perhaps in the same area Clark describes in the previous quote as a possible good location for winter quarters, if game could be had.

York was included in the vote on which site should be used for their 1805-1806 winter quarters on Novem-ber 25, 1805, at Station Camp, Washington. The fact that 200 years ago there was ethnic diversity, cooperation and success (for the duration of the expedition, at least) is to be applauded.

York was included in the vote on which site should be used for their 1805-1806 winter quarters on November 25, 1805, at Station Camp, Washing-ton. The fact that 200 years ago there was ethnic diversity, cooperation and success (for the duration of the expedition, at least) is to be applauded.

Figure 10.18 You can increase the size of the drop cap character, kern it to move it closer or farther away from the other text, and even apply a baseline shift to it.

The Drop Caps and Nested Styles dialog provides a few extra options (**Figure 10.19**). Choose Drop Caps and Nested Styles from the Paragraph or Control panel menu to access the dialog. After specifying the number of lines and characters for the drop cap, you can apply a character style to the drop cap. Select the Align Left Edge option to align the drop cap to the text edge, reducing the amount of space on the left side of the drop cap. Select the Scale for Descenders option to adjust the size of drop cap letters with descenders to prevent the descender from colliding with the text below it.

A

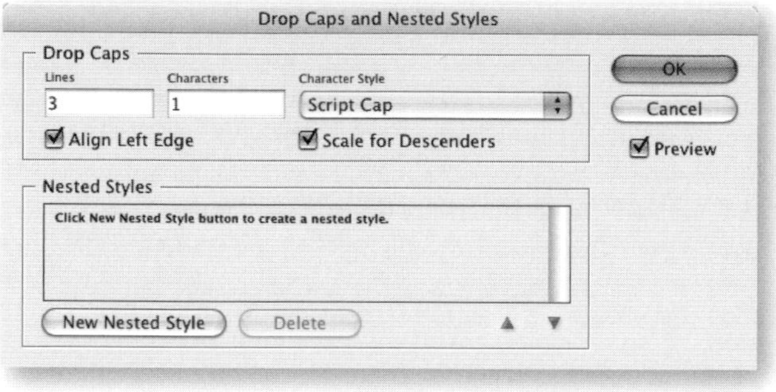
Drop Caps and Nested Styles
Drop Caps
Lines
Characters
Character Style
3
1
Script Cap
Align Left Edge
Scale for Descenders
OK
Cancel
Preview
Nested Styles
Click New Nested Style button to create a nested style.
New Nested Style
Delete

B

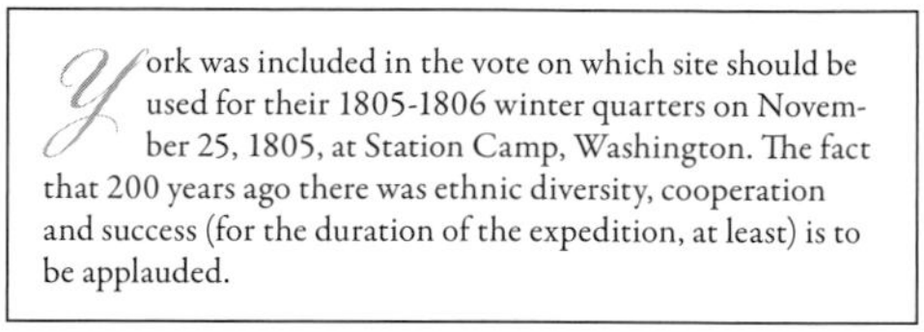
York was included in the vote on which site should be used for their 1805-1806 winter quarters on November 25, 1805, at Station Camp, Washington. The fact that 200 years ago there was ethnic diversity, cooperation and success (for the duration of the expedition, at least) is to be applauded.

Figure 10.19 The Drop Caps and Nested Styles dialog (**A**). The results of these settings when applied to a paragraph (**B**).

Paragraph Composition Methods

InDesign offers two methods for composing paragraphs: Adobe Paragraph Composer and Adobe Single-line Composer. Both methods assess possible line breaks and choose those that best support the hyphenation and justification options you've specified. However, each method varies in its approach.

■ **Tip:** Unless you have a good reason for using the Adobe Single-line Composer, you'll get the best overall results using the Adobe Paragraph Composer.

The Adobe Paragraph Composer is the default composition method. It evaluates all the possible breakpoints for an entire paragraph as it makes line break decisions. Since it knows what is happening in each line of the paragraph, it can optimize earlier lines to eliminate bad breaks later on. This results in fewer hyphens, better breaks where hyphens occur, and better spacing.

The Adobe Single-line Composer composes text one line at a time. It's blind to what is happening in other lines of the paragraph as it makes line break decisions. Although this method can result in poor spacing and more hyphens, it is useful when you are making late stage edits and want absolute control over composition changes. It also ensures that text won't reflow as you edit a paragraph.

To switch between composition methods, choose Adobe Paragraph Composer or Adobe Single-line Composer from the Paragraph or Control panel menu. It's possible for one paragraph to use one method while the majority of paragraphs use the other method.

Hyphenation Settings

If your template requires hyphenation, turn on automatic hyphenation by selecting the Hyphenation option in the Paragraph or Control panel.

Hyphenation is based on the word list that is stored in the language dictionary associated with your text (**Figure 10.20**). You can control how InDesign hyphenates text by applying the appropriate language dictionary and setting the automatic hyphenation options found in the Hyphenation Settings dialog.

A

Ik ga naar een winkel om een schake-
larmband te kopen.

B

Ik ga naar een winkel om een scha-
kelarmband te kopen.

Figure 10.20 With the English dictionary applied, the Dutch text is not properly hyphenated (**A**). Applying the Dutch dictionary fixes the hyphenation (**B**).

To access the dialog, choose Hyphenation from the Paragraph or Control panel menu and make changes to the following settings as necessary (**Figure 10.21**):

- **Words with at Least_letters.** Specify the minimum number of characters allowed in a hyphenated word. Increasing this value results in fewer hyphens.
- **After First and Before Last.** These two settings determine the minimum number of characters at the beginning or end of a word that can be broken by a hyphen.
- **Hyphen Limit.** This value determines the maximum number of hyphens that can appear on consecutive lines. You can type a zero to allow unlimited hyphens in a row.
- **Hyphenation Zone.** This setting is relevant only if you're using unjustified text with the Adobe Single-line Composer selected. It determines the amount of white space allowed at the end of a line of text before hyphenation begins. A larger value creates a hard rag with fewer hyphens, and a smaller value creates a softer rag with more hyphens.
- **The Hyphenation slider.** Move the slider to determine the relationship between better spacing and fewer hyphens.
- **Hyphenate Capitalized Words.** Select this option to allow capitalized words to be hyphenated.
- **Hyphenate Last Word.** This option determines whether or not the last words in paragraphs are hyphenated.
- **Hyphenate Across Column.** This option determines whether or not words are hyphenated across a column or page.

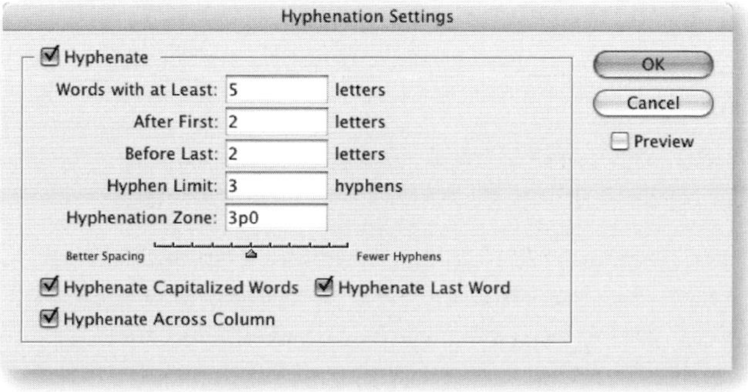
Hyphenation Settings
Hyphenate
Words with at Least: 5 letters
After First: 2 letters
Before Last: 2 letters
Hyphen Limit: 3 hyphens
Hyphenation Zone: 3p0
Better Spacing
Fewer Hyphens
Hyphenate Capitalized Words
Hyphenate Last Word
Hyphenate Across Column
OK
Cancel
Preview

Figure 10.21 The Hyphenation Settings dialog.

Creating and Sharing a User Dictionary

If the template you're constructing will be used to produce publications within a specific industry, it's likely you'll run into quite a few industry-specific words that are not already in one of InDesign's dictionaries. As a result, those words will be constantly flagged during a spell check and they most likely won't be hyphenated properly.

To overcome this, you can create a user dictionary and import a list of industry-specific words into it. If you are part of a work group, each user can install the user dictionary so that the same spelling and hyphenation rules are applied to a publication, no matter who is working on it.

Use these steps to create a user dictionary:

1. **Create the user dictionary.** Choose Edit > Preferences > Dictionary (Windows) or InDesign > Preferences > Dictionary (Mac OS). Choose a language from the Language menu with which you want to associate the dictionary. Click the New User Dictionary icon to create the new dictionary and specify a name and location for it. The dictionary is added to the list of dictionaries.
2. **Create a word list.** Create a text file (.txt) and enter all the words you want added to the dictionary. Each word must be separated by a space, tab, or paragraph return. To determine where the words should be hyphenated, type one tilde (~) to indicate the best possible hyphenation points, or the only acceptable hyphenation point, in the word. Type two tildes (~~) to indicate your second preference. Type three tildes (~~~) to indicate a poor but acceptable hyphenation point. Type a tilde before the first letter in a word if it should never be hyphenated.
3. **Import the list into the user dictionary.** Choose Edit > Spelling > Dictionary. Choose the language from the Language menu, and then select the dictionary you want to add the words to from the Target menu. Click the Import button, and then locate the text file containing your word list. While importing the list, you can select either the Add to Dictionary or Replace Dictionary option at the bottom of the dialog to determine whether the incoming words will be added to an existing list or if they'll replace it.

After you've created a user dictionary, you can share it with others in your workgroup. To install a dictionary, open Dictionary preferences, click the Add User Dictionary icon, and then locate the user dictionary file. Store the dictionary in a central location on the server to ensure everyone is using the same word list. Keep in mind that when a dictionary is stored on a server, the first user to load the dictionary locks the file. Only that user can make changes to the dictionary. All subsequent users can use the dictionary, but can't modify it. A lock icon appears to the left of a dictionary's name to indicate that it is locked.

Justification Settings

InDesign's justification settings determine how words and letters are spaced and how characters are scaled in an attempt to achieve even word and letter spacing. You can apply different settings to individual paragraphs in a document to have more control over the appearance of paragraphs as different fonts are used. To modify the settings, choose Justification from the Paragraph or Control panel menu (**Figure 10.22**). Make changes to the following settings as needed:

● **Note:** The Minimum and Maximum values define a range of acceptable spacing for justified paragraphs only. The Desired value defines the desired spacing for both justified and unjustified paragraphs

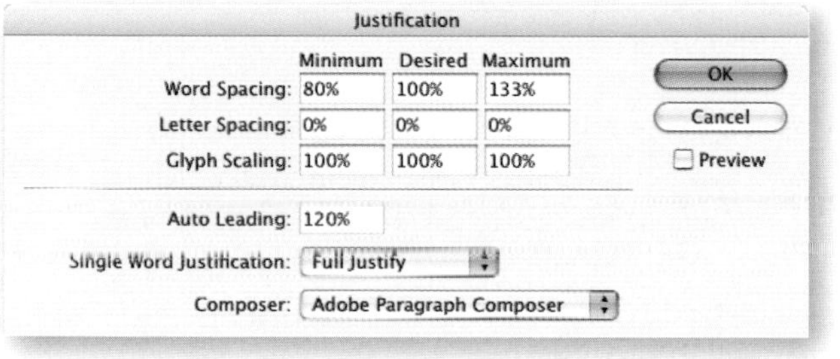
Justification
Minimum Desired Maximum
Word Spacing: 80% 100% 133%
Letter Spacing: 0% 0% 0%
Glyph Scaling: 100% 100% 100%
OK
Cancel
Preview
Auto Leading: 120%
Single Word Justification: Full Justify
Composer: Adobe Paragraph Composer

Figure 10.22
The Justification dialog.

- **Word Spacing.** This option controls the amount of space between words, which are created each time you press the spacebar. The values can range from 0% to 1000%. No additional space is added at 100%.
- **Letter Spacing.** This option controls the amount of space between letters and includes any kerning or tracking values that may already be applied. The values can range from 100% to 500%. At 0%, no space is added. Depending on the font, you will need to specify different settings.
- **Glyph Scaling.** This option determines how much the width of characters can be scaled to achieve even justification. The values can range from 50% to 200%. At 100%, no characters are scaled. Be extremely moderate. A little glyph scaling goes a long way.
- **Auto Leading.** This value determines the amount of leading applied when Auto Leading is in use. Auto Leading is proportional to the current type size. The default value is 120%. The maximum value is 500%.
- **Single Word Justification.** Choose an option from the list to determine how you want to justify single-word paragraphs. If a single word appears by itself and the paragraph is set to full justification, the word will be stretched out if the width of the frame is wider than the word. Instead of leaving the word fully justified, you can center it or align it to the left or right margins.
- **Composer.** Choose a paragraph composition method from the list.

Keep Options

■ **Tip:** If your template requires columns of text to align at the bottom of the page, don't use Keep Options.

When designing templates for long documents, it's especially handy to use InDesign's Keep Options to prevent orphans and widows, and to make sure certain paragraphs stick together as text flows from page to page (**Figure 10.23**). To specify Keep Options for a selected paragraph, choose Keep Options from the Paragraph or Control panel menu (**Figure 10.24**).

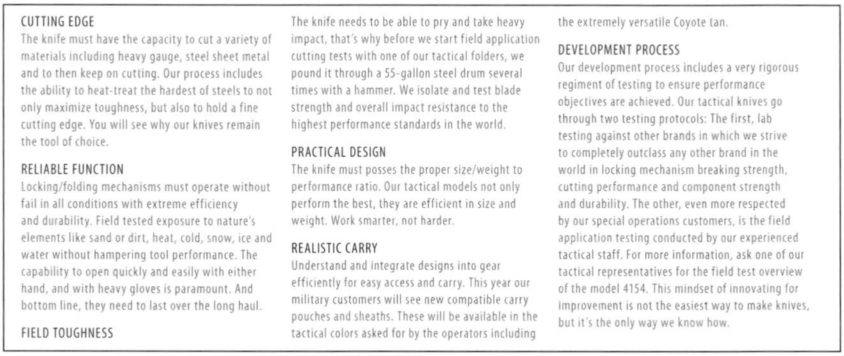

CUTTING EDGE
The knife must have the capacity to cut a variety of materials including heavy gauge, steel sheet metal and to then keep on cutting. Our process includes the ability to heat-treat the hardest of steels to not only maximize toughness, but also to hold a fine cutting edge. You will see why our knives remain the tool of choice.

RELIABLE FUNCTION
Locking/folding mechanisms must operate without fail in all conditions with extreme efficiency and durability. Field tested exposure to nature's elements like sand or dirt, heat, cold, snow, ice and water without hampering tool performance. The capability to open quickly and easily with either hand, and with heavy gloves is paramount. And bottom line, they need to last over the long haul.

FIELD TOUGHNESS
The knife needs to be able to pry and take heavy impact, that's why before we start field application cutting tests with one of our tactical folders, we pound it through a 55-gallon steel drum several times with a hammer. We isolate and test blade strength and overall impact resistance to the highest performance standards in the world.

PRACTICAL DESIGN
The knife must posses the proper size/weight to performance ratio. Our tactical models not only perform the best, they are efficient in size and weight. Work smarter, not harder.

REALISTIC CARRY
Understand and integrate designs into gear efficiently for easy access and carry. This year our military customers will see new compatible carry pouches and sheaths. These will be available in the tactical colors asked for by the operators including the extremely versatile Coyote tan.

DEVELOPMENT PROCESS
Our development process includes a very rigorous regiment of testing to ensure performance objectives are achieved. Our tactical knives go through two testing protocols: The first, lab testing against other brands in which we strive to completely outclass any other brand in the world in locking mechanism breaking strength, cutting performance and component strength and durability. The other, even more respected by our special operations customers, is the field application testing conducted by our experienced tactical staff. For more information, ask one of our tactical representatives for the field test overview of the model 4154. This mindset of innovating for improvement is not the easiest way to make knives, but it's the only way we know how.

Figure 10.23 When no Keep Options are specified, headlines can become stranded and the last line in a paragraph can end up starting a new column.

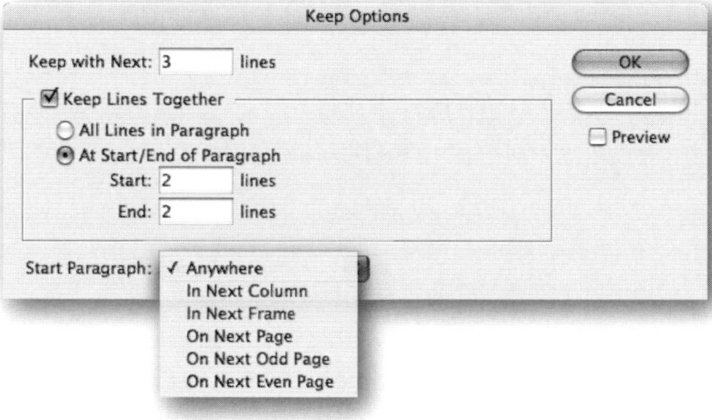
Keep Options
Keep with Next: 3 lines
Keep Lines Together
All Lines in Paragraph
At Start/End of Paragraph
Start: 2 lines
End: 2 lines
Start Paragraph:
✓ Anywhere
In Next Column
In Next Frame
On Next Page
On Next Odd Page
On Next Even Page
OK
Cancel
Preview

Figure 10.24 The Keep Options dialog.

Specify the following options as necessary:

- **Keep with Next_lines.** This value determines how many lines in the following paragraph remain with the last line of the current paragraph as text moves between frames. You can specify a value up to five. For example, if a value of **3** is entered and the first three lines of the next paragraph move to another frame, the last line of the current paragraph will move with them. This is very useful for making sure a subhead always stays with the next few lines of the following paragraph.

- **Keep Lines Together.** Select this option to keep the lines within a paragraph together. You can choose to keep all the lines together and prevent the paragraph from breaking by selecting All Lines In Paragraph; or select At Start/End of Paragraph and specify the number of lines that must appear at the beginning or end of the paragraph. This option is useful for preventing orphans and widows.
- **Start Paragraph.** Choose an option from the list to determine where the selected paragraph should begin. If Anywhere is selected, the start position is determined by the other Keep Options settings. If any of the other options are selected, the paragraph will be forced to start from the chosen position.

Balance Ragged Lines Option

Using the Balance Ragged Lines option reduces the amount of manual intervention necessary to achieve visual balance in a paragraph (**Figure 10.25**). When applied, InDesign automatically breaks the paragraph in a way that balances ragged aligned text across multiple lines, saving you the hassle of forcing line breaks or entering nonbreaking spaces. Choose Balance Ragged Lines from the Paragraph or Control panel menu to apply the option to a selected paragraph. It's particularly useful for headings, pull-quotes, and centered paragraphs.

● **Note:** Balance Ragged Lines only takes effect when the Adobe Paragraph Composer is selected.

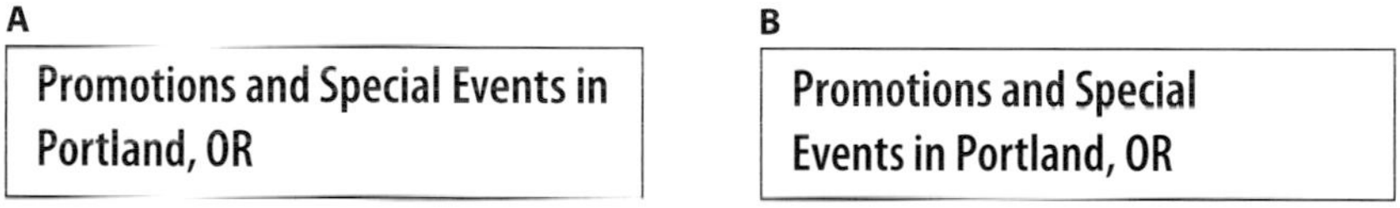
A
Promotions and Special Events in
Portland, OR
B
Promotions and Special
Events in Portland, OR

Figure 10.25 Before applying the Balance Ragged Lines option (**A**). After applying it, the heading is automatically improved (**B**).

Paragraph Rules

Paragraph rules are lines that can appear above and/or below a paragraph. If the paragraph moves, the rules follow it, preventing you from having to manually reposition the lines when the text reflows. InDesign's Paragraph Rules feature is an invaluable tool and should be utilized in any template that calls for rules in its design (**Figure 10.26**).

To add a rule above or below a paragraph, choose Paragraph Rules from the Paragraph or Control panel menu (**Figure 10.27**). Then choose either Rule Above or Rule Below from the menu at the top of the Paragraph Rules dialog and select Rule On to activate the rule. To see what the rule looks like as you create it, select Preview.

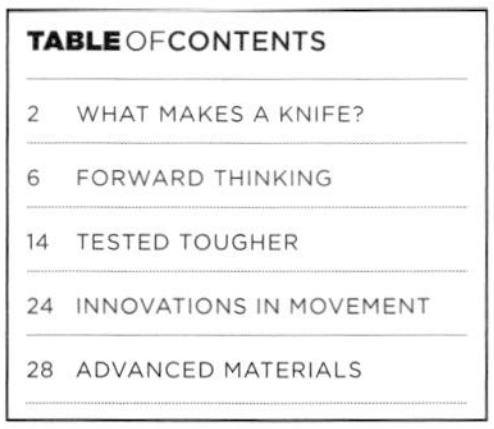
TABLE OF CONTENTS
2 WHAT MAKES A KNIFE?
6 FORWARD THINKING
14 TESTED TOUGHER
24 INNOVATIONS IN MOVEMENT
28 ADVANCED MATERIALS

Figure 10.26 Since paragraph rules were used to create this table of contents, entries can be added or deleted, and the lines will automatically reposition as necessary.

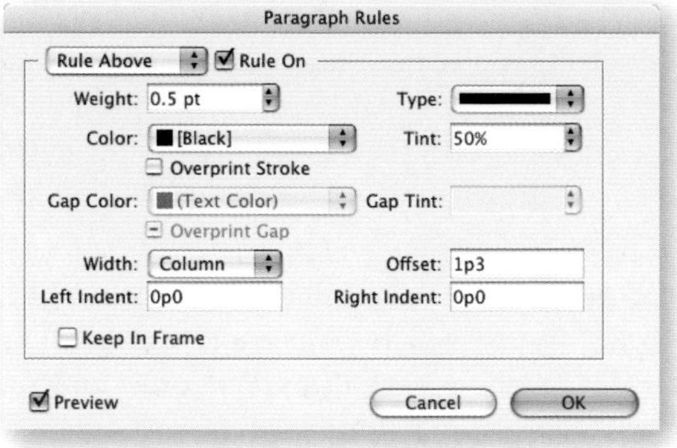
Paragraph Rules
Rule Above
Rule On
Weight: 0.5 pt
Type:
Color: [Black]
Tint: 50%
Overprint Stroke
Gap Color: (Text Color)
Gap Tint:
Overprint Gap
Width: Column
Offset: 1p3
Left Indent: 0p0
Right Indent: 0p0
Keep In Frame
Preview
Cancel
OK

Figure 10.27 The Paragraph Rules dialog.

■ **Tip:** You can add a rule above and below the paragraph by selecting the Rule On option for both Rule Above and Rule Below.

● **Note:** The offset for a rule above is measured from the baseline of the top line of text to the bottom of the rule. The offset for a rule below is measured from the baseline of the last line of text to the top of the rule.

Type a weight value to determine the thickness of the rule. For Type, specify the kind of rule you want to create. Next, choose a color and tint value for the rule. The colors listed are those already in the Swatches panel. If you specified a line type other than solid, choose a gap color and/or gap tint value to add color to the area between dashes, dots, or lines. Select Overprint Stroke or Overprint Gap to ensure that the line overprints any underlying inks on the printing press.

To determine how wide the rule should be, choose either Column or Text from the Width menu. To specify the vertical position of the rule, type a value into the Offset field. You can also set a left and/or right indent for the rule by typing values into the Left Indent and Right Indent fields. Select the Keep in Frame option when creating a rule above to make sure the rule is drawn within the text frame.

Bulleted and Numbered Lists

InDesign offers two productive methods for creating bulleted and numbered lists: setting up a hanging indent or using the Bullets and Numbering feature.

SETTING UP A HANGING INDENT

■ **Tip:** If a bullet character is a different font from the body text, the bullet may not vertically align properly. Apply a baseline shift to adjust it.

To set up a hanging indent, select the paragraphs that will become the list, specify a left indent value, and then specify a negative first-line left indent value (**Figure 10.28**). All the lines in each selected paragraph are indented except for the first line. To align the text in the first line with the subsequent lines in the paragraph, you must insert a tab character after the bullet or number character. If a space is used, the text in the first line won't properly align. You can also use the Tabs dialog to create a hanging indent (Figure 10.16).

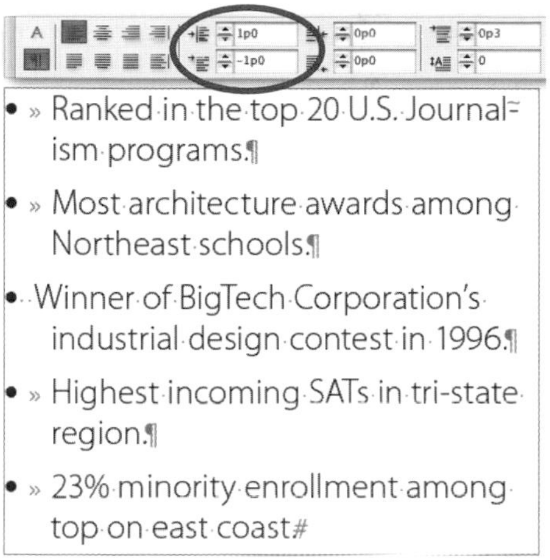
1p0
-1p0
0p0
0p0
0p3
0
• » Ranked in the top 20 U.S. Journal-
ism programs.¶
• » Most architecture awards among
Northeast schools.¶
• Winner of BigTech Corporation's
industrial design contest in 1996.¶
• » Highest incoming SATs in tri-state
region.¶
• » 23% minority enrollment among
top on east coast#

Figure 10.28 It's common to specify a negative first-line left indent value that is equal to the value you enter for the left indent. Notice how the two spaces in the third paragraph are causing it to misalign.

USING THE BULLETS AND NUMBERING FEATURE

InDesign's Bullets and Numbering feature automatically generates bulleted and numbered lists in a single click. Even the numbers in numbered lists are updated as you add or remove paragraphs in the list, making this feature a valuable component of many templates.

To create a bulleted or numbered list, select the paragraphs that will become the list, and then click the Bulleted List or Numbered List button in the Control panel (**Figure 10.29**). You can also use these buttons to turn off a list or switch between bullets and numbers. The actual bullet and number characters aren't inserted into the text and cannot be selected with the Type tool. To edit their formatting, you'll have to use the Bullets and Numbering dialog. To access it, choose Bullets and Numbering from the Paragraph or Control panel menu.

A **B**

Figure 10.29 The Bulleted List button (**A**); The Numbered List button (**B**).

To format a bullet character, choose Bullets from the List Type menu (**Figure 10.30**). Select a bullet character from the Bullet Character grid. If you don't want to use one of the existing characters, click Add and locate the character you want to use (**Figure 10.31**). By default, the Text After field contains a tab space (^t). To insert a different character, click the triangle to the right of the field. You can even apply a character style to the bullet by choosing one from the Character Style menu.

■ **Tip:** You can convert the bullets or numbers in a list to actual text by choosing Convert Numbering To Text or Convert Bullets To Text from the Paragraph panel menu.

● **Note:** If you are tempted to use the Indent to Here character to create bulleted and numbered lists, think twice. To create lists with this character, you have to manually insert it into each line in a list, potentially costing you hours of labor. It's useful in rare situations, but not in templates.

- When the text you are going to import does not already contain bullet or number characters. This is often the case when using Data Merge to merge a data source file with a document.
- If you plan to repurpose the text for another publication or Web site and only want to change the appearance of the text in the current InDesign document. Since the bullet and number characters aren't actually inserted into the text, they cannot be exported or pasted into another application, allowing you to repurpose just the text.

Setting Tabs

Tabs position text at specific locations in a line of text. They are commonly used to create bulleted and numbered lists, and for separating columns of information into a table-like layout. You can set left-justified, center-justified, right-justified, and decimal or special-character tabs.

■ **Tip:** Click the magnet icon at the bottom-right corner of the Tabs dialog to snap the dialog above the text frame. If the text frame is too close to the top of the document window, the Tabs dialog will not snap to the frame.

Before you set tabs, you must first insert tabs where you want to add horizontal space. For example, to create a four-column layout, insert three tab characters—one between each column. At this point, you're not concerned with how the text appears, so don't worry if lines of text are breaking as you insert tabs. You'll clean all that up in the next step.

After you've entered the necessary tabs, select the paragraphs you want to set tabs for, and then choose Type > Tabs to open the Tabs dialog. To set a tab, first click a tab-alignment button (left, center, right, or decimal) to determine how text will align to the tab's position, and then click a location on the tab ruler to position the new tab (**Figure 10.33**). You can also type a specific value into the X field and press Enter or Return.

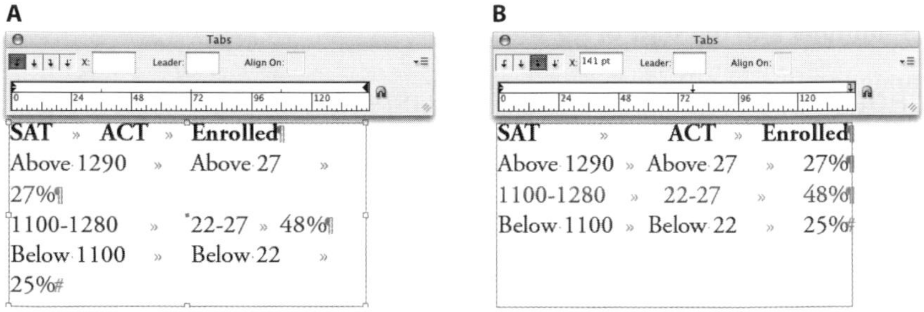
A
Tabs
X:
Leader:
Align On:
0
24
48
72
96
120
SAT » ACT » Enrolled
Above 1290 » Above 27 »
27%
1100-1280 » 22-27 » 48%
Below 1100 » Below 22 »
25%
B
Tabs
X: 141 pt
Leader:
Align On:
0
24
48
72
96
120
SAT » ACT » Enrolled
Above 1290 » Above 27 » 27%
1100-1280 » 22-27 » 48%
Below 1100 » Below 22 » 25%

Figure 10.33 A list before tabs are set (**A**) and the list after they are set (**B**). A center-justified tab centers the middle column and a right-justified tab aligns the last column.

CREATING DECIMAL TABS

When using the decimal tab, you can set a tab to align to any character you choose, such as a decimal point (.) or a dollar sign ($). Click the decimal tab-alignment button and then click the location on the tab ruler where you want to align the special character. In the Align On field, type the character to which you want to align and press Enter or Return (**Figure 10.34**).

A B

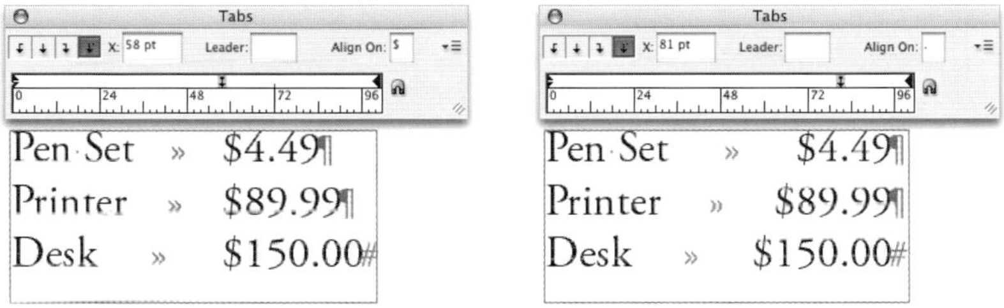
Tabs
X: 58 pt
Leader:
Align On: $
Pen Set » $4.49
Printer » $89.99
Desk » $150.00
Tabs
X: 81 pt
Leader:
Align On: .
Pen Set » $4.49
Printer » $89.99
Desk » $150.00

Figure 10.34 A price list aligning on a dollar sign (**A**) and the same list aligning on a decimal point (**B**).

CREATING TAB LEADERS

You can use the Tabs dialog to insert a tab leader, such as a series of dots or dashes, between a tab and the following text. Using this feature keeps you from having to manually do the work. Select a tab stop on the ruler and then type a pattern of up to eight characters into the Leader field (**Figure 10.35**). You can even select the tab leader and apply formatting to it.

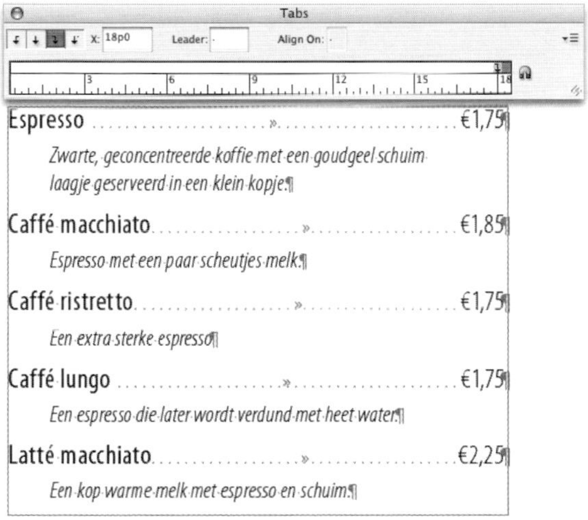
Tabs
X: 18p0
Leader: .
Align On:
Espresso €1,75
Zwarte, geconcentreerde koffie met een goudgeel schuim laagje geserveerd in een klein kopje
Caffé macchiato €1,85
Espresso met een paar scheutjes melk
Caffé ristretto €1,75
Een extra sterke espresso
Caffé lungo €1,75
Een espresso die later wordt verdund met heet water
Latté macchiato €2,25
Een kop warme melk met espresso en schuim

Figure 10.35 The tab leaders in this list are a period (.) followed by a space character. The size and color of the period were also changed.

Paragraph and Character Styles

Paragraph and character styles are collections of typographical attributes that can be applied to text with a single click. Character styles contain character-level formatting and paragraph styles contain both character-level and paragraph-level formatting (**Figure 10.36**). As their names imply, paragraph styles are applied to entire paragraphs and character styles are applied to specific characters and words within paragraphs. When you modify a style sheet, all the text to which it is applied instantly updates with the new changes. If you've avoided style sheets in the past, it's a good time to embrace them now and make them part of every template you create.

Figure 10.36 The New Paragraph Style dialog (**A**); The New Character Style dialog (**B**).

A

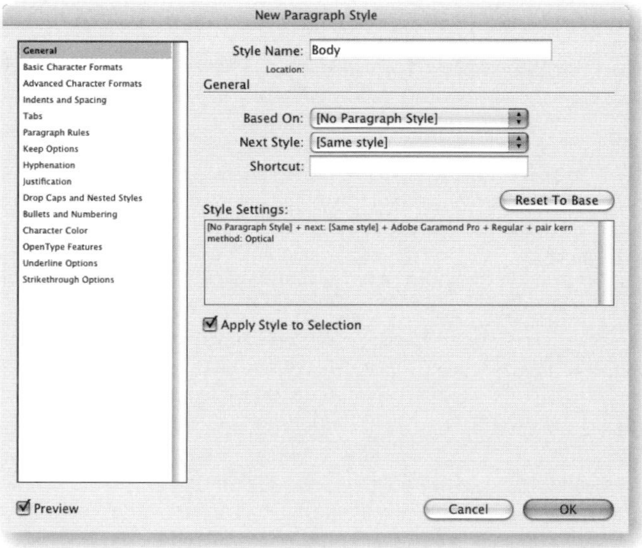
New Paragraph Style
General
Basic Character Formats
Advanced Character Formats
Indents and Spacing
Tabs
Paragraph Rules
Keep Options
Hyphenation
Justification
Drop Caps and Nested Styles
Bullets and Numbering
Character Color
OpenType Features
Underline Options
Strikethrough Options
Style Name: Body
Location:
General
Based On: [No Paragraph Style]
Next Style: [Same style]
Shortcut:
Reset To Base
Style Settings:
[No Paragraph Style] + next: [Same style] + Adobe Garamond Pro + Regular + pair kern method: Optical
Apply Style to Selection
Preview
Cancel
OK

B

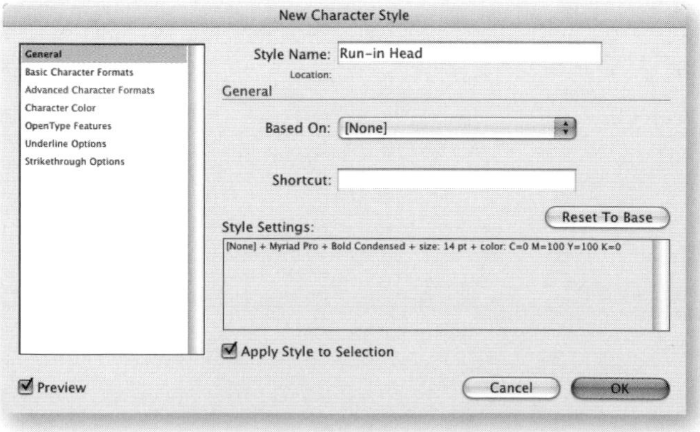
New Character Style
General
Basic Character Formats
Advanced Character Formats
Character Color
OpenType Features
Underline Options
Strikethrough Options
Style Name: Run-in Head
Location:
General
Based On: [None]
Shortcut:
Reset To Base
Style Settings:
[None] + Myriad Pro + Bold Condensed + size: 14 pt + color: C=0 M=100 Y=100 K=0
Apply Style to Selection
Preview
Cancel
OK

Before setting up any paragraph and character styles, make sure all the textual elements are represented and formatted the way you want them to look. This way the bulk of the work is already done. All you have to do then is generate style sheets based on the sample text in your mock-up layout.

Keep in mind that style sheets do not have to lock you into one static design. Even if they just serve as a starting point from which you can tailor the formatting to a publication's specific needs, they are an indispensable tool.

Creating Paragraph Styles

By default, every document contains the [Basic Paragraph] style, which is applied to all text as you type. You can't delete or rename this style, but you can edit its attributes. Double-click the [Basic Paragraph] style to edit it.

■ **Tip:** Edit the [Basic Paragraph] style so that it utilizes one of the main fonts used in your template.

Follow theses steps to create a paragraph style based on existing text:

1. Place the type cursor into the sample text that represents the formatting of the paragraph style you want to create.
2. Click the Create New Style button at the bottom of the Paragraph Styles panel. "Paragraph Style 1" appears in the panel. If it's the second style you've created, it will be called "Paragraph Style 2," and so on.
3. Double-click the new paragraph style to name it and add any additional formatting to the style if necessary. Choose a name that identifies the intended purpose of the style. Notice that when you double-clicked the paragraph style, you also simultaneously applied it to the sample text.

● **Note:** You can also create a new paragraph style by choosing New Paragraph Style from the Paragraph Styles panel menu. Be sure to check Apply Style to Selection before clicking OK.

Creating Character Styles

Before you create any character styles, it's very important to make paragraph styles and apply them to your sample text first. Only the attributes that are different from those defined by the applied paragraph style—such as the type style and character color—are made part of the character style. All other attributes are left undefined (**Figure 10.37**). This important first step prevents character styles from applying attributes that are already applied by a paragraph style and keeps you from having to edit both paragraph and character styles when the text formatting in your template needs to be modified.

A

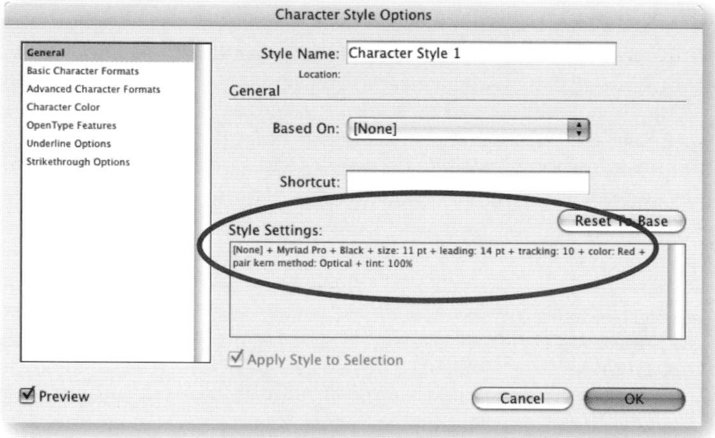
Character Style Options
General
Basic Character Formats
Advanced Character Formats
Character Color
OpenType Features
Underline Options
Strikethrough Options
Style Name: Character Style 1
Location:
General
Based On: [None]
Shortcut:
Style Settings:
Reset To Base
[None] + Myriad Pro + Black + size: 11 pt + leading: 14 pt + tracking: 10 + color: Red + pair kern method: Optical + tint: 100%
Apply Style to Selection
Preview
Cancel
OK

B

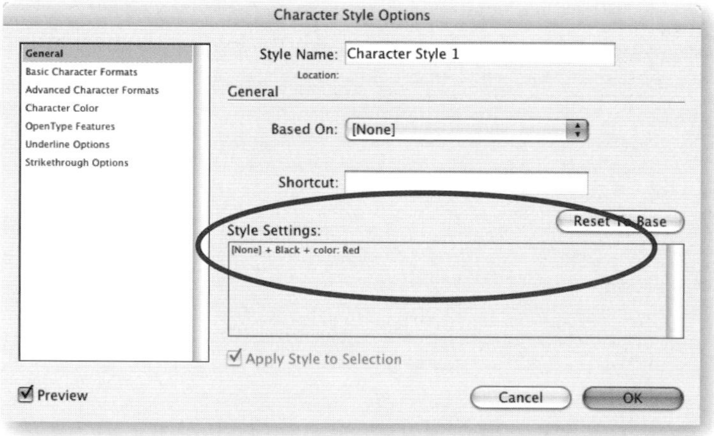
Character Style Options
General
Basic Character Formats
Advanced Character Formats
Character Color
OpenType Features
Underline Options
Strikethrough Options
Style Name: Character Style 1
Location:
General
Based On: [None]
Shortcut:
Style Settings:
Reset To Base
[None] + Black + color: Red
Apply Style to Selection
Preview
Cancel
OK

Figure 10.37 A character style created before a paragraph style was applied (**A**) and the same character style created after a paragraph style is applied (**B**). Read the Style Settings overview each time you make a new character style to determine what attributes it picked up.

Follow these steps to create a character style based on existing text:

1. Select the text that represents the formatting of the character style you want to create.
2. Click the Create New Style button at the bottom of the Character Styles panel. The new character style appears in the panel.
3. Double-click the new character style to name it. Choose a name that identifies the purpose of the style. Note that when you double-clicked the character style, you also simultaneously applied it to the selected text.

■ **Tip:** When setting up nested styles, it's important to append an extra word or character, such an asterisk (*), to the paragraph style's name. If another designer uses the template or even when you come back to it months later, you can immediately recognize where all the formatting is coming from as you apply and manage style sheets.

Setting Up Nested Styles

A nested style is a character style that is embedded into a paragraph style and applied to a specified range of text within the paragraph you apply the paragraph style to. In other words, nested styles allow you to apply paragraph styles and character styles at the same time in just one mouse click, taking automation to a whole new level.

Nested styles play a major role in any template containing text formatting that follows a consistent pattern. They are especially useful for bulleted and numbered lists, run-in headings, and so on (**Figure 10.38**).

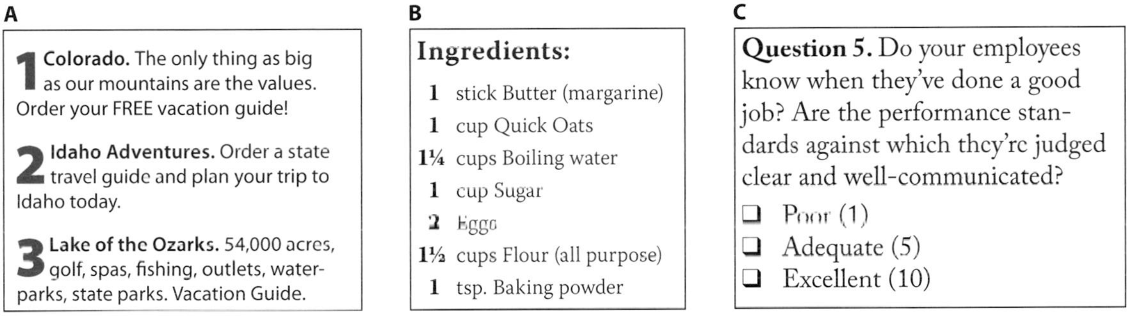
A
1 Colorado. The only thing as big as our mountains are the values. Order your FREE vacation guide!
2 Idaho Adventures. Order a state travel guide and plan your trip to Idaho today.
3 Lake of the Ozarks. 54,000 acres, golf, spas, fishing, outlets, water-parks, state parks. Vacation Guide.
B
Ingredients:
1 stick Butter (margarine)
1 cup Quick Oats
1¼ cups Boiling water
1 cup Sugar
2 Eggs
1½ cups Flour (all purpose)
1 tsp. Baking powder
C
Question 5. Do your employees know when they've done a good job? Are the performance standards against which they're judged clear and well-communicated?
❑ Poor (1)
❑ Adequate (5)
❑ Excellent (10)

Figure 10.38 Common uses for nested styles.

To add nested styles to a paragraph style, double-click the paragraph style and click Drop Caps and Nested Styles (**Figure 10.39**). Choose New Nested Style and do the following for each nested style you add:

1. Choose a character style from the first menu to determine the appearance of the specified range of text within the paragraph.

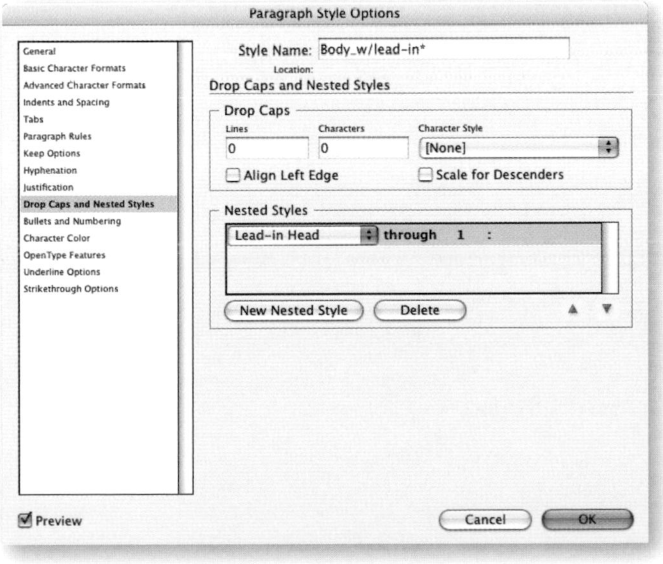
Paragraph Style Options
General
Basic Character Formats
Advanced Character Formats
Indents and Spacing
Tabs
Paragraph Rules
Keep Options
Hyphenation
Justification
Drop Caps and Nested Styles
Bullets and Numbering
Character Color
OpenType Features
Underline Options
Strikethrough Options
Style Name: Body_w/lead-in*
Location:
Drop Caps and Nested Styles
Drop Caps
Lines
Characters
Character Style
0
0
[None]
Align Left Edge
Scale for Descenders
Nested Styles
Lead-in Head
through
1
:
New Nested Style
Delete
Preview
Cancel
OK

Figure 10.39 Creating a nested style. You won't see a menu or be able to modify a nested style option until you first click it.

■ **Tip:** Before adding a nested style, remove any applied character styles from the sample text that the paragraph style is applied to. You can then properly preview the results of the nested style as you create it.

2. Choose an option from the last menu to determine where the character style should stop applying its formatting (**Figure 10.40**). You can also type a character, such as a colon (:) or a specific letter or number, but you cannot type a word. If you type a string of characters, such as a period followed by a comma and a colon (.,:), InDesign will look for only one of those characters, but not the whole string. This is useful when you cannot predict which character will appear in the text.

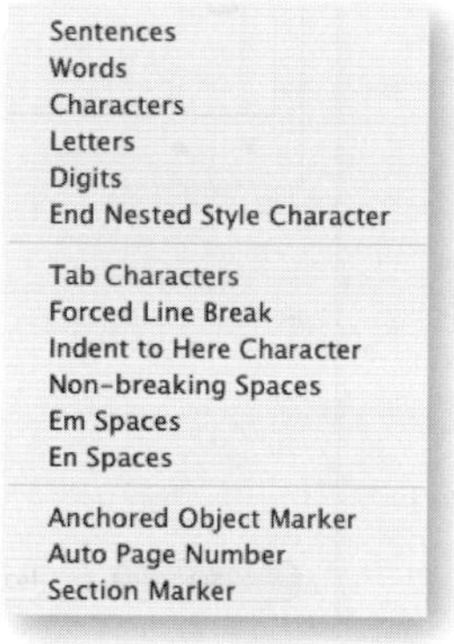
Sentences
Words
Characters
Letters
Digits
End Nested Style Character
Tab Characters
Forced Line Break
Indent to Here Character
Non-breaking Spaces
Em Spaces
En Spaces
Anchored Object Marker
Auto Page Number
Section Marker

Figure 10.40 This menu offers several items to choose from for ending the character style formatting.

3. Specify how many instances of the selected item (such as characters, words, or a specific character) are required.
4. Choose Through or Up To from the second menu. Choosing Through includes the character that ends the nested style, whereas choosing Up To only formats those characters that precede this character.
5. Click the Up button or Down button to change the order of the styles. This determines the order in which the character formatting is applied. When two or more nested styles exist within a paragraph, one takes over from where the previous one ends.
6. After you've added two or more nested styles, you can set them up to loop. Create an additional nested style, choose [Repeat] from the first menu, and then specify how many nested styles will be repeated (**Figure 10.41**).

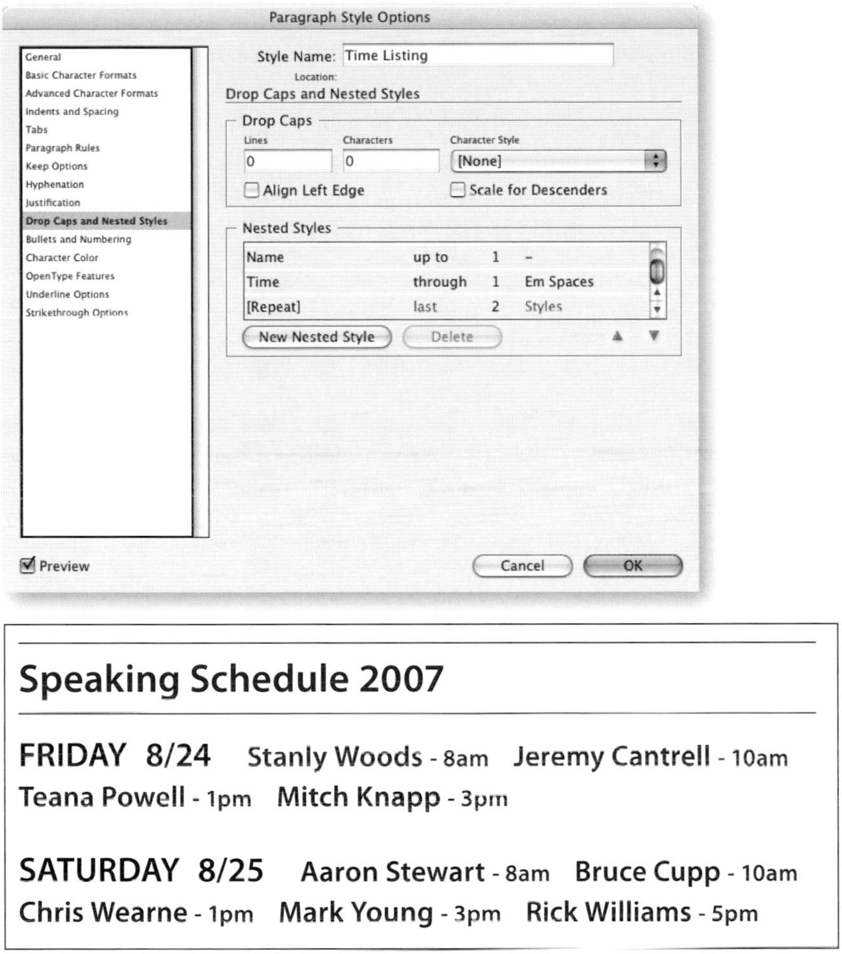

Paragraph Style Options
General
Basic Character Formats
Advanced Character Formats
Indents and Spacing
Tabs
Paragraph Rules
Keep Options
Hyphenation
Justification
Drop Caps and Nested Styles
Bullets and Numbering
Character Color
OpenType Features
Underline Options
Strikethrough Options
Style Name: Time Listing
Location:
Drop Caps and Nested Styles
Drop Caps
Lines
Characters
Character Style
0
0
[None]
Align Left Edge
Scale for Descenders
Nested Styles
Name up to 1 -
Time through 1 Em Spaces
[Repeat] last 2 Styles
New Nested Style
Delete
Preview
Cancel
OK
Speaking Schedule 2007
FRIDAY 8/24 Stanly Woods - 8am Jeremy Cantrell - 10am
Teana Powell - 1pm Mitch Knapp - 3pm
SATURDAY 8/25 Aaron Stewart - 8am Bruce Cupp - 10am
Chris Wearne - 1pm Mark Young - 3pm Rick Williams - 5pm

Figure 10.41 Since this time schedule contains a consistent alternating pattern, the last two nested styles were set up to loop. Even if you add or remove words in the paragraph, the looping pattern continues.

Productivity Tips

When creating style sheets, there are several ways to increase their productivity:

- **Use the Next Style option.** This unassuming option lives a twofold existence. At minimum, it determines which paragraph style is automatically applied to the next paragraph when you are typing text directly into InDesign. Even more powerful is its ability to automatically apply a series of individual styles to multiple paragraphs in one click. You can apply a paragraph style, which in turn applies the specified Next Style to the second paragraph.

If that next paragraph also has the Next Style option defined, the next style will be applied to the third paragraph, and so on.

To specify the Next Style option, choose a paragraph style from the Next Style menu in the Paragraph Styles Options dialog. To apply sequential styles to multiple paragraphs, select the paragraphs you want to apply the styles to, right-click (Windows) or Control-click (Mac OS) the parent style, and then choose Apply [*Style Name*] then Next Style. Using the Next Style option can save hours of formatting labor whenever the text formatting in a publication follows a consistent pattern (**Figure 10.42**).

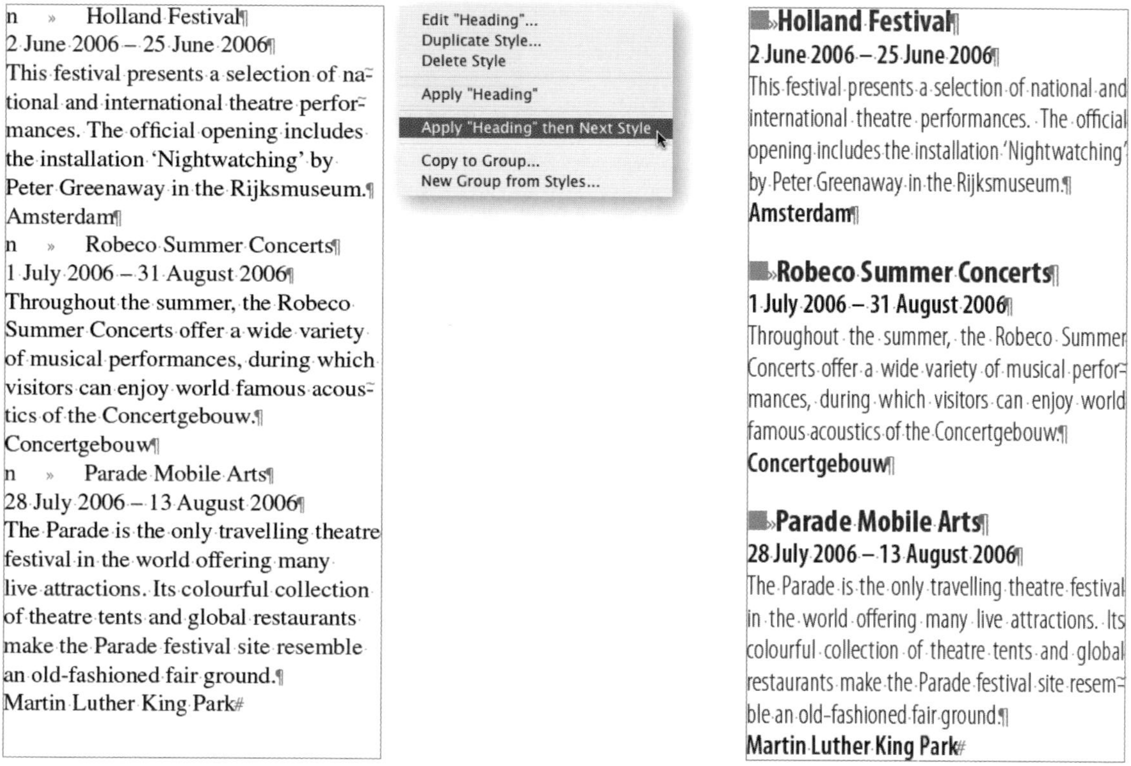
n » Holland Festival¶
2 June 2006 – 25 June 2006¶
This festival presents a selection of national and international theatre performances. The official opening includes the installation 'Nightwatching' by Peter Greenaway in the Rijksmuseum.¶
Amsterdam¶
n » Robeco Summer Concerts¶
1 July 2006 – 31 August 2006¶
Throughout the summer, the Robeco Summer Concerts offer a wide variety of musical performances, during which visitors can enjoy world famous acoustics of the Concertgebouw.¶
Concertgebouw¶
n » Parade Mobile Arts¶
28 July 2006 – 13 August 2006¶
The Parade is the only travelling theatre festival in the world offering many live attractions. Its colourful collection of theatre tents and global restaurants make the Parade festival site resemble an old-fashioned fair ground.¶
Martin Luther King Park#
Edit "Heading"...
Duplicate Style...
Delete Style
Apply "Heading"
Apply "Heading" then Next Style
Copy to Group...
New Group from Styles...
Holland Festival¶
2 June 2006 – 25 June 2006¶
This festival presents a selection of national and international theatre performances. The official opening includes the installation 'Nightwatching' by Peter Greenaway in the Rijksmuseum.¶
Amsterdam¶
Robeco Summer Concerts¶
1 July 2006 – 31 August 2006¶
Throughout the summer, the Robeco Summer Concerts offer a wide variety of musical performances, during which visitors can enjoy world famous acoustics of the Concertgebouw.¶
Concertgebouw¶
Parade Mobile Arts¶
28 July 2006 – 13 August 2006¶
The Parade is the only travelling theatre festival in the world offering many live attractions. Its colourful collection of theatre tents and global restaurants make the Parade festival site resemble an old-fashioned fair ground.¶
Martin Luther King Park#

Figure 10.42 Four styles are used in this example: Heading, Dates, Description, and City. The Next Style for Heading is Dates, for Dates it's Description, for Description it's City, and to complete the loop, the Next Style for City is Heading. By applying sequential styles, it's possible to format this entire block of text with a single click.

- **Base the style on another.** This option makes it possible to link paragraph styles together, so that if changes are made to the parent style, all the styles based on it are automatically updated with those changes. To base a style on another, choose an existing paragraph style from the Based On menu.

  It's important to carefully consider the use of this option. It can act as your best friend, preventing you from having to redefine one style at a time when several styles need the same update. But, it can also work against you when you want to restrict formatting changes to one style. Whenever you choose to base a style on another, be sure to identify it somehow when naming the style so you can keep track of the formatting changes you make.

- **Organize the list of styles sheets.** You can drag styles to different locations within the Paragraph Styles panel to make them easier to locate. A thick line appears, indicating where the style will drop when you release the mouse button. Organize the styles into a logical order that makes the most sense for your template and workflow requirements.

- **Create Style Groups.** You can organize styles into style groups, making them easy to find and manage (**Figure 10.43**). This is especially useful when a template contains many style sheets. To create a style group, choose New Style Group from the Paragraph Styles panel menu, and then choose a name that clearly identifies its purpose. Once created, you can drag styles in and out of the style group to add or remove them.

● **Note:** If a paragraph style other than [Basic Paragraph] is applied to text when you create a new style, the new style will be automatically based on the currently applied style.

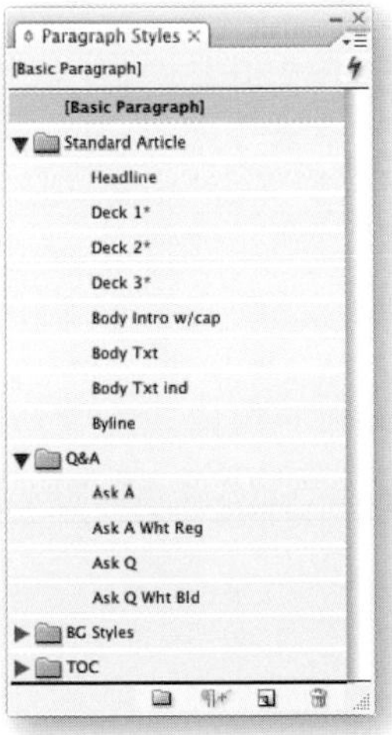
Paragraph Styles
[Basic Paragraph]
[Basic Paragraph]
Standard Article
Headline
Deck 1*
Deck 2*
Deck 3*
Body Intro w/cap
Body Txt
Body Txt ind
Byline
Q&A
Ask A
Ask A Wht Reg
Ask Q
Ask Q Wht Bld
BG Styles
TOC

Figure 10.43 This template makes good use of style groups. The styles have been organized within each group to make them easier to find.

- **Redefine style sheets.** When constructing a template, it's not uncommon to frequently update its style sheets as you modify the design. Instead of editing a style directly, you may find it easier to change the formatting of an existing paragraph in your mock-up layout, and then redefine the style based on the new formatting. To redefine a style, choose Redefine Style from the Paragraph Styles or Character Styles panel menu.

Importing Style Sheets

If you've already created paragraph and character styles in another InDesign document, you can import them into the template you're building. Choose Load All Text Styles from either the Paragraph Styles or Character Styles panel menu, and then locate the document containing the style sheets you want to import. In the Load Styles dialog, select the styles you want to import (**Figure 10.44**).

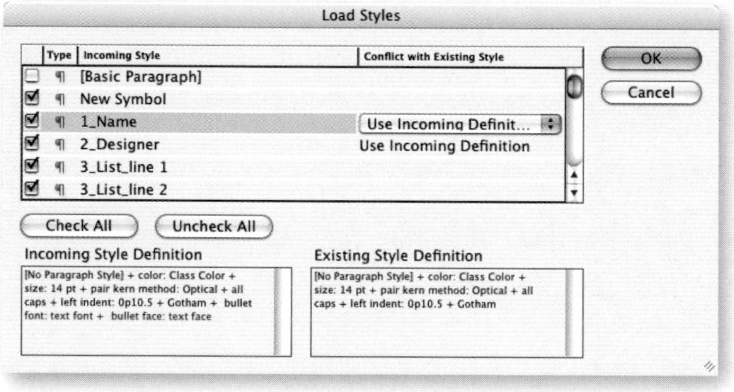
Load Styles
Type
Incoming Style
Conflict with Existing Style
OK
Cancel
[Basic Paragraph]
New Symbol
1_Name
Use Incoming Definit...
2_Designer
Use Incoming Definition
3_List_line 1
3_List_line 2
Check All
Uncheck All
Incoming Style Definition
[No Paragraph Style] + color: Class Color + size: 14 pt + pair kern method: Optical + all caps + left indent: 0p10.5 + Gotham + bullet font: text font + bullet face: text face
Existing Style Definition
[No Paragraph Style] + color: Class Color + size: 14 pt + pair kern method: Optical + all caps + left indent: 0p10.5 + Gotham

Figure 10.44 The Load Styles dialog. When a style conflict exists, you can compare the incoming style definition with the existing style definition at the bottom of the dialog.

If an existing style has the same name as one of the incoming styles, choose either Use Incoming Style Definition or Auto-Rename in the Conflict With Existing Style column to determine how the conflict should be resolved. If you choose Use Incoming Style Definition, the existing style will be overwritten with the imported style and all the text in the document will be updated with any new style attributes. If you choose Auto-Rename, the incoming style will be renamed so that both styles can exist within the same document. So, if both documents have a style called "Bullet List," the imported style is renamed "Bullet List copy" in the current document.

11

Formatting Frames and Generating Object Styles

ONE OF THE BIG ADVANTAGES OF USING INDESIGN CS3 FOR DESIGNING AND producing your publications is the feature-rich toolset it provides for formatting frames. An abundance of formatting options are available—from a simple fill and stroke color to a stunning combination of various transparency effects. It's important that you become familiar with each of these options and learn to apply them in the most efficient ways.

This chapter provides detailed information about InDesign's most essential frame formatting tools and teaches you how to generate object styles based on the sample design elements in a mock-up layout. With object styles, you'll be able to generate consistent publications and significantly speed up labor-intensive production tasks.

Essential Frame Formatting

Tip: You can apply a fill color to grayscale or monochrome (1-bit) images by selecting the image with the Direct Selection tool and then specifying a color.

All of the formatting that can be applied to text frames, graphics frames, and unassigned frames is collectively referred to as object-level formatting. You'll find the various formatting controls in a number of different panels and dialogs throughout InDesign.

A detailed description of the most essential formatting follows. Keep in mind that you'll need to select a frame with the Selection tool before you can apply formatting to it. And if you're working with a frame inside a group, use the Direct Selection tool.

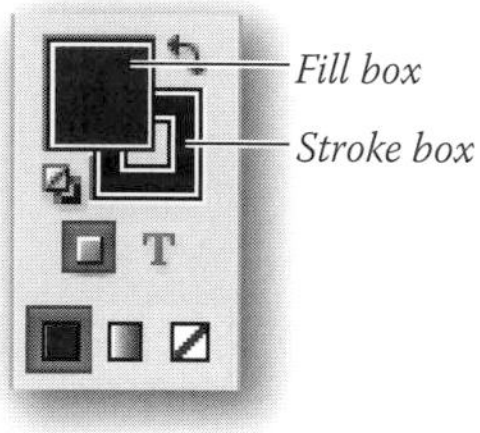
Fill box
Stroke box

Figure 11.1 The fill and stroke area of the toolbox. Both controls are also available in the Color panel and Swatches panel.

Applying a Fill and Stroke Color

You can add color to a frame's fill, stroke (border), or both. To do so, select the Fill box or the Stroke box in the toolbox to specify whether you want to add color to the frame's fill or stroke, and then select a color swatch in the Swatches panel or mix a color in the Color panel (**Figure 11.1**). You can't simultaneously apply a fill and a stroke color unless both options are applied with an object style.

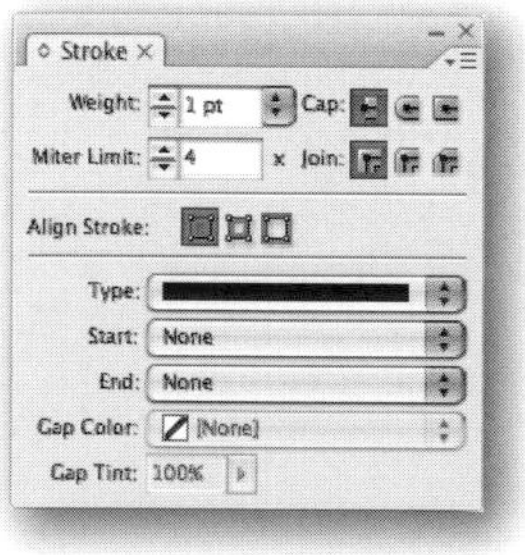
Stroke
Weight: 1 pt
Cap:
Miter Limit: 4
x Join:
Align Stroke:
Type:
Start: None
End: None
Gap Color: [None]
Gap Tint: 100%

Figure 11.2 The Stroke panel. Choose Show Options from the panel menu to display all the available options.

Stroke Options

The Stroke panel contains quite a few options that provide control over the weight and appearance of a frame's stroke (**Figure 11.2**). Let's start from the top of the panel and work down:

- **Weight.** Specify a value to determine how wide you want the stroke to be. Avoid making strokes thinner than 0.25 pt, because you can't see them very well when they're printed on a high-resolution output device.
- **Cap styles.** Select one of the three cap styles to specify how you want the ends of an open path to appear. Butt Cap, which is the default setting, creates squared ends that stop at the endpoints. Round Cap creates semicircular ends that extend past the endpoints. Projecting Cap creates squared ends and makes the stroke surround the path evenly in every direction (**Figure 11.3**).

Butt Cap
Round Cap
Projecting Cap

Figure 11.3 The three cap styles in use. The Round Cap and the Projecting Cap styles extend half the stroke width past the endpoints, adding length to the stroke.

- **Join options.** Select one of the three join options to specify how you want the stroke at the corner points of a frame to appear. Miter Join, which is the default setting, creates pointed corners. Round Join creates rounded corners, and Bevel Join creates squared-off corners (**Figure 11.4**).

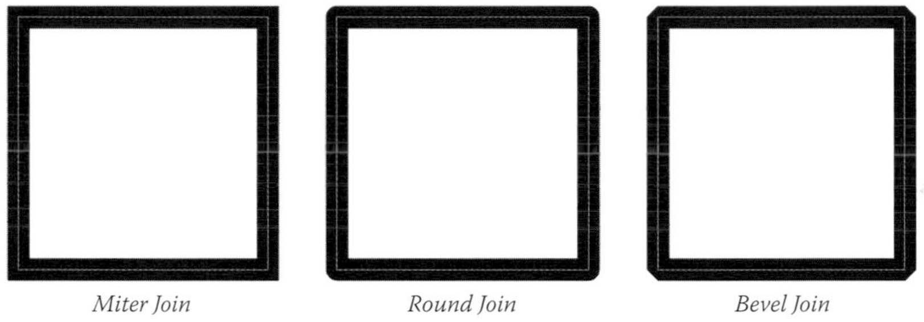
Miter Join
Round Join
Bevel Join

Figure 11.4 The three join options in use.

- **Miter Limit.** At first, this option can seem a bit obscure. To simplify it for you, the miter limit value only applies to frames to which the Miter Join option has been applied. The specified value determines how long a corner point can be before InDesign switches from a miter join to a bevel join. The default miter limit is 4, which means that when the length of the corner point reaches four times the stroke weight, the point becomes squared-off (**Figure 11.5**). Enter a value between 1 and 500.

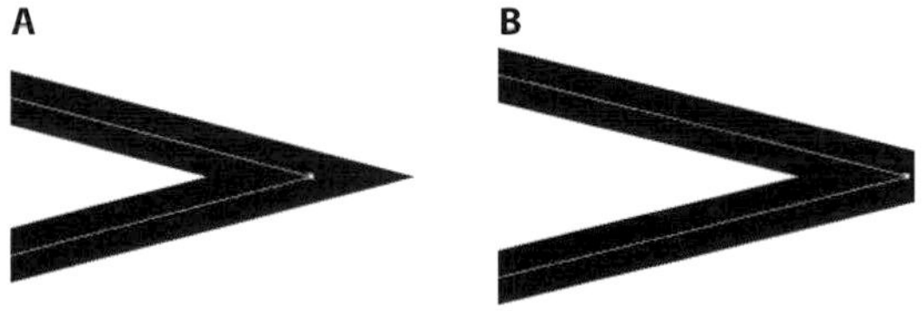
A
B

Figure 11.5 The corner point of this triangle (**A**) is getting close to the maximum allowable length, as specified by the miter limit value. Once the threshold is reached, the miter join is converted to a bevel join (**B**).

- **Align Stroke.** Click one of the three icons to specify a desired alignment method. Strokes can be aligned along the center, inside, or outside of a path or frame (**Figure 11.6**). By default, strokes are center aligned.

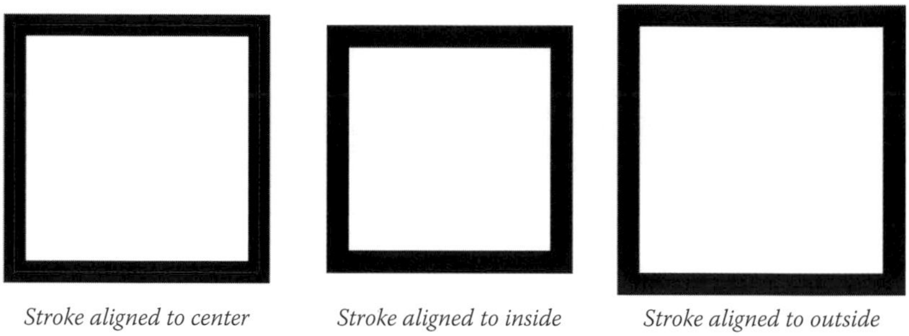
Stroke aligned to center
Stroke aligned to inside
Stroke aligned to outside

Figure 11.6 Each of the Align Stroke options in use. The layer color these frames are on is red to make the frame edges more visible.

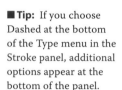

■ **Tip:** If you choose Dashed at the bottom of the Type menu in the Stroke panel, additional options appear at the bottom of the panel.

Having these three choices comes in handy when aligning paths and frames to guides on the page. For instance, to quickly create a border within the page margins, you can snap a frame to the margin guides and align the stroke along the inside of the frame. If the stroke was aligned to the center of theframe, you would have to carefully nudge the frame until the edge of the stroke touches the margin guide.

- **Type.** Choose one of the many stroke types available in this menu (**Figure 11.7**). If your mock-up layout calls for a unique stroke type, you can create a custom stroke style by choosing Stroke Styles from the Stroke panel menu. You can make a striped, dotted, or dashed stroke and define its pattern, corner attributes, and cap style.
- **Start and End.** Select a start and/or end shape to specify how you want the beginning and end of an open path to appear (**Figure 11.8**).
- **Gap Color and Gap Tint.** Choose a gap color and gap tint to add color to the area between dots, lines, or dashes.

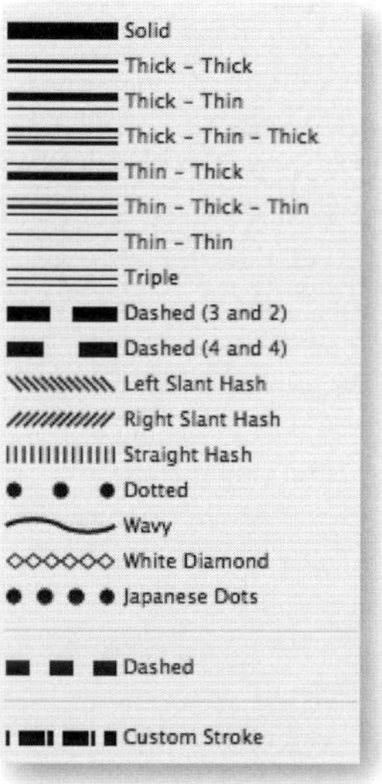
Solid
Thick - Thick
Thick - Thin
Thick - Thin - Thick
Thin - Thick
Thin - Thick - Thin
Thin - Thin
Triple
Dashed (3 and 2)
Dashed (4 and 4)
Left Slant Hash
Right Slant Hash
Straight Hash
Dotted
Wavy
White Diamond
Japanese Dots
Dashed
Custom Stroke

Figure 11.7 The Type menu in the Stroke panel displays all the stroke types available in a document. Custom stroke styles appear at the bottom of the menu.

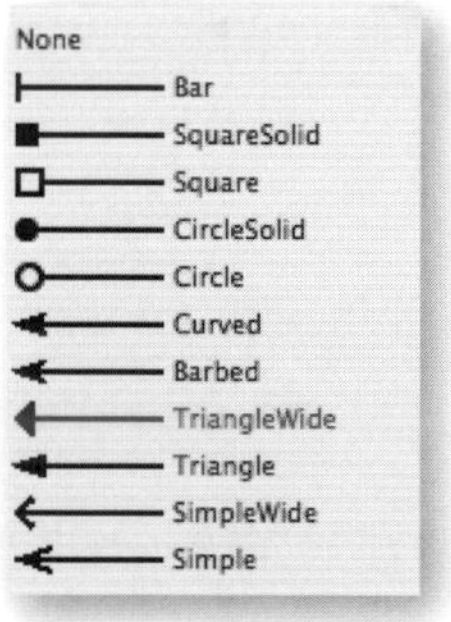
None
Bar
SquareSolid
Square
CircleSolid
Circle
Curved
Barbed
TriangleWide
Triangle
SimpleWide
Simple

Figure 11.8 The Start and End menus in the Stroke panel provide several shapes to choose from.

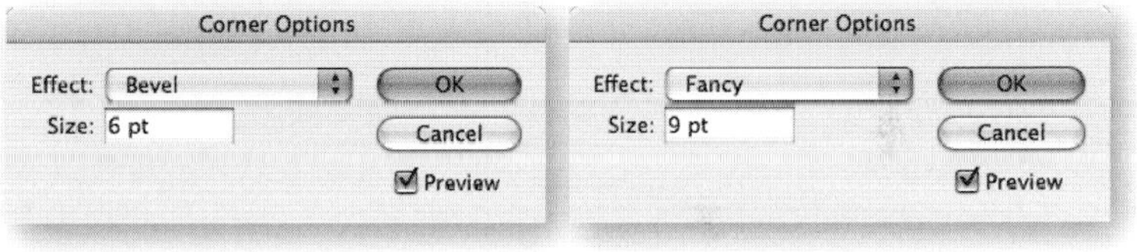
Corner Options
Effect: Bevel
Size: 6 pt
OK
Cancel
Preview
Corner Options
Effect: Fancy
Size: 9 pt
OK
Cancel
Preview

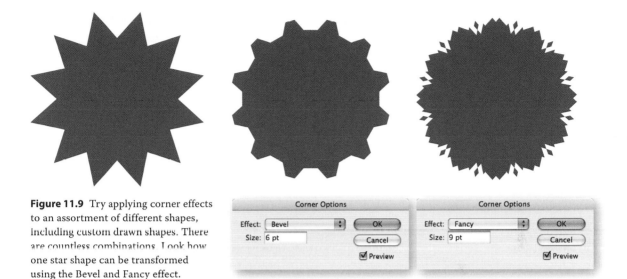

Figure 11.9 Try applying corner effects to an assortment of different shapes, including custom drawn shapes. There are countless combinations. Look how one star shape can be transformed using the Bevel and Fancy effect.

Applying Corner Effects

InDesign provides several corner effects that you can apply to frames to quickly enhance their shape. You can round off the corners of a simple square and even add some excitement to an ordinary polygon. To apply a corner effect, select an object that has corners and choose Object > Corner Options. From the Effect menu in the Corner Options dialog, choose the effect you want to apply. Type a value into the Size field to specify how far the effect extends from each corner point of the selected object (**Figure 11.9**). After you've applied a corner effect, you can go back and modify the settings again, because the effects are nondestructive.

■ **Tip:** The Pathfinder panel contains several buttons for converting the shape of a frame. When you convert a frame into one of the predefined shapes that have a corner effect, the radius size is based on the size value in the Corner Options dialog. With nothing selected on the page, change the size value to modify the default setting.

Text Frame Options

InDesign provides an assortment of invaluable formatting attributes that can be applied to text frames including multiple columns, inset spacing (margins), vertical justification, and a custom baseline grid. To apply any one of these attributes to a selected text frame, choose Object > Text Frame Options (**Figure 11.10**).

■ **Tip:** Hold Alt (Windows) or Option (Mac OS) and double-click a text frame with the Selection tool to quickly access the Text Frame Options dialog.

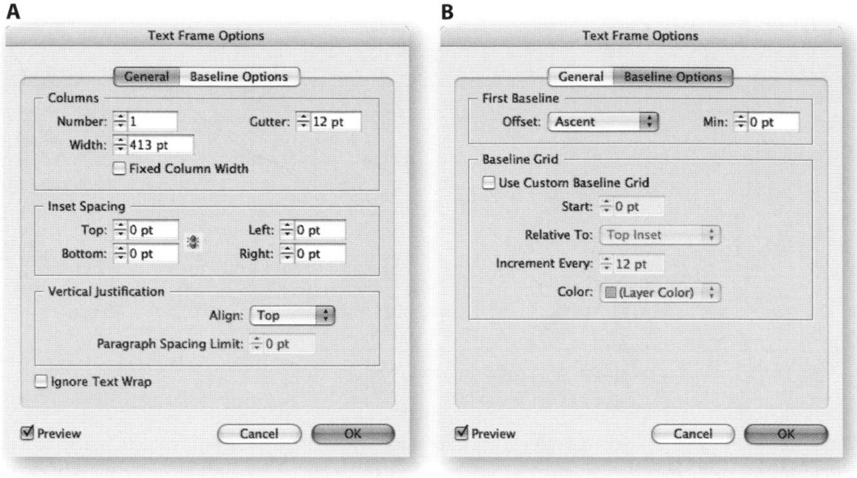
A
Text Frame Options
General
Baseline Options
Columns
Number: 1
Gutter: 12 pt
Width: 413 pt
Fixed Column Width
Inset Spacing
Top: 0 pt
Left: 0 pt
Bottom: 0 pt
Right: 0 pt
Vertical Justification
Align: Top
Paragraph Spacing Limit: 0 pt
Ignore Text Wrap
Preview
Cancel
OK
B
Text Frame Options
General
Baseline Options
First Baseline
Offset: Ascent
Min: 0 pt
Baseline Grid
Use Custom Baseline Grid
Start: 0 pt
Relative To: Top Inset
Increment Every: 12 pt
Color: (Layer Color)
Preview
Cancel
OK

Figure 11.10 The General area (**A**) and the Baseline Options area (**B**) of the Text Frame Options dialog. Select Preview at the bottom to see the results of the specified settings before clicking OK.

Here's a look at each option and some of the benefits of each:

- **Columns.** Specify the number of columns, the gutter space between each column, and the desired width of each column. By adding columns to a specific text frame, you can break away from the boundaries imposed by the layout grid on the page. For detailed information on working with columns, see the "Columns" section in Chapter 7, "Setting Up the Framework of a Template."
- **Inset Spacing.** Specify the desired offset distance for the top, left, bottom, and right sides of a text frame. The need for an inset value might not be apparent until you apply a stroke or fill to the frame and realize that the text is touching the frame's edges (**Figure 11.11**). If the frame you're adding inset spacing to has a nonrectangular shape or a corner effect applied to it, only the Inset option is available. All the other fields become unavailable.

■ **Tip:** When you select a text frame with the Selection tool, the right side of the Control panel displays options for changing the number of columns in the frame and for specifying the different vertical alignment methods.

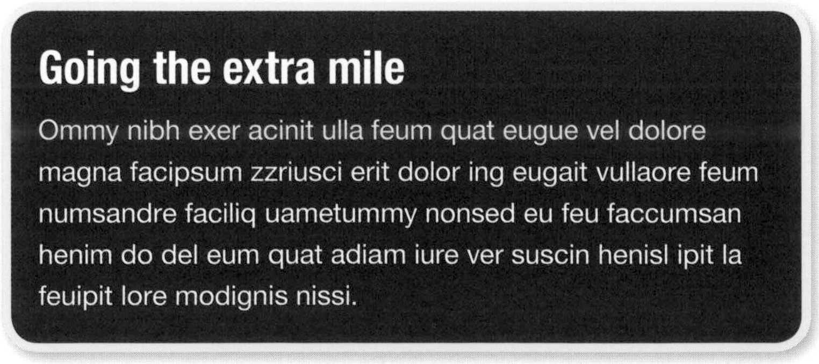
Going the extra mile
Ommy nibh exer acinit ulla feum quat eugue vel dolore magna facipsum zzriusci erit dolor ing eugait vullaore feum numsandre faciliq uametummy nonsed eu feu faccumsan henim do del eum quat adiam iure ver suscin henisl ipit la feuipit lore modignis nissi.

Figure 11.11 Instead of using two separate frames to create this design element, it's more productive to use one frame with inset spacing to keep the text from touching the frame's edges.

- **Vertical Justification.** Choose an option from the Align menu to vertically align text to the top, center, or bottom of a text frame. These alignment options come in very handy in many situations. For instance, to quickly position the last line of type in a frame along a guide, snap the base of the frame to the guide and then bottom align the text to the frame. In addition, by vertically centering text that is also horizontally centered, you can position the text right at the midpoint of a frame (**Figure 11.12**). Keep in mind that you cannot vertically align text within a frame that has a non-rectangular shape.

ESSENTIAL MINERALS
24

Figure 11.12 The page number at the bottom of this layout is both horizontally and vertically centered within one frame. The section heading is aligned to the bottom of its frame, which is snapped to a ruler guide.

Another option available in the Align menu is Justify, which allows you to fill a frame from top to bottom with text regardless of the leading value being used (**Figure 11.13**). The lines of text are also evenly distributed. To expand the space between paragraphs, specify a Paragraph Spacing Limit value. Avoid vertically justifying multicolumn text frames. When the last column contains just a few lines of text, too much space appears between each line.

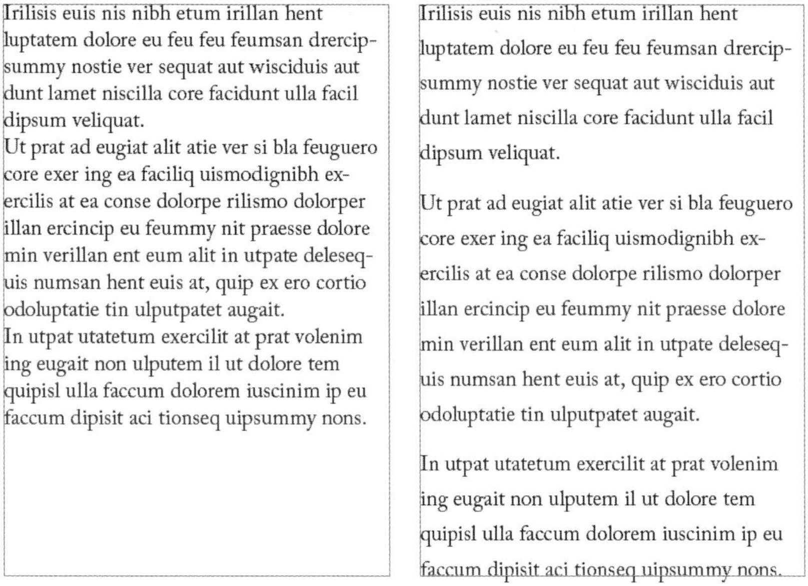
Irilisis euis nis nibh etum irillan hent luptatem dolore eu feu feu feumsan drercipsummy nostie ver sequat aut wisciduis aut dunt lamet niscilla core facidunt ulla facil dipsum veliquat.
Ut prat ad eugiat alit atie ver si bla feuguero core exer ing ea faciliq uismodignibh exercilis at ea conse dolorpe rilismo dolorper illan ercincip eu feummy nit praesse dolore min verillan ent eum alit in utpate delesequis numsan hent euis at, quip ex ero cortio odoluptatie tin ulputpatet augait.
In utpat utatetum exercilit at prat volenim ing eugait non ulputem il ut dolore tem quipisl ulla faccum dolorem iuscinim ip eu faccum dipisit aci tionseq uipsummy nons.
Irilisis euis nis nibh etum irillan hent luptatem dolore eu feu feu feumsan drercipsummy nostie ver sequat aut wisciduis aut dunt lamet niscilla core facidunt ulla facil dipsum veliquat.
Ut prat ad eugiat alit atie ver si bla feuguero core exer ing ea faciliq uismodignibh exercilis at ea conse dolorpe rilismo dolorper illan ercincip eu feummy nit praesse dolore min verillan ent eum alit in utpate delesequis numsan hent euis at, quip ex ero cortio odoluptatie tin ulputpatet augait.
In utpat utatetum exercilit at prat volenim ing eugait non ulputem il ut dolore tem quipisl ulla faccum dolorem iuscinim ip eu faccum dipisit aci tionseq uipsummy nons.

Figure 11.13 On the left, the text is top aligned. On the right, the same text is vertically justified and a Paragraph Spacing Limit value has been applied.

● **Note:** Vertically justified text cannot wrap around objects. When you place an object with a text wrap above vertically justified text, the text becomes aligned to the top of the frame, unless the Ignore Text Wrap option in the Text Frame Options dialog is selected.

- **Ignore Text Wrap.** Select this option when you want to prevent a text wrap from affecting the text in a specific frame. It's especially useful to apply this option to certain placeholder text frames on a master page, such as folios, headings, and anything else that you don't want to be affected by a text wrap.

■ **Tip:** When vertically centering a single line of text within a frame, it might not appear perfectly centered until you choose either Cap Height or X Height from the Offset menu.

- **First Baseline.** Select one of the options in the Offset menu to determine where the first line of text starts in relation to the top of the text frame (**Figure 11.14**):
  - **Ascent.** Positions the height of the ascent character in the font to the top of the frame.
  - **Cap Height.** Aligns the top of the uppercase letters to the top of the frame.
  - **Leading.** Uses the text's leading value as the distance between the baseline of the text and the top of the frame.
  - **X Height.** Aligns the tops of the main body of lowercase letters (more or less the height of the lowercase letter x) to the top of the frame.
  - **Fixed.** Allows you to specify a custom distance between the baseline of the text and the top of the frame.
  - **Min.** Enter a value into the Min field to increase the distance. Positive values move the text downward.

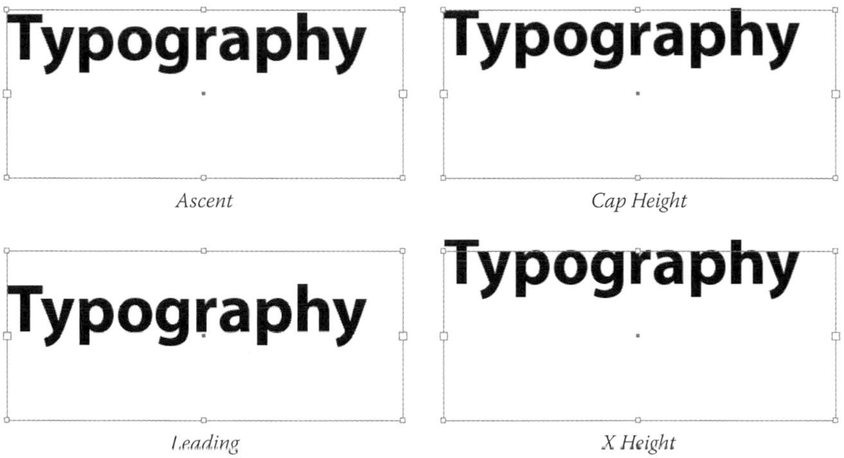
Typography
Ascent
Typography
Cap Height
Typography
Leading
Typography
X Height

Figure 11.14 The different Offset options in use. The Fixed option isn't shown.

If inset spacing is applied to the top of the frame, the first line of text is measured from the top inset. When text is bottom aligned, the baseline of the last line of text is always aligned to the bottom of the frame regardless of the option that is specified in the Offset menu.

- **Baseline Grid.** This section of the Text Frame Options dialog allows you to set up a baseline grid within a frame that functions independently from the document baseline grid. Each text frame can potentially have its own baseline grid. For a detailed description of each setting, see the "Baseline Grid" section in Chapter 7.

■ **Tip:** Optical Margin Alignment is applied at the story level, which means that all the text within the story is affected by it. To turn off Optical Margin Alignment for individual paragraphs, choose Ignore Optical Margin from the Paragraph or Control panel menu.

Optical Margin Alignment

When text is left aligned or right aligned, the edges of a column might still appear misaligned due to punctuation marks and the shape of certain letters such as "W" and "A." To fix this, InDesign provides Optical Margin Alignment, which causes certain punctuation marks (such as quotation marks, commas, periods, and dashes) and the edges of offending letters to hang slightly outside the text frame to create a smoother looking edge—also known as hanging punctuation (**Figure 11.15**).

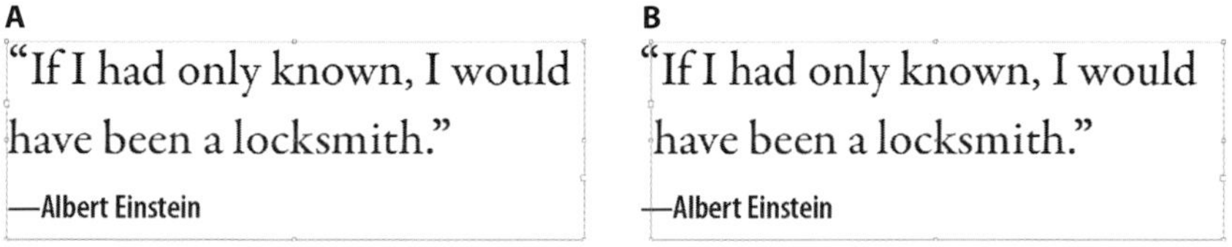
A
"If I had only known, I would have been a locksmith."
—Albert Einstein
B
"If I had only known, I would have been a locksmith."
—Albert Einstein

Figure 11.15 Before (**A**) and after (**B**) applying Optical Margin Alignment.

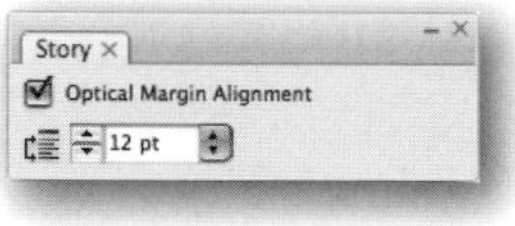
Story
Optical Margin Alignment
12 pt

Figure 11.16
Interestingly, the Story panel is the only panel in InDesign with one feature.

To turn on Optical Margin Alignment, select a text frame, choose Type > Story, and then select the option in the Story panel (**Figure 11.16**). Specify a font size to determine the desired amount of overhang. Depending on the size of the text, you'll want to use different values. For a good start, use the same size as the text and then make modifications as necessary. Use this special effect in moderation. It's great for pull quotes, but it's generally not a good idea to use it for body text.

Wrapping Text Around Objects

InDesign's Text Wrap feature is quite versatile and provides a number of ways to wrap text around any object, including text frames and imported images. The various controls for creating and controlling text wraps are found in the Text Wrap panel (**Figure 11.17**).

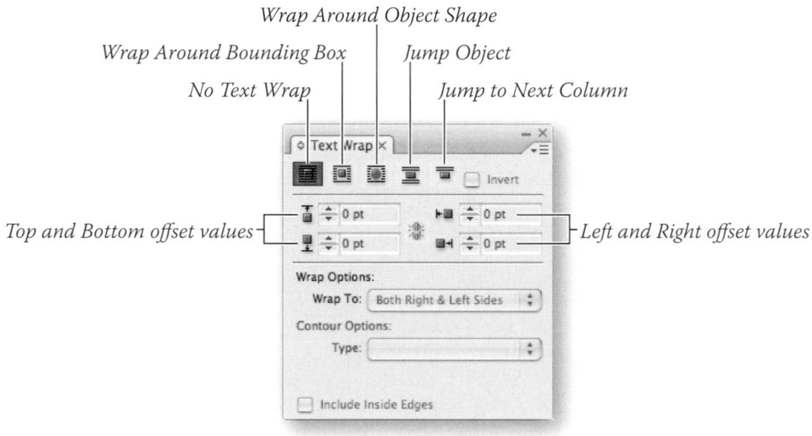
Wrap Around Object Shape
Wrap Around Bounding Box
Jump Object
No Text Wrap
Jump to Next Column
Text Wrap
Invert
Top and Bottom offset values
0 pt
0 pt
0 pt
0 pt
Left and Right offset values
Wrap Options:
Wrap To:
Both Right & Left Sides
Contour Options:
Type:
Include Inside Edges

Figure 11.17 The various settings in the Text Wrap panel aren't available until you activate a wrap option.

To apply a text wrap to an object, select it and choose the desired wrap option. InDesign creates a non-printing boundary around the object, which repels surrounding text (**Figure 11.18**). To adjust the distance between the object and the text, specify offset values. Positive values move the text away from the frame and negative values allow the text to move within the frame.

With images, you can apply a text wrap to either the container frame (using the Selection tool) or the content (using the Direct Selection tool). It's useful to apply the text wrap to the content when it doesn't fill the entire space available in its container frame.

Figure 11.18 The text wrap boundary is visible when the frame is selected.

Here's a look at each wrap option in detail:

- **Wrap Around Bounding Box.** This option creates a wrap that conforms to the width and height of the selected object's bounding box.
- **Wrap Around Object Shape.** This option generates a text wrap boundary that follows the contour of the object's shape within its bounding box (**Figure 11.19**). If the object is an imported image, the contour options in the Text Wrap panel become available, providing you with additional choices (**Figure 11.20**).

Merging Words with Shapes and Images
Forming Ideas Into Solutions | 49

Figure 11.19 You can wrap text around imported images and shapes that you draw in InDesign.

Text Wrap
Invert
0 pt
10 pt
10 pt
10 pt
Wrap Options:
Wrap To:
Contour Opt
Type:
Path:
Include
Bounding Box
Detect Edges
Alpha Channel
✓ Photoshop Path
Graphic Frame
Same as Clipping
User-Modified Path

Figure 11.20 The Type menu in the Text Wrap panel. Notice that when wrapping text around an object's shape, only one offset value is available.

● **Note:** When using Photoshop Path, Alpha Channel, or the Detect Edges option to generate a text wrap around an object's shape, you might have to move the image below the text for it to properly wrap around the shape. If you're importing a native Photoshop image (.psd) that has a transparent background, the image can be above or below the text. However, to prevent the text from interacting with the transparency in unexpected ways when the file is printed, keep the image below the text.

Choose the option that makes the most sense for the image you've imported. If the image has a clipping path applied to it, you might choose Same as Clipping. If the image contains one or more Photoshop paths, you might choose the Photoshop Path option. The Path menu appears, letting you select the path you want to use for generating the text wrap. And if the image contains one or more alpha channels, you might choose Alpha Channel. The Alpha menu appears from which you can then select the alpha channel you want to use for generating the text wrap.

If the image doesn't contain a Photoshop path or alpha channel, you might choose Detect Edges. In that case, InDesign generates the text wrap using automatic edge detection. If your image contains large open white spaces (such as the hole in the handle of a coffee mug), select Include Inside Edges at the bottom of the panel to allow the text to appear within the white space. You can also do this when using the Alpha Channel option.

The Bounding Box option creates a text wrap around the bounding box of the image within the container frame. The Graphic Frame option creates the text wrap around the container frame, but applies it to the content, so you'll have to select the content with the Direct Selection tool to see and edit the text wrap boundary.

- **Jump Object.** This keeps surrounding text away from the left and right sides of the object, forcing text to jump over it. In multiple column layouts, the text wrap only affects the columns that the object is within.
- **Jump to Next Column.** This forces surrounding text to jump over the object and start over at the top of the next column or text frame.
- **Invert.** Select this option to invert the text wrap boundary so that text can fill the inside of the wrap object (**Figure 11.21**). You can create some nice effects by applying Invert to images that use the Wrap Around Object Shape option.

Na consed exerostie feugait, core feummolore dionullum del ing euissed te dunt dignim dignim inibh el eliquiscipis dolor suscipit alismod modolore mo-diam, sed minim esent nulput iliquat praesto odolore eu faccummy nim etum ex
eugait luptatie vullum
iril in ullam nulput eliquisim
dolor alisit nos digna aut amet ute
eum adipsustie ver ipsustrud tie magna
faccum incillu ptatio erostisim exer iuscinci
bla feuguer ostrud magna feu faciliquis dolor sum vullan et autat.lobore magna feuisi ex
elesed magna adiate tismoloreet num volenis el
diamet nos endigna cortion sequatisl dignim
zzrit velendipisit lametuerit doluptatem
iusciduipit eui enim dipiscil ulput prat
at at. Duiscilit atis et, si blaore eu
feummy nisim verillum vel
eniat, venibh euip
euisciduis num vel ex eugue et luptat ipisiscil del illuptat alit dolore mincidu iscidunt nulput lor iusciduip enim iliquiscil ullaorem del iustismolor autpatum velessectem incipsuscil el ulla ad do consecte minis aut ut amet la autat. Nonsed modolutpat duis nis dolobor ipisim ate corem et am vel iniamet vercillaor irilit iurem volor in ut accum dolor adignibh el ut ing eniat. Ut non eum ing euguer adion hendre ver autat doloreet lut exer senit, quipit nis nos euisl.

Figure 11.21 This circle has no fill or stroke and the text wrap is inverted to create this effect. Try experimenting with a variety of shapes to add some flavor to your publications.

CUSTOMIZING A TEXT WRAP

It's sometimes necessary to customize the shape of an object's text wrap boundary. By doing so, you can control exactly where the text wraps around the object (**Figure 11.22**). To edit a text wrap, select the object with the Direct Selection tool. The text wrap boundary becomes visible and behaves just like a regular path. Select and modify individual anchor points and direction points, or even use the Pen tool to add and delete anchor points. After editing a text wrap, you can no longer enter an offset value and the User-Modified Path contour option is automatically selected. To revert back to the original path, select the original contour option.

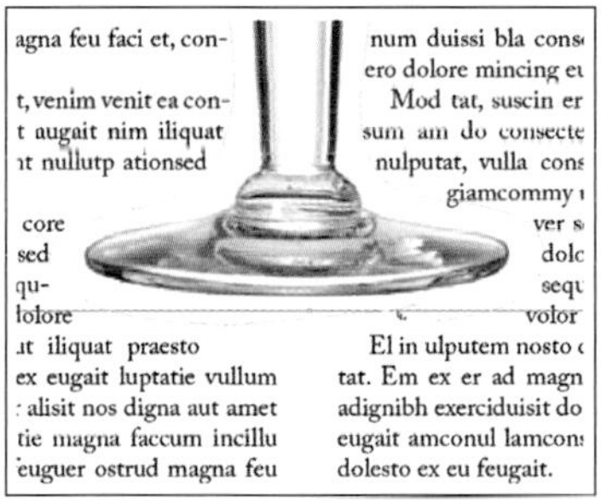
agna feu faci et, con-
t, venim venit ea con-
t augait nim iliquat
nt nullutp ationsed
core
sed
qu-
lolore
num duissi bla cons
ero dolore mincing et
Mod tat, suscin er
sum am do consecte
nulputat, vulla cons
giamcommy
ver s
dolc
sequ
volor
at iliquat praesto
ex eugait luptatie vullum
alisit nos digna aut amet
tie magna faccum incillu
euguer ostrud magna feu
El in ulputem nosto
tat. Em ex er ad magn
adignibh exerciduisit do
eugait amconul lamcon
dolesto ex eu feugait.

Figure 11.22 The text wrap boundary at the bottom of this martini glass was edited to improve the wrap in the paragraph below it.

SPECIFYING THE WRAP OPTIONS

Several options are available in the Wrap To menu that allow you to control which side of an object the text wraps to (**Figure 11.23**). By default, InDesign wraps text around both the right and left sides of an object. But you can also wrap it to just the left side or the right side. When working with facing pages, you might choose to wrap text to the side of the object that faces the spine or to wrap text to the side that faces away from the spine. You can then move the object between pages, and the text wrap is smart enough to change the wrap direction, depending on which side of the spine it's on.

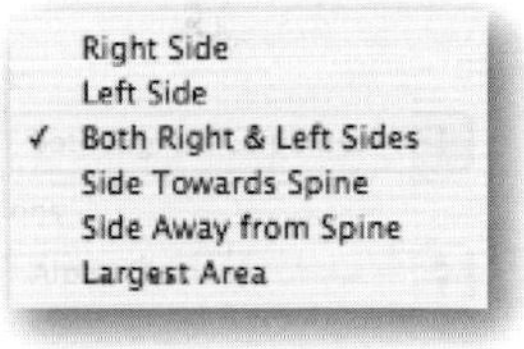
Right Side
Left Side
✓ Both Right & Left Sides
Side Towards Spine
Side Away from Spine
Largest Area

Figure 11.23 The Wrap To menu in the Text Wrap panel.

CONTROLLING TEXT WRAP ON MASTER PAGE ITEMS

After applying a text wrap to a master page item, you can choose whether the text wrap affects only the text on the master page or if it affects text on both master pages and document pages. To switch between these two behaviors, select a master page item and then select or deselect Apply to Master Page Only from the Text Wrap panel menu. If selected, you must override the master page item on a document page to wrap text around it.

● **Note:** The wrap options are only available if you've selected Wrap Around Bounding Box or Wrap Around Object Shape.

SETTING THE TEXT WRAP PREFERENCES

You should be aware of three text wrap preferences because they have a significant affect on all the text-wrapped objects in a document (**Figure 11.24**). To enable or disable a preference, choose Edit > Preferences > Composition (Windows) or InDesign > Preferences > Composition (Mac OS). Here's a short description of each option:

- **Justify Text Next to an Object.** Selecting this option forces text to become justified next to wrap objects that are surrounded by left or right aligned text. So when a wrap object is placed in a column of text, the text is always aligned on both the left and right sides of the object.
- **Skip By Leading.** This option is selected by default. It ensures that wrapped text moves to the next available leading increment as the wrap object pushes the text downward. With this option deselected, the lines of text might not be able to line up across multiple columns.
- **Text Wrap Only Affects Text Beneath.** With this option selected, text that is stacked above a wrap object isn't affected by the text wrap. When it's deselected, you can place wrap objects above or below text, and the text wrap will still affect the surrounding text.

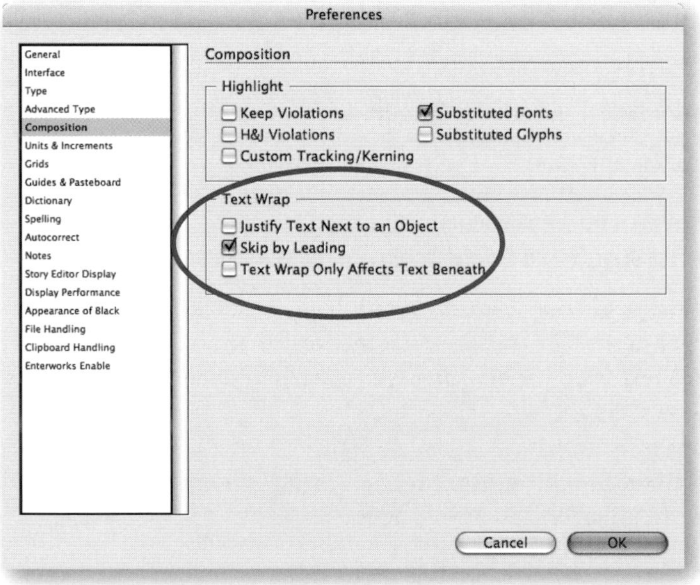
Preferences
General
Interface
Type
Advanced Type
Composition
Units & Increments
Grids
Guides & Pasteboard
Dictionary
Spelling
Autocorrect
Notes
Story Editor Display
Display Performance
Appearance of Black
File Handling
Clipboard Handling
Enterworks Enable
Composition
Highlight
Keep Violations
H&J Violations
Custom Tracking/Kerning
Substituted Fonts
Substituted Glyphs
Text Wrap
Justify Text Next to an Object
Skip by Leading
Text Wrap Only Affects Text Beneath
Cancel
OK

Figure 11.24 The Text Wrap preferences are saved in your template and affect all future documents based on it, so make sure to specify the appropriate settings, depending on the publication's design requirements.

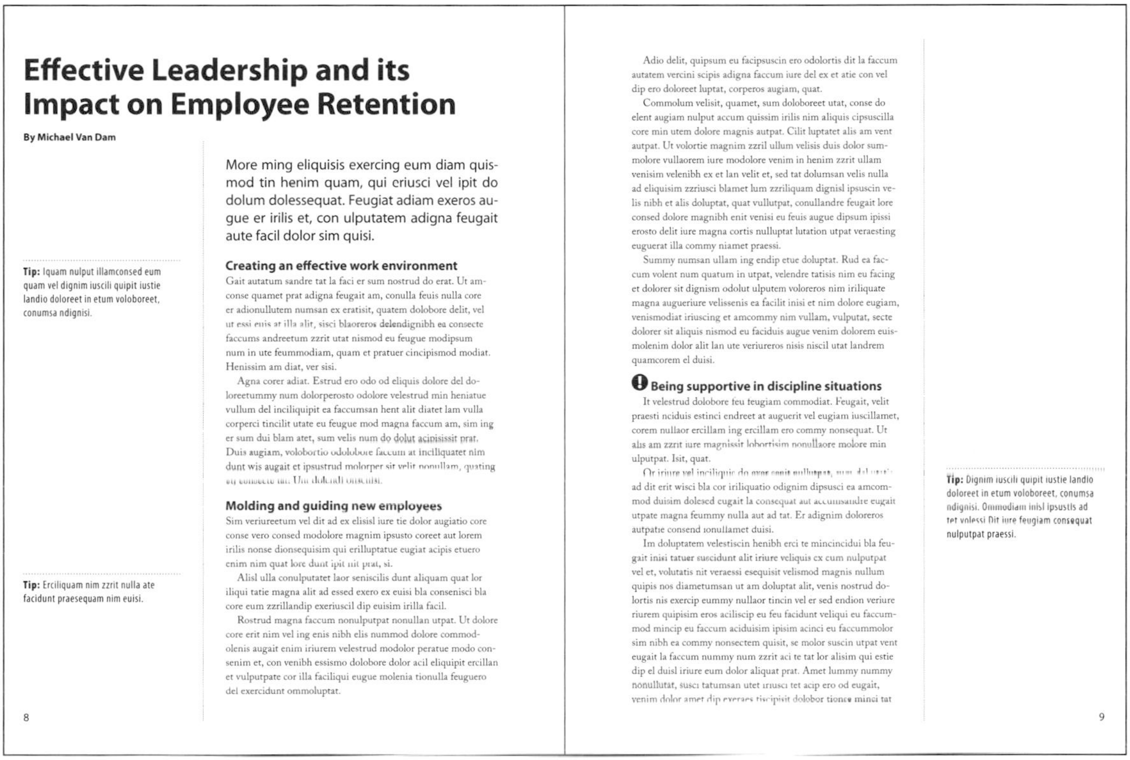
Effective Leadership and its Impact on Employee Retention
By Michael Van Dam
More ming eliquisis exercing eum diam quismod tin henim quam, qui eriusci vel ipit do dolum dolessequat. Feugiat adiam exeros augue er irilis et, con ulputatem adigna feugait aute facil dolor sim quisi.
Tip: Iquam nulput illamconsed eum quam vel dignim iuscili quipit iustie landio doloreet in etum voloboreet, conumsa ndignisi.
Creating an effective work environment
Molding and guiding new employees
Tip: Erciliquam nim zzrit nulla ate facidunt praesequam nim euisi.
Being supportive in discipline situations
Tip: Dignim iuscili quipit iustie landio doloreet in etum voloboreet, conumsa ndignisi. Ommodiam inisl ipsustis ad tet volessi Dit iure feugiam consequat nulputpat praessi.
8
9

Figure 11.25 The exclamation point icon and all the sidebar elements in this journal are anchored to specific text. If the text reflows, the designer won't have to go back and reposition every sidebar element, because they'll flow right along, even when the text moves to another page.

Working with Anchored Objects

While the primary purpose of a text frame is to contain text, it can also contain objects such as graphics frames and other text frames. When you insert an object into a text frame, it is *anchored* to specific text, so if the text in the document reflows, the anchored object travels with the text it's attached to. If the publication you're designing a template for uses sidebars, figures, captions, icons, or any other design element that must flow with specific text, you'll definitely want to utilize the power of anchored objects (**Figure 11.25**).

You can create an anchored object in two ways:

- **Anchor an existing object.** Select an object, cut or copy it, and then position your cursor within the text where you want the object to appear. Then paste the object into the frame. By default the anchored object's position

■ **Tip:** You can anchor an image directly into a text frame as you import it by placing your cursor into the text and then placing the image.

is inline, which means the object is placed in sequence with the other characters. You can drag the object up or down with the Selection tool, but you cannot drag it left or right. If necessary, you can also reposition the object above the line of text to which it is anchored, or you can completely customize its position—which is discussed in the next section.

- **Insert a new empty frame.** If an element has yet to be created, you can insert an empty frame, which might become a figure or sidebar that has yet to be written. Position your cursor within the text where you want the object to appear, and then choose Object > Anchored Object > Insert. The Insert Anchored Object dialog appears from which you can specify the type of frame you want to create, as well as its size and formatting attributes (**Figure 11.26**). In addition, you can determine how the object is positioned within the text frame (see next section). After clicking OK, the anchored object is created according to your specified settings.

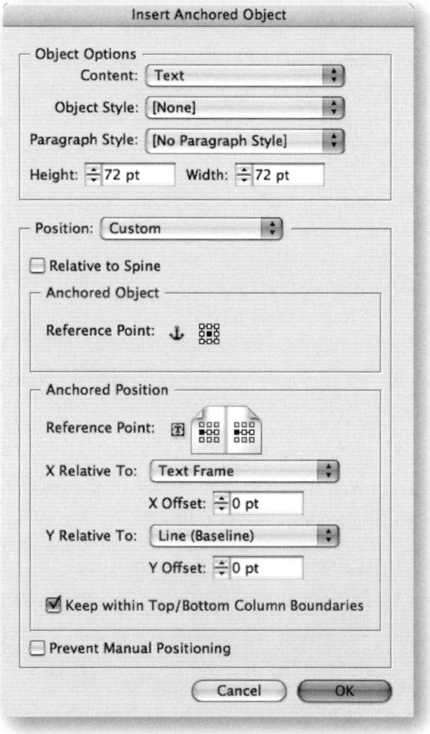
Insert Anchored Object
Object Options
Content: Text
Object Style: [None]
Paragraph Style: [No Paragraph Style]
Height: 72 pt
Width: 72 pt
Position: Custom
Relative to Spine
Anchored Object
Reference Point:
Anchored Position
Reference Point:
X Relative To: Text Frame
X Offset: 0 pt
Y Relative To: Line (Baseline)
Y Offset: 0 pt
Keep within Top/Bottom Column Boundaries
Prevent Manual Positioning
Cancel
OK

Figure 11.26 When inserting an empty frame, you can apply an object style to it and even a paragraph style if you're creating a text frame.

● **Note:** When an anchored object has a text wrap applied to it, the lines of text preceding the object are not affected by the text wrap. When using the Above Line or Custom position options, the text wrap also doesn't affect the line of text to which it is anchored.

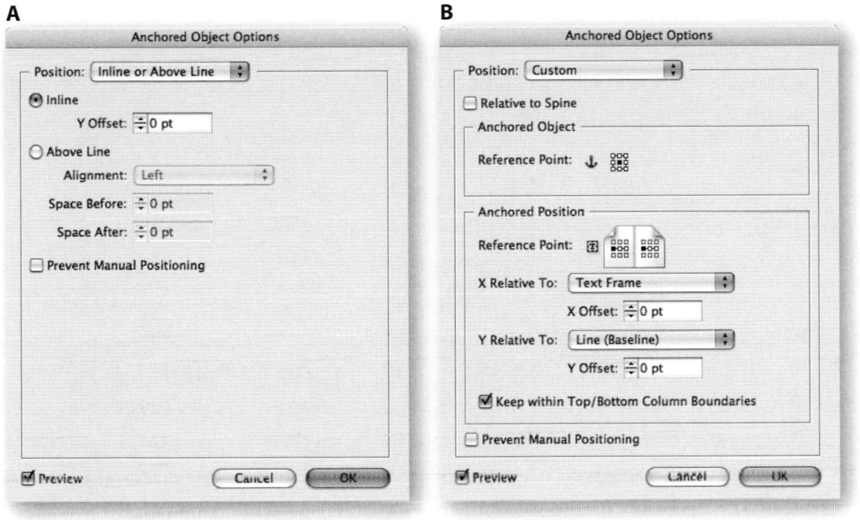
A
Anchored Object Options
Position: Inline or Above Line
Inline
Y Offset: 0 pt
Above Line
Alignment: Left
Space Before: 0 pt
Space After: 0 pt
Prevent Manual Positioning
Preview
Cancel
OK
B
Anchored Object Options
Position: Custom
Relative to Spine
Anchored Object
Reference Point:
Anchored Position
Reference Point:
X Relative To: Text Frame
X Offset: 0 pt
Y Relative To: Line (Baseline)
Y Offset: 0 pt
Keep within Top/Bottom Column Boundaries
Prevent Manual Positioning
Preview
Cancel
OK

Figure 11.27 The Anchored Object Options dialog is divided into two sections: Inline or Above Line (**A**) and Custom (**B**). Choose an option from the Position menu to switch between both sections. Click Preview at the bottom to see the results before clicking OK.

POSITIONING ANCHORED OBJECTS

You can position an anchored object in three ways: inline, above line, or custom. When inserting a new empty frame, you can specify its position attributes in the Insert Anchored Object dialog (Figure 11.26). To edit the position of an existing anchored object, select it with the Selection tool, choose Object > Anchored Object > Options, and then specify the following options as necessary (**Figure 11.27**):

- **Inline.** This option aligns the bottom of the anchored object with the baseline of the text to which it is attached (**Figure 11.28**). Specify a Y Offset value to move the object up or down. Positive values move the object above the baseline, and negative values move it below the baseline. The bottom of the object can't be moved above the top of the leading height, and the top of the object can't be moved below the baseline. To relocate the object within the body of text, you'll have to select it with the Text tool and then cut and paste it. To overcome these constraints, choose Custom from the Position menu.
- **Above Line.** This option places the anchored object above the line of text to which it is attached (**Figure 11.29**). If necessary, select one of the following alignment options from the Alignment menu: Left, Center, Right, Away From Spine, Towards Spine, or (Text Alignment). All of these options, except (Text Alignment), align the object within the entire column, ignoring any indent values applied to the paragraph. Type values into the Space Before and/or Space After fields to adjust the space between the object and the text above and below it.

■ **Tip:** When using the Inline position method, the anchored object can run into text above or below it. To fix this problem, you might add space above the paragraph that contains the inline object, specify a larger leading value, or resize the object.

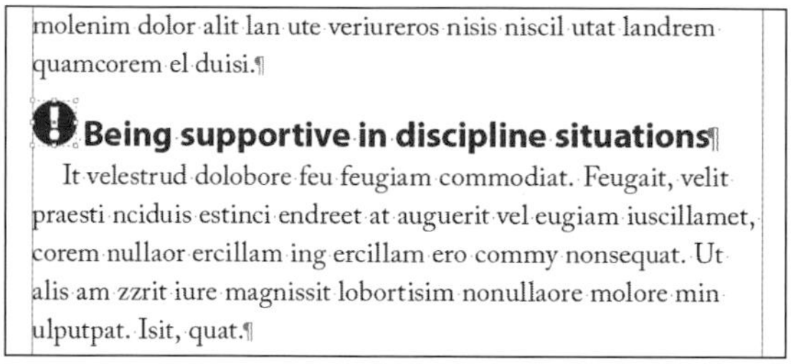
molenim dolor alit lan ute veriureros nisis niscil utat landrem quamcorem el duisi.¶
Being supportive in discipline situations¶
It velestrud dolobore feu feugiam commodiat. Feugait, velit praesti nciduis estinci endreet at auguerit vel eugiam iuscillamet, corem nullaor ercillam ing ercillam ero commy nonsequat. Ut alis am zzrit iure magnissit lobortisim nonullaore molore min ulputpat. Isit, quat.¶

Figure 11.28 This anchored icon is using the Inline position option.

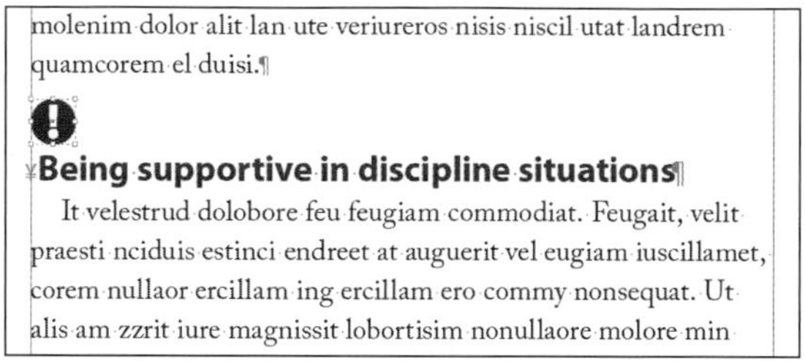
molenim dolor alit lan ute veriureros nisis niscil utat landrem quamcorem el duisi.¶
Being supportive in discipline situations¶
It velestrud dolobore feu feugiam commodiat. Feugait, velit praesti nciduis estinci endreet at auguerit vel eugiam iuscillamet, corem nullaor ercillam ing ercillam ero commy nonsequat. Ut alis am zzrit iure magnissit lobortisim nonullaore molore min

Figure 11.29 This anchored icon is using the Above Line position option.

- **Custom.** If the preceding options don't satisfy your design requirements, you can choose the Custom option so that you can freely position an anchored object anywhere on the page or spread. When you customize the position of an anchored object, InDesign places an anchor symbol ⚓ on the anchored object and an anchor marker ¥ at the point within the text where the object is anchored. In addition, a dashed line can appear between the anchor marker and its associated anchored object. These markers allow you to easily identify the point at which the object is anchored (**Figure 11.30**).

Coming up next is a detailed description of all the options you can specify to customize an anchored object's position.

■ **Tip:** You can cut and paste the anchor marker to attach the anchored object to another position within the text. Be careful not to accidentally delete the anchor marker while editing text, or the anchored object will be deleted.

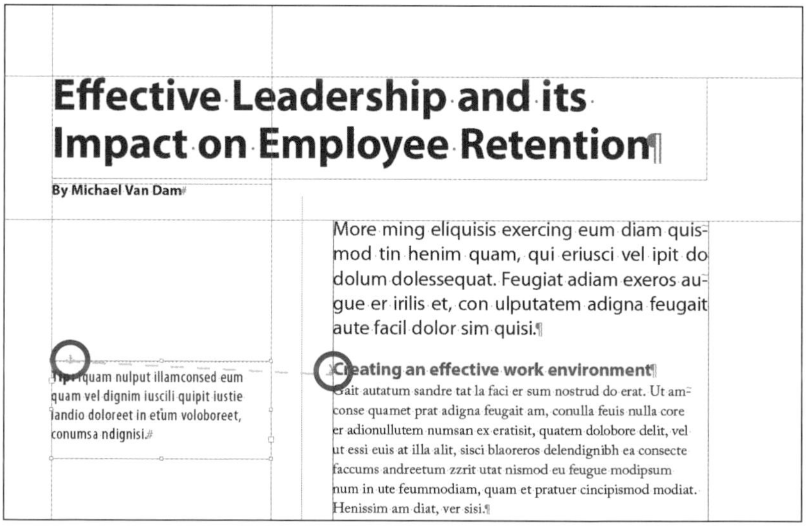
Effective Leadership and its Impact on Employee Retention¶
By Michael Van Dam
More ming eliquisis exercing eum diam quismod tin henim quam, qui eriusci vel ipit do dolum dolessequat. Feugiat adiam exeros augue er irilis et, con ulputatem adigna feugait aute facil dolor sim quisi.¶
quam nulput illamconsed eum quam vel dignim iuscili quipit iustie iandio doloreet in etum voloboreet, conumsa ndignisi.
eating an effective work environment¶
ait autatum sandre tat la faci er sum nostrud do erat. Ut amconse quamet prat adigna feugait am, conulla feuis nulla core er adionullutem numsan ex eratisit, quatem dolobore delit, vel ut essi euis at illa alit, sisci blaoreros delendignibh ea consecte faccums andreetum zzrit utat nismod eu feugue modipsum num in ute feummodiam, quam et pratuer cincipismod modiat. Henissim am diat, ver sisi.¶

Figure 11.30 To view the anchor markers, choose Type > Show Hidden Characters. To view anchor symbols, choose View > Show Frame Edges. To view a dashed line from an anchor marker to its associated anchored object, select the object and choose View > Show Text Threads.

CUSTOMIZING THE POSITION OF ANCHORED OBJECTS

The Custom section of the Anchored Object Options dialog contains four main options: Relative to Spine, Anchored Object, Anchored Position, and Prevent Manual Positioning (Figure 11.27). These options work together to specify an anchored object's location. At first you might find them a bit confusing, but with a little experimentation you'll soon understand how they all work.

● **Note:** As you gain more experience in customizing the position of anchored objects you'll realize that you can specify the options in any order necessary to achieve the desired results.

Anchored Object. Start with the Anchored Object option. Click a point on the reference point locator to specify the location on the anchored object that you want aligned to the location on the page (as specified by the Anchored Position reference point). So, if you want to align the left side of the object with a page item, such as the margin guide, click one of the leftmost reference points.

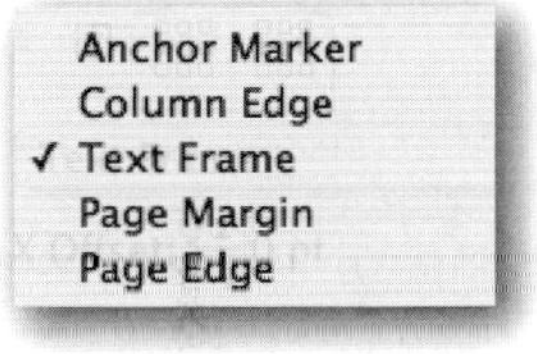
Anchor Marker
Column Edge
✓ Text Frame
Page Margin
Page Edge

Figure 11.31 The X Relative To menu.

Anchored Position. Next, specify the various Anchored Position options. Click a point on the reference point locator to specify the location on the page to which you want the anchored object aligned. The page location is defined by the combination of the X and Y Relative To options:

- **X Relative To.** The option you select in the X Relative To menu determines which page item you want to use as the basis for horizontal alignment (**Figure 11.31**). So if Text Frame is selected, the anchored object can align to the left, center, or right side of the text frame. In the X Offset field, specify a value to move the object left or right. The exact point at which the object aligns horizontally depends on the selected reference points and the specified X Offset value.

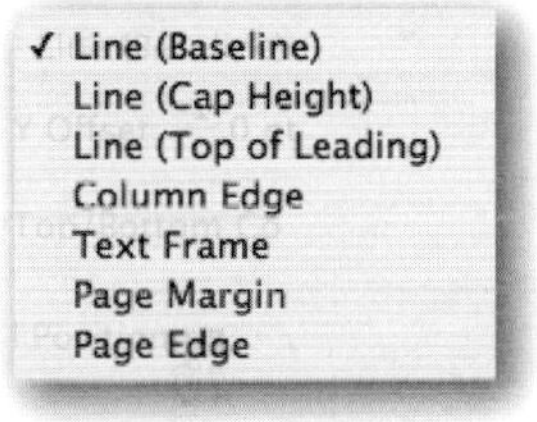
✓ Line (Baseline)
Line (Cap Height)
Line (Top of Leading)
Column Edge
Text Frame
Page Margin
Page Edge

Figure 11.32 The Y Relative To menu.

- **Y Relative To.** The option you select in the Y Relative To menu determines what the anchored object vertically aligns with (**Figure 11.32**). So if Line (Baseline) is selected, the top, center, or bottom of the object can be aligned to the baseline of the text to which it is anchored. Similarly, if Column Edge is selected, the object can be aligned to the top, center, or bottom of the column. In the Y Offset field, specify a value to move the object up or down. Positive values move the object downward. The exact point at which the object aligns vertically depends on the selected reference points and the specified Y Offset value.

● **Note:** Depending on which option is selected in the Y Relative To menu, the Anchored Position reference point locator displays either three or nine available points. The line options provide only three points to choose from (middle left, center, and middle right), because the vertical position of the anchored object is established by where it is located in the text.

- **Keep within Top/Bottom Column Boundaries.** Select this option to keep the anchored object inside of the text frame when one of the line options, such as Line (Baseline), is selected in the Y Relative To menu. So if text reflows, the anchored object won't go past the boundaries of the frame.

Relative to Spine. Select this option at the top of the dialog to align an anchored object relative to the document spine. For instance, if the object on the left-facing page is positioned on the outside margin, it will remain on the outside margin if the text reflows to the right-facing page. With this option selected, the Anchored Object reference point locator displays as a two page spread, with both pages mirroring each other (**Figure 11.33**). For long documents with a lot of sidebar elements—such as the one displayed in Figure 11.25—it's essential that you select Relative to Spine.

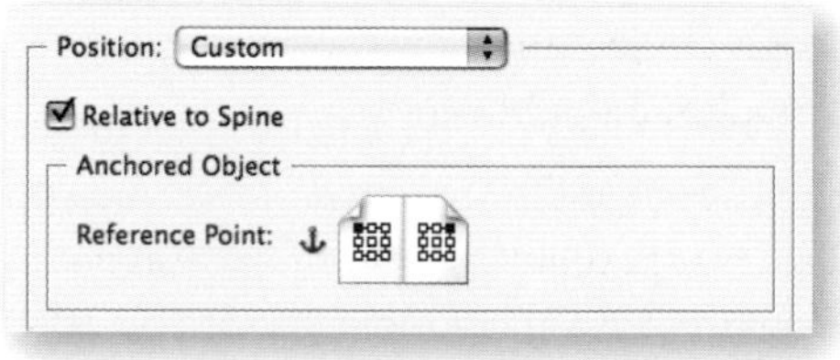
Position: Custom
Relative to Spine
Anchored Object
Reference Point:

Figure 11.33 With the top-left reference point selected on the left-page icon, the top-right reference point on the right-page icon is automatically selected. The anchored object will then always appear in the outside margin regardless of what side of the spread it's on.

Prevent Manual Positioning. This option locks the anchored object so you can't accidentally drag or nudge it on the page. You can unlock its position without opening the Anchored Object Options dialog by choosing Object > Unlock Position. To relock it, choose Object > Lock Position.

● **Note:** The Prevent Manual Positioning option is available in both the Inline or Above Line and Custom sections of the Anchored Object Options dialog.

Here are a few tips for working with custom positioned anchored objects:

- After specifying the settings in the Anchored Object Options dialog, you can manually drag the object to set the X and Y Offset values. This method is often easier than typing values in the dialog.
- Select one of the line options in the Y Relative To menu to keep an object aligned with a specific line of text. Then the object will stay with that text if it reflows.
- If you don't want the object to move with a specific line of text, choose any option (other than a line option) in the Y Relative To menu. If the text to which the object is anchored reflows to another page, the object moves to the same relative position on the next page.
- The Custom position settings can be combined in a multitude of ways to achieve different results. You don't want to repeat the process of setting up all those options for each anchored object you create. Either incorporate the settings into an object style or save an often-used anchored object to an object library.

Frame Fitting Options

You can associate fitting options to empty placeholder frames so that when new content is placed into them, the prespecified fitting options are automatically applied. Select an empty frame and choose Object > Fitting > Frame Fitting Options to specify the range of options. See Chapter 8, "Setting Up Master Pages, Libraries, and Layers," for detailed information.

Applying Transparency Effects

InDesign CS3 provides a wealth of transparency effects that can be creatively applied to any object—even imported images. Many of the special effects you once had to create in Photoshop or Illustrator can now be created within InDesign, speeding up the time it takes to produce a publication. Best of all, you can use object styles to quickly apply frequently used transparency effects and manage their consistent use throughout a publication.

● **Note:** If you select a graphic with the Direct Selection tool, any applied transparency effects will only affect the graphic. If you select a group, any applied effects will affect all the objects and text in the group, so use the Direct Selection tool to apply effects to objects within a group.

All of the various controls for working with transparency can be found in the Effects panel—previously called the Transparency palette in InDesign CS2 (**Figure 11.34**). It lets you apply transparency effects and choose whether they are applied to an object, its stroke, its fill, or its text.

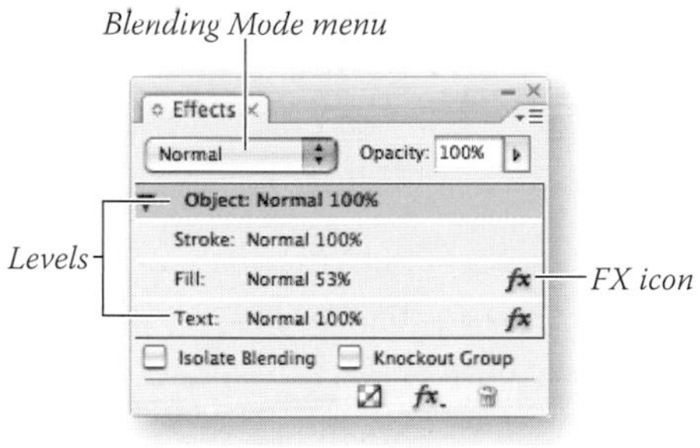
Blending Mode menu
Effects
Normal
Opacity: 100%
Object: Normal 100%
Stroke: Normal 100%
Fill: Normal 53%
Text: Normal 100%
Levels
FX icon
Isolate Blending
Knockout Group

Figure 11.34 The Effects panel. The different levels display the blending mode and Opacity settings for each part of the selected object (Object, Stroke, Fill, and Text). The FX icon appears on each level that you've applied transparency effects to, such as a drop shadow.

To apply transparency effects, select an object and click a level in the Effects panel to determine which part(s) of the object you want to change. To select multiple levels, hold Ctrl/Command as you click each level you want to include. Then apply the desired settings. A brief description of the different effects you can apply follows.

OPACITY

The most basic form of transparency that you can apply to an object is opacity. In the Effects panel, specify a value for Opacity or click the arrow next to the Opacity field and drag the slider. You can vary the value from 100% (completely opaque) to 0% (completely transparent), so as you decrease the opacity of an object, the underlying objects become visible through its surface (**Figure 11.35**).

● **Note:** You cannot apply opacity to individual text characters.

Figure 11.35 An opacity value of 50% is applied to the yellow circle, so you can see through to the blue circle behind it. The magenta circle on top is not affected by the opacity change, because transparency settings only affect the objects that are behind the transparent object.

BLENDING MODES

Blending modes allow you to control how colors in transparent objects blend with the colors of objects behind them (**Figure 11.36**). InDesign provides a list of blending modes to choose from (**Figure 11.37**). The same blending modes can be found in Photoshop and Illustrator, so if you're familiar with using them in those applications, you're already familiar with using them in InDesign. For a complete description of how each blending mode option works, choose Help > InDesign Help, and then type "specify how colors blend" into the Search field.

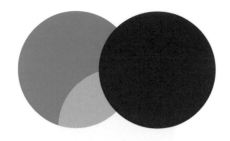

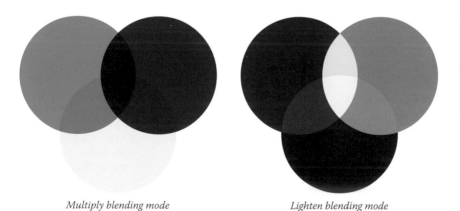

Multiply blending mode *Lighten blending mode*

Figure 11.36 By using different blending modes, these different colored circles can take on new appearances. In this example, the blending mode is applied to each circle.

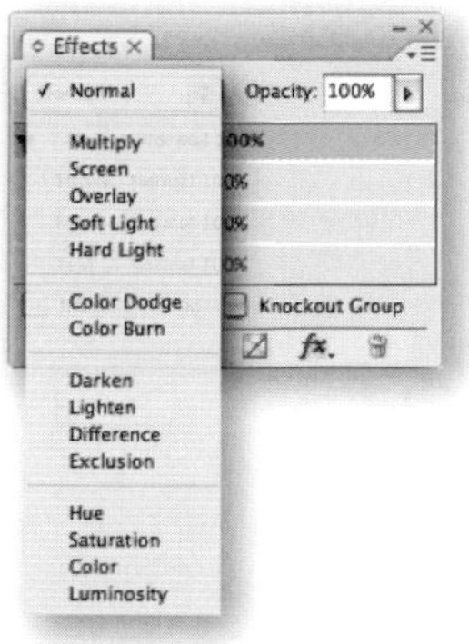
Effects
Normal
Opacity: 100%
Multiply
Screen
Overlay
Soft Light
Hard Light
Color Dodge
Color Burn
Knockout Group
Darken
Lighten
Difference
Exclusion
Hue
Saturation
Color
Luminosity

Figure 11.37 The Blending Mode menu. By default, Normal is applied to all objects.

EFFECTS

InDesign provides nine special effects that you can apply in your layouts. Click the FX button at the bottom of the Effects panel to choose an effect (**Figure 11.38**). You can also choose Object > Effects, and then choose an effect name. After selecting an effect, the Effects dialog appears. Here you can specify the various settings for that effect (**Figure 11.39**). To apply more effects to an object, select the check box next to the names of the effects you want to apply. Click the name of an effect to view and specify its settings.

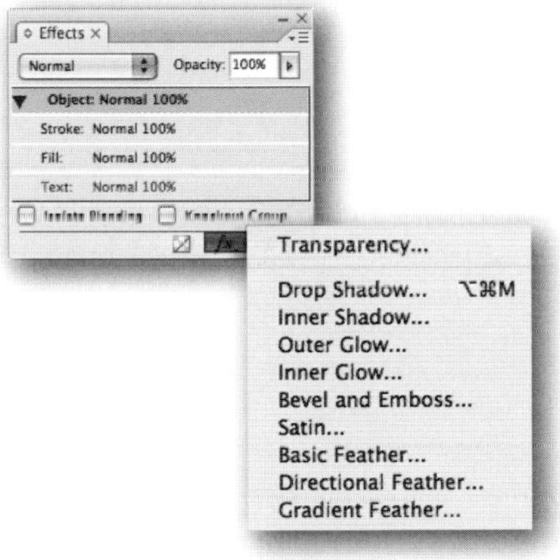
Effects
Normal
Opacity: 100%
Object: Normal 100%
Stroke: Normal 100%
Fill: Normal 100%
Text: Normal 100%
Transparency...
Drop Shadow... ⌥⌘M
Inner Shadow...
Outer Glow...
Inner Glow...
Bevel and Emboss...
Satin...
Basic Feather...
Directional Feather...
Gradient Feather...

Figure 11.38 All of the transparency effects are nondestructive, which means you can always go back and edit an effect after you've applied it.

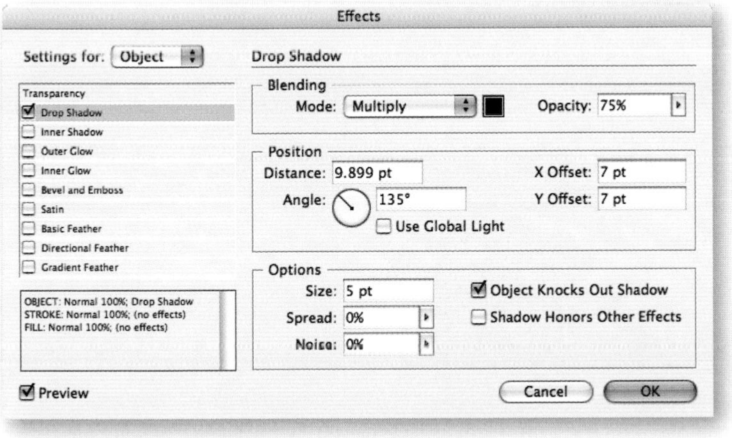
Effects
Settings for: Object
Drop Shadow
Transparency
Drop Shadow
Inner Shadow
Outer Glow
Inner Glow
Bevel and Emboss
Satin
Basic Feather
Directional Feather
Gradient Feather
Blending
Mode: Multiply
Opacity: 75%
Position
Distance: 9.899 pt
X Offset: 7 pt
Angle: 135°
Y Offset: 7 pt
Use Global Light
Options
Size: 5 pt
Object Knocks Out Shadow
Spread: 0%
Shadow Honors Other Effects
Noise: 0%
OBJECT: Normal 100%; Drop Shadow
STROKE: Normal 100%; (no effects)
FILL: Normal 100%; (no effects)
Preview
Cancel
OK

Figure 11.39 If you're used to applying effects in Photoshop, this dialog will look familiar. Many of the settings and options are the same across the different effects, so it won't be long before you become familiar with all the controls.

After applying an effect, you can quickly edit it by double-clicking the level in the Effects panel that the effect is applied to. So if a drop shadow was applied to just the text, double-click the Text level to edit the drop shadow settings. You can copy the effects between objects by selecting the object that contains the effect you want to copy and then dragging the FX icon to another object. You can only drag and drop one level at a time. To quickly remove all the transparency effects that are applied to an object, click the Clear All Effects button at the bottom of the Effects panel.

The number of combined transparency effects you can apply to objects in your layouts is immeasurable (**Figure 11.40**). The only advice I'll give you is to keep your designs simple. Don't make them more complex than necessary. The more complex the design, the more possible hang-ups you'll run into during output.

The Best of
New York
Jellena Virt

Figure 11.40 This book cover utilizes a combination of several transparency effects. "New York" is vertically centered within a white filled text frame. A gradient feather and an opacity value of 50% is applied to just the fill. To make the text pop out a little, an outer glow is applied to it.

Creating Object Styles

■ **Tip:** You can edit the default object styles by double-clicking their names in the Object Styles panel and then modifying their settings.

An object style is a collection of object-level formatting attributes—from a basic fill and stroke to a combination of transparency effects—that can be applied to frames with a single click (**Figure 11.41**). When you modify an object style, all the frames to which it is applied are instantly updated with the new changes, making object styles an indispensable component of almost any template.

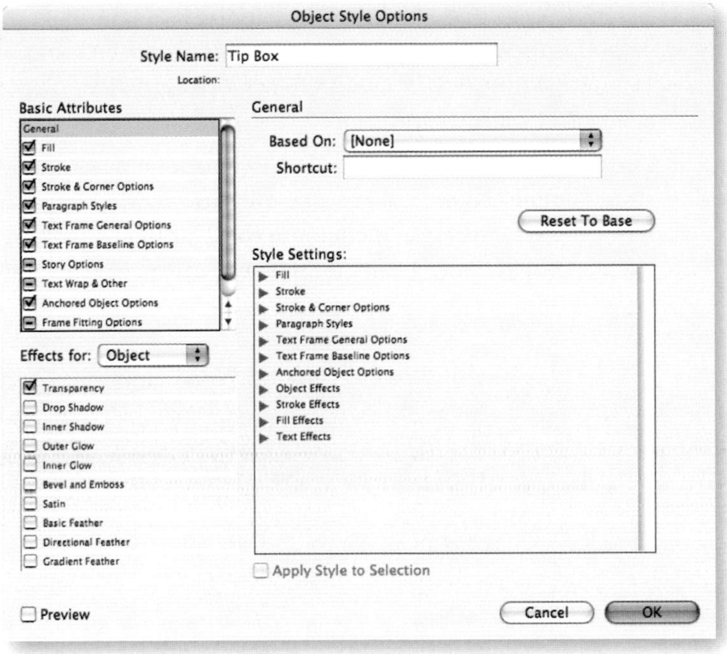
Object Style Options
Style Name: Tip Box
Location:
Basic Attributes
General
Fill
Stroke
Stroke & Corner Options
Paragraph Styles
Text Frame General Options
Text Frame Baseline Options
Story Options
Text Wrap & Other
Anchored Object Options
Frame Fitting Options
Effects for: Object
Transparency
Drop Shadow
Inner Shadow
Outer Glow
Inner Glow
Bevel and Emboss
Satin
Basic Feather
Directional Feather
Gradient Feather
General
Based On: [None]
Shortcut:
Reset To Base
Style Settings:
Fill
Stroke
Stroke & Corner Options
Paragraph Styles
Text Frame General Options
Text Frame Baseline Options
Anchored Object Options
Object Effects
Stroke Effects
Fill Effects
Text Effects
Apply Style to Selection
Preview
Cancel
OK

Figure 11.41 The Object Style Options dialog. All the formatting described earlier in this chapter can be made part of an object style's definition. After applying an object style, all of the object-level formatting options can be modified from one convenient location.

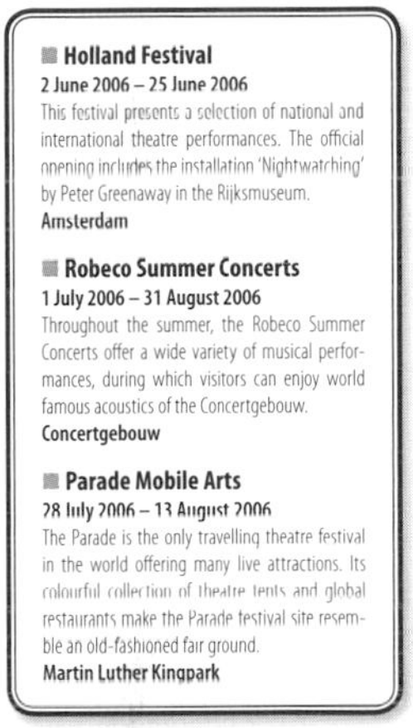
Holland Festival
2 June 2006 – 25 June 2006
This festival presents a selection of national and international theatre performances. The official opening includes the installation 'Nightwatching' by Peter Greenaway in the Rijksmuseum.
Amsterdam
Robeco Summer Concerts
1 July 2006 – 31 August 2006
Throughout the summer, the Robeco Summer Concerts offer a wide variety of musical performances, during which visitors can enjoy world famous acoustics of the Concertgebouw.
Concertgebouw
Parade Mobile Arts
28 July 2006 – 13 August 2006
The Parade is the only travelling theatre festival in the world offering many live attractions. Its colourful collection of theatre tents and global restaurants make the Parade festival site resemble an old-fashioned fair ground.
Martin Luther Kingpark

Figure 11.42 All the formatting applied to this frame and the text within it can be applied with a click of one object style. How's that for automation?

Before setting up any object styles, make sure all the design elements are represented and formatted the way you want them to look. With that taken care of, all the hard work that went into formatting the various objects can then be automated (**Figure 11.42**). All you have to do is generate object styles based on the sample objects in your mock-up layout.

By default, every document contains two object styles: [Basic Graphics Frame] and [Basic Text Frame] (**Figure 11.43**). The [Basic Graphics Frame] style is automatically applied to all new paths and unassigned frames. It is not applied to the frames often referred to as graphics frames, which are created with the Rectangle Frame tool. The [Basic Text Frame] style is automatically applied to all new text frames.

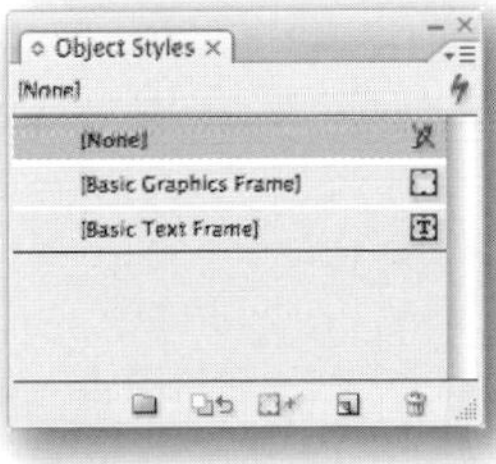
Object Styles
[None]
[None]
[Basic Graphics Frame]
[Basic Text Frame]

Figure 11.43 The Object Styles panel with the default object styles.

Follow theses steps to create an object style based on the formatting you've already applied to an object:

1. Select the frame that uses the formatting you want the object style to include.
2. Click the Create New Style button at the bottom of the Object Styles panel or choose New Object Style from the panel menu. Give the style a name that identifies its intended purpose. At this point, it's also a good idea to determine whether or not you want to base the style on another object style. If not, choose [None] from the Based On menu.

● **Note:** When you base a style on another style, the styles become linked to each other. So when you edit the base style, any shared attributes that appear in the styles based on it are also changed. If you don't want this behavior in your template, be sure to not base styles on other styles.

3. Select any other categories that contain formatting you might need to edit or define, and specify the options as necessary. To edit an effect, first choose an option in the Effects For menu (Object, Stroke, Fill, or Text), and then select an effect category to specify its settings.
4. Click the check box to the left of each category to determine whether it should be turned on, turned off, or ignored in the style (**Figure 11.44**). Only the formatting in the checked categories is included in the style. The formatting in unchecked categories is excluded from the style. And categories containing a small box (Windows) or a hyphen (Mac OS) are ignored.

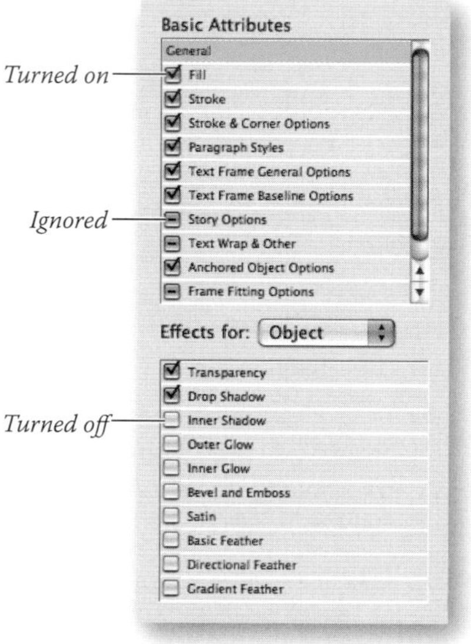
Turned on
Ignored
Turned off
Basic Attributes
General
Fill
Stroke
Stroke & Corner Options
Paragraph Styles
Text Frame General Options
Text Frame Baseline Options
Story Options
Text Wrap & Other
Anchored Object Options
Frame Fitting Options
Effects for: Object
Transparency
Drop Shadow
Inner Shadow
Outer Glow
Inner Glow
Bevel and Emboss
Satin
Basic Feather
Directional Feather
Gradient Feather

Figure 11.44 Object styles have many categories. Think carefully about the purpose of each object style you create and make sure that the categories you want the style to control or ignore are in the appropriate state.

● **Note:** The categories under Basic Attributes can only be turned on or ignored. All of the effects, except for Transparency, can be turned on, turned off, or ignored.

● **Note:** If the Clear Overrides When Applying Style option is not selected in the Object Styles panel menu, any formatting already applied to an object is preserved when the style is applied to it, even if the previously applied formatting doesn't match the style's definition. In this case, the style becomes overridden.

So by placing a check in the Drop Shadow check box, you are indicating that you want the drop shadow formatting included in the object style. Removing the check excludes the drop shadow, so if the style is applied to an object containing a drop shadow, the shadow is removed from the object, because it doesn't match the style's definition. If you add a drop shadow to an object with that style already applied to it, the style will appear overridden (as indicated by the plus [+] symbol to the right of its name).

By setting the category to be ignored, the drop shadow will be omitted from the style, so if the style is applied to an object containing a drop shadow, the shadow is preserved. And if a drop shadow is added to an object with that style already applied to it, the style does not become overridden.

Productivity Tips

When creating object styles, there are several ways to increase your productivity:

- **Create object styles for all repeating design elements.** Object styles don't have to lock you into one static design. Even if they just serve as a starting point from which you tailor the formatting to a publication's specific needs, they are an indispensable tool. Then later, as your designs veer far away from the original style, you can select an object and choose Break Link to Style from the Object Styles panel menu. This will retain all your custom formatting and break the link to the style so that future updates to the style definition won't affect that object.
- **Add keyboard shortcuts to frequently used object styles.** Enter the desired keyboard shortcut into the Shortcut field in the General section of the Object Style Options dialog. Make sure Num Lock is turned on, and then hold down any combination of Shift, Alt, and Ctrl (Windows) or Shift, Option, and Command (Mac OS), and choose a number from the numeric keypad. You cannot use letters or nonkeypad numbers for defining style shortcuts.
- **Organize the list of styles.** Object styles can be relocated within the Object Styles panel. Simply drag a style to a new location. A thick line appears, indicating where the style will drop when you release the mouse button. You might also choose to sort the list in alphabetical order. Choose Sort By Name from the Object Styles panel menu to do so.
- **Create style groups.** To organize a long list of object styles, separate them into style groups. To create a style group, choose New Style Group from the Object Styles panel menu, and then choose a name that clearly identifies its purpose. Once created, you can drag styles in and out of the style group to add or remove them.
- **Redefine an object style's definition.** As you construct a template, you'll often find that an object style needs to be updated to reflect new design changes. Instead of editing the style directly, you can select an object that contains the new formatting, and then choose Redefine Style from the Object Styles panel menu. The style is updated to match the formatting of the object. Keep in mind that the Redefine Style command does not redefine ignored categories.
- **Include the Paragraph Styles category.** By default, this category is ignored the first time you create a new object style. To dramatically improve your level of efficiency, you can include this category in object styles that will be applied to text frames. When the object style is applied, the paragraph

■ **Tip:** The Frame Fitting Options category is also ignored by default the first time you create a new object style. After creating the style, be sure to turn on this category if you want it to be included in the style's definition.

style is applied in the same click. And if the paragraph style includes any nested styles, they will be applied in that instance as well. Select Apply Next Style if the selected paragraph style contains a Next Style definition (**Figure 11.45**).

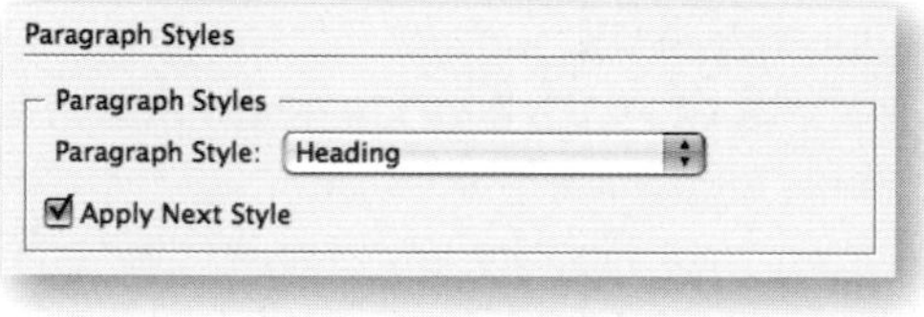
Paragraph Styles
Paragraph Styles
Paragraph Style: Heading
Apply Next Style

Figure 11.45 The Paragraph Styles area of the Object Style Options dialog. See Figure 11.42 for an example of this setup in use.

Importing Object Styles

If you've already created object styles in another InDesign document, you can import them into the template you're building. Choose Load Object Styles from the Object Styles panel menu and then locate the document containing the object styles you want to import. In the Load Styles dialog, select all the object styles you want to import (**Figure 11.46**).

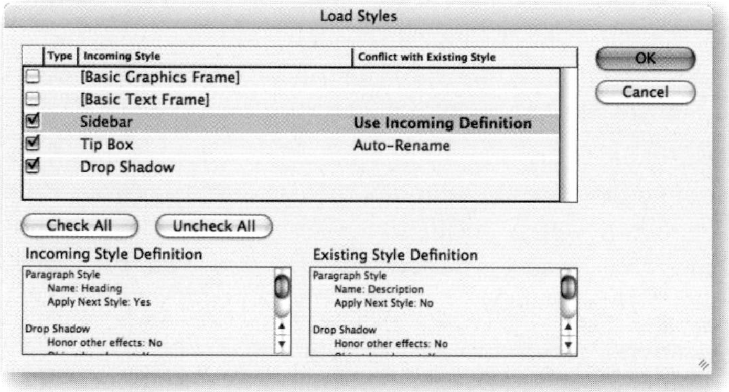
Load Styles
Type
Incoming Style
Conflict with Existing Style
[Basic Graphics Frame]
[Basic Text Frame]
Sidebar
Use Incoming Definition
Tip Box
Auto-Rename
Drop Shadow
OK
Cancel
Check All
Uncheck All
Incoming Style Definition
Paragraph Style
Name: Heading
Apply Next Style: Yes
Drop Shadow
Honor other effects: No
Existing Style Definition
Paragraph Style
Name: Description
Apply Next Style: No
Drop Shadow
Honor other effects: No

Figure 11.46 The Load Styles dialog. When a style conflict exists, you can compare the incoming style definition with the existing style definition at the bottom of the dialog.

If an existing object style has the same name as one of the incoming object styles, choose either Use Incoming Definition or Auto-Rename in the Conflict With Existing Style column to determine how the conflict should be resolved. If you choose Use Incoming Definition, the existing style will be overwritten with the imported style and all the objects in the document will be updated with any new style attributes. If you choose Auto-Rename, the incoming style will be renamed so that both styles can exist within the same document. So, if both documents have an object style called "Tip Box," the imported style is renamed "Tip Box copy."

12

Formatting Tables and Generating Table and Cell Styles

WHEN MOST DESIGNERS HEAR THE WORD "TABLES," THEY USUALLY THINK OF spreadsheets: rows, columns, cells, and endless amounts of boring data. If you wanted to spend your time dealing with tables and spreadsheets you would have been an accountant, not a designer, right? The reality is that all sorts of information can be presented very effectively using tables, and using InDesign's table features can reduce the pain factor and even make it fun to work with tables.

For many years I've been a big fan of Edward Tufte's writing on the design and display of information. Tables might not sound like the most exciting part of your day, but you can be proud to bring great design and clarity to even the most boring parts of a document. In this chapter, you'll learn how to efficiently format tables and how to create table and cell styles based on samples in your mock-up layout.

Creating Tables

A few years ago, InDesign introduced tables to the world of page layout, allowing you to work with tables—complete with editable content and easy formatting—just as easily as working with any other text content. Tables can flow from frame to frame and page to page, intermingled with text threads, just like any other text content in a layout.

You have several options for getting table content into an InDesign layout:

- **Creating a table from scratch.** You can create a text frame, insert the text cursor, and choose Table > Insert Table to create tables from scratch with InDesign and then type the data by hand, but you're not likely to use this method in a template workflow. It's a tedious, error-prone process that doesn't lend itself to time-saving strategies.
- **Converting text to a table.** For a more common workflow, you can place delimited text in your layout, select the text, and then choose Table > Convert Text to Table. This is the best option if you receive content as text files, commonly referred to as a "data dump," that have been exported from a spreadsheet or database.
- **Placing Microsoft Word documents.** You can place Microsoft Word documents that include tables, and the tables are retained as tables in InDesign.
- **Placing Microsoft Excel documents.** Microsoft Excel documents are arguably the most common source of table data. Not only are they the most likely source, but when configured properly, you can save a lot of time with a well-designed template. Place an .xls document just like a text file, and the table will thread just like a normal text story. Simply placing a file is probably the easiest option for users of your template.
- **Copying and Pasting.** You can also copy cells from Microsoft Excel or tabbed text from a text editing application and paste directly into an InDesign table. Just make sure you select a table cell before you paste. The top-left table cell you select will be the top-left corner of any cells you paste.

Selecting Tables

Through many years of training and consulting, one of the things I repeat all the time is, "You must select it to affect it." And this is true of tables as well as any other kind of page content. Whether you're designing a mock-up or layout applying table and cell styles, you need to know how to navigate through tables. You can rely on the menu commands found by choosing Table > Select, or you can use the methods described below.

Selecting Tables and Cells

To Select This...	Do This...
Cell	Use the Text tool, click in the cell, and drag just beyond the cell boundaries.
Cell	When you're editing text in a cell, press the Esc key.
Range of cells	Use the Text tool to click and drag across the range of cells.
Column	Use the Text tool, hover over the top edge of the column, and click when the cursor changes to a down arrow.
Row	Use the Text tool, hover over the left edge of the row, and click when the cursor changes to a right arrow.
Entire table	Use the Text tool to click the top-left corner of the table when the cursor changes to a diagonal arrow cursor.

Formatting Essential Cell Options

Tables are composed of cells just like sentences are composed of words and words are composed of letters. Because cells are the essential building blocks of tables, that's where you'll start in your exploration of table design. In fact, cell formatting combines with table formatting very much like character and paragraph styles combine to form nested paragraph styles (see Chapter 10, "Formatting Type and Generating Style Sheets"), so you'll start at the "bottom" and work your way up.

The best place to start is to use a complete mock-up of the table design and formatting you have in mind. Begin by creating a basic table and filling the cells with representative content. It's crucial that you use a variety of content samples at this point in an effort to anticipate many different scenarios. Ensuring that your table design can reasonably accommodate content of varying length (text), size (images), and complexity (merged and split cells) will save you a lot of time down the road.

You can learn about cell formatting attributes by selecting a cell or a range of cells and choosing Table > Cell Options > Text or by pressing Alt-Ctrl-B (Windows) or Option-Command-B (Mac OS) (**Figure 12.1**). You might notice that the Cell Options dialog that appears includes several options that are also available in the Control and Table panels. While there's nothing wrong with creating your table mock-up using the options available in those other panels, they do intermingle various cell and table options. The fact that the Cell Options dialog contains only cell formatting controls can be a helpful delineation as you learn effective ways to combine cell and table formatting.

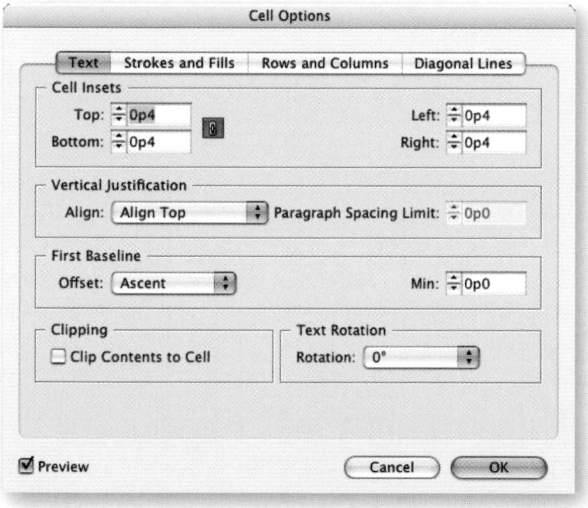
Cell Options
Text
Strokes and Fills
Rows and Columns
Diagonal Lines
Cell Insets
Top: 0p4
Bottom: 0p4
Left: 0p4
Right: 0p4
Vertical Justification
Align: Align Top
Paragraph Spacing Limit: 0p0
First Baseline
Offset: Ascent
Min: 0p0
Clipping
Clip Contents to Cell
Text Rotation
Rotation: 0°
Preview
Cancel
OK

Figure 12.1 The Cell Options dialog conveniently displays only cell formatting options and is a great learning tool because it distinguishes between cell and table formatting options.

Enable the Preview option in the lower-left corner of the dialog so you immediately see the effects of the various cell formatting controls. The following sections contain a summary of several of the available options.

Text Formatting for Cells

Use the Text tab options to format text in each cell:

- **Cell Insets.** This is the padding between the cell perimeter and the cell content. Cell insets can be changed individually on each side, or all sides can be synchronized with the link icon.
- **Vertical Justification.** This option controls how content is aligned vertically inside the cell. The Paragraph Spacing Limit value is only available when you choose to Justify Vertically, and it limits the maximum amount of space between paragraphs to achieve the vertically justified effect.
- **First Baseline.** The cell baseline options behave just like normal baseline options for text frames, but in this case each cell behaves like its own text frame. See "Text Frame Options" in Chapter 11, "Formatting Frames and Generating Object Styles," for detailed information on each option.
- **Clipping.** If you have an inline graphic in a cell that is taller than the vertical dimension of the cell, you can control whether the content is clipped to the cell area or bleeds outside the boundaries.
- **Text Rotation.** Set the rotation angle of text in a cell. Setting the angle to 90° or 270° is perfect for column labels and 180° is a great way to format answers to quizzes and trivia questions.

Strokes and Fills for Cells

Use the Strokes and Fills tab options to change the format of the cells:

- **Cell Stroke.** You can control normal stroke attributes including weight, color, type, tint, and gap options (**Figure 12.2**). By default, these stroke attributes are applied to all edges of selected cells. If you want to control different edges of the cells independently, click the edges of the cell mock-up at the top of the dialog. Edges of the cell mock-up that are highlighted in blue are the strokes that are affected by the current settings. Toggle a cell edge by clicking it in the example cell and then change the settings accordingly. Note that if more than one cell is selected, the mock-up will reflect that, so the strokes between cells can also be affected.
- **Cell Fill.** Arguably, some of the most frequently used cell formatting options, these settings allow you to select a color swatch and tint for the selected cells. If you plan to use a repeating pattern of alternating row or column fills, save that for later when you apply table formatting options.

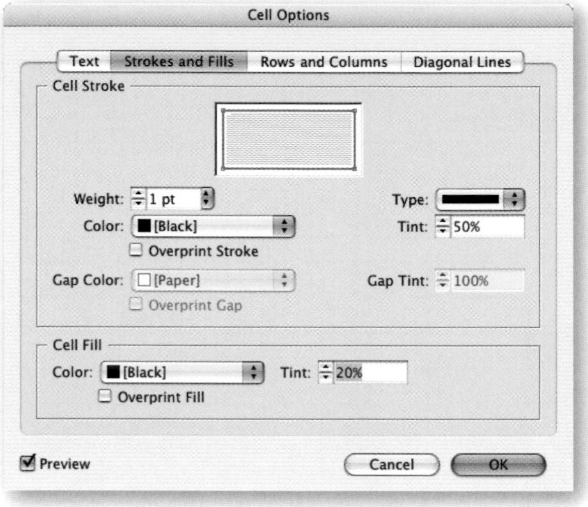
Cell Options
Text
Strokes and Fills
Rows and Columns
Diagonal Lines
Cell Stroke
Weight: 1 pt
Type:
Color: [Black]
Tint: 50%
Overprint Stroke
Gap Color: [Paper]
Gap Tint: 100%
Overprint Gap
Cell Fill
Color: [Black]
Tint: 20%
Overprint Fill
Preview
Cancel
OK

Figure 12.2 Customize stroke and fill settings for individual cells in the Cell Options dialog.

Rows and Columns for Cells

Use the Rows and Columns tab options to control the height and width of rows and columns:

- **Row Height.** Table content of varying lengths can produce rows with different heights, which isn't always the most pleasing table design. To solve this common problem, InDesign lets you set all table rows to an exact height or at least a specific common minimum (**Figure 12.3**).

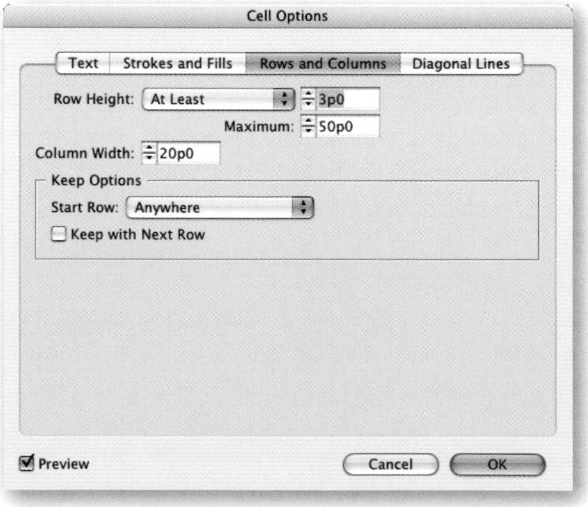
Cell Options
Text
Strokes and Fills
Rows and Columns
Diagonal Lines
Row Height: At Least
3p0
Maximum: 50p0
Column Width: 20p0
Keep Options
Start Row: Anywhere
Keep with Next Row
Preview
Cancel
OK

Figure 12.3 Achieving evenly spaced rows and columns is easy with the Rows and Columns tab in the Cell Options dialog.

- **Column Width.** This option allows you to quickly adjust table columns with mathematical precision.
- **Keep Options.** For very detailed table layouts, you can control the flow of table rows across multiple columns, frames, and pages.

While it's helpful to understand what options are available as a designer, it's important to know that the row and column size attributes for table cells are not captured as a part of cells styles. Instead, you should rely on placeholder tables or library items to retain specific row and column size settings.

Diagonals Lines in Cells

Use the Diagonal Lines tab options to create strikeouts in table cells:

- **Stroke Style.** Diagonal lines in cells are a good way to indicate information that is out of date, invalid, or corrected. It's also a good way to indicate that you've left a table cell empty on purpose. Click one of the buttons at the top of the dialog to choose the format of the diagonal line you want to use, if any (**Figure 12.4**).
- **Line Stroke.** You can control typical stroke options such as weight, type, color, tint, and gap options.
- **Draw.** You can even choose whether the content or the diagonal stroke is in front.

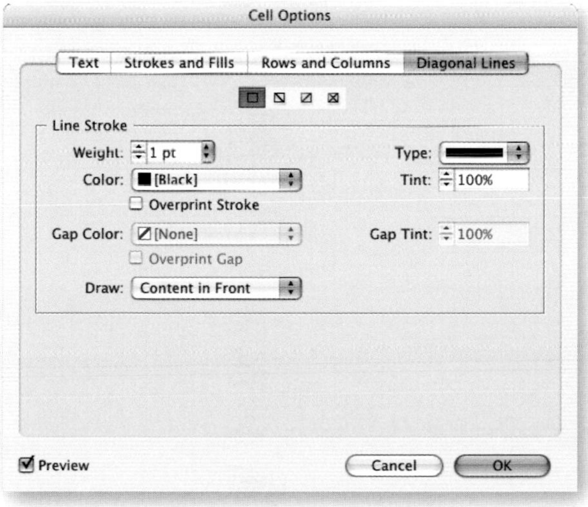
Cell Options
Text
Strokes and Fills
Rows and Columns
Diagonal Lines
Line Stroke
Weight: 1 pt
Type:
Color: [Black]
Tint: 100%
Overprint Stroke
Gap Color: [None]
Gap Tint: 100%
Overprint Gap
Draw: Content in Front
Preview
Cancel
OK

Figure 12.4 You probably won't use diagonal cell lines often, but it sure beats drawing diagonal lines by hand.

Creating Cell Styles

■ **Tip:** Cell styles will override table style formatting, so plan to use cell styles for localized formatting. Good candidates for cell styles include header rows, footer rows, summary cells, and any other cells that you want to bring to the attention of your readers.

Now that you've customized your cell design using all of the available options, it's time to capture the results of your design as a cell style. The process of creating a mock-up and then capturing a style is similar to the process of capturing paragraph and character styles based on sample text formatting (see Chapter 10).

Before you capture your first cell style, note that there is no [Basic Cell] style because, by default, cell formatting is based on the [Basic Table] style. Instead, there's a [None] style that can be used to remove cell formatting. Follow these steps to create a new cell style:

1. Select a cell from your table mock-up and choose New Cell Style from the Cell Styles panel menu (**Figure 12.5**).

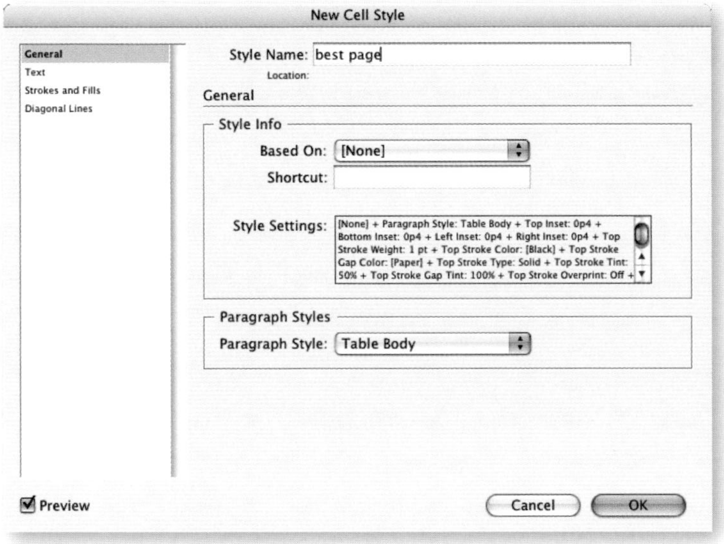
New Cell Style
General
Text
Strokes and Fills
Diagonal Lines
Style Name: best page
Location:
General
Style Info
Based On: [None]
Shortcut:
Style Settings: [None] + Paragraph Style: Table Body + Top Inset: 0p4 + Bottom Inset: 0p4 + Left Inset: 0p4 + Right Inset: 0p4 + Top Stroke Weight: 1 pt + Top Stroke Color: [Black] + Top Stroke Gap Color: [Paper] + Top Stroke Type: Solid + Top Stroke Tint: 50% + Top Stroke Gap Tint: 100% + Top Stroke Overprint: Off +
Paragraph Styles
Paragraph Style: Table Body
Preview
Cancel
OK

Figure 12.5 Creating a cell style based on a mock-up table design captures the details of your formatting example.

2. Use the New Cell Style dialog to give your cell style a useful name based on its purpose in the design.
3. Enable the Preview check box in the bottom-left corner of the dialog so you can see the effects of any changes instantly.
4. Decide if you want to base the cell style on another cell style. This can be very helpful if you need several cell styles to share common attributes such as cell strokes but have them differ in other attributes such as fill color. By basing multiple cell styles on one common cell style and varying only the fill color, you can save a lot of time and make future adjustments easily.

5. If you want, you can assign a keyboard shortcut to your cell style. Windows users can use a combination of Shift, Alt, Ctrl and numbers from the numeric keypad. Macintosh users can combine Shift, Option, Command and numbers from the numeric keypad.
6. InDesign lets you specify a paragraph style to automatically apply to text inside a styled table cell, which is possibly one of the most time-saving table features in the entire application. Use this option to control the formatting of a cell and its content with one click instead of formatting them separately.
7. Review the settings that you've captured in your cell style. If there are other formatting options you need to change, make the appropriate changes in the Text, Strokes and Fills, and Diagonal Lines sections of the New Cell Style dialog.
8. Click OK to save the new cell style.

● **Note:** Unfortunately, you cannot use letters or nonkeypad numbers as part of your style shortcuts.

If you need to edit the cell style down the road, just double-click the style in the Cell Styles panel and make any necessary corrections or updates. Any changes made to a cell style will change the style definition and any cells formatted with that cell style. On the other hand, if you need to remove cell formatting and start from scratch, just select the cells and apply the [None] cell style.

If you've paid close attention, you might have noticed that not all cell formatting attributes can be captured as a part of a cell style. The options that aren't captured in a cell style include row heights, column widths, keep options, and any merging or splitting of cells. If your template includes complicated table designs with irregular cell arrangements, you should consider saving those table structures as library items. You can then reuse the table layout, copy and paste data into the table cells, and then format the table with the necessary table and cell styles.

Formatting Essential Table Options

By now you should have a good understanding of how to format and style table cells, but if you designed your tables one cell at a time, it would be an incredibly slow and tedious process. Instead, you'll build on what you've learned and move on up to table formatting. You can control some of these table formatting options in the Control and Table panels, but consider using the Table Setup command (Table > Table Options > Table Setup) because it consolidates all the available table formatting options in one place and filters out any cell-specific settings. Here's a quick rundown of notable table formatting options.

Table Setup

Use the Table Setup tab of the Table Options dialog to adjust general table formatting options:

- **Table Dimensions.** When you create a table by placing Microsoft Word or Excel data, InDesign automatically creates the correct number of rows and columns required to accommodate all the source information. However, if you're creating a table from scratch, you'll want to use the Table Dimensions controls in the Table Options dialog (**Figure 12.6**). Enable the Preview option, enter the number of rows and columns and how many rows should repeat as running header and footer rows, and InDesign will create the cells for you. This is a helpful option if you want to design the table layout in your template and then copy and paste the cell data during the production phase.

Table Options
Table Setup
Row Strokes
Column Strokes
Fills
Headers and Footers
Table Dimensions
Body Rows: 6
Columns: 4
Header Rows: 1
Footer Rows: 0
Table Border
Weight: 0 pt
Type:
Color: [Black]
Tint:
Overprint
Gap Color: [Paper]
Gap Tint: 100%
Overprint
Preserve Local Formatting
Table Spacing
Space Before: 0p4
Space After: -0p4
Stroke Drawing Order
Draw: Best Joins
Preview
Cancel
OK

Figure 12.6 You can customize table dimensions, but those options cannot be captured as part of a table style.

● **Note:** Table and cell borders are an example of how table and cell formatting options can conflict. For example, what happens if you have a table border set to two points and a cell border set to one point? Which setting wins out? The order of precedence is custom cell formatting, cell styles, cell styles from table styles, custom table formatting, and then table styles.

- **Table Border.** While cell borders surround just individual cells, table borders apply a stroke to the outside perimeter of the entire table. You can format the table border with typical stroke attributes including weight, type, color, tint, and gap options.
- **Table Spacing.** You can apply a default amount of spacing before and after your tables, which is essentially the same as the paragraph spacing options discussed in Chapter 10. If you're already using paragraph spacing after your paragraphs, you can set the spacing before a table to zero. However, if you aren't using any spacing after paragraphs, you'll want to add a bit of spacing before your tables.

It usually works well to make your paragraph spacing and table spacing match. For example, you can set the spacing before paragraphs and tables to zero and you can use the same space after value for paragraphs and tables for consistent spacing.

One exception to the strategy of using the same paragraph and table spacing would be if you use a caption or figure number after your tables. In that case you'd probably want to use no spacing before your tables but use a small space after your tables to offset the table caption, and then use paragraph spacing after the paragraph style you use for your caption. Enabling Preview in the Table Options dialog is especially helpful in a situation like this where you are considering the simultaneous interactions of so many different options.

- **Stroke Drawing Order.** The last option in the Table Setup tab of the Table Options dialog, the Stroke Drawing Order feature lets you control how row and column strokes interact. For example, if your row strokes are one color or style and your column strokes are a different color or style, you can choose which one is displayed on top. You can even control how double strokes intersect using the Best Joins and InDesign 2.0 Compatibility options.

Row Strokes

Row strokes are the horizontal lines between rows of cells and include standard stroke options such as weight, type, color, tint, and gap options. You can also use a pattern of alternating row strokes if you want the strokes to reinforce the organization of your data without overwhelming the design (**Figure 12.7**).

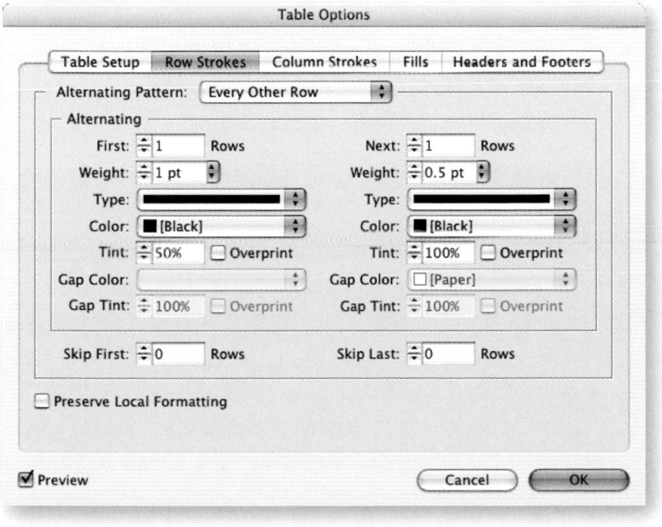
Table Options
Table Setup
Row Strokes
Column Strokes
Fills
Headers and Footers
Alternating Pattern: Every Other Row
Alternating
First: 1 Rows
Next: 1 Rows
Weight: 1 pt
Weight: 0.5 pt
Type:
Type:
Color: [Black]
Color: [Black]
Tint: 50%
Overprint
Tint: 100%
Overprint
Gap Color:
Gap Color: [Paper]
Gap Tint: 100%
Overprint
Gap Tint: 100%
Overprint
Skip First: 0 Rows
Skip Last: 0 Rows
Preserve Local Formatting
Preview
Cancel
OK

Figure 12.7 Row strokes and column strokes can help improve readability of long or complex tables, but don't overdo it.

Column Strokes

Column strokes function the same as row strokes, except on the vertical axis. Remember that the interaction between row and column strokes is controlled by the Stroke Drawing Order options in the Table Setup tab.

Fills

You can greatly enhance the readability of table data with subtle use of row and column fill patterns. If you expect your readers to scan up and down columns of information, you can use one of the alternating patterns for columns; if readers will be scanning across rows of related information, you should choose one of the row patterns.

After you've chosen your alternating pattern, you need to decide which color swatches you'll use to fill the rows and columns, and any tinting you want to use. Even a simple alternating pattern of every other row filled with a 20% black swatch can make it easier for readers to digest lots of tabular data (**Figure 12.8**). Notice that you can skip a specific number of first and last rows, but don't use this feature to create the effect of running header and foot rows because you'll configure those in the next step.

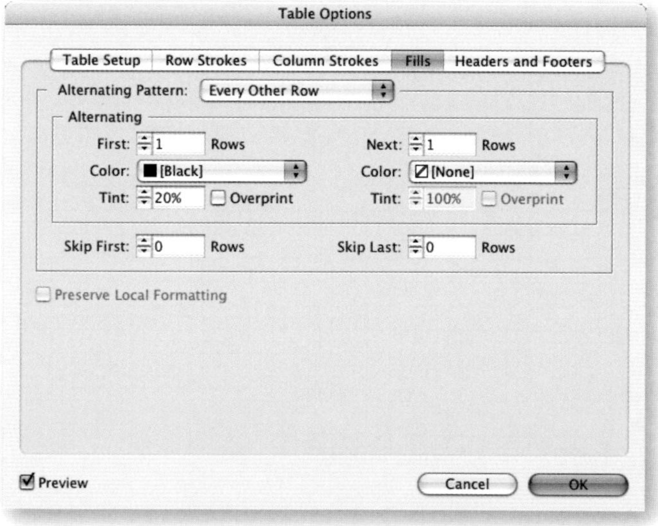
Table Options
Table Setup
Row Strokes
Column Strokes
Fills
Headers and Footers
Alternating Pattern:
Every Other Row
Alternating
First:
1
Rows
Next:
1
Rows
Color:
[Black]
Color:
[None]
Tint:
20%
Overprint
Tint:
100%
Overprint
Skip First:
0
Rows
Skip Last:
0
Rows
Preserve Local Formatting
Preview
Cancel
OK

Figure 12.8 A subtle alternating fill pattern using light tints can significantly improve readability of a table without making the table look like a distracting checkerboard.

Headers and Footers

If you have long tables that thread across multiple columns, frames, or pages, it's very easy to lose the context of the table data. For example, if you have a long table of weather data spanning multiple pages that includes lows, highs, and averages, it might not be clear on later pages what the numbers refer to on page three if the only column labels are all the way back on page one.

● **Note:** Remember that running table headers and footers are automatically excluded from table fill patterns, so you don't have to subtract them from the design manually.

The solution is to use column headers and footers that help readers understand the data they're looking at. Table headers are great for labeling the table data, and table footers are effective for notes, legal disclaimers, and other explanatory notes. If headers and footers make sense for your table mock-up, determine how many header and footer rows to use, and how often they should repeat (**Figure 12.9**). Based on your settings, your running table headers and footers will repeat at every new text column, frame, or page where your table is threaded.

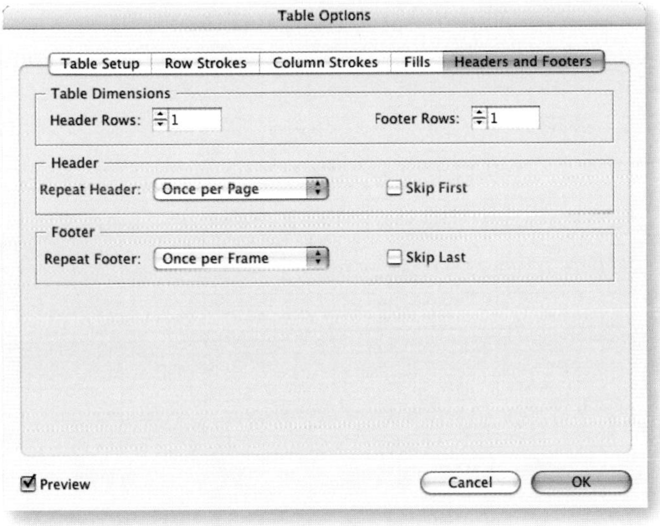
Table Options
Table Setup
Row Strokes
Column Strokes
Fills
Headers and Footers
Table Dimensions
Header Rows: 1
Footer Rows: 1
Header
Repeat Header: Once per Page
Skip First
Footer
Repeat Footer: Once per Frame
Skip Last
Preview
Cancel
OK

Figure 12.9 Create automatic running headers and footers for tables that span multiple frames or pages.

■ **Tip:** Instead of manually formatting header and footer cells to be unique aspects of the table design, consider using cell styles. You'll see in the next section that this is a smart approach for a variety of reasons.

Creating Table Styles

You're quickly approaching the grand finale of sound table design: a fully automated table style. You understand the various components, including paragraph styles, cell formatting, cell styles, and table formatting. You're about to combine all of these pieces into a single time-saving table style. Table styles are a great feature in InDesign CS3.

Before you create a table style, you should make sure you've already generated all the color swatches and cell styles you plan to incorporate in the final table design. Creating these swatches and styles ahead of time will significantly streamline the rest of the process. Follow these steps to create a table style:

1. Create a mock-up table using representative sample data for your publication. Format the table with cell styles, which should specify paragraph styles for the text formatting.
2. After you complete the cell formatting, add table-level formatting to your mock-up by selecting Table > Table Options. Customize row and column strokes, create alternating fills, and assign header and footer rows, as necessary.
3. Select the table and choose New Table Style from the Table Styles panel menu to create a new table style and then further customize the various settings. Enable the Preview option to get instant feedback for any changes you need to make to the style (**Figure 12.10**).

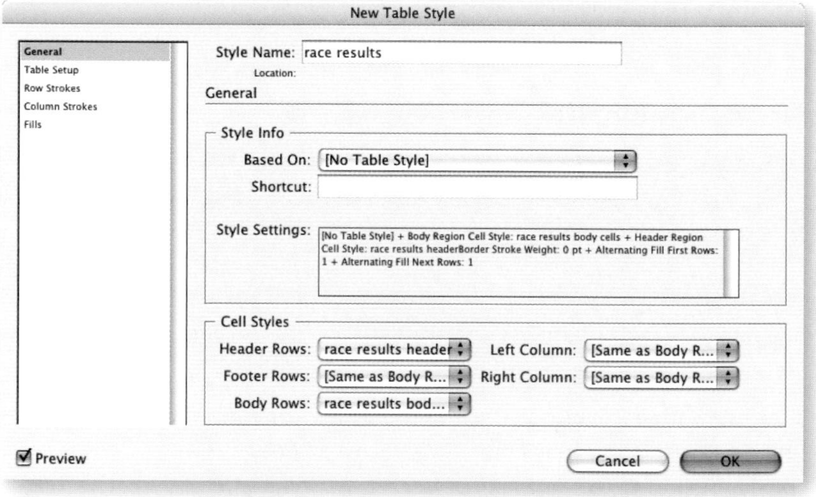
New Table Style
General
Table Setup
Row Strokes
Column Strokes
Fills
Style Name: race results
Location:
General
Style Info
Based On: [No Table Style]
Shortcut:
Style Settings: [No Table Style] + Body Region Cell Style: race results body cells + Header Region Cell Style: race results headerBorder Stroke Weight: 0 pt + Alternating Fill First Rows: 1 + Alternating Fill Next Rows: 1
Cell Styles
Header Rows: race results header
Footer Rows: [Same as Body R...
Body Rows: race results bod...
Left Column: [Same as Body R...
Right Column: [Same as Body R...
Preview
Cancel
OK

Figure 12.10 Create a table style by capturing the formatting of your table mock-up.

4. In the General section of the dialog give your new table style a useful name, decide if the style should be based on another table style, and give your style a custom keyboard shortcut if you plan to use the style frequently. Remember that shortcuts for styles can only consist of keyboard modifiers and numbers from the numeric keypad.
5. The magic of table styles occurs in the Cell Styles area of the General section. These options let you tie together table styles and cell styles, much like paragraph styles and character styles combine to create nested styles.

If you have header or footer rows in your table, make sure they've been defined by selecting Table > Convert Rows > To Header or Table > Convert Rows > To Footer, and then choose which cell styles should automatically apply to those components of the table. Next, decide if your left or right columns should be formatted with a certain cell style. Then choose a cell style for your body rows, which are all of the remaining cells. It might seem unnecessary to assign a cell style to your body rows, but it will make any future updates faster and easier.

Tip: You can automatically apply text formatting to tables by including paragraph styles in cell styles which are included in table styles.

6. The remaining categories include Table Setup, Row Strokes, Column Strokes, and Fills, and correspond with the table formatting options you've already seen in the Table Options dialog. Make any necessary changes to these table style options.

Note: Table Setup attributes including the number of rows, columns, header rows, and footer rows are not captured in a table style. You should configure these attributes in a placeholder table or save the table mock-up in an InDesign library.

The process of combining color swatches, text styles, cell styles, and table styles takes a bit of planning but will save lots of production time in the future. The trickiest part is remembering which formatting options apply to a cell, which options apply to a table, and which options aren't captured as part of styles. With a bit of practice you'll get the hang of it, and you'll love the power of formatting a very complex table with a single click of the mouse.

Understanding the [Basic Table] Style

You've learned how to create table styles that will save you lots of time, but if you really want to reach the highest levels of efficiency, you'll need to understand the [Basic Table] style. You can't delete or rename the [Basic Table] style, but if there's a certain table format you plan to use over and over again in your layout, you can edit its settings. Double-click the [Basic Table] style in the Table Styles panel (**Figure 12.11**), make all necessary adjustments, including referencing existing cell styles, and click OK.

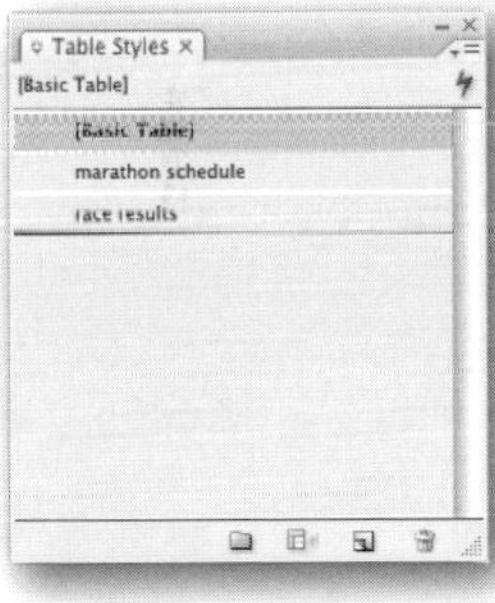
Table Styles
[Basic Table]
marathon schedule

Figure 12.11 Customize the [Basic Table] style to give yourself a better starting point for new basic tables.

Now every time you create a new table in your template, it will use the formatting dictated by the [Basic Table] style. This is helpful even if you don't use complicated table formatting. For example, customizing the [Basic Table] style is an easy way to adjust global attributes such as table borders, space before and after, and alternating fills.

Applying Styles

Applying cell and table styles is a pretty straightforward process. Insert your text cursor anywhere in a table and click the name of a table style in the Table Styles panel. The style is applied to the entire table even if it threads across multiples frames and pages. If you need to apply a cell style to a particular cell or group of cells, you can select those cells in the table, and then click the name of a cell style in the Cell Styles panel.

Perhaps the easiest way to apply table styles is when you place a Microsoft Excel source file. Choose File > Place, select the .xls file you want to use, and enable the Show Import Options check box. Click Open to view the Microsoft Excel Import Options dialog and set the table formatting option to Unformatted Table. Choosing this option enables the Table Style menu where you can choose which table style to assign to the table automatically as it's placed in your layout (**Figure 12.12**).

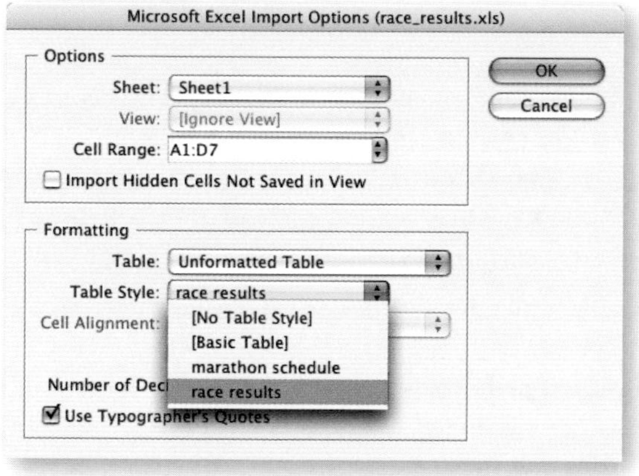
Microsoft Excel Import Options (race_results.xls)
Options
Sheet: Sheet1
View: [Ignore View]
Cell Range: A1:D7
Import Hidden Cells Not Saved in View
OK
Cancel
Formatting
Table: Unformatted Table
Table Style: race results
Cell Alignment:
[No Table Style]
[Basic Table]
marathon schedule
race results
Number of Dec
Use Typographer's Quotes

Figure 12.12 For the ultimate in table formatting efficiency, format your tables with table styles as part of the Place process (File > Place).

If you find you're applying the same cell styles repeatedly, try to designate those cell styles as part of a table style. If there's no predictable pattern to your need for cell styles, your best bet is to apply the cell styles manually. But if the special cell style is in a consistent part of the table and can't be captured as a table style (header rows, footer rows, left column, or right column), creating a placeholder table in your template and copying and pasting cell data into the table might save you some time.

■ **Tip:** Before you apply a table style for the first time, select the table, right-click/Control-click on the table style name in the Table Styles panel, and choose "Apply table style, Clear Overrides." This clears all formatting from the table before applying the table style and ensures you're starting with a blank slate. This is a good test for your table style because if the formatting applies as you expect, you can proceed. If all the formatting doesn't work as planned, it's time for some troubleshooting.

Clearing Overrides

In some situations you'll want to customize a table design beyond what you've designated with table and cell styles, and there's nothing wrong with that. However, other times you'll get to the point where your table design includes formatting attributes that aren't part of your styles. These overrides are indicated by a plus sign next to the applied table style in the Table Styles panel (**Figure 12.13**).

To clear attributes that aren't part of your table styles, select the table, and then do *either* of the following:

- Alt/Option-click the appropriate style name.
- Click the Clear Overrides button at the bottom of the Table Styles panel.

If you clear the overrides from your table styles and the design still doesn't look right, select any cells that need to be reformatted and clear any overrides in the Cell Styles panel. If the table formatting looks correct but the text formatting is inconsistent, you might need to clear overrides for any paragraph styles used in the table cells.

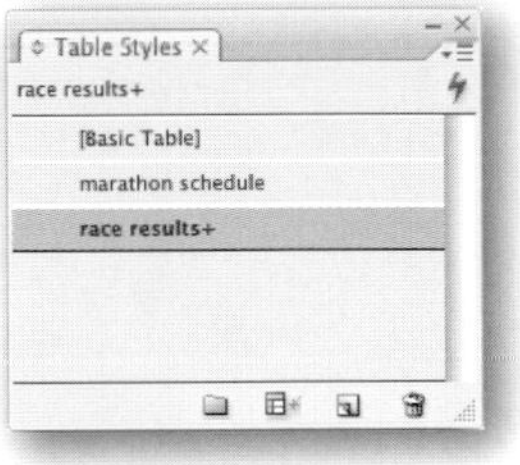
Table Styles
race results+
[Basic Table]
marathon schedule
race results+

Figure 12.13 Remove table style overrides for consistently formatted tables.

■ **Tip:** If you're not sure why you have a style with an override, just hover your cursor over the style name in the panel, and InDesign displays a tool tip that shows you which formatting options don't match the style.

Redefining Table and Cell Styles

As hard as you might try, it's unlikely you'll get the perfect combination of paragraph, cell, and table styles on the first attempt. Sometimes the problem can be solved with a simple tweak to a table or cell style, but other times you might have bigger mistakes to fix. If that's the case, consider changing the cell formatting in your template mock-up instead of editing the corresponding styles.

After you've made the necessary adjustments to cell and table formatting, select the appropriate part of the table mock-up and then choose Redefine Style from the Table Styles or Cell Styles panel menu. Now, instead of seeing an override indicator in the panel, InDesign updates the selected style to match the selected table mock-up.

Using Linked Content

Throughout this chapter you've learned about several creative solutions that will save you a lot of time when working with tables, but every production artist knows how often table content can change, even at the last minute. This means that even if the appropriate InDesign features have been employed in your template, it could still mean a lot of rework for last-minute table data such as product specifications, financial data, and schedules.

Fortunately, there's an InDesign preference you can enable that helps minimize a lot of this rework. Press Ctrl/Command-K to open the application Preferences and choose the Type category on the left. At the very bottom of this pane is the option Create Links When Placing Text and Spreadsheet Files. This setting is disabled by default, but I encourage you to turn it on (**Figure 12.14**). Even better, enable this option with no InDesign documents open so that it affects all new documents you create.

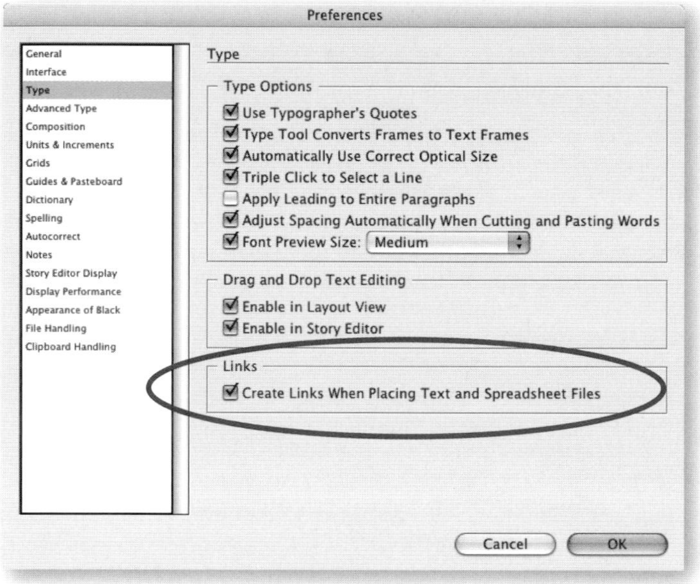
Preferences
General
Interface
Type
Advanced Type
Composition
Units & Increments
Grids
Guides & Pasteboard
Dictionary
Spelling
Autocorrect
Notes
Story Editor Display
Display Performance
Appearance of Black
File Handling
Clipboard Handling
Type
Type Options
Use Typographer's Quotes
Type Tool Converts Frames to Text Frames
Automatically Use Correct Optical Size
Triple Click to Select a Line
Apply Leading to Entire Paragraphs
Adjust Spacing Automatically When Cutting and Pasting Words
Font Preview Size: Medium
Drag and Drop Text Editing
Enable in Layout View
Enable in Story Editor
Links
Create Links When Placing Text and Spreadsheet Files
Cancel
OK

Figure 12.14 Enable the linked text option in the application preferences to streamline last-minute content updates.

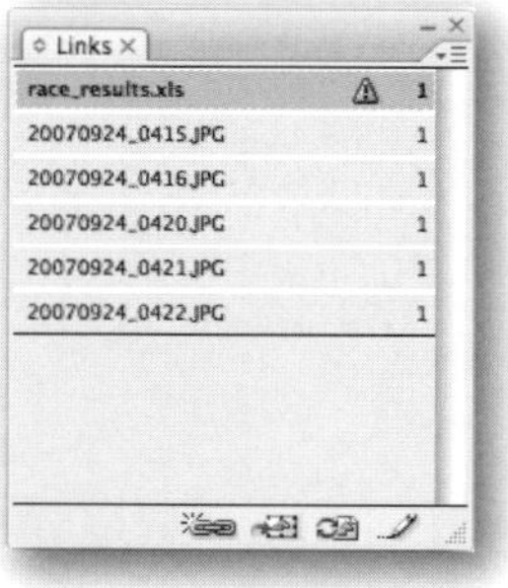
Links
race_results.xls
20070924_0415.JPG
20070924_0416.JPG
20070924_0420.JPG
20070924_0421.JPG
20070924_0422.JPG

Figure 12.15 Links to Excel spreadsheets show up in the Links panel just like any other linked file.

With this option enabled, InDesign behaves in an interesting hybrid way when placing text and spreadsheet files. The source content, such as .doc and .xls files behave as links in that they appear in the Links panel and display a yellow triangle icon when they are out of date (**Figure 12.15**). Linked documents are tracked by InDesign as if they were linked graphics. So if a source file, such as an Excel spreadsheet, gets updated and the production artist updates the link, the layout will update with the new content and the formatting of the table will be retained because it's dictated by table and cell styles. Overrides of paragraph and character styles are eliminated by this update process, but this could be a great time-saver if you enable this option in your templates.

The InDesign document doesn't rely on linked text and spreadsheet files in the same way it relies on linked graphics. Linked graphics are obviously required to output the final layout for professional printing, but the linked .doc and .xls files are not required for final output. That's the essence of this hybrid behavior. As a template designer you can create a link relationship for easy updates without the extra file dependencies usually required for final printing.

Productivity Tips

Now that you understand how to use table and cell styles to streamline the process of formatting tables in your publications, it's time to explore a few extra productivity tips.

- **Importing cell and table styles from other documents.** Creating really great cell and table styles isn't exactly rocket science, but it does take a bit of planning and testing. Once you've designed a table style, you might want to use it in multiple InDesign templates. To streamline that process and to avoid having to re-create your table and cell style from scratch, choose the Load Cell Styles or Load Table Styles commands from the Cell Styles or Table Styles panel menu, select another InDesign document, and load the styles (**Figure 12.16**).

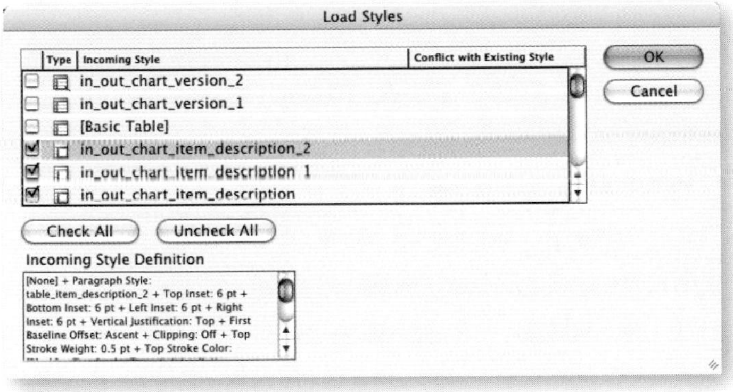
Load Styles
Type
Incoming Style
Conflict with Existing Style
OK
Cancel
in_out_chart_version_2
in_out_chart_version_1
[Basic Table]
in_out_chart_item_description_2
in_out_chart_item_description 1
in_out_chart_item_description
Check All
Uncheck All
Incoming Style Definition
[None] + Paragraph Style: table_item_description_2 + Top Inset: 6 pt + Bottom Inset: 6 pt + Left Inset: 6 pt + Right Inset: 6 pt + Vertical Justification: Top + First Baseline Offset: Ascent + Clipping: Off + Top Stroke Weight: 0.5 pt + Top Stroke Color:

Figure 12.16 Load table and cell styles from another document instead of re-creating them from scratch.

- **Organizing and grouping styles.** If you work with a lot of cell and table styles, keeping them organized is a good idea for you and anyone else who needs to use your template. By default, InDesign lists your styles in the order they were created with the newest ones at the top. Instead, consider sorting the styles by their frequency of use. Just click and drag the styles up and down in the panel, remembering that default styles listed in brackets cannot be moved. You can also organize the styles alphabetically by choosing the Sort by Name command in the Table Styles and Cell Styles panel menus. If you're overwhelmed by too many styles, consider creating style groups to keep things tidy. Just click the New Style Group button at the bottom of the panel, double-click the group folder icon to give it a useful name, and drag your styles into the appropriate group (**Figure 12.17**).

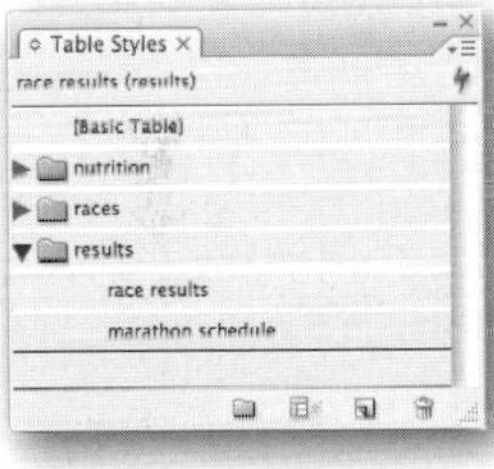
Table Styles
race results (results)
[Basic Table]
nutrition
races
results
race results
marathon schedule

Figure 12.17 As your list of table and cell styles grows, you might want to organize them into groups.

- **Breaking a link to a style.** In a perfect world you'd be able to anticipate all possible variables with perfect table styles. However, real-world experience tells you that's not always possible. When your table designs veer away from your original style, you might want to select the table and choose the Break Link to Style command in the Table Styles or Cell Styles panel menu. This will retain all your custom formatting and break the link to the style so that future updates to the style definition won't affect your table formatting.

● **Note:** If you import a table style that references cell styles, those cell styles are automatically imported as well. This means you can't deselect a required cell style until you deselect the related table style. And in turn, if the cell styles use paragraph styles, those are also loaded. And if the paragraph styles use nested styles, the corresponding character styles are loaded, too.

- **Using color in table and cell styles.** Did you notice that when you choose colors for alternating fills and cell, row, and column strokes you can only choose from existing swatches and tints of existing swatches? Ensure a smooth workflow by creating your color swatches before you create your cell and table styles.
- **Placing images in cells.** Don't forget that you can place images in table cells as inline anchored objects. This can be especially helpful when designing templates for catalogs and sales sheets. If your image is larger than the cell it's placed in, you can enable the Clip Contents to Cell option in the Cell Options dialog, but note this is only helpful if the image is too wide for the cell. If the image is too tall for the cell, you'll need to shrink the image or increase the height of the cell, because the Clip Contents option doesn't affect images that are too tall.
- **Eliminating overset cells.** You can create overset table cells just like you can create overset text frames. Instead of seeing the red plus sign indicator, InDesign indicates a cell is overset by displaying a small red dot in the cell (**Figure 12.18**). Your options are to either reduce the amount of content, decrease the size of the content by changing the formatting, or increase the size of the cells. If you attempt to print or export your design when there are overset cells or text frames, InDesign warns you of the problem and asks if you want to proceed before fixing the overset.

Race	State	Time	Pace
Chicago Marathon	IL	3:47:27	8:40
Pittsburgh Marathon	PA	3:38:49	8:20
Derby Festival Marathon	KY	3:58:39	9:06
Boulder Backroads Mara-	CO	4:00:06	9:10
Milwaukee Lakefront	WI	3:49:04	8:45
Rock 'n' Roll Marathon	AZ	3:35:26	8:13

Figure 12.18 Any placeholder tables that contain overset table cells should be fixed before distributing the template.

13

Adding Support for Long Documents

PRODUCING LONG DOCUMENTS, SUCH AS BOOKS, CATALOGS, AND JOURNALS can be demanding work. If the template you're designing will be used to construct a long document, you'll want to incorporate several production-enhancing features into it, depending on the needs of the publication. Will it contain a lot of tables or figures that need to be carefully numbered? Will it require footnotes at the bottom of the page? Will you have to produce complex multilevel lists or generate a table of contents? If so, read on.

Creating Running Lists

InDesign's Define Lists feature is a simple, yet powerful tool for generating and maintaining running lists of numbered information. Unlike a normal numbered list, a defined list can span multiple stories and even different documents in a book file. For instance, you can create a defined list to track a list of tables throughout a book. As you add or delete tables, they are automatically renumbered, which prevents you from having to manually renumber them—one at a time (**Figure 13.1**).

● **Note:** The Default list can't run across stories, so it's best to create a new list instead of using the default.

To create a running list, you first need to define a new list for the item you want to number. Choose Type > Bulleted and Numbered Lists > Define Lists. In the Define Lists dialog, click New to create a new list, and then type a name for it. Next, choose Continue Numbers across Stories, or Continue Numbers from Previous Document in Book, or both (**Figure 13.2**). One template can contain several defined lists, each used to track a different type of item—instructions, questions and answers, figures, and so on.

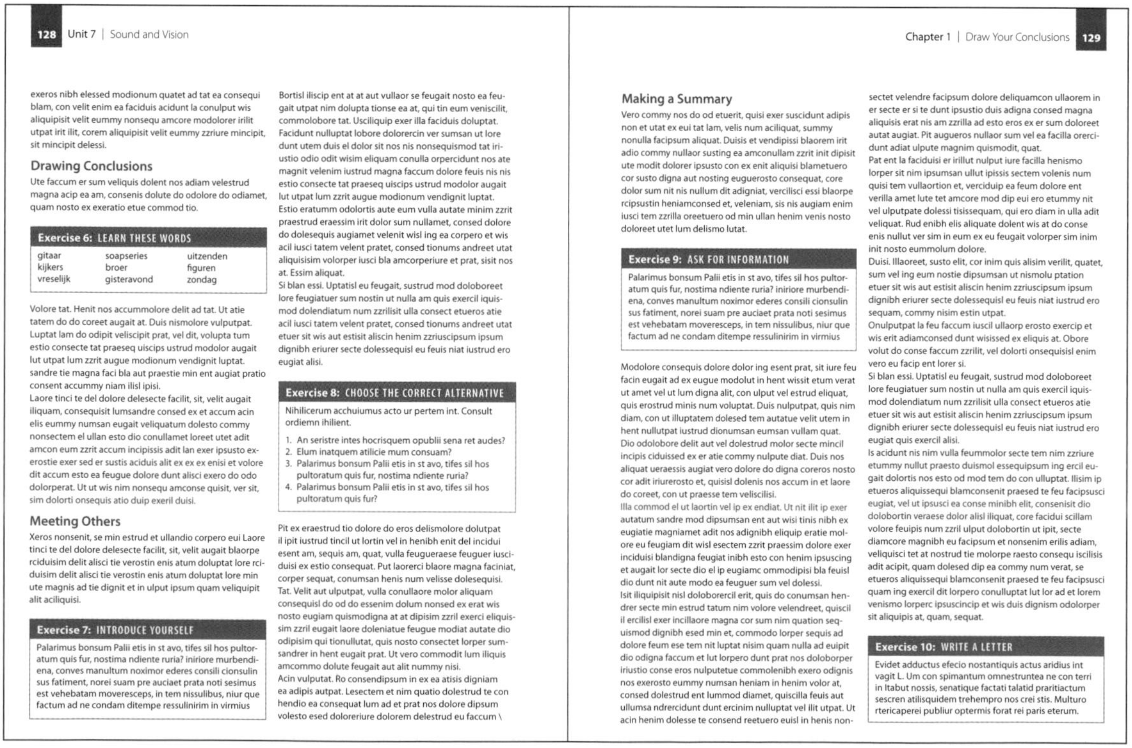
128 Unit 7 | Sound and Vision
Drawing Conclusions
Exercise 6: LEARN THESE WORDS
gitaar soapseries uitzenden
kijkers broer figuren
vreselijk gisteravond zondag
Meeting Others
Exercise 7: INTRODUCE YOURSELF
Exercise 8: CHOOSE THE CORRECT ALTERNATIVE
Chapter 1 | Draw Your Conclusions 129
Making a Summary
Exercise 9: ASK FOR INFORMATION
Exercise 10: WRITE A LETTER

Figure 13.1 A defined list was created to track the exercises throughout this book. Although each exercise is in its own table and is separated by text, InDesign still numbers them consecutively.

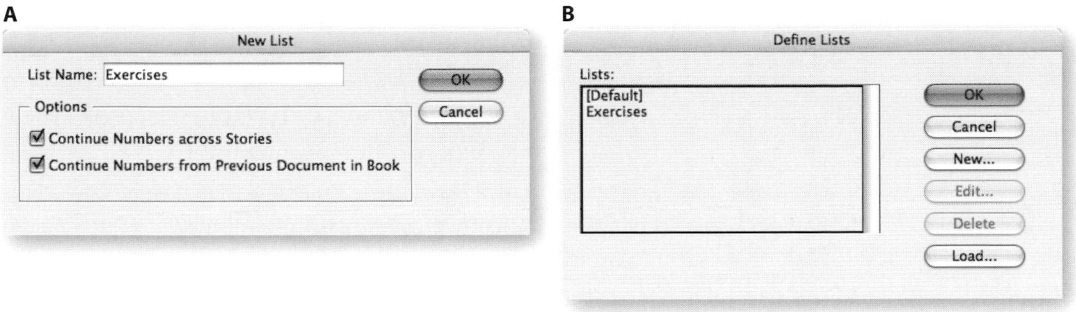
A
New List
List Name: Exercises
OK
Cancel
Options
Continue Numbers across Stories
Continue Numbers from Previous Document in Book
B
Define Lists
Lists:
[Default]
Exercises
OK
Cancel
New...
Edit...
Delete
Load...

Figure 13.2 Choose a name that describes the purpose of the list (**A**). After the list is created, it appears in the Define Lists dialog (**B**).

After defining a list, the next step is to create a paragraph style that will be applied to all the text in the running list. If one already exists, you can just edit it. On the left side of the Paragraph Style Options dialog, click Bullets and Numbering. Choose Numbers from the List Type menu and then select the defined list you created earlier from the List menu (**Figure 13.3**). Determine how you want the numbers to appear and specify all the other options accordingly.

● **Note:** See Chapter 10, "Formatting Type and Generating Style Sheets," for detailed information on how to format a numbered list.

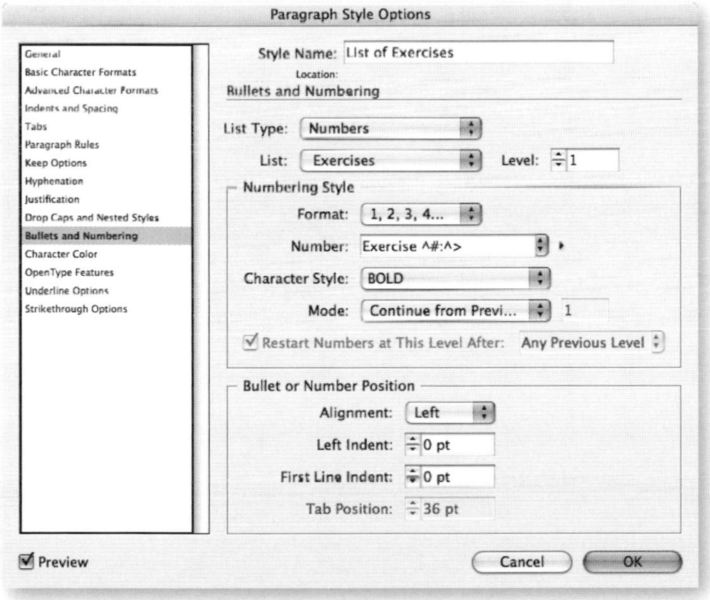
Paragraph Style Options
General
Basic Character Formats
Advanced Character Formats
Indents and Spacing
Tabs
Paragraph Rules
Keep Options
Hyphenation
Justification
Drop Caps and Nested Styles
Bullets and Numbering
Character Color
OpenType Features
Underline Options
Strikethrough Options
Style Name: List of Exercises
Location:
Bullets and Numbering
List Type: Numbers
List: Exercises
Level: 1
Numbering Style
Format: 1, 2, 3, 4...
Number: Exercise ^#:^>
Character Style: BOLD
Mode: Continue from Previ...
1
Restart Numbers at This Level After: Any Previous Level
Bullet or Number Position
Alignment: Left
Left Indent: 0 pt
First Line Indent: 0 pt
Tab Position: 36 pt
Preview
Cancel
OK

Figure 13.3 This paragraph style is set up to track the list of exercises shown in Figure 13.1. The expression in the Number field (Exercise ^#:^>) results in the word Exercise followed by a space, the current number, a colon, and an En Space.

With the paragraph style set up, apply it to each paragraph that you want to be part of the list. The first paragraph you apply the style to is assigned the number 1 and the next paragraph is assigned number 2, even if it appears in a different frame several pages later. Since both paragraphs are part of the same defined list, they are numbered consecutively.

Creating Multilevel Lists

In Chapter 10, "Formatting Type and Generating Style Sheets," you learned how to create basic numbered lists. Now you'll learn how to take your numbered lists to the next level. InDesign let's you set up a system of paragraph styles that work together to automatically number and maintain a list of up to nine levels. By creating a multilevel list, you can display paragraphs of information in a hierarchical structure (**Figure 13.4**).

Figure 13.4 Multilevel lists are often used in textbooks and technical documentation. This particular list has three levels.

1870 – 1900: Liberalism and Ethical Politics in Holland

1. Important Changes Between 1870 – 1900
   - 1.1 When was the Suez Canal opened?
   - 1.2 Why was it so important to the colonials?
   - 1.3 What were the motives behind modern imperialism?
2. Economical Changes: Initiatives and Expansion
   - 2.1 Why were the liberals against the Cultuurstelsel?
   - 2.2 What political changes were the result of the Dutch constitution?
   - 2.3 What is the name of the person who organized a demonstration against the Dutch constitution?
     - a. Karel van Echem
     - b. David Van Dam
     - c. Norah Heutz
   - 2.4 What were the consequences of the Agrarian Law in 1890?
3. Social Changes
   - 3.1 Who profited the most from the rise in education?
   - 3.2 What two important Indonesian political parties came into existence?

To create a multilevel list, choose Type > Bulleted and Numbered Lists > Define Lists, and define a new list. Then create a paragraph style for each level in the list. So, a list with three levels requires three paragraph styles.

In the Paragraph Style Options dialog, click Bullets and Numbering. Choose Numbers from the List Type menu and then select the defined list you created earlier from the List menu. Each paragraph style that is part of the multilevel list needs to be assigned the same defined list. Next, enter a number into the Level field to describe the level of the list that the style is applied to. Specify the other options as necessary to determine the numbering scheme and format for that level.

When you apply the paragraph styles to each level in a list, InDesign automatically numbers the entries for you. As entries are added or deleted, they are automatically renumbered, saving you a lot of work.

Here are some tips for creating multilevel lists:

- **Create a style group.** Place all the paragraph styles associated with a particular list into a style group (**Figure 13.5**).
- **Base each style on another style.** You might choose a style from the Based On menu to base each style on the style that will be assigned to the level above it. So, a change to the parent style instantly updates the styles based on it.
- **Use the Next Style option.** If a multilevel list follows a predictable pattern, choose the style from the Next Style menu that will be assigned to the subsequent level in the list. Then, as you type each level of the list, the styles are automatically applied. And after importing a list, you can format the entire list with one click of a button by selecting it, right-clicking/Control-clicking the parent style, and then choosing Apply [*Style Name*] then Next Style.
- **Use the Number field to your advantage.** Several metacharacters are available in the menu to the right of the Number field that can be combined in different ways. For example, you can include the first-level prefix when numbering the second level of a list, such as 1.1, 1.2, 1.3, and so on. This is achieved by entering a number placeholder for the first level (^1) followed by a period (.), the current level number (^#), and a tab space (^t). See Figure 13.4 for an example of this numbering scheme.

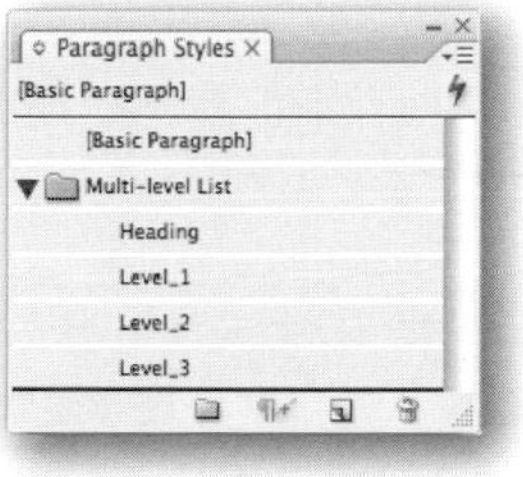
Paragraph Styles
[Basic Paragraph]
[Basic Paragraph]
Multi-level List
Heading
Level_1
Level_2
Level_3

Figure 13.5 With all the related paragraph styles together, it's easy to find them and quickly format a multilevel list.

Setting the Document Footnote Options

Footnotes are often used in textbooks and manuals. They are notes located at the bottom of a page that provide additional information about something mentioned in the text above. InDesign makes it easy to insert and format footnotes.

To insert a footnote, place your cursor into the text where you want the footnote reference number to appear, and then choose Type > Insert Footnote. The number appears in the text and its corresponding footnote text appears at the bottom of the column (**Figure 13.6**). The cursor is also repositioned within the footnote area so you can immediately start adding text to it. As you type, the footnote area expands upward, as necessary, to accommodate all the text.

● **Note:** InDesign also lets you import footnotes from Word or RTF documents.

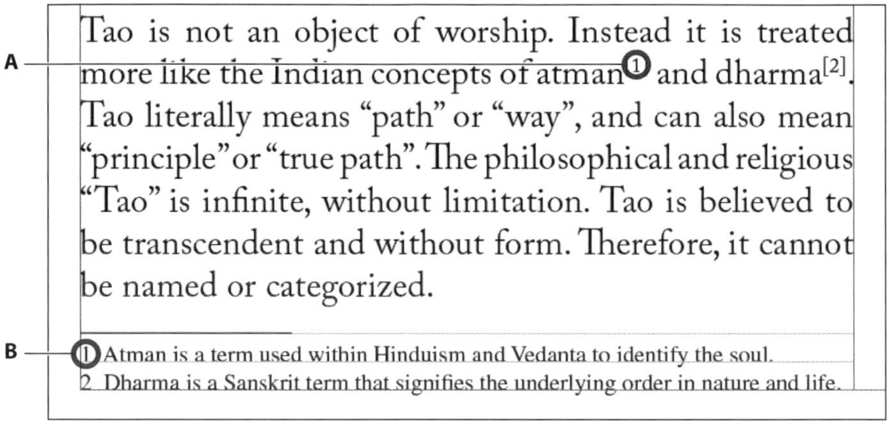
A
B
Tao is not an object of worship. Instead it is treated more like the Indian concepts of atman① and dharma[2]. Tao literally means "path" or "way", and can also mean "principle" or "true path". The philosophical and religious "Tao" is infinite, without limitation. Tao is believed to be transcendent and without form. Therefore, it cannot be named or categorized.
1 Atman is a term used within Hinduism and Vedanta to identify the soul.
2 Dharma is a Sanskrit term that signifies the underlying order in nature and life.

Figure 13.6 The reference number (A) and its corresponding footnote text (B). As footnotes are added or deleted, the footnotes are automatically renumbered.

To change the appearance of the reference number and the footnote text, choose Type > Document Footnote Options. These options control the numbering, formatting, and layout for all the footnotes in a document. By specifying these options in your template, you ensure that all new publications based on it will use the same settings.

The options in the Numbering and Formatting tab let you determine how the footnotes should be numbered and formatted (**Figure 13.7**).

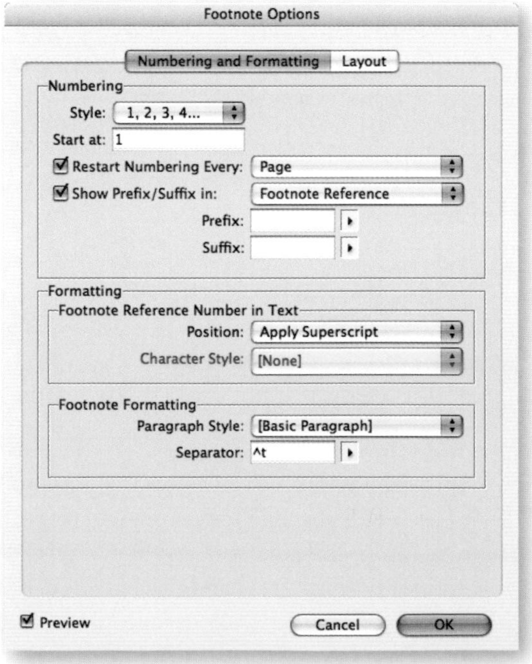
Footnote Options
Numbering and Formatting
Layout
Numbering
Style: 1, 2, 3, 4...
Start at: 1
Restart Numbering Every: Page
Show Prefix/Suffix in: Footnote Reference
Prefix:
Suffix:
Formatting
Footnote Reference Number in Text
Position: Apply Superscript
Character Style: [None]
Footnote Formatting
Paragraph Style: [Basic Paragraph]
Separator: ^t
Preview
Cancel
OK

Figure 13.7 The Numbering and Formatting tab in the Footnote Options dialog. Select Preview at the bottom to see the results of the changes you made before clicking OK.

Specify the following settings as necessary:

- **Style.** Choose the numbering style you want to use for the footnote reference numbers (**Figure 13.8**).

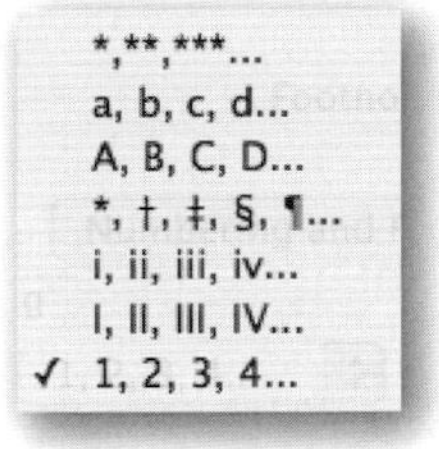
*, **, ***...
a, b, c, d...
A, B, C, D...
*, †, ‡, §, ¶...
i, ii, iii, iv...
I, II, III, IV...
✓ 1, 2, 3, 4...

Figure 13.8 Choose from seven numbering styles available in the Style menu.

- **Start at.** Specify the number that the first footnote in a story will use. Keep in mind that footnote numbering starts over in each story, so it's important to flow all the text within one story.
- **Restart Numbering Every.** If you select this option, you can choose to restart the footnote numbering on every page, spread, or section within the document. You might choose Page or Spread when using symbols (*, §) for the numbering style.
- **Show Prefix/Suffix in.** Select this option to insert a prefix or suffix in the footnote reference, footnote text, or both. For instance, you might want to add closing parenthesis after the number in the footnote text. Adding a hair space or thin space to the prefix of the footnote reference is a good idea if the number is too close to the preceding text. Click the icon next to the Prefix field to display a menu and insert one of these spacing options.

■ **Tip:** When working with multiple documents in a book file, you might want to continue the footnote numbering sequence from one document to another by specifying the next consecutive number in the Start at field in each document.

- **Position.** This option allows you to control the position of the footnote reference number. You can choose Apply Superscript (default), Apply Subscript, or Apply Normal. Choose Apply Normal if you would rather use a character style that includes OpenType superscript settings to determine the number's position.
- **Character Style.** Choose a character style to format the footnote reference number. For instance, you might want make the number bold or italic. Only the character styles already in the document are available in the menu.
- **Paragraph Style.** You might want to choose a paragraph style other than [Basic Paragraph] to format the footnote text at the bottom of the column. Only the paragraph styles already in the document are available in the menu. The style you choose is applied to all the footnote text in the document.

■ **Tip:** If you want to control the formatting of individual reference numbers and footnote text, you can select them separately and apply paragraph and/or character styles to them.

- **Separator.** Any character typed into this field appears between the footnote number and the start of the footnote text. The tab character (^t) is the default separator. You can replace it with another character, such as an em space (^m). Click the icon next to the Separator field for a menu of other possible characters to use. You can even insert multiple characters.

The options in the Layout tab let you control the formatting that is applied to the footnote section at the bottom of the page (**Figure 13.9**).

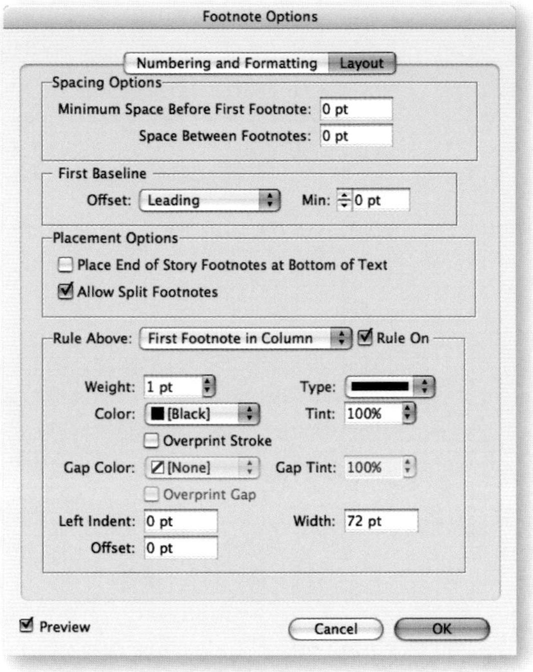
Footnote Options
Numbering and Formatting
Layout
Spacing Options
Minimum Space Before First Footnote: 0 pt
Space Between Footnotes: 0 pt
First Baseline
Offset: Leading
Min: 0 pt
Placement Options
Place End of Story Footnotes at Bottom of Text
Allow Split Footnotes
Rule Above: First Footnote in Column
Rule On
Weight: 1 pt
Type:
Color: [Black]
Tint: 100%
Overprint Stroke
Gap Color: [None]
Gap Tint: 100%
Overprint Gap
Left Indent: 0 pt
Width: 72 pt
Offset: 0 pt
Preview
Cancel
OK

Figure 13.9 The Layout tab in the Footnote Options dialog.

Specify the following settings as necessary:

- **Minimum Space Before First Footnote**. Enter a value to determine the minimum amount of space between the last line of text in the column and the first footnote.
- **Space Between Footnotes.** Enter a value to determine the distance between footnote entries in a column.
- **First Baseline Offset.** This option controls the distance between the first line of footnote text and the top of the footnote area (as indicated by the divider line). Choose an option from the Offset menu to determine which part of the text the top of the footnote area is measured from (**Figure 13.10**). Enter a value into the Min field to increase the distance.
- **Place End of Story Footnotes at Bottom of Text.** If you select this option, and the last column of text in a story doesn't fill the entire frame, the footnote will appear just below the text instead of at the bottom of the column.
- **Allow Split Footnotes.** Select this option to allow footnotes to split across a column when they exceed the amount of available space in a column. If this option is deselected, the entire footnote moves to the next column, or the text frame becomes overset.

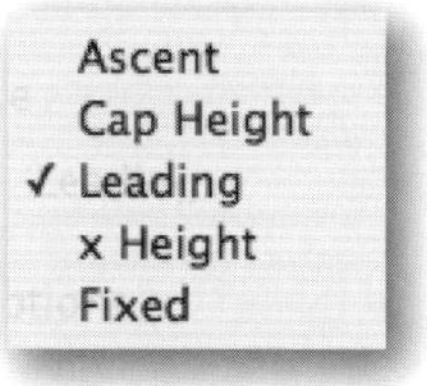
Ascent
Cap Height
✓ Leading
x Height
Fixed

Figure 13.10 Choose from five options in the Offset menu. By default, the text's leading value is used.

■ **Tip:** You can control where a footnote splits by choosing Type > Insert Break Character > Column Break.

- **Rule Above.** This option lets you create a divider line between the footnote text and the last line of text in a column. By choosing either First Footnote in Column or Continued Footnotes from the Rule Above menu, you can specify a separate appearance for rules above the footnote text or rules above any footnote text continued in another frame. Specify the rule you want to change the settings for and then select Rule On to activate it.

  Type a weight value to determine the thickness of the rule. For Type, specify the kind of rule you want to create. Next, choose a color and tint value for the rule. The colors listed are those already in the Swatches panel. If you specified a line type other than solid, choose a gap color and/or gap tint value to add color to the area between dashes, dots, or lines. Select Overprint Stroke or Overprint Gap if you want the line to overprint any underlying inks on the printing press.

  Type a value into the Left Indent field to set a left indent for the rule. Type a value into the Width field to determine how wide the rule should be. To specify the rule's vertical position, type a value into the Offset field.

Creating a Table of Contents Style

If the publication you're constructing a template for requires a table of contents, you'll want to create a table of contents style (TOC style), which is a collection of settings used to automatically build a table of contents. The TOC style is conveniently stored in the template document, so whenever designers need to generate a table of contents, all they have to do is utilize the TOC style you've set up. This saves a lot of production time and ensures a consistent design.

Tip: One template can contain multiple TOC styles. You might have one for a list of chapters and another for a list of figures, photo credits, or advertisers.

Before creating a TOC style, let's take a look at how InDesign generates a table of contents. The process requires three main steps. The first and most important step is to carefully apply paragraph styles to every heading, subhead, and other text elements that will compose your table of contents. The second step is to specify which paragraph styles are used in the table of contents and determine how it is formatted. The third step is to create the table of contents and place it into your document. The content for each entry is pulled directly from the text in the document. In other words, the text that the specified paragraph styles are applied to gets copied into the table of contents (**Figure 13.11**). After the table of contents is generated, you can move pages and edit headings, and then simply update the table of contents with a couple of mouse clicks.

B
CONTENTS
A
ANCIENT ROME
8
9
ANCIENT ROME
Roman Forum
10
ANCIENT ROME
Arch of Constantine
11

Figure 13.11 Since paragraph styles were applied to each chapter title and heading in this book (**A**), that information is used to create this table of contents (**B**).

To set up a TOC style, create a mock-up layout of the table of contents, and then make any necessary paragraph and character styles based on its formatting. You'll use these styles to format the table of contents. Next, choose Layout > Table Of Contents Styles (**Figure 13.12**). Click New and type a name for the style you're creating. In the Title field, type the name that you want to appear at the top of the table of contents, such as "Contents." From the Style menu choose one of the paragraph styles that you created earlier to format the title.

● **Note:** By default, every InDesign document has two paragraph styles available for formatting a table of contents: TOC Title and TOC Body Text. The styles don't appear in the Paragraph Styles panel unless they are used when creating a table of contents.

A

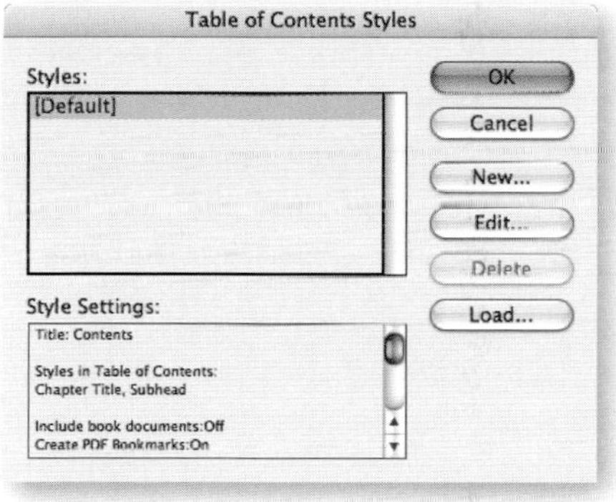
Table of Contents Styles
Styles:
[Default]
OK
Cancel
New...
Edit...
Delete
Load...
Style Settings:
Title: Contents
Styles in Table of Contents:
Chapter Title, Subhead
Include book documents:Off
Create PDF Bookmarks:On

B

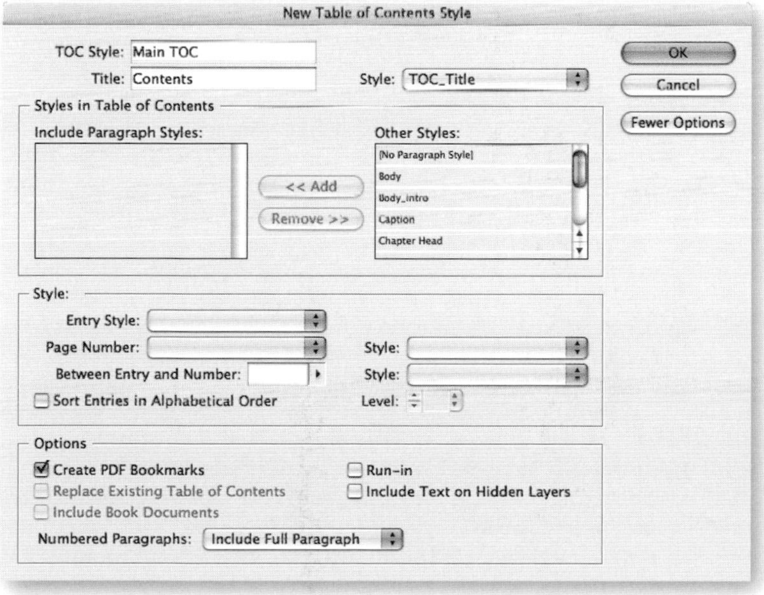
New Table of Contents Style
TOC Style: Main TOC
Title: Contents
Style: TOC_Title
OK
Cancel
Fewer Options
Styles in Table of Contents
Include Paragraph Styles:
<< Add
Remove >>
Other Styles:
[No Paragraph Style]
Body
Body_intro
Caption
Chapter Head
Style:
Entry Style:
Page Number:
Style:
Between Entry and Number:
Style:
Sort Entries in Alphabetical Order
Level:
Options
Create PDF Bookmarks
Run-in
Replace Existing Table of Contents
Include Text on Hidden Layers
Include Book Documents
Numbered Paragraphs: Include Full Paragraph

Figure 13.12 The Table of Contents Styles dialog contains a list of all the TOC styles stored in a document (**A**). The New Table of Contents Style dialog (**B**). Click the More Options button to show all the available formatting options.

● **Note:** Only the paragraph styles currently in your template show up in the Other Styles list. So before creating a TOC style, you must first make all the paragraph styles that will be applied to the content you want included in the table of contents.

Next, determine which content you want to include in the table of contents by moving paragraph styles from the Other Styles list to the Include Paragraph Styles list. To move a style, select it and click the Add button (or double-click it). It's a good idea to move the styles in the same order the entries will appear in the table of contents. By default, each style you add is set one level lower than the previously added style. You can change this hierarchy by selecting a style and specifying a new level number in the Level field. You might also need to relocate the styles within the list by dragging them to a new position.

After moving the necessary styles to the Include Paragraph Styles list, you can specify how you want the text in the table of contents formatted. The formatting you apply to each style in the list determines the appearance of the associated entries in the table of contents (**Figure 13.13**). Specify the following settings for each style as necessary:

- **Entry Style.** Select the paragraph style you want applied to the associated entry in the table of contents.
- **Page Number.** Choose to place the page number before the entry, to place it after the entry, or to have no page number at all. In Figure 13.11, the chapter title entries aren't followed by a page number, whereas the subhead entries are. You might also format the page number by selecting a character style from the Style menu to the right of Page Number option.

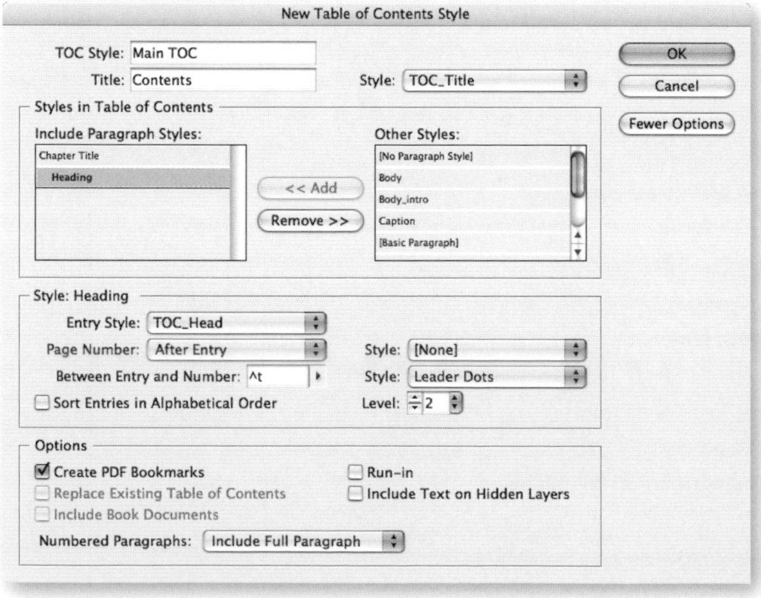
New Table of Contents Style
TOC Style: Main TOC
Title: Contents
Style: TOC_Title
OK
Cancel
Fewer Options
Styles in Table of Contents
Include Paragraph Styles:
Chapter Title
Heading
<< Add
Remove >>
Other Styles:
[No Paragraph Style]
Body
Body_intro
Caption
[Basic Paragraph]
Style: Heading
Entry Style: TOC_Head
Page Number: After Entry
Style: [None]
Between Entry and Number: ^t
Style: Leader Dots
Sort Entries in Alphabetical Order
Level: 2
Options
Create PDF Bookmarks
Run-in
Replace Existing Table of Contents
Include Text on Hidden Layers
Include Book Documents
Numbered Paragraphs: Include Full Paragraph

Figure 13.13 The settings in the Style section apply only to the currently selected style in the Include Paragraph Styles list. You can specify different formatting options for each style.

- **Between Entry and Number.** Specify which character(s) you want inserted between the table of contents entry and its page number. A tab space (^t) is inserted by default. Click the menu to the right of the field to insert other characters, such as an Em Space or Right Indent Tab. You might also format the space between the entry and the page number by selecting a character style from the Style menu to the right of the Between Entry and Number option. In Figure 13.11, the paragraph style applied to each subhead entry includes a tab leader setting, so applying a character style to the tab space formats the leader dots.
- **Sort Entries in Alphabetical Order.** Select this option if you want the entries arranged in alphabetical order. Although it isn't useful for a listing of chapters in a book or magazine, this option is very useful for sorting a list of figures or advertisers.

● **Note:** The sort order for the table of contents is determined by the document's default language setting.

After you've specified the formatting for each style, you then need to consider a few options at the bottom of the New Table of Contents Style dialog:

- **Create PDF Bookmarks.** Select this option if you want PDF bookmarks for each entry in the table of contents to be created when you export the document to PDF. The entries will appear in the Bookmarks panel of Adobe Acrobat or Adobe Reader.
- **Run-in.** Select this option to make the entries run into a single paragraph (**Figure 13.14**). Each entry is separated by a semicolon followed by a space (;).

CONTENTS

9 Ancient Rome
Roman Forum; Arch of Constantine; Teatro di Marcello; Capitoline Hill; Colosseum

17 Rome's Best Museums
Capitoline Museums; Vatican Museums; Galleria Borghese; Etruscan Museum at Villa Giulia

25 Romantic Rome
La Terrazza; Pincio; Le Jardin du Russie, Campidoglio; Ponte Sant' Angelo

31 Rome's Best Hotels
Eden; Hassler; Hotel de Russie; Santa Maria; Villa San Pio

37 Shopping in Rome
Martina Novelli; Franchi; Castroni; Fuori Orario; Via Sannio

43 Dining in Rome
Taverna del Campo; Dar Poeta; Insalata Ricca; Trattoria Monti; Caffé delle Arti

Figure 13.14 By running the entries together into one paragraph, you can set up a table of contents that looks like this. Notice that the page numbers are placed before the chapter title entries in this design.

- **Include Text on Hidden Layers.** All the information that makes up the table of contents has to be on a page somewhere in the document. But sometimes information that needs to be included in the table of contents shouldn't appear on a page. So, you can place that information on a hidden layer and then select this option in the TOC style. The paragraphs on hidden layers are then included in your table of contents when it's generated.
- **Numbered Paragraphs.** If certain text elements—chapter titles, headings, and subheads—use numbering, specify whether the entries in the table of contents will include the full paragraph (both numbers and text), just the numbers, or just the paragraph.

14

Preparing Your Template for Success

CONGRATULATIONS! YOUR TEMPLATE IS ALMOST COMPLETE. YOU'VE SET UP THE underlying framework, master pages, and libraries. You've generated style sheets for text, objects, and maybe even tables. And you might have set up a table of contents style or a few other long document features. Most important, you've considered the smallest details along the way and have produced a template that is optimized for its intended purpose. Now it's time to tie up any loose ends and prepare your template for the job it was created to do: facilitate fast and efficient page layout.

This chapter walks you through the process of finalizing your template, testing it, and packaging it for final implementation. It also shows you how to create a style guide to accompany more complex templates for distribution to a workgroup.

Finalizing Your Template

When you start a document based on a template, the new document is an exact duplicate of that template. Everything, including any problems and inconsistencies, are carried over to each new document based on the template. Therefore, it's critical that you clean up your template and specify its various default settings before using it in a live production workflow.

No matter how careful you are when constructing a template, you will always make a few unintentional mistakes during the process. This important step ensures that your template is shipshape, efficient, and easy to use. Each time you use the template to create a new document, you'll be able to start working immediately without having to sort anything out first, such as deleting unnecessary objects, fixing font problems, or looking for missing links.

Cleaning Up the Template

Your ultimate goal in this step is to get rid of unnecessary elements and prevent printing problems from occurring. Here are some common gotchas to look for. At least some or all of them will apply to your template, depending on its level of complexity. This process should be quick and painless if you paid close attention to accuracy and detail while constructing your template:

● **Note:** If you plan on creating a style guide, be sure to save a copy of the template with all of its sample elements intact, so you can use them to make the guide.

- **Eliminate sample layout elements.** Any sample elements left over from the mock-up layout should be removed unless they serve a specific purpose. Basically, if a designer has to delete an element before he or she can begin using your template, it's creating unnecessary work and should be deleted. However, there is an exception. If a frame is holding useful placeholder text, it may be better to keep it on the page. In most cases, though, it's faster to apply paragraph and character styles than it is to select and replace text.
- **Delete extra pages.** If there are extra pages in the document, get rid of them. Keep only the pages or spreads that are necessary for starting a new document. For example, a brochure template will begin with two pages—one for each side. Also, remove any superfluous master pages that won't ever be used.
- **Clean up the pasteboard.** Remove objects from the pasteboard unless they have been strategically placed to be used during production. Even if you think an object has good reason for being there, consider adding it to an object library instead.
- **Remove excessive style sheets.** It's easy to create more style sheets than you actually need. Try to minimize the number of style sheets in your template by creating them for just the elements that frequently repeat throughout the design. If a style sheet will hardly ever be used, consider

deleting it. With a smaller list of style sheets to choose from, your template will be easier to use and you'll be far more productive.

- **Clear overrides from default style sheets.** While building your template, you might have unintentionally overridden the default paragraph style or default graphics frame style by changing a setting while nothing was selected.

  For instance, after changing the type size and selecting a new font, you realize that you forgot to select some text first. Since nothing was selected when you changed the formatting, you inadvertently overrode the default paragraph style. From now on, that formatting will be initially applied to all new text that you type.

  It can be quite an inconvenience to those using your template if you save it without clearing the overrides. If a style sheet has been overridden, it will display a plus sign (+) next to its name. To clear the overrides, hold Alt/Option as you click the style.

● **Note:** It's possible to override the default character style if one has been specified. However, it's not possible to override the default text frame style or table style.

- **Check font usage.** Look for missing fonts or any extra fonts in use that shouldn't be. An easy way to do this is to use the Find Font command by choosing Type > Find Font. If a font is used anywhere in the template, including master pages and the pasteboard, it will be listed (**Figure 14.1**).

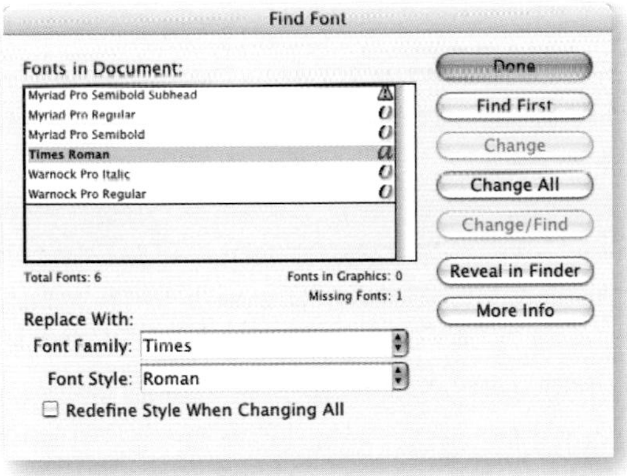
Find Font
Fonts in Document:
Myriad Pro Semibold Subhead
Myriad Pro Regular
Myriad Pro Semibold
Times Roman
Warnock Pro Italic
Warnock Pro Regular
Total Fonts: 6
Fonts in Graphics: 0
Missing Fonts: 1
Replace With:
Font Family: Times
Font Style: Roman
Redefine Style When Changing All
Done
Find First
Change
Change All
Change/Find
Reveal in Finder
More Info

Figure 14.1 The Find Font dialog lists all the fonts in use. To the right of each item is an icon that displays the type of font it is or its current condition. If a font is missing, a yellow caution symbol is displayed.

  If an extra font is being used, select it in the list and click Find First to locate it. Once located, choose Done to close the dialog, and then apply the correct font or delete the text that uses the font to fix the issue. Most likely you accidentally created an extra text frame on the page or somewhere on the pasteboard that is using the unwanted font. If there is a missing font, install it or replace the text using the font with the appropriate one. Continue this procedure until all the font problems are found and resolved.

- **Remove extra layers.** Look for any unnecessary layers you might have created and delete them.

- **Clean up the list of swatches.** Make sure every swatch has been given a useful name based on its function in the template. Also, if a swatch exists within the Swatches panel that will rarely if ever be used, delete it. Most likely you'll want to delete cyan, magenta, yellow, red, green, and blue. They are InDesign's default swatches and probably don't serve a purpose in your template.

  It's easy to accumulate a lot of swatches, but try to keep the list as small as possible. This makes it easier for designers to find a specific color when they need it. At times, they might have to create a new one, but that is far easier than scrolling through an endless list of swatches.

  Also, if any spot colors exist within the template, convert them to process colors unless you are actually planning to print with them.

- **Check the links.** Check the list of imported graphics in the Links panel to make sure there are no missing or modified links (**Figure 14.2**). If a linked file is missing, you won't be able to print successfully, because the original file was moved to a different location after you imported it. To fix the connection, select the link, choose Relink from the Links panel menu, and then locate the file.

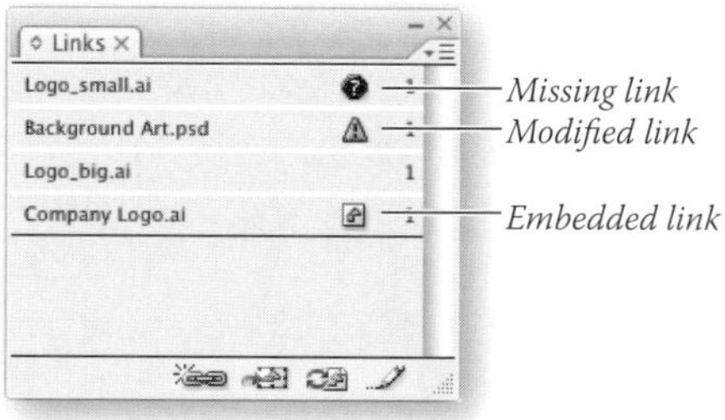
Links
Logo_small.ai
Background Art.psd
Logo_big.ai
1
Company Logo.ai
Missing link
Modified link
Embedded link

Figure 14.2 All files placed in a document are listed in the Links panel. If a graphic has been modified, is missing, or is embedded, an icon will appear on the right side of the link to display its status.

Note: You can use InDesign's preflight utility to check for issues with both fonts and linked graphics at the same time by choosing File > Preflight.

  If a linked file shows that it has been modified, the version of the file on disk is more recent than the version in your document. Select the link and choose Update Link from the Links panel menu to fix it.

  You might choose to embed some graphics, such as a company logo, into the template document to break their connection to the original file. InDesign will no longer try to manage them. Keep in mind that whenever you embed a file, the size of your template file also increases. So, try to keep the number of embedded graphics to a minimum.

- **Check the resolution of imported images.** When you resize raster images, you also change their resolution. If the resolution becomes to low for your intended output device, the image will lose detail and appear jagged on the printed page.

If your template contains any images, such as background art and logos, it's important to check their resolution. You can do this by opening the Info panel and selecting an image (**Figure 14.3**). The image's resolution is displayed as both actual pixels per inch (the resolution of the native image file) and effective pixels per inch (the resolution of the image after it has been resized).

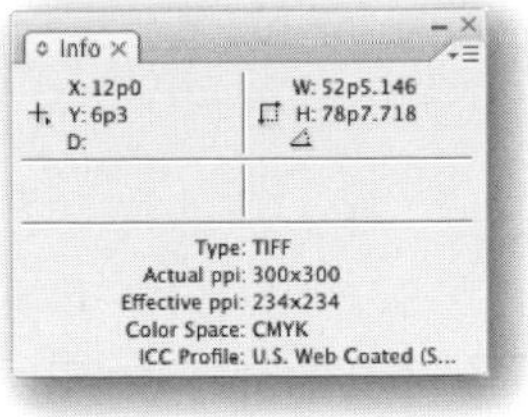
Info
X: 12p0
Y: 6p3
D:
W: 52p5.146
H: 78p7.718
Type: TIFF
Actual ppi: 300x300
Effective ppi: 234x234
Color Space: CMYK
ICC Profile: U.S. Web Coated (S...

Figure 14.3 The results of a scaled image are shown in the Info panel. As you scale down an image, its resolution increases. As you scale up an image, its resolution decreases.

- **Look for potential transparency problems.** If your template uses any transparent effects, such as drop shadows and gradient feathers, use the Flattener Preview panel to locate and preview which areas of the document will be flattened when printing the file (**Figure 14.4**). Fix any issues you run into to prevent them from reoccurring in every new document based on the template.

  A common problem occurs when type is too close to transparent objects, because it might interact with the objects in unexpected ways. For example, a single character may be converted to an outline, resulting in a thicker stroke width, while the other characters in the same line of text print normally. To overcome this, move the text frame to the top of the stacking order or relocate it to a higher layer in the Layers panel, as long as the design permits.

  Also, if your template contains spot color objects that use a blending mode, be prepared for unexpected results and avoid the following blending modes: Difference, Exclusion, Hue, Saturation, Color, and Luminosity.

  For a complete reference and troubleshooting guide on how transparency affects output, see the documents "Achieving Reliable Print Output with Transparency" and "A Designer's Guide to Transparency for Print Output" on the Adobe Web site.

■ **Tip:** Choose View > Overprint Preview to get a better idea of how spot inks that overprint or interact with transparent objects will appear in the final printed document. Just make sure to turn Overprint Preview off when you're done using it.

A
B
C
Flattener Preview
Highlight: All Rasterized Regions
Auto Refresh Highlight
Refresh
Preset: [High Resolution]
Ignore Spread Overrides
Apply Settings to Print
Lorem Ipsum
Lorem Ipsum

Figure 14.4 Using the Flattener Preview panel to discover any possible rasterized regions (**A**). The Gradient Feather effect was used to fade the bottom of this frame into the headline below it (**B**). Since the headline is behind the transparent object in the stacking order, the type will be rasterized wherever the top frame overlaps it (**C**).

Specifying the Default Settings

Default settings determine the initial behavior of a document and the objects it contains. You can specify default settings at the application level, document level, or object level. If you change a setting when no documents are open, your changes are applied at the application level, which means that all new documents will use those default settings. If you change a setting when a document is open, your changes affect that document only. If you change object-level settings when no objects are selected, your changes specify the defaults for all new objects you create within that document.

Keep in mind that if the default settings at the application level are different from those at the document level, the document's settings will always override the application's settings when the document is open. So, when designers start a new document based on your template, they will automatically be using the default settings you've defined instead of their own. By specifying the defaults in your template, you're enforcing standards, ensuring consistency, and setting other designers up for increased productivity.

To specify the default settings for your template, deselect all the objects on the page by choosing Edit > Deselect All, and then change InDesign's various settings found in the menus, dialogs, and panels. Here's a list of suggested settings to specify as defaults in your templates. They are all optional and should be set up as necessary:

- **Show frame edges.** Viewing the frame edges on a page can be as irritating as it is useful. With templates, it's especially helpful to see them, because you can clearly see where the placeholder text and graphics frames sit on the page (**Figure 14.5**). When other designers use your template, they'll find it much easier to select and modify the various elements as they produce a document.
- **Show guides and grids.** From the moment you start a new document based on a template, you want to see the layout grid so you know immediately where to start placing the various elements onto the page. Choose View > Grids & Guides > Show Guides if they aren't already visible. If your template uses the baseline grid or document grid, make them visible as well. Choose View > Grids & Guides, and then choose Show Baseline Grid or Show Document Grid as necessary.
- **Ruler guide color.** You can change the default ruler guide color so that each new guide you create uses that color. This can be useful to keep the guides you create separate from those already coming from a master page. With no ruler guides selected, choose Layout > Ruler Guides, and then select a color from the Color menu.

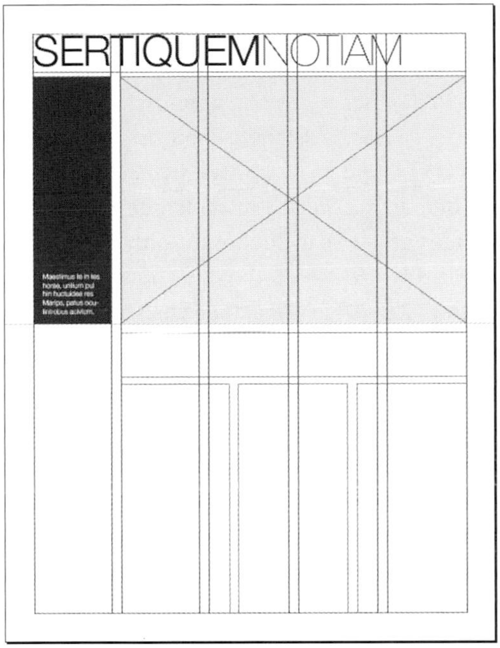
SERTIQUEMNOTIAM

Figure 14.5 This template page contains several placeholder frames. If the frame edges were not visible, it would be difficult to see that the placeholder text frames for the headline and body text don't adhere to the five-column grid.

- **Unlock guides.** It's best not to lock all the guides in your template. When they are locked, you won't be able to select or move any guides on the page, which is especially frustrating when you try to modify the location of a guide you've just created and can't. If the guides are currently locked, choose View > Grids & Guides > Lock Guides to disable the option. If you need to lock a few guides, place them on a separate layer and lock just that layer.
- **Lock column guides.** Make sure the column guides are locked to prevent them from being accidentally relocated. Choose View > Grids & Guides > Lock Column Guides to enable the option.
- **Show hidden characters.** If the nonprinting characters such as spaces, tabs, forced line breaks, and paragraph returns are currently hidden, you might choose to make them visible. They are especially useful when applying paragraph styles, because you can see where each paragraph begins and ends. When applying paragraph styles that contain nested styles, viewing the nonprinting characters also makes it easy to ensure the correct character is being used to end each nested style (**Figure 14.6**). Choose Type > Show Hidden Characters to view the nonprinting characters.

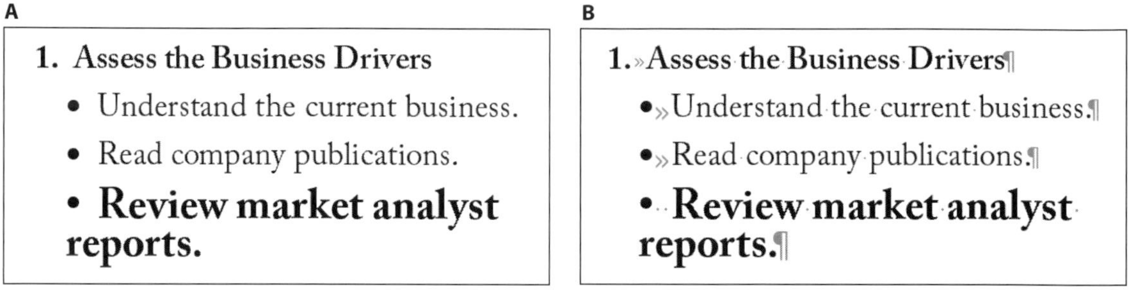
A
1. Assess the Business Drivers
• Understand the current business.
• Read company publications.
• Review market analyst reports.
B
1.»Assess the Business Drivers¶
•»Understand the current business.¶
•»Read company publications.¶
• Review market analyst reports.¶

Figure 14.6 When the nonprinting characters are hidden (**A**), it can difficult to spot potential problems, such as extra paragraph returns and spaces. With the nonprinting characters visible, you can easily see that the last paragraph in this list needs a tab after the bullet character instead of two spaces to make the nested style work (**B**).

- **Show text threads.** If your template will be used to create documents that contain many linked text frames, you might find it useful to make the threads visible. This makes it easier to identify which frames are part of a story and is especially useful for newspaper and magazine templates (**Figure 14.7**). Choose View > Show Text Threads to make the threads visible. When you select a text frame, a visual thread indicates the frames it is linked to; otherwise, nothing is displayed when no text frames are selected.

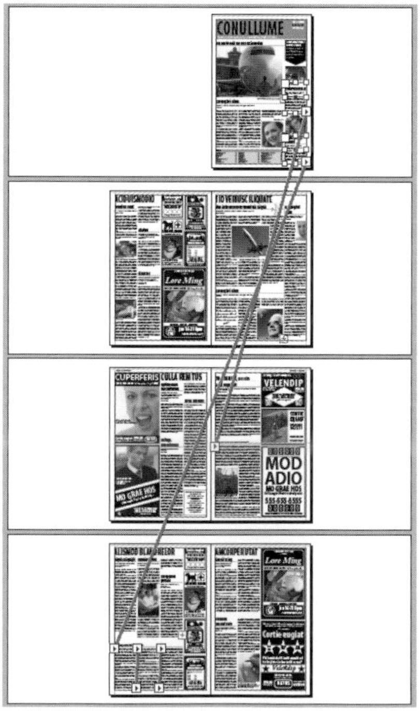

Figure 14.7 By making the text threads visible, you can easily track a story when it jumps from one page to another in a document.

- **Normal view mode.** Make sure your template is in Normal view mode; otherwise, you won't be able to see the frame edges, layout grid, nonprinting characters, text threads, or objects on the pasteboard. Choose View > Screen Mode > Normal or use the Normal Mode button at the bottom of the toolbox.
- **Enable or Disable Layout Adjustment.** You might have used the layout adjustment feature while building your template, so it's likely still enabled. Decide whether or not you want to keep it enabled by default, choose Layout > Layout Adjustment, and then enable or disable the feature as needed. Keeping Layout Adjustment enabled can result in unexpected modifications to a layout, such as when a new master page is applied. However, if well planned, this feature can be a powerful production tool. If you decide to keep it enabled, make sure you communicate that to other designers who will be using your template so they are aware that it's enabled.
- **Layers panel settings.** Double-check the Layers panel to make sure the layers are locked or unlocked and visible or not as required by your template. Also, if there are multiple layers, select the layer that you want to designate as the default layer.
- **Default master pages.** If your template contains multiple master pages, apply the primarily used master page(s) to each document page as needed. You will then be set up with the correct layout grid and placeholder frames the moment you start a new document. Also, override any elements you need immediate access to so you don't have to repeat the override process each time you start a new document.
- **Default style sheets.** By setting specific paragraph styles, object styles, and table styles as defaults in your template, you can control the formatting that is initially applied to text, objects, and tables as you create them.

  With paragraph styles, you can either edit the [Basic Paragraph] style or specify a new default style. To edit the [Basic Paragraph] style, double-click it and modify its formatting options as needed. To specify a new default style, deselect everything on the page and then click a style other than [Basic Paragraph]. You can also specify a default character style, but it's best not to, because it will be applied to all the text you type or import and conflict with the formatting already applied by the paragraph style. So, make sure that [None] is selected in the Character Styles panel.

  There are two default object styles: [Basic Graphics Frame] and [Basic Text Frame] (**Figure 14.8**). You can either edit the current default object styles or reassign new defaults. To edit them, double-click each style and modify their formatting options as necessary. To reassign the default style

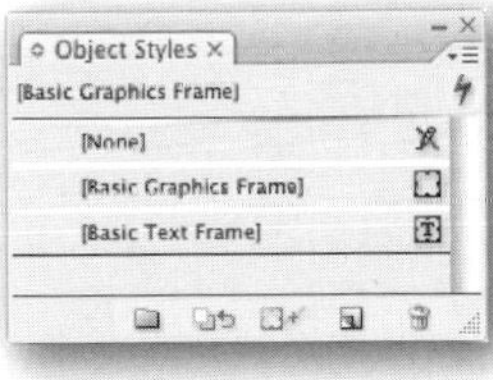
Object Styles
[Basic Graphics Frame]
[None]
[Basic Graphics Frame]
[Basic Text Frame]

Figure 14.8 The default object styles can be identified by the icon to the right of their name. The Text Frame icon marks the default style for text frames. The Graphics Frame icon marks the default style for unassigned frames.

● **Note:** The [Basic Graphics Frame] style is only applied to paths and unassigned frames. There is no default object style applied to frames created with the Rectangle Frame Tool, which are often referred to as graphics frames.

for text frames, choose Default Text Frame Style from the Object Styles panel menu, and then select an object style. To reassign the default style for unassigned frames, choose Default Graphic Frame Style from the Object Styles panel menu, and then select an object style.

To specify a default cell style, you have to make it part of the default table style's definition. You can't just select a cell style when no table is selected. Even if you do, the cell style won't be initially applied to the tables you create.

- **Document window size, page number, and magnification level.** Each time you start a new document based on your template, the size of the document window, last page you were on, and level of magnification will be the same as when you last saved the template. So, if you are on page 3, zoomed in on a particular object, and the document window is quite small when you save the template, each new document you create based on it will start the same way. To make your template more straightforward, adjust the document window to an optimal size, activate the first page, and then fit the page or spread into the window.

  To resize the document window, drag the size box at the bottom right of the window. To activate a page, double-click its icon in the Pages panel. To fit either the page or spread into the document window, choose View > Fit Page in Window or View > Fit Spread in Window.

- **Measurement system.** If your template has been created for a specific team of designers, and you know what measurement system they prefer to use, specify that measurement system. If you're not sure which measurement system to use, choose the system that is most appropriate for the majority of designers who will be using the template. Right-click/Control-click a ruler and choose the desired system from the context menu. By right-clicking/Control-clicking at the intersection of the horizontal and vertical rulers, you can change the system for both rulers at the same time.

Testing Your Template

When everything is finalized, you can save your template into the template file format and put it to the test. Think of this step as the final quality inspection of your page production machine. You want to make sure all of its parts are functioning properly and ready to go. Thorough testing ensures that problems are addressed ahead of time, preventing costly mistakes later on. It also helps you discover better ways to streamline production tasks, making your template even more efficient.

To test your template, simply walk through a live production scenario. Start a new document based on your template and create a sample layout. As you work, you'll naturally run into elements that need to be fixed or improved.

Here are some testing principles that will guide you through the process:

- **Use goal-oriented tasks.** It's important to produce actual pages while testing your template to fully optimize it for the publications it's going to create. This helps you determine how much time it takes to complete a series of tasks and provides you with the information you need to come up with better solutions.
- **Use representative content.** Whenever possible, use text and graphics from an actual project to test your template. Include a complete range of possible variations in image size, image resolution, and text length. This gives you a real production experience and ensures that your template will function as anticipated.
- **Test for speed.** As you walk through a production scenario, continually look for areas of performance improvement. Does your template require too many steps to produce a layout? Can one or two steps be eliminated or automated somehow? Can the template be organized more efficiently? In many cases, you can substantially increase productivity by combining various InDesign features to produce pages in fewer steps.

  For example, you can set up nested styles to apply paragraph and character styles in just one click. You can also set up an object style to apply a paragraph style at the same time you apply the object style. If that paragraph style contains a nested style, you are combining even more steps into one automated solution.
- **Test for accuracy.** While testing for speed, it's a good idea to test for accuracy as well. This ensures that your template reproduces the design as intended. It's not uncommon, for example, to apply a paragraph style, only to find that it applies the wrong formatting.
- **Test for ease-of-use.** Your template's success also depends on its level of organization and user-friendliness. Unclear naming conventions, overlapping frames, and excessive color swatches, paragraph styles and master pages all make for an unwieldy template that is difficult to use. Consequently, this contributes to a counterproductive template.
- **Consider your initial goals.** Continually ask yourself if the template meets your initial goals or not. This keeps you heading in the right direction, ensuring that your final template is fully optimized for its intended purpose.

■ **Tip:** Keep the original template file open as you build and test a sample layout. When changes need to be made, you can quickly switch to the original template, make the necessary changes, and then go back to testing the sample file.

- **Look for conflicting InDesign features.** While testing, you might discover that using one particular feature is preventing you from using another feature. If so, you may be forced to make a compromise. Refer back to your initial objectives and create the most optimal solution that considers all aspects of your project.

Don't be surprised if you find yourself continually updating a template as you test it. No template is ever complete on your first attempt. There are always at least a few small details that are overlooked. Template design is a process where you design, test, and evaluate new possibilities. This process may need to be repeated until your template is ready for implementation.

Implementing Your Template

With your template finalized and thoroughly tested, you're ready to implement it into a live production workflow. To prepare it for a smooth deployment, it's important to add metadata to the template and collect all of its elements into one tidy package.

Adding Metadata to a Template

● **Note:** Some duplicate fields are found in different sections of the File Info dialog. If you enter information into one field, that information will automatically be copied into each duplicate field.

When you save your template, some metadata (file information) is automatically saved with the file, including a thumbnail preview, its color swatches, and a list of the fonts being used. You can add additional metadata to your template by choosing File > File Info.

The File Info dialog contains several sections where you can enter various types of metadata; however, you don't need to fill in all the available fields. In fact, most of the sections are used for viewing metadata in the graphics and images that are linked to an InDesign document.

It's a good idea to at least identify your template by inserting the document's title, your name, a short description, and some keywords into the Description section of the dialog. You might also add more detailed information into the IPTC Contact section as necessary. All of the metadata added to the template becomes searchable in Adobe Bridge and makes it easy to organize a collection of templates (**Figure 14.9**). Chapter 15, "Managing Templates with Adobe Bridge CS3," shows you how to take full advantage of metadata.

A

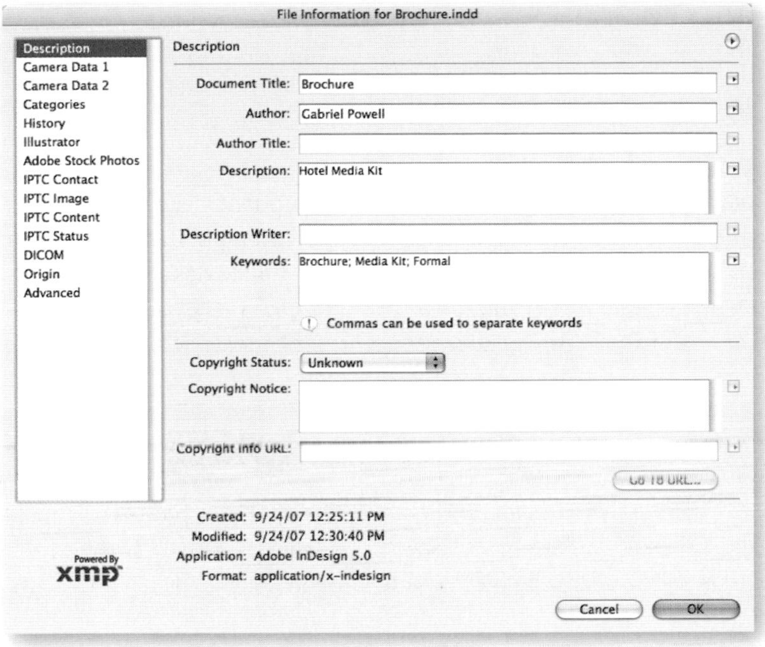
File Information for Brochure.indd
Description
Camera Data 1
Camera Data 2
Categories
History
Illustrator
Adobe Stock Photos
IPTC Contact
IPTC Image
IPTC Content
IPTC Status
DICOM
Origin
Advanced
Description
Document Title: Brochure
Author: Gabriel Powell
Author Title:
Description: Hotel Media Kit
Description Writer:
Keywords: Brochure; Media Kit; Formal
Commas can be used to separate keywords
Copyright Status: Unknown
Copyright Notice:
Copyright Info URL:
Go To URL...
Created: 9/24/07 12:25:11 PM
Modified: 9/24/07 12:30:40 PM
Application: Adobe InDesign 5.0
Format: application/x-indesign
Powered By xmp
Cancel
OK

B

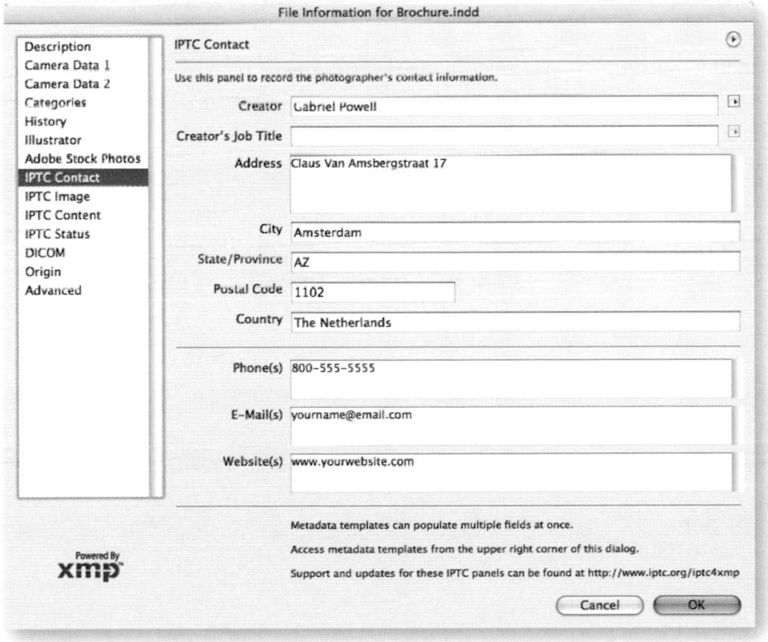
File Information for Brochure.indd
Description
Camera Data 1
Camera Data 2
Categories
History
Illustrator
Adobe Stock Photos
IPTC Contact
IPTC Image
IPTC Content
IPTC Status
DICOM
Origin
Advanced
IPTC Contact
Use this panel to record the photographer's contact information.
Creator Gabriel Powell
Creator's Job Title
Address Claus Van Amsbergstraat 17
City Amsterdam
State/Province AZ
Postal Code 1102
Country The Netherlands
Phone(s) 800-555-5555
E-Mail(s) yourname@email.com
Website(s) www.yourwebsite.com
Metadata templates can populate multiple fields at once.
Access metadata templates from the upper right corner of this dialog.
Support and updates for these IPTC panels can be found at http://www.iptc.org/iptc4xmp
Powered By xmp
Cancel
OK

C

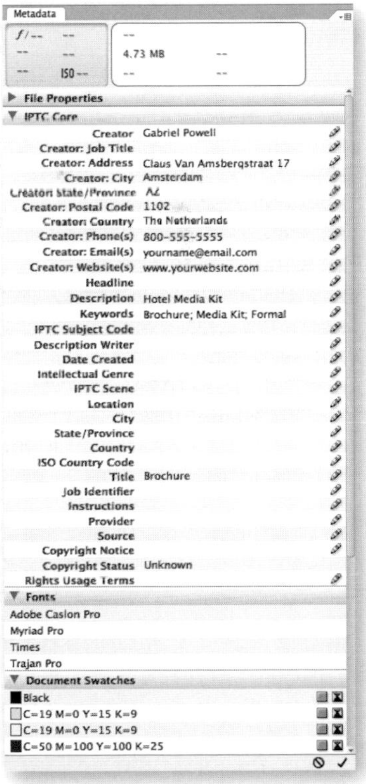
Metadata
4.73 MB
File Properties
IPTC Core
Creator Gabriel Powell
Creator: Job Title
Creator: Address Claus Van Amsbergstraat 17
Creator: City Amsterdam
Creator: State/Province AZ
Creator: Postal Code 1102
Creator: Country The Netherlands
Creator: Phone(s) 800-555-5555
Creator: Email(s) yourname@email.com
Creator: Website(s) www.yourwebsite.com
Headline
Description Hotel Media Kit
Keywords Brochure; Media Kit; Formal
IPTC Subject Code
Description Writer
Date Created
Intellectual Genre
IPTC Scene
Location
City
State/Province
Country
ISO Country Code
Title Brochure
Job Identifier
Instructions
Provider
Source
Copyright Notice
Copyright Status Unknown
Rights Usage Terms
Fonts
Adobe Caslon Pro
Myriad Pro
Times
Trajan Pro
Document Swatches
Black
C=19 M=0 Y=15 K=9
C=19 M=0 Y=15 K=9
C=50 M=100 Y=100 K=25

Figure 14.9 Metadata was added to the Description section (**A**) and IPTC Contact section (**B**) of the File Info dialog. Within Adobe Bridge, you can view a document's metadata in the Metadata panel (**C**).

Packaging a Template for Distribution

By creating a package, your template and all of its supporting elements are kept together in one central folder, allowing other designers to easily find everything they need to start producing documents. This also allows you to save and track versions of your template, which in turn aids template revisions down the road.

For simple templates, you'll need to at least include the fonts and graphic links in the package. More complex templates can require even more components, such as an object library, an Adobe Swatch Exchange file, a print preset file, glyph sets, scripts, a user dictionary, and a style guide.

InDesign's package utility can do most of the work for you. When you package a document, a folder is created that contains a copy of the InDesign file, any fonts used in the file, linked graphics, and a customized report (**Figure 14.10**). This report includes a list of all used fonts, links, and inks required to print the document, as well as the print settings that were last saved with it. Here are the steps for packaging an InDesign document:

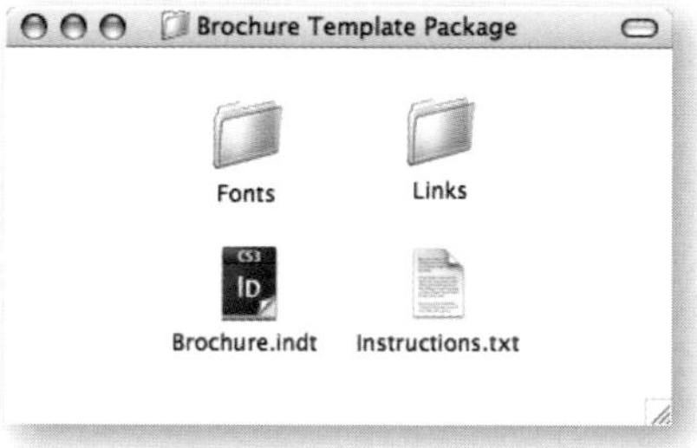
Brochure Template Package
Fonts
Links
Brochure.indt
Instructions.txt

Figure 14.10 This brochure template has been packaged together and is now ready to implement into a live production workflow.

1. Choose File > Package. InDesign performs a final preflight check prior to creating the package. If problem areas are detected, a dialog appears to alert you to the issues.
2. If no alert appears, it means your document passed the preflight inspection and is ready to be packaged.

   If an alert does appear, click View Info to open the Preflight dialog where you can get further information and correct any unforeseen problems (**Figure 14.11**). If any issues need to be resolved, click Cancel and fix them. Otherwise, click Package to continue the packaging process.

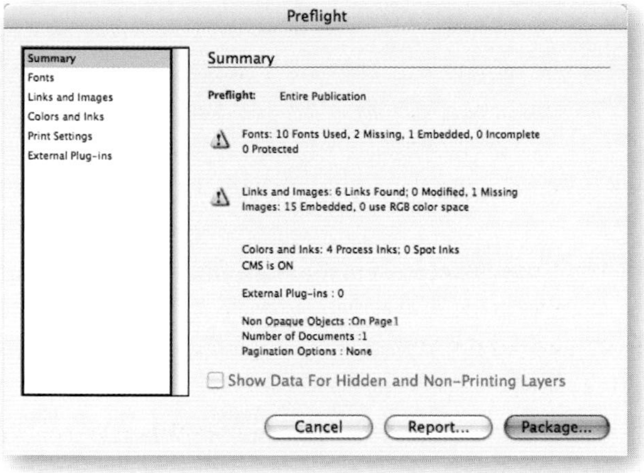
Preflight
Summary
Fonts
Links and Images
Colors and Inks
Print Settings
External Plug-ins
Summary
Preflight: Entire Publication
Fonts: 10 Fonts Used, 2 Missing, 1 Embedded, 0 Incomplete
0 Protected
Links and Images: 6 Links Found; 0 Modified, 1 Missing
Images: 15 Embedded, 0 use RGB color space
Colors and Inks: 4 Process Inks; 0 Spot Inks
CMS is ON
External Plug-ins : 0
Non Opaque Objects :On Page1
Number of Documents :1
Pagination Options : None
Show Data For Hidden and Non-Printing Layers
Cancel
Report...
Package...

Figure 14.11
The Preflight dialog. If potential problems exist within the document, an alert icon appears to the left of each problem category in the Summary section. To see more detailed information about each issue, click through the sections at the left of the dialog.

3. In the Printing Instructions dialog, fill in the optional information and click Continue (**Figure 14.12**). If you choose not to fill in these fields now, you can do it later in the report that is generated when the package folder is created.

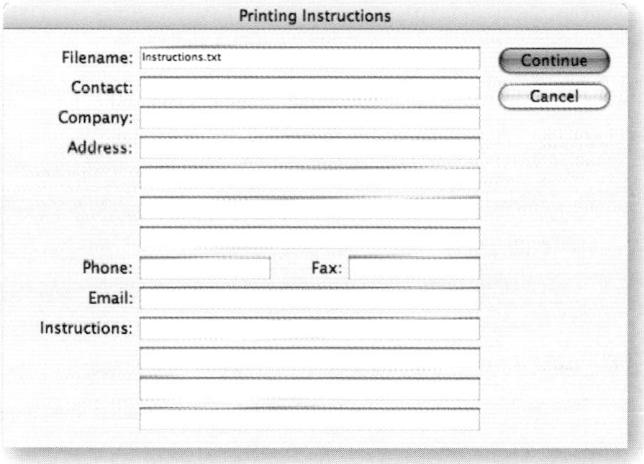
Printing Instructions
Filename:
Instructions.txt
Contact:
Company:
Address:
Phone:
Fax:
Email:
Instructions:
Continue
Cancel

Figure 14.12
The Printing Instructions dialog.

4. In the Create Package Folder dialog, type a name for the package folder, specify a location for it, and then select the following as necessary (**Figure 14.13**):

   Copy Fonts (Except CJK). Copies all the fonts used in the document. It will not copy a type style, such as bold or italic, if it hasn't been used on a page somewhere. CJK (Chinese, Japanese, Korean) fonts will also not be copied into the folder. To include an entire font family, you'll have to manually copy the font files into the package folder, so I recommend not selecting this option when packaging a template.

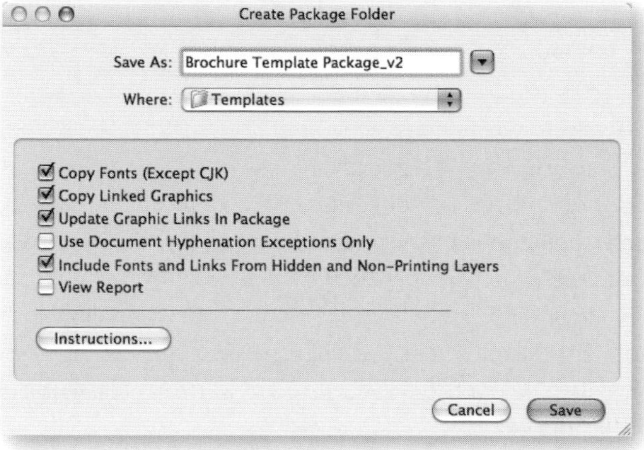
Create Package Folder
Save As: Brochure Template Package_v2
Where: Templates
Copy Fonts (Except CJK)
Copy Linked Graphics
Update Graphic Links In Package
Use Document Hyphenation Exceptions Only
Include Fonts and Links From Hidden and Non-Printing Layers
View Report
Instructions...
Cancel
Save

Figure 14.13 The Create Package Folder dialog.

■ **Tip:** When naming the package folder, include the version number at the end of the name so you can track the various iterations of your template as you modify and improve it.

Copy Linked Graphics. Copies all linked graphic files into the package folder.

Update Graphic Links in Package. Changes the graphic links to the package folder location, allowing InDesign to quickly find the links in their new place.

Use Document Hyphenation Exceptions Only. When this option is selected, the document is prevented from composing text with an external user dictionary, and the document's hyphenation exceptions list is prevented from merging with an external user dictionary. This is useful when you are sending the document to a print service provider. Otherwise, when packaging a template, it's better to leave the option deselected.

Include Fonts and Links From Hidden and Non-Printing Layers. Packages the objects located on hidden layers and layers that have the Print Layer option deselected.

View Report. Opens the instructions report right after the package is created. Click the Instructions button at the bottom of the dialog if you want to edit the report prior to completing the packaging process.

5. Click Save to continue packaging the document.

● **Note:** You cannot save gradients, tints, mixed inks, or the Registration swatch into an Adobe Swatch Exchange file.

ADDITIONAL PACKAGE ELEMENTS

In addition to packaging the basic elements, you should consider adding several other elements to the package. InDesign doesn't automatically package these elements for you, so you'll need to manually copy them to the package folder:

- **Object library.** If you've set up an object library, you'll definitely want to copy it to your template package. The library should always accompany the template wherever it may go (**Figure 14.14**).

CS
LIBRARY

Figure 14.14 InDesign Library file.

- **Adobe Swatch Exchange file.** You might want to save the template's solid color swatches to an Adobe Swatch Exchange file (.ase) for use in Photoshop, Illustrator, or other InDesign documents. Other designers can simply import the file into their application and use those color swatches instead of having to re-create them in each new document. The colors appear exactly the same across each application as long as your color management settings are synchronized. This ensures that each designer in a workgroup uses the same consistent color. When the project comes together, you won't have to deal with conflicting colors.

  To create an Adobe Swatch Exchange file, select the process and spot color swatches you want to share. Choose Save Swatches from the Swatches panel menu and save the file into your template package folder (**Figure 14.15**).

ASE

Figure 14.15 Adobe Swatch Exchange file.

- **Print presets.** If your template will be used by a workgroup that regularly outputs to different printers, you can automate the printing process by saving all the various output settings into print presets. To back them up or make them readily available to your service providers, clients, or others in your workgroup, you can save the presets as separate files and add them to your template package.

  To create a print preset, choose File > Print Presets > Define, and then click New. In the dialog that appears, give the preset a name and adjust the print settings. Click OK and a preset is created and added to the list. To save a print preset as a separate file, choose File > Print Presets > Define. Select one or more presets in the list and click Save. Specify a name and save the file into your package folder (**Figure 14.16**).

PRESETS

Figure 14.16 InDesign Printer Presets file.

- **Glyph sets.** If you've set up a glyph set, you might want to copy it to your template package folder for others to use. When you create a glyph set, it is stored in the Glyph Sets folder, which is located in a different location depending on your operating system. Copy glyph set files to and from this folder to share them with others. See Chapter 10, "Formatting Type and Generating Style Sheets," for more information on using the Glyphs panel and creating Glyph sets.

Glyph Sets Folder Locations

Mac OS: Users/[*username*]/Library/Preferences/Adobe InDesign/[*version*]/Glyph Sets

Windows XP: Documents and Settings\[*username*]\Application Data\Adobe\InDesign\[*version*]\Glyph Sets

Windows Vista: Users\[*username*]\AppData\Roaming\Adobe\InDesign\[*version*]\Glyph Sets

- **Scripts.** If there are any scripts you want to include with your template, be sure to copy them to your package folder. For more information on using and writing scripts, see the Adobe Web site. There's a wealth of learning resources available. Check out the documents, "Adobe Introduction to Scripting," and "Adobe InDesign CS3 Scripting Tutorial" for an introduction to scripting. There are also in-depth scripting guides available for each of the scripting languages compatible with InDesign: AppleScript, JavaScript, and VBScript. When you create or receive a script, place it in the Scripts folder so that it shows up in the Scripts panel.

Scripts Folder Locations

Mac OS: Users/[*username*]/Library/Preferences/Adobe InDesign/[*version*]/Scripts

Windows XP: Documents and Settings\[*username*]\Application Data\Adobe\InDesign\[*version*]\Scripts

Windows Vista: Users\[*username*]\AppData\Roaming\Adobe\InDesign\[*version*]\Scripts

DICT.

Figure 14.17 InDesign User Dictionary file.

- **User dictionary.** If you've created a user dictionary for your template, it's important to copy it to the package folder so that others outside of your network have access to it (**Figure 14.17**). See Chapter 10, "Formatting Type and Generating Style Sheets," for more information on creating and sharing a user dictionary.
- **Style guide.** If a style guide will be accompanying the template, add it to the package folder as well so whoever picks up the template will know exactly how to use it.

Creating a Style Guide

A style guide identifies the components of a template and demonstrates the appropriate use of each typographic and graphical element that constitutes the design. You might think of it as a rule book for designers, ensuring a consistent design (**Figure 14.18**). Ultimately, the style guide you create should provide all the information a designer needs to accurately reproduce a document with your template.

In large organizations and for more complex publications, a style guide is a necessity. In small organizations or where just a few designers will be using the template—and the design is stored in their minds—a style guide is optional.

Creating a style guide is relatively simple. Essentially, you create a sample layout that represents a typical publication and then label each template element. The following guidelines will help you develop a style guide that is suitable for your template's needs:

- **Determine how detailed the style guide should be.** A style guide can't always be exhaustive. Try to give designers just the information they need to successfully produce documents with your template. By not overwhelming them with too many details, your style guide will be straightforward and easy to use.
- **Create a cover page.** Although not completely necessary, you might want to create a cover page for the style guide. This makes it more official and provides a place for additional information, such as the document's trim size and bleed information, and a list of all the elements within the template package folder. You might also create a key that provides additional explanation for any symbols or abbreviations used to label the various elements (**Figure 14.19**).
- **Represent each layout.** Create sample pages that represent each layout in the publication you've designed the template for. One way to do this is to apply every master page to a document page and then add sample text, images, and graphics to complete the layout. Be sure to demonstrate the preferred use and treatment of each major text and graphic element in the publication's design. You can use the mock-up layout you created as a great starting point.
- **Create a separate document for the style guide.** For more complex templates, it's best to create a separate document for the style guide. However, if your template is quite simple, you can create a separate layer for any necessary template usage instructions instead. Keep the layer hidden so the information is available when needed, but is otherwise kept out of view and won't ever print.

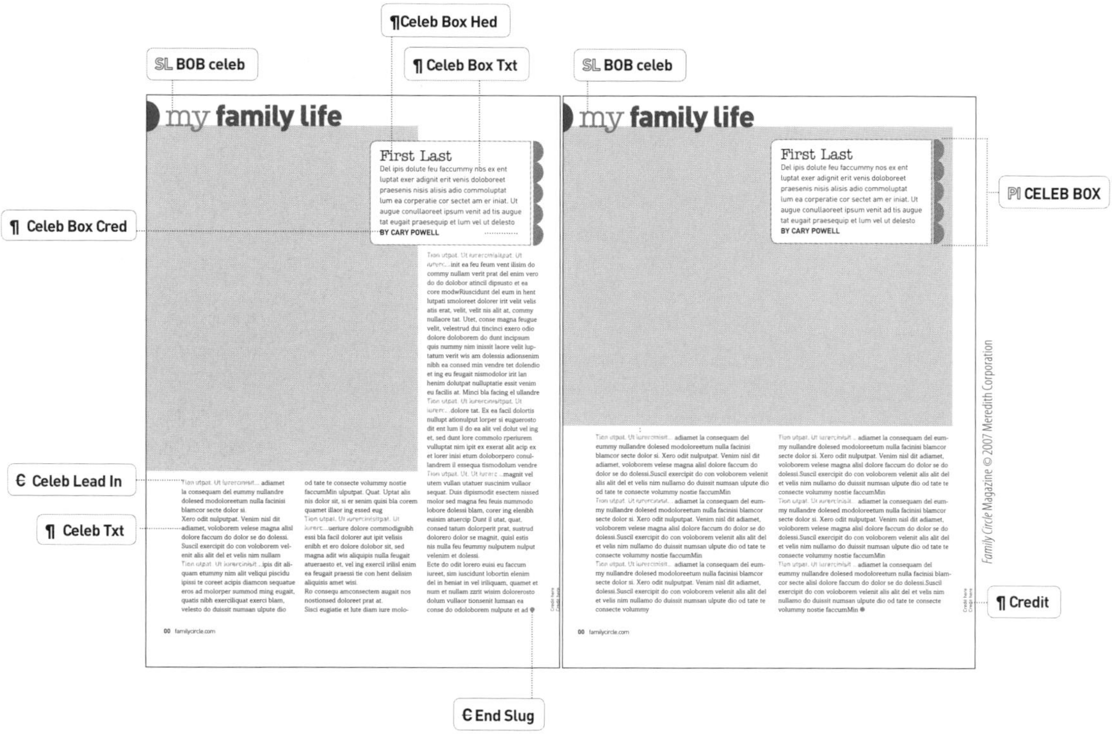
¶Celeb Box Hed
SL BOB celeb
¶ Celeb Box Txt
SL BOB celeb
my family life
First Last
BY CARY POWELL
my family life
First Last
BY CARY POWELL
¶ Celeb Box Cred
PI CELEB BOX
€ Celeb Lead In
¶ Celeb Txt
¶ Credit
Family Circle Magazine © 2007 Meredith Corporation
€ End Slug

SL HEALTH dave left
¶ Slug Dek
€ Slug Byline
SL HEALTH dave right
ask dr. dave
HOW TO MANAGE YOUR MOODS, YOUR RELATIONSHIPS, YOUR LIFE. BY DAVE JOHNSON, M.D.
ask dr. dave
HOW TO MANAGE YOUR MOODS, YOUR RELATIONSHIPS, YOUR LIFE. BY DAVE JOHNSON, M.D.
¶ Ask Q Wht Bld
¶ Ask A Wht Reg
¶ Ask Q
¶ Ask A
Family Circle Magazine © 2007 Meredith Corporation
PI DAVE bio left
¶ Credit
PI DAVE bio right

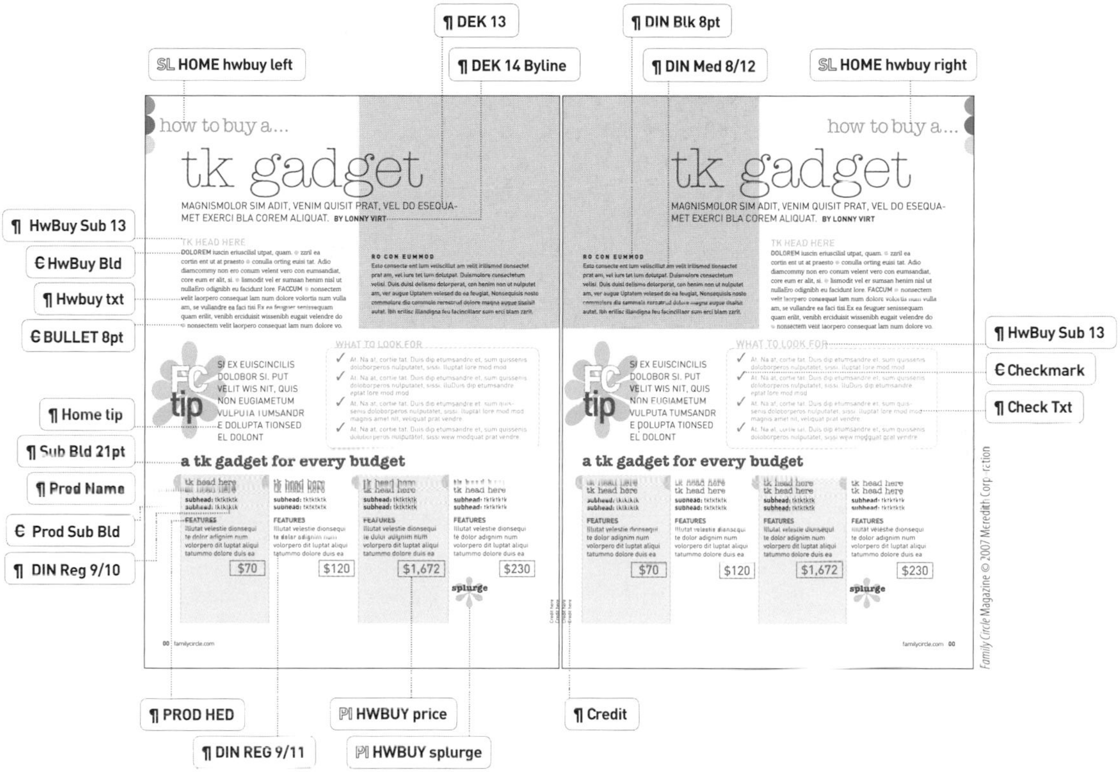
¶ DEK 13
¶ DIN Blk 8pt
SL HOME hwbuy left
¶ DEK 14 Byline
¶ DIN Med 8/12
SL HOME hwbuy right
how to buy a...
tk gadget
MAGNISMOLOR SIM ADIT, VENIM QUISIT PRAT, VEL DO ESEQUA-MET EXERCI BLA COREM ALIQUAT. BY LONNY VIRT
¶ HwBuy Sub 13
€ HwBuy Bld
¶ Hwbuy txt
€ BULLET 8pt
TK HEAD HERE
WHAT TO LOOK FOR
FC tip
SI EX EUISCINCILIS DOLOBOR SI. PUT VELIT WIS NIT, QUIS NON EUGIAMETUM VULPUTA TUMSANDR E DOLUPTA TIONSED EL DOLONT
¶ Home tip
¶ Sub Bld 21pt
¶ Prod Name
€ Prod Sub Bld
¶ DIN Reg 9/10
a tk gadget for every budget
$70
$120
$1,672
$230
splurge
¶ HwBuy Sub 13
€ Checkmark
¶ Check Txt
Family Circle Magazine © 2007 Meredith Corporation
¶ PROD HED
Pl HWBUY price
¶ Credit
¶ DIN REG 9/11
Pl HWBUY splurge

Figure 14.18 These three spreads are from the *Family Circle* Magazine style guide. They are an excellent example of how a detailed style guide should look. Each design element is clearly identified with labels. Alternative layout variations are also demonstrated. The gray-filled frames indicate the preferred position, width, and height of images.

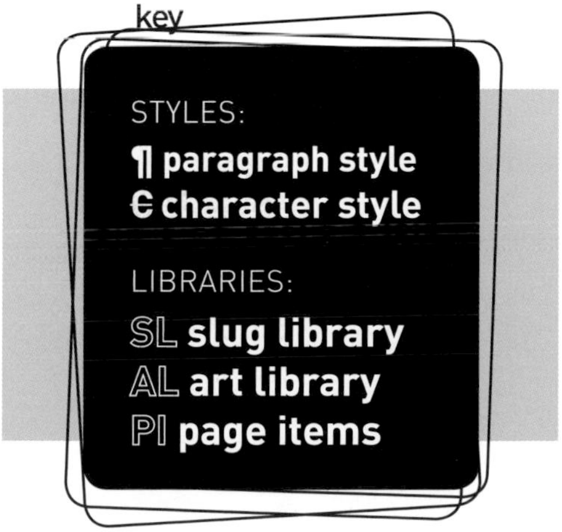
key
STYLES:
¶ paragraph style
€ character style
LIBRARIES:
SL slug library
AL art library
PI page items

Figure 14.19 The *Family Circle* Magazine style guide uses this key on its cover page to explain the meaning of the symbols and abbreviations used for identifying character styles, paragraph styles, and the object library in which a particular object can be found in.

One way to set up a style guide is to generate a PDF file for each sample page or spread, import each PDF into a new InDesign document, and then label all the elements. You might even include the visible guides and grids when you create the PDF file if you want to see the layout grids in the style guide. The advantage to this method is that you can shrink the layout to fit on a page size that your printer accommodates and still have enough room for all the labels.

- **Label each template element.** Identify the first use of each element in a layout with a label. Each label should include the element's name and a symbol or abbreviation that identifies the element's type. You might even color code the labels for more clarity.

  Label every character style, paragraph style, object style, table style, and cell style. Label any library items and specify which object library they come from, if more than one exists. You might also specify the required measurements between elements that require hand positioning.

  Every template is different, so look for anything else that needs a label or requires additional explanation. However, try not to clutter a page with too many labels. If a page is getting full, try labeling some repeating elements on another page.

- **Create a color palette.** If your template restricts the use of color, add a color palette to the style guide. This may seem like a no-brainer, but it's good to have documented rules on color usage. Label each color with the name you used in the Swatches panel to make it easy for designers to locate the colors as they need them.

15

Managing Templates with Adobe Bridge CS3

ADOBE BRIDGE CS3 IS A FILE BROWSER THAT SITS AT THE HUB OF THE ADOBE Creative Suite 3 and is fully integrated with it. This multifaceted tool lets you locate, browse, and organize the assets you need for any project—without ever leaving the Creative Suite.

In many ways, Bridge functions like a typical window in Mac OS X or Windows. You can open, move, and copy files on your computer or a connected network folder. You can also create folders and rename them. Beyond that, Bridge offers additional capabilities that can significantly improve your creative process. You can append XMP (Extensible Metadata Platform) metadata such as descriptions and keywords to your files to make them more searchable; organize your files with ratings and labels, and then use filtering methods to narrow down the number of files that are displayed; browse the contents of an InDesign template document without opening it in InDesign—the list goes on and on.

Here are the most significant features that make Bridge the ideal application.

Launching Bridge

Figure 15.1 The Go to Bridge button.

Bridge is an independent application that you can access on its own or from within Adobe InDesign and other Creative Suite 3 applications. From InDesign, choose File > Browse or click the Go to Bridge button on the right side of the Control panel (**Figure 15.1**). You might also choose to launch Bridge from the Programs menu (Windows) or the Dock (Mac OS X).

You can quickly switch from Bridge to the previously opened Creative Suite application by choosing File > Return to [*application*]. This only works if you used the Bridge button or chose Browse from the File menu to switch to Bridge.

Exploring the Interface

By default, Bridge has one window that is divided into five panes (**Figure 15.2**). Each pane consists of one or more panels. The top-left pane contains the Favorites and Folders panels. The Content panel in the middle is the largest and displays the contents of a selected folder. When you select a file, a preview of it is displayed in the Preview panel and its file information shows up in the Metadata panel. The Keywords panel shows any keywords that are attached to the file. The Filter panel lets you sort and filter the files that show up in the Content panel.

■ **Tip:** Press the Tab key to quickly show or hide all the panels at once.

You can rearrange and resize the panels to suit your particular working style. To relocate them, drag a panel by its tab into another pane. To make them smaller or larger, drag the horizontal and vertical divider bars between panels. To open or close individual panels, choose Window, and then the name of the panel you want to open or close. You can temporarily collapse a panel by double-clicking its tab.

It's also possible to open more than one Bridge window at a time. This makes it easier to move or copy files from one location to another. Or, you might want to browse multiple folders at the same time. Choose File > New Window to open a new window.

Images
Favorites
Folders
Content
Preview
Bridge Home
Computer
Version Cue
Start Meeting
Adobe Stock Photos
Adobe Photographers Directory
Desktop
Templates
gabriel_mini
Filter
Sort Manually
Keywords
No Keywords 25
Date Created
8/2/04 19
10/28/03 1
10/20/03 1
7/1/03 1
6/18/03 1
6/16/03 1
Date Modified
Today 1
8/2/04 24
Orientation
Landscape 18
Portrait 7
25 items, one hidden, 1 selected - 52 KB
Metadata
Keywords
540 x 360
52 KB 72 ppi
RGB
File Properties
Filename ks15651.jpg
Document Type JPEG file
Date File Modified
Dimensions 540 x 360
Dimensions (in inches)
Resolution 72 ppi
Bit Depth 8
Color Mode RGB
IPTC Core
Creator
Creator: Job Title
Creator: Address
Creator: City
Creator: State/Province
Creator: Postal Code
Creator: Country

Figure 15.2 The default workspace.

Navigating Folders

Bridge provides several ways to navigate folders. The Folders panel lets you access any disc, drive, or other network volume that is connected to your computer (**Figure 15.3**). You can move through a folder structure by clicking the triangle in front of each folder. When you want to see a folder's contents, click the folder icon. You can also double-click a folder in the Content panel to open it. If you want to move back and forward between the most recently open folders, click the Go Back and Go Forward buttons at the top-left side of the Bridge window.

The Favorites panel allows you to save your favorite and most used folders into one central location for quick and easy access (**Figure 15.4**). By default, a few folders have already been added. However, it's possible to customize it as you wish. You can add any folder or file to the Favorites panel by dragging it to the panel. To reposition an item, simply drag it up or down within the panel. To delete a favorite, select it and choose File > Remove from Favorites.

■ **Tip:** When browsing a large folder of files, you can start typing the name of a file and Bridge will select it in the Content panel for you.

Folders
Desktop
Project Library
Stock Photography
Amana
Comstock
Image Source
Zefa
Templates
Computer
gabrielp
Macintosh HD
Network
Windows HD
Version Cue

Figure 15.3 The Folders panel. Increase the size of the panel to easily view the folder structure.

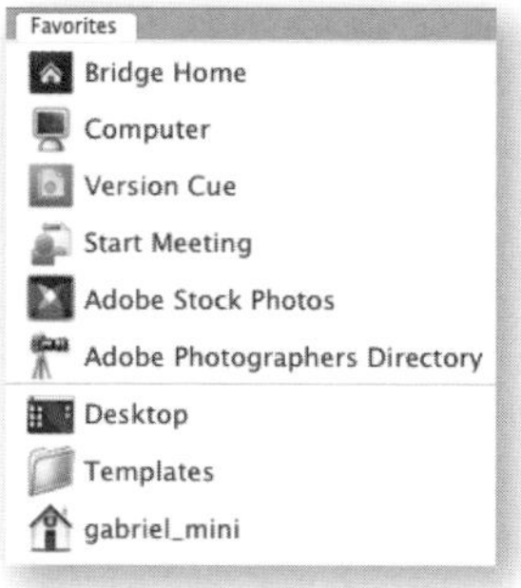
Favorites
Bridge Home
Computer
Version Cue
Start Meeting
Adobe Stock Photos
Adobe Photographers Directory
Desktop
Templates
gabriel_mini

Figure 15.4 The Favorites panel. You can add a folder of templates that you need frequent access to.

Scaleable Thumbnail Previews

The Content panel displays thumbnails of each file in a selected folder and will fit as many as it can across and down based on their size. You can dynamically scale the preview size by dragging the slider at the bottom of the Bridge window (**Figure 15.5**). At smaller sizes, you can see more documents at once, which is useful if you're looking for something by name. At larger sizes, the thumbnails are much bigger, making it easier to identify a document by appearance.

Images
Images
Content
ks1465.jpg
ks3806.jpg
ks4641.jpg
ks4697.jpg
ks4701.jpg
ks4730.jpg
ks4871.jpg
ks15651.jpg
ks5792.jpg
ks6016.jpg
ks6546.jpg
ks11732.jpg
25 items, one hidden

Figure 15.5 Drag the Thumbnail slider to dynamically scale the preview size of the icons.

When you select a document, its thumbnail is displayed in the Preview panel. If multiple documents are selected, they all appear and automatically adjust to fit within the panel. You can increase the size of the Preview panel to make the thumbnails even bigger. This is particularly beneficial when browsing an InDesign template file (.indt), because you can look through its individual pages without having to open the document (**Figure 15.6**).

You can further magnify parts of a document's thumbnail with the Loupe tool (**Figure 15.7**). To access it, click anywhere on a thumbnail in the Preview panel. The area you click on becomes magnified at 100 percent. To relocate the Loupe tool, drag it to another location or click somewhere else on the thumbnail. To zoom in and out, use the mouse scroll wheel or press the plus sign (+) or minus sign (-) key. You can increase the magnification up to 800 percent. To hide the Loupe tool, just click it.

■ **Tip:** When you first open a folder to view its contents, it may take some time for Bridge to build a thumbnail preview for each file. Bridge builds a cache file for each folder as you open it the first time. Once you've opened a folder, it will open much faster the next time you navigate to it. To speed up the process, you can choose to build a cache file for a folder and its subfolders simultaneously by selecting it and choosing Tools > Cache > Build and Export Cache.

● **Note:** If a preview image was not saved with a template file, Bridge will not build a preview for it. Instead, you'll see the standard InDesign template icon.

Preview
SGO
Product Catalog.indt
6
/6

Figure 15.6 The Preview panel. Click the left and right arrows or type a page number to navigate to a specific page within a template file.

Preview
SGO
TAT ACCUM EX
INIT LOREET VELLS AL
123 Everywhere
City, ST 00000
adobe@adobe.c
Product Catalog.indt (100%)
6
/6

Figure 15.7 The Loupe tool in use. The position of the pointed corner determines the magnified area.

Flexible Workspaces

Bridge offers a lot of flexibility when it comes to customizing the default workspace. You can rearrange and resize panels as necessary, or you can select one of the preconfigured Bridge workspaces.

To switch between workspaces, choose Window > Workspace, and then choose the desired workspace. You can also click one of the workspace buttons at the bottom right of the Bridge window (**Figure 15.8**). At times, you may want to save your own custom configuration. In that case, choose Window >

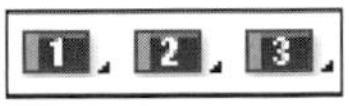
1
2
3

Figure 15.8 The workspace buttons.

Workspace > Save Workspace. Your saved workspace will appear in the Window menu along with the other workspaces.

■ **Tip:** Each workspace button can have a different workspace assigned to it. Click and hold the button and choose the desired workspace from the pop-up list.

■ **Tip:** If more than one Bridge window is open, each can use a different workspace.

You might use the Light Table workspace to sort through a collection of photos or Metadata Focus to efficiently view and append metadata to a list of files. The Horizontal Filmstrip workspace is extremely useful when you want to quickly browse through a collection of files and still take advantage of large thumbnail previews. It displays a list of small thumbnails across the bottom and a large preview of the selected file in the Preview panel above them. If multiple files are selected, each will be displayed and will automatically adjust to fit within the Preview panel (**Figure 15.9**).

Images
Images
Favorites
Folders
Preview
Bridge Home
Computer
Version Cue
Start Meeting
Adobe Stock Photos
Adobe Pho...s Directory
Desktop
Templates
gabriel_mini
Filter
Sort Manually
Keywords
No Keywords 25
Date Created
8/2/04 19
10/28/03 1
10/20/03 1
7/1/03 1
6/18/03 1
6/16/03 1
2/9/03 1
Date Modified
Yesterday 1
8/2/04 24
Orientation
Landscape 18
Portrait 7
Content
25 items, one hidden, 6 selected - 1.010 MB

Figure 15.9 The Horizontal Filmstrip workspace.

Compact Mode

■ **Tip:** To prevent a window in Compact mode from always floating on top of all windows, deselect Compact Window Always On Top from the panel menu that becomes available in Compact mode.

You can quickly shrink a Bridge window by switching to Compact mode. This hides all the panels except for the Content panel and keeps the window floating on top of all other windows, making it always available as you work in different applications. For instance, you can drag multiple graphic files from the Bridge window into one of your layouts in InDesign.

To switch to Compact mode, click the Switch To Compact Mode button on the top-right side of the Bridge window (**Figure 15.10**). You can further minimize a window and completely hide the Content panel by clicking the Switch To Ultra Compact Mode button. To return the window to normal size, click the Switch To Full Mode button.

A
B

Figure 15.10 The Switch To Compact Mode button (**A**) also serves as the Switch To Full Mode button when a window is in Compact mode. The Switch To Ultra Compact Mode button (**B**).

Organizing Files

One of the biggest advantages of using Bridge is its unique ability to organize your files and projects. Instead of using Windows Explorer (Windows) or the Finder (Mac OS X) to access your files, you can use Bridge to more quickly collect the files you need by rating and labeling them. Then you can sort and filter your files in the Content panel, making them easier to find and manage.

■ **Tip:** You can use keyboard shortcuts to apply ratings. Press Command-1 to give your template a one star rating, Command-2 to give it a two star rating, and so on (in Windows press Ctrl-1, Ctrl-2, etc.). To remove the rating, press Command-0 (Ctrl-0 in Windows).

Rating and Labeling Files

While browsing a collection of templates, you may find it useful to rate them with zero to five stars (**Figure 15.11**). Each template can be rated in terms of its level of importance or whatever rules you choose. You can rate a single document or multiple documents at the same time by selecting them and choosing the desired number of stars from the Label menu.

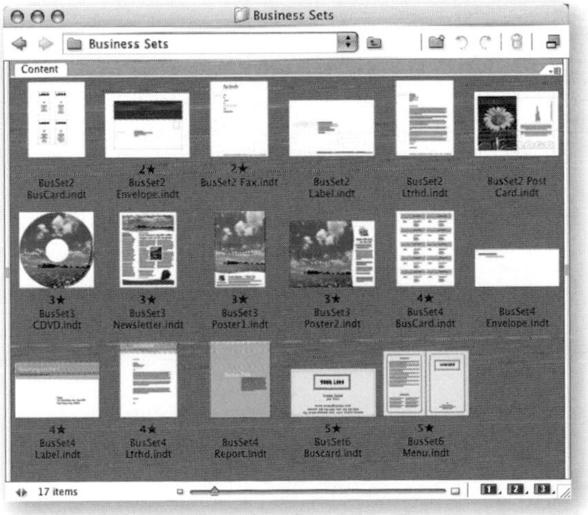
Business Sets
Business Sets
Content
BusSet2 BusCard.indt
2★ BusSet2 Envelope.indt
2★ BusSet2 Fax.indt
BusSet2 Label.indt
BusSet2 Ltrhd.indt
BusSet2 Post Card.indt
3★ BusSet3 CDVD.indt
3★ BusSet3 Newsletter.indt
3★ BusSet3 Poster1.indt
3★ BusSet3 Poster2.indt
4★ BusSet4 BusCard.indt
BusSet4 Envelope.indt
4★ BusSet4 Label.indt
4★ BusSet4 Ltrhd.indt
BusSet4 Report.indt
5★ BusSet6 Buscard.indt
5★ BusSet6 Menu.indt
17 items

Figure 15.11 After you've rated a file, its rating appears next to its filename.

In addition to rating your templates, you can label them with up to five color labels (Red, Yellow, Green, Blue, or Purple). Simply select the documents you want to label and choose a label color from the Label menu. Any meaning can be attributed to each color as you see fit (**Figure 15.12**). By default, the labels are prenamed: Select, Second, Approved, Review, To Do. You can change the names of each label by choosing Edit > Preferences (Windows) or Bridge > Preferences (Mac OS) and clicking Labels (**Figure 15.13**).

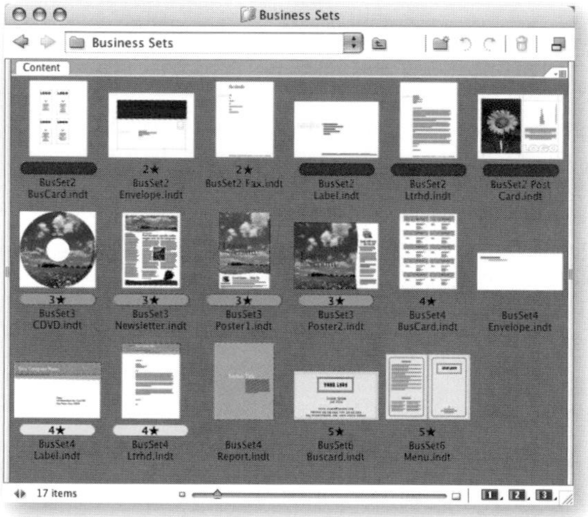
Business Sets
Business Sets
Content
17 items

Figure 15.12 After you've labeled a file, its label color appears with its rating next to the filename.

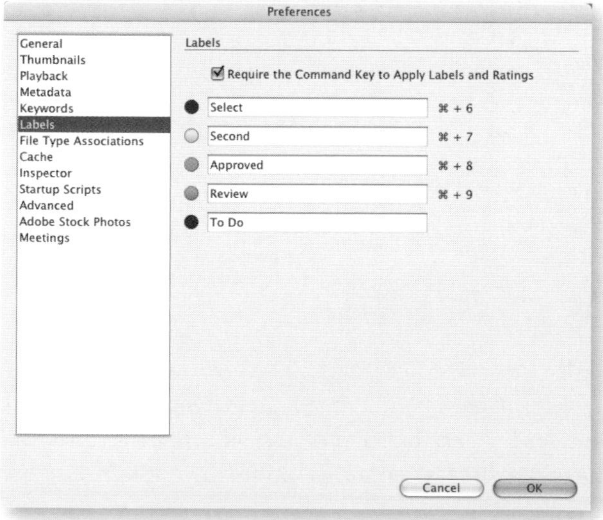
Preferences
General
Thumbnails
Playback
Metadata
Keywords
Labels
File Type Associations
Cache
Inspector
Startup Scripts
Advanced
Adobe Stock Photos
Meetings
Labels
Require the Command Key to Apply Labels and Ratings
Select
⌘ + 6
Second
⌘ + 7
Approved
⌘ + 8
Review
⌘ + 9
To Do
Cancel
OK

Figure 15.13 Labels preferences.

■ **Tip:** You can use keyboard shortcuts to apply labels. Press Command-6 for Red, Command-7 for Yellow, Command-8 for Green, and Command-9 for Blue (in Windows, press Ctrl and numbers 6–9 for the same results). Purple doesn't have a keyboard shortcut.

Sorting and Filtering Methods

After rating and/or labeling a collection of templates, you can sort them so that all the templates sharing the same rating or label are grouped together in the Content panel. In addition to sorting by *Label* and *Rating*, you can sort by *Document Kind, Dimensions, File Size,* and more. To sort by any of these options, choose View > Sort and select the sorting method you want to use. You can also choose a sorting option from the Sort menu at the top-right side of the Filter panel.

In addition to sorting, you can narrow down the view of a particular folder to show just a few specific documents. For example, you might want to view just the templates that have a five star rating. Or maybe you only want to see the templates you've assigned a yellow label to. This can all be done using the Filter panel. Simply place a checkmark in front of the label, rating, or any other criteria you want to view. The Content panel will update, showing only the files that meet the criteria of the checked categories. You can choose just one category or a combination of categories if you like (**Figure 15.14**).

■ **Tip:** You can choose to display the entire contents of a folder and its subfolders in the Content panel without having to navigate through each subfolder, such as when you want to view a template, its image links, and fonts at the same time. Click the Flatten View button at the top-left side of the Filter panel. Click the button again to turn off this behavior.

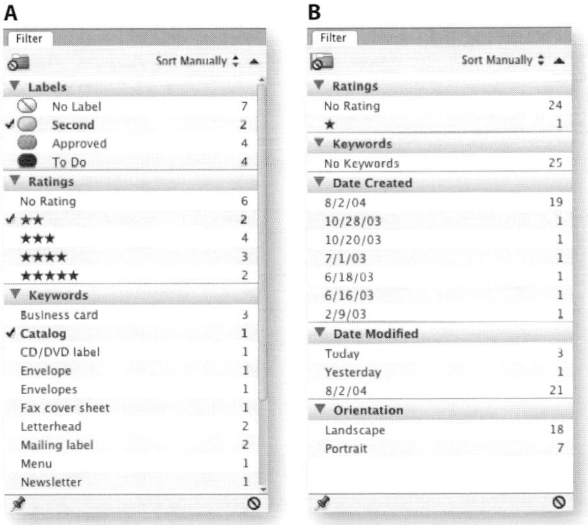
A
Filter
Sort Manually
Labels
No Label 7
Second 2
Approved 4
To Do 4
Ratings
No Rating 6
★★ 2
★★★ 4
★★★★ 3
★★★★★ 2
Keywords
Business card 3
Catalog 1
CD/DVD label 1
Envelope 1
Envelopes 1
Fax cover sheet 1
Letterhead 2
Mailing label 2
Menu 1
Newsletter 1
B
Filter
Sort Manually
Ratings
No Rating 24
★ 1
Keywords
No Keywords 25
Date Created
8/2/04 19
10/28/03 1
10/20/03 1
7/1/03 1
6/18/03 1
6/16/03 1
2/9/03 1
Date Modified
Today 3
Yesterday 1
8/2/04 21
Orientation
Landscape 18
Portrait 7

Figure 15.14 These Filter settings (**A**) allow just the templates with a yellow label, a two star rating, and the assigned Catalog keyword to be displayed in the Content panel. When viewing a collection of images, the Filter categories change to represent the displayed files (**B**).

The Filter panel is context sensitive, updating its categories based on the metadata found in the assortment of files in the Content panel. For instance, if the Content panel contains images, the Filter panel will contain an Orientation category. If any one of the images contains a rating, the Ratings category will appear, and so on.

Entering Metadata

Metadata is a set of data that describes and gives information about the files on your computer. Most documents contain at least some metadata. Images commonly contain information such as their dimensions, resolution, and color mode. InDesign documents even contain a list of the fonts being used and any existing color swatches (**Figure 15.15**). The big advantage of metadata is that it makes your files searchable and allows you to more easily organize your files. For example, you can search for all of your InDesign templates that use a particular font, and Bridge will find and gather them in the Content panel.

● **Note:** Much of the metadata in a file is searchable with Spotlight in Mac OS X.

■ **Tip:** Choose the Metadata Focus workspace to optimize the size and arrangement of the Metadata and Keywords panels.

Bridge makes it possible to view metadata and add additional information to a file through the Metadata panel (**Figure 15.16**). Select one or more documents and enter your information into the IPTC Core category or one of the other categories. When you're finished, click the Apply button at the bottom-right corner of the Metadata panel. It looks like a checkmark. Most of this data actually travels with the file and is searchable by other applications, including asset management systems. If it isn't possible to store the information in the file, metadata is stored in a separate sidecar file instead.

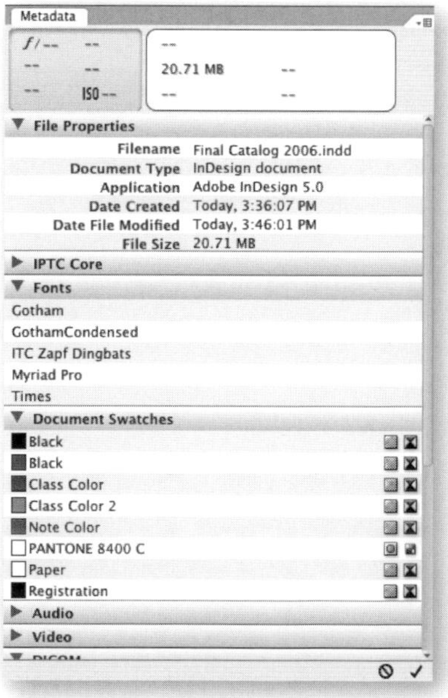
Metadata
20.71 MB
File Properties
Filename Final Catalog 2006.indd
Document Type InDesign document
Application Adobe InDesign 5.0
Date Created Today, 3:36:07 PM
Date File Modified Today, 3:46:01 PM
File Size 20.71 MB
IPTC Core
Fonts
Gotham
GothamCondensed
ITC Zapf Dingbats
Myriad Pro
Times
Document Swatches
Black
Black
Class Color
Class Color 2
Note Color
PANTONE 8400 C
Paper
Registration
Audio
Video

Figure 15.15 Scroll toward the bottom of the Metadata panel to view the fonts and color swatches being used in a selected InDesign document.

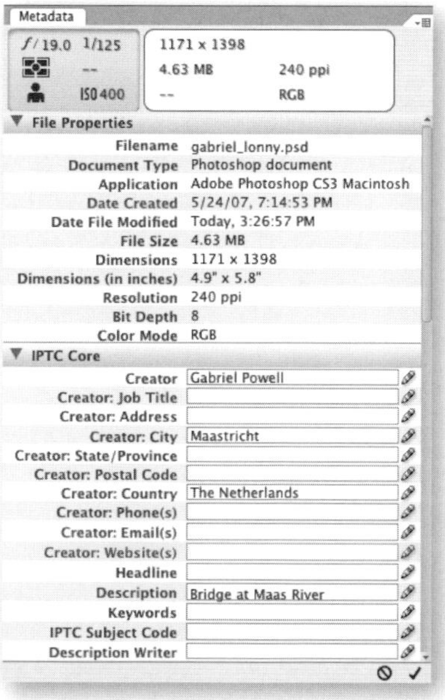
Metadata
f/19.0 1/125
ISO 400
1171 x 1398
4.63 MB 240 ppi
RGB
File Properties
Filename gabriel_lonny.psd
Document Type Photoshop document
Application Adobe Photoshop CS3 Macintosh
Date Created 5/24/07, 7:14:53 PM
Date File Modified Today, 3:26:57 PM
File Size 4.63 MB
Dimensions 1171 x 1398
Dimensions (in inches) 4.9" x 5.8"
Resolution 240 ppi
Bit Depth 8
Color Mode RGB
IPTC Core
Creator Gabriel Powell
Creator: Job Title
Creator: Address
Creator: City Maastricht
Creator: State/Province
Creator: Postal Code
Creator: Country The Netherlands
Creator: Phone(s)
Creator: Email(s)
Creator: Website(s)
Headline
Description Bridge at Maas River
Keywords
IPTC Subject Code
Description Writer

Figure 15.16 Click inside a metadata field to enter data.

Another way to add metadata to a file is through the File Info dialog (**Figure 15.17**). Select one or more files and choose File > File Info. Any existing data will display in one of several categories on the left side of the dialog. Enter your desired information and click OK. If you plan on using the same information again and again, you can create a metadata template to use as a starting point for populating metadata in other InDesign documents. Choose Save Metadata Template from the File Info dialog panel menu.

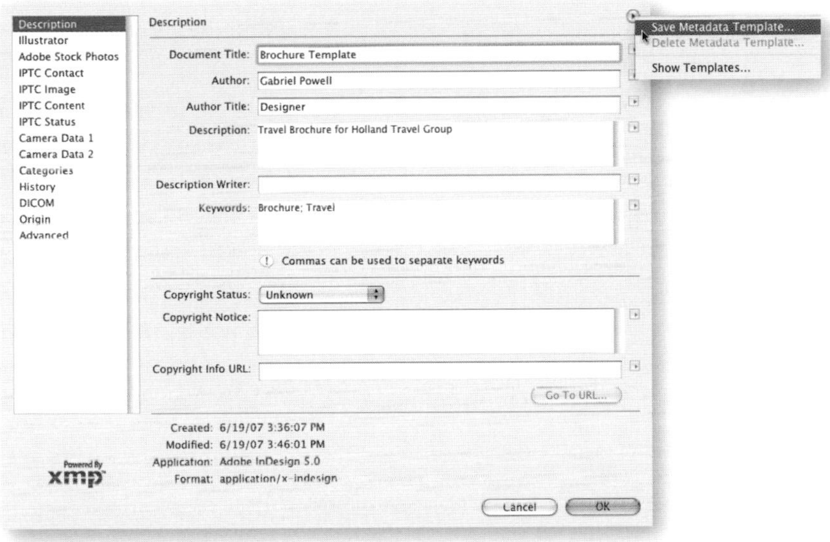
Description
Illustrator
Adobe Stock Photos
IPTC Contact
IPTC Image
IPTC Content
IPTC Status
Camera Data 1
Camera Data 2
Categories
History
DICOM
Origin
Advanced
Description
Save Metadata Template...
Delete Metadata Template...
Show Templates...
Document Title: Brochure Template
Author: Gabriel Powell
Author Title: Designer
Description: Travel Brochure for Holland Travel Group
Description Writer:
Keywords: Brochure; Travel
Commas can be used to separate keywords
Copyright Status: Unknown
Copyright Notice:
Copyright Info URL:
Go To URL...
Created: 6/19/07 3:36:07 PM
Modified: 6/19/07 3:46:01 PM
Application: Adobe InDesign 5.0
Format: application/x-indesign
Powered By xmp
Cancel
OK

Figure 15.17 The File Info dialog.

The next time you want to append that set of metadata to another document, choose Tools > Append Metadata, and then select the desired template. To totally replace any preexisting metadata, choose Tools > Replace Metadata, and then select a template.

Assigning Keywords

Bridge also makes it easy to assign keywords to your files, which are another form of metadata. You might assign keywords such as Business, Brochure, or Sales Sheet to your templates as you create them. Later, when you need to find a brochure template, you can conduct a search for its keyword and all the templates that contain the Brochure keyword will show up in the Content panel.

A number of preset keywords ship with Bridge. Use the Keywords panel to view or delete them (**Figure 15.18**). You can also create new keywords and categories as you need them. To assign a keyword, select one or more

Keywords
Assigned Keywords: Birthday; New York
Events 3
Birthday
Graduation
Wedding
People 2
Matthew
Ryan
Places 5
New York
Paris
San Francisco
San Jose
Tokyo

Figure 15.18 The Keywords panel.

documents and click the check box in front of each keyword that you want to assign. All the keywords assigned to a file will be listed at the top of the Keywords panel. To remove keywords from a file, deselect the box in front of each keyword that you want to remove. You can organize keywords into sets and subsets by dragging them onto other keywords.

When you click on a file, its assigned keywords appear italic in the Other Keywords category if you haven't already added them to the Keywords panel. These are considered temporary and will be removed from the panel when you quit and reopen Bridge. If you prefer to keep a temporary keyword in the Keywords panel, drag it to another set. You can also right-click (Windows) or Control-click (Mac OS) the keyword and choose Make Persistent from the context menu.

Finding Files

Because you've taken the time to label your templates, enter metadata information, and assign keywords to them, you can easily search for your templates. Bridge offers a powerful find feature that allows you to search within any folder, disc, or connected network volume on your computer.

To search for a document, choose Edit > Find to bring up the Find dialog and enter your search criteria (**Figure 15.19**). Bridge can search for information such as *Rating, Label, Document Type, Keywords,* and *Description.* You can even add search criteria by clicking the plus sign. For example, you might want to search for templates with a three star rating that also have the Brochure keyword assigned to them.

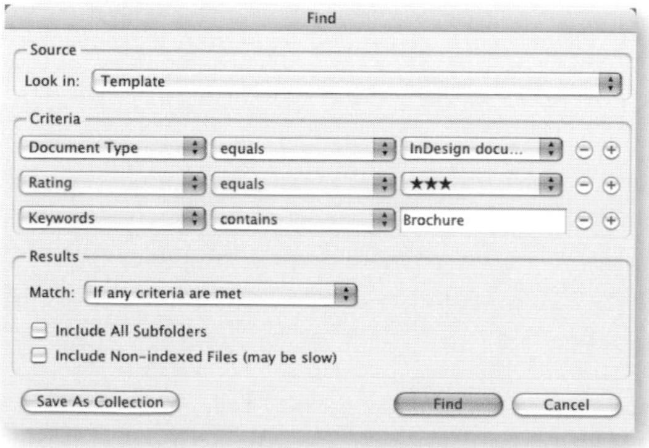
Find
Source
Look in: Template
Criteria
Document Type
equals
InDesign docu...
Rating
equals
★★★
Keywords
contains
Brochure
Results
Match: If any criteria are met
Include All Subfolders
Include Non-indexed Files (may be slow)
Save As Collection
Find
Cancel

Figure 15.19 The Find dialog.

Saving and Using Collections

If you continually perform the same search, you can choose to save your search criteria as a collection. The next time you want to perform that search, simply double-click a collection file and Bridge will show all the files that match its criteria, even if files were added after the collection file was created.

To create a collection, choose Edit > Find, set up your desired search criteria, and then click the Save As Collection button at the bottom of the Find dialog. A dialog appears allowing you to name and save the collection file to a specific location (**Figure 15.20**). Select the Add to Favorites option to add the collection to the Favorites panel once it is created.

A

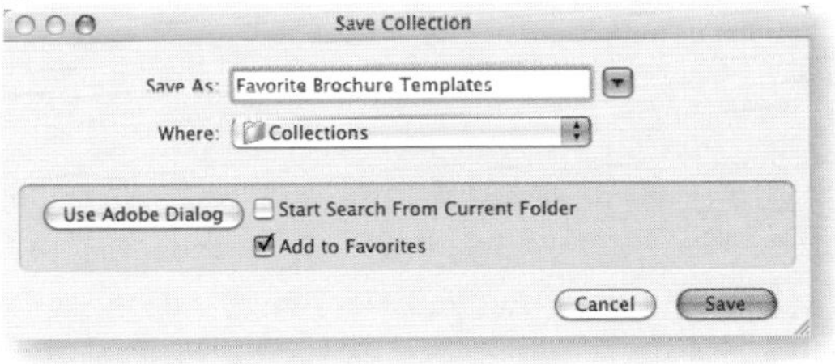
Save Collection
Save As: Favorite Brochure Templates
Where: Collections
Use Adobe Dialog
Start Search From Current Folder
Add to Favorites
Cancel
Save

B

COLLECT

Figure 15.20 The Save Collection dialog (**A**) and the Collection file icon (**B**).

16

Automating Layouts with XML

WELCOME TO THE FUTURE OF PUBLISHING—WRITE A DOCUMENT ONCE, PUSH a button, and deliver it anywhere from print to the Web to mobile devices and beyond. Together, the powerful page layout capabilities of InDesign and the inherent benefits of XML are making this a reality for creative professionals all over the world.

InDesign provides several ways of working with XML. You can export XML content from a publication to reuse it in another form of media, or you can import XML content and format it using InDesign's array of formatting tools. If you have a publication with a structured design, you can even set up an XML-ready template for it and then automate subsequent publications.

This chapter focuses on how to create a template that is specifically designed to automate a layout with imported XML content. You'll first learn what XML is and how it works. Then you'll learn how to create an XML-ready template and import XML content into InDesign.

What Is XML?

XML (eXtensible Markup Language) is a flexible data format used to distribute content to multiple destinations. It can store and organize just about any kind of information in a form customized to your needs, such as a magazine article, catalog of products, or a database of numbers. As an open standard, XML is not tied to any particular platform or application, making it easy to share data between previously incompatible applications.

If you're familiar with HTML, you'll notice that XML looks similar. However, these languages are fundamentally different from each other. HTML was designed to display data and control its formatting. Whereas XML was designed to structure data and describe what the information is. Since it is stored in a plain-text file, the actual appearance of the XML content is determined by the destination application. For instance, you can use a CSS style sheet to format XML content for a Web site, or you can use paragraph and character styles to format the same XML content in an InDesign document.

XML content can originate from a database (FileMaker Pro, Microsoft Access), an XML-capable application (InDesign), or be manually written with an XML editor. An XML editor lets you read and compose XML, and often comes with services that prevent mistakes and make your documents more reader friendly. A number of editors are available, ranging in quality and expense. Although you can use a simple plain-text editor to work with XML, such as TextEdit on the Mac and Notepad on Windows, they are quite limited in comparison to a professional XML editor, such as XMLSpy, Oxygen, or Stylus Studio.

XML Terminology and Markup Rules

Let's take a look at the building blocks of an XML document and how they all fit together. As a designer, you might at first find some of the terminology a bit foreign. But stick with it and you'll soon discover that XML is actually quite easy to understand. To keep it simple, only the most essential information you need to know for automating a layout is covered. For a deeper understanding of XML, I encourage you to study a book dedicated to the subject.

Markup. XML uses symbols, called *markup*, to identify the various parts of a document and determine how they relate to each other. The markup must follow certain syntax rules. An XML document that follows these rules is considered *well-formed*.

Element. The most fundamental building block is called an *element*. Elements are information containers, which can hold text or other elements. One big element might contain a group of elements, which in turn contain other elements, and so on down to the data. This creates a hierarchical structure that defines the organization of the data (**Figure 16.1**).

```
<?xml version="1.0" encoding="UTF-8"?>

<businesscards>

    <Card>
        <Name>Adam McCoy</Name>
        <Position>Director of Marketing</Position>
        <Addressln1>5034 SE 44th Avenue</Addressln1>
        <Addressln2>Portland, Oregon 97543</Addressln2>
        <Phone>503-248-9876 direct</Phone>
        <Email>adam@metafusiontraining.com</Email>
    </Card>

    <Card>
        <Name>Jeremy Cantrell</Name>
        <Position>Sales Associate</Position>
        <Addressln1>25 NW 23rd Place, Suite 6-122</Addressln1>
        <Addressln2>Portland, Oregon 97210</Addressln2>
        <Phone>503-248-9876 direct</Phone>
        <Email>jeremy@metafusiontraining.com</Email>
    </Card>

    <Card>
        <Name>Dale Erwing</Name>
        <Position>Trainer</Position>
        <Addressln1>5131 Buffalo Ave. #20</Addressln1>
        <Addressln2>Sherman Oaks, CA 91423</Addressln2>
        <Phone>310-795-8943 cell</Phone>
        <Email>dale@metafusiontraining.com</Email>
    </Card>

    <Card>
        <Name>Jim Conner</Name>
        <Position>Trainer</Position>
        <Addressln1>25 NW 23rd Place, Suite 6-122</Addressln1>
        <Addressln2>Portland, Oregon 97210</Addressln2>
        <Phone>503-515-2376 cell</Phone>
        <Email>jim@metafusiontraining.com</Email>
    </Card>

</businesscards>
```

Figure 16.1 A typical XML document containing information for a set of business cards. The businesscards element contains several Card elements. Each Card element contains a set of elements that contain the contact information for each employee. Spaces and paragraph returns were added to make the data reader friendly.

Start and end tag. Each element is made up of a *start tag* and an *end tag*, which mark the boundaries of the contained data and describe what it is. The start tag consists of an opening angle bracket (<) followed by the element's name and a closing angle bracket (>). After the start tag is the element's *content* and then the end tag. The end tag consists of an opening angle bracket and a slash (</) followed by the element's name and a closing angle bracket (**Figure 16.2**). As you get used to looking at XML, you'll use the tags as markers to navigate visually through a document.

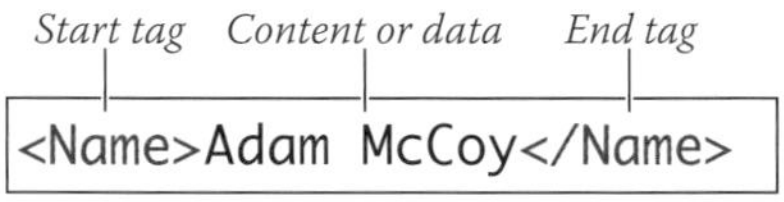
Start tag
Content or data
End tag
<Name>Adam McCoy</Name>

Figure 16.2 The syntax for an element. Color has been used to make it easier to identify each part.

● **Note:** InDesign assigns an href attribute to images when you assign a tag to them in a layout. The href attribute indicates the file path and file name of the image. InDesign can export these attributes to an XML document and can also process them on import. If the file path and file name are found, the actual image is placed into the layout.

Attributes. Start tags may also contain optional *attributes*, which provide additional information about an element. Attributes are often used to append metadata to specific data or uniquely identify a number of elements that have the same name. In a set of business cards, you could use an attribute to identify the version number of each card, allowing you to track each card as changes are made to it. Or you might have a catalog with hundreds of products. If you don't identify each one with an attribute, it would be difficult to refer to a particular product when you need information about it.

An attribute is a name-value pair. When a start tag contains an attribute, it begins with an opening angle bracket followed by the element's name as usual. After that is the attribute name, an equals sign (=), a value in quotes, and a closing angle bracket (**Figure 16.3**). There's no limit to the number of attributes an element can have, as long as no two attributes within the element have the same name.

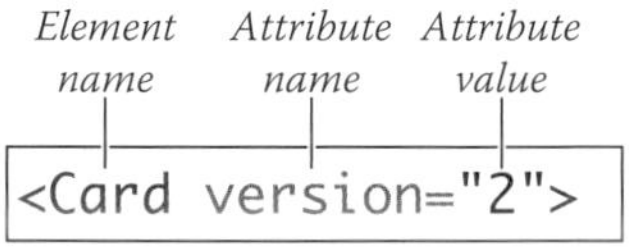
Element name
Attribute name
Attribute value
<Card version="2">

Figure 16.3 The syntax for a start tag that contains an attribute.

Comment. Another type of markup you'll sometimes find in an XML document is a *comment*. Comments are notes within the document that are not interpreted by an XML processor. They are often used to identify the purpose of different sections in the document and help you navigate through the clutter of elements. Comments can go anywhere in the document except before the XML declaration (see Figure 16.5) and inside tags. A comment starts with the delimiter <!-- and ends with the delimiter -->. The comment goes between these two delimiters (**Figure 16.4**)

A

Start delimiter *End delimiter*

```
<!-- contents of Adam McCoy -->
```

B

```
<Card version="2">
<!-- contents of Adam McCoy  -->
    <Name>Adam McCoy</Name>
    <Position>Director of Marketing</Position>
    <Addressln1>5034 SE 44th Avenue</Addressln1>
    <Addressln2>Portland, Oregon 97543</Addressln2>
    <Phone>503-248-9876 direct</Phone>
    <Email>adam@metafusiontraining.com</Email>
</Card>
```

Figure 16.4 The syntax for a comment (**A**). An XML document showing a comment and an attribute in use (**B**).

Element Naming Convention

Several important rules must be followed when naming elements. The name can contain any alphanumeric characters (a–z, A–Z, and 0–9), accented characters, or characters from non-Latin scripts (Greek, Arabic). The only punctuation permitted in the name are the hyphen (-), underscore (_), and period (.). You can't use the colon (:), since it is used for another purpose. The name can't contain spaces and can only begin with a letter or underscore. Names are case-sensitive, so Body, body, and BODY are three different elements. Also, the names in the start and end tags must be identical.

Besides those rules, you can define your own element names. XML tags are not predetermined like they are in HTML. This allows you to create documents based on your specific needs. That is what the term "extensible" refers to.

Document tree. XML documents are represented in a structural form called a *document tree*. It's tree-like because it originates from one point and branches out into leaves. Each point where a branching occurs is called a *node*. An XML document consists of one outermost node, called the *root element*, which contains many branch nodes and some leaf nodes. It may also contain some optional administrative information at the top of the document, collectively referred to as the *document prolog* (**Figure 16.5**).

XML declaration

Document type declaration

Document prolog

Document tree

```
<?xml version="1.0" encoding="UTF-8"?>

<!DOCTYPE nutrition_directory SYSTEM "///Users/gabrielp/Desktop/
nutrition_directory.dtd">

<nutrition_directory>
    <food>
        <name>Avocado Dip</name>
        <mfr>Sunnydale</mfr>
        <serving units="g">29</serving>
        <calories total="110" fat="100"/>
        <total-fat>11</total-fat>
        <saturated-fat>3</saturated-fat>
        <cholesterol>5</cholesterol>
        <sodium>210</sodium>
        <carb>2</carb>
        <fiber>0</fiber>
        <protein>1</protein>
        <vitamins>
            <a>0</a>
            <c>0</c>
        </vitamins>
        <minerals>
            <ca>0</ca>
            <fe>0</fe>
        </minerals>
    </food>
    <food>
        <name>Bagels, New York Style </name>
        <mfr>Thompson</mfr>
        <serving units="g">104</serving>
        <calories total="300" fat="35"/>
        <total-fat>4</total-fat>
        <saturated-fat>1</saturated-fat>
        <cholesterol>0</cholesterol>
        <sodium>510</sodium>
        <carb>54</carb>
        <fiber>3</fiber>
        <protein>11</protein>
        <vitamins>
            <a>0</a>
            <c>0</c>
        </vitamins>
        <minerals>
            <ca>8</ca>
            <fe>20</fe>
        </minerals>
    </food>
</nutrition_directory>
```

Figure 16.5 Parts of an XML document, which contains information for a nutrition directory. Can you tell the difference between the markup and the data? Without the markup, the data would not be organized or have any meaning.

Document prolog. The document prolog, if you use one, starts at the top of the document, before the root element. There are two main parts: an *XML declaration* and a *document type declaration*. The XML declaration prepares an XML processor with information it needs to work with the document. If used, it must always appear in the first line. The document type declaration is an instruction that associates the document with a document type definition (DTD). This line isn't required unless you want a parser to validate your document's structure against a set of rules provided in a DTD file.

● **Note:** Don't confuse document type declaration with document type definition (DTD). They are two different things.

DTD. A DTD defines the document structure with a list of permissible elements and attributes. It enforces agreed upon parameters that an XML document must conform to (**Figure 16.6**). If the structure is incorrect or an undeclared element or attribute is used, the document will be considered *invalid*. When a document properly adheres to the DTD, it is considered *valid*. To test an XML document against a DTD, you need a professional XML editor or you can import the DTD file into InDesign and test any existing XML content within a document.

● **Note:** Schemas are similar to DTDs but have additional capabilities. Although they are often preferred over DTDs, Schema files aren't currently compatible with InDesign.

```
<!ELEMENT nutrition_directory (#PCDATA | food)*>
<!ELEMENT food (name, mfr?, serving, calories, total-fat, saturated-fat,
cholesterol, sodium, carb, fiber, protein, vitamins,  minerals)>
<!ELEMENT name (#PCDATA)>
<!ELEMENT mfr (#PCDATA)>
<!ELEMENT serving (#PCDATA)>
<!ATTLIST serving units CDATA #IMPLIED>
<!ELEMENT calories (#PCDATA)>
<!ATTLIST calories total CDATA #IMPLIED>
<!ATTLIST calories fat CDATA #IMPLIED>
<!ELEMENT total-fat (#PCDATA)>
<!ELEMENT saturated-fat (#PCDATA)>
<!ELEMENT cholesterol (#PCDATA)>
<!ELEMENT sodium (#PCDATA)>
<!ELEMENT carb (#PCDATA)>
<!ELEMENT fiber (#PCDATA)>
<!ELEMENT protein (#PCDATA)>
<!ELEMENT vitamins (#PCDATA | a | c)*>
<!ELEMENT minerals (ca | fe)*>
<!ELEMENT ca (#PCDATA)>
<!ELEMENT fe (#PCDATA)>
<!ELEMENT a (#PCDATA)>
<!ELEMENT c (#PCDATA)>
```

Figure 16.6 The DTD file for the nutrition directory shown in Figure 16.5. Each of the permissible elements and attributes have been declared. It also specifies what information is permitted within each element and in what order the elements must be in.

To successfully share XML data with others, it's important to agree on a structure and a standard set of element names and attributes, and then use a DTD file to ensure that everyone conforms to those standards. For example, in a magazine article, you could specify that a story must begin with a headline and a byline followed by the body. If you have a project that requires a DTD, you can use an industry-standard DTD that meets your requirements or write your own. Many XML editors can even auto-generate a DTD file for you. However, a good working knowledge of writing and editing DTDs still comes in very handy.

That's XML markup in a nutshell. Once you've written an XML document or exported it from a database, you're ready to import it into an XML-capable application and put it to use. Every program that works with XML first has to parse the data. *Parsing* is the process of reading the XML, validating it, and passing it along for further processing. If a document isn't well-formed or doesn't conform to a referenced DTD, the parser catches it and reports the problem.

InDesign's XML Tools

● **Note:** You can drag elements from the Structure pane to frames on the page to populate them with XML data. However, when automating a layout with XML, this routine isn't necessary.

InDesign provides two tools for working with XML content: the Structure pane and the Tags panel (**Figure 16.7**). When XML content exists within an InDesign document, the Structure pane displays all the elements in their hierarchical structure. It also lets you add, edit, and manage different types of XML content, including elements, attributes, and comments. To show the Structure pane, choose View > Structure > Show Structure. You can adjust the width of the Structure pane by dragging the bar that separates the pane from the document page. To expand or collapse an element—showing or hiding its child elements—click the triangle to the left of it.

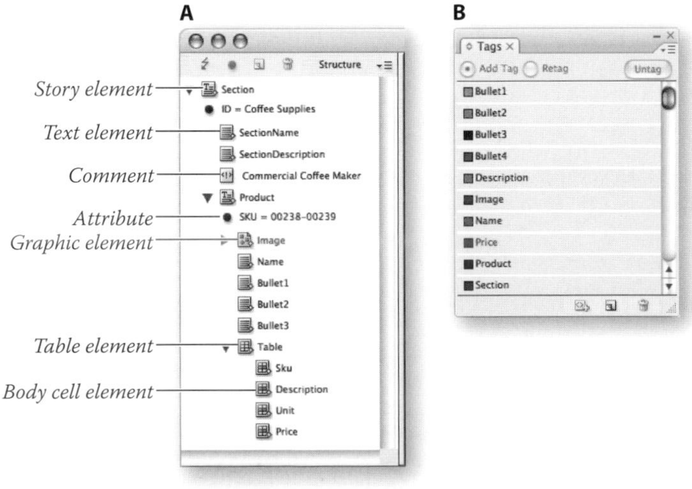
A
B
Structure
Story element
Section
ID = Coffee Supplies
Text element
SectionName
SectionDescription
Comment
Commercial Coffee Maker
Product
Attribute
SKU = 00238-00239
Graphic element
Image
Name
Bullet1
Bullet2
Bullet3
Table element
Table
Sku
Body cell element
Description
Unit
Price
Tags
Add Tag
Retag
Untag
Bullet1
Bullet2
Bullet3
Bullet4
Description
Image
Name
Price
Product
Section

Figure 16.7 The Structure pane (**A**) makes it easy to identify each element and its position within the hierarchical structure. An icon to the left of each element indicates what type of content it holds. The Tags panel (**B**) lets you import, export, add, delete, and rename tags. Each tag has a unique color assigned to it.

The Tags panel displays a list of tags available in the document. It is used to assign element tags to content you plan to export to XML, or to assign tags to text and graphics placeholders before importing XML content into them. To show the Tags panel, choose Window > Tags.

Understanding the Workflow

Setting up an automated XML workflow within InDesign is less complicated than you might think. All that's required is a basic understanding of XML, strategic use of InDesign's toolset, and keen attention to detail. In fact, if you've already used Data Merge, you'll find the process quite similar.

To begin, you need to generate an XML document, which contains the content for the layout you'll be producing. In the best scenario, all your data is stored in a database so you can simply export the information you need from the database to an XML document. In other situations, you might be able to export the XML content from another InDesign file. And as a last resort, you might choose to manually write the XML, which really defeats the very purpose of automation.

The next step is to create an XML-ready template, which is an InDesign document that contains placeholder text and graphics frames, and any boilerplate design elements that remain the same throughout each iteration of the layout. XML tags are assigned to each placeholder, which identify where the imported XML content should be placed. The formatting applied to each placeholder determines how the XML content will appear.

Once the template is set up, you can start a new document based on it and then import the XML content. If the assigned tags match by name and by structural hierarchy in the Structure pane, InDesign merges the XML content, replacing any existing content in the document. During import, several options must be considered and correctly specified to ensure the desired import results. See "Importing the XML Document," later in this chapter for information on each import option.

There are two ways to set up a template:

- **Set up multiple instances of a sample layout.** This method works well for a publication such as a set of business cards. You set up a sample business card layout that contains all the necessary components and assign XML tags to each placeholder. Then you duplicate the layout several times and arrange each instance on the page. When you import the XML document with the correct import options selected, InDesign populates the tagged placeholders with the corresponding XML data. Each duplicate layout on the page is populated with the repeating elements found in the XML content (**Figure 16.8**).

A

```
<?xml version="1.0" encoding="UTF-8" standalone="yes"?>
<businesscards>
    <Card>
        <!-- contents of Adam McCoy  -->
        <employeeName>Adam McCoy</employeeName>
        <employeePosition>Director of Marketing</employeePosition>
        <employeeAddressln1>5034 SE 44th Avenue</employeeAddressln1>
        <employeeAddressln2>Portland, Oregon 97543</employeeAddressln2>
        <employeePhone>503-248-9876 direct</employeePhone>
        <employeeEmail>adam@metafusiontraining.com</employeeEmail>
    </Card>

    <Card>
        <!-- contents of Gabriel Powell  -->
        <employeeName>Gabriel Powell</employeeName>
        <employeePosition>Senior Training Director</employeePosition>
        <employeeAddressln1>25 NW 23rd Place, Suite 6-122</employeeAddressln1>
        <employeeAddressln2>Portland, Oregon 97210</employeeAddressln2>
        <employeePhone>503-515-5404 direct</employeePhone>
        <employeeEmail>gabriel@metafusiontraining.com</employeeEmail>
    </Card>

    <Card>
        <!-- contents of Jeremy Cantrell  -->
        <employeeName>Jeremy Cantrell</employeeName>
        <employeePosition>Sales Associate</employeePosition>
        <employeeAddressln1>25 NW 23rd Place, Suite 6-122</employeeAddressln1>
        <employeeAddressln2>Portland, Oregon 97210</employeeAddressln2>
        <employeePhone>503-248-9876 direct</employeePhone>
        <employeeEmail>jeremy@metafusiontraining.com</employeeEmail>
    </Card>

    <Card>
        <!-- contents of Dale Erwing  -->
        <employeeName>Dale Erwing</employeeName>
        <employeePosition>Trainer</employeePosition>
        <employeeAddressln1>5131 Buffalo Ave. #20</employeeAddressln1>
        <employeeAddressln2>Sherman Oaks, CA 91423</employeeAddressln2>
        <employeePhone>310-795-8943 cell</employeePhone>
        <employeeEmail>dale@metafusiontraining.com</employeeEmail>
    </Card>

    <Card>
        <!-- contents of Jim Conner  -->
        <employeeName>Jim Conner</employeeName>
        <employeePosition>Trainer</employeePosition>
        <employeeAddressln1>25 NW 23rd Place, Suite 6-122</employeeAddressln1>
        <employeeAddressln2>Portland, Oregon 97210</employeeAddressln2>
        <employeePhone>503-515-2376 cell</employeePhone>
        <employeeEmail>jim@metafusiontraining.com</employeeEmail>
    </Card>

    <Card>
        <!-- contents of Sheila Baily  -->
        <employeeName>Sheila Baily</employeeName>
        <employeePosition>Assistant Training Director</employeePosition>
        <employeeAddressln1>25 NW 23rd Place, Suite 6-122</employeeAddressln1>
        <employeeAddressln2>Portland, Oregon 97210</employeeAddressln2>
        <employeePhone>503-481-7243 mobile</employeePhone>
        <employeeEmail>sheila@metafusiontraining.com</employeeEmail>
    </Card>

    ...
</businesscards>
```

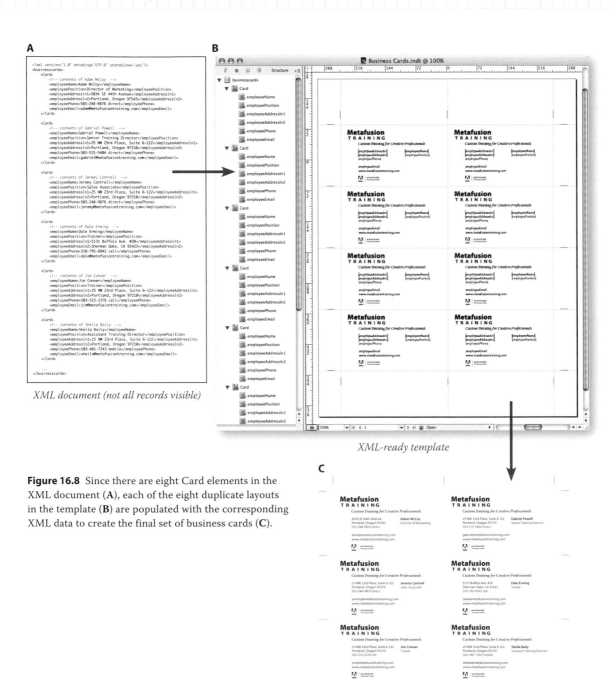

XML document (not all records visible)

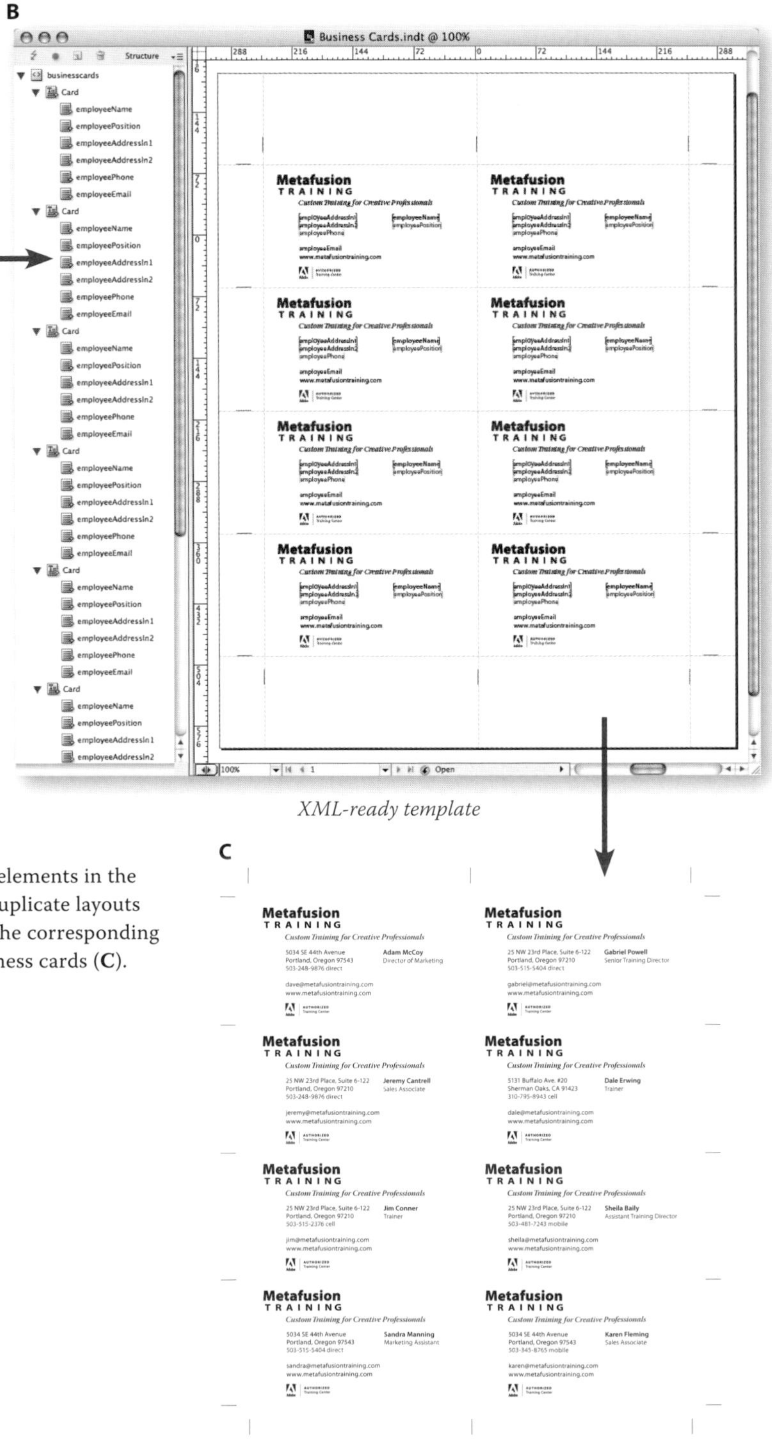
B
Business Cards.indt @ 100%
Structure
businesscards
Card
employeeName
employeePosition
employeeAddressln1
employeeAddressln2
employeePhone
employeeEmail
Metafusion
TRAINING
XML-ready template
C
Metafusion
TRAINING
Custom Training for Creative Professionals
Final merged document

Figure 16.8 Since there are eight Card elements in the XML document (**A**), each of the eight duplicate layouts in the template (**B**) are populated with the corresponding XML data to create the final set of business cards (**C**).

- **Set up a sample layout that is automatically cloned to create other instances.** This method works well for a publication such as a product catalog. If a typical product contains a name, a bulleted list, a table of information, and an image, you would set up just one sample product design that contains those components and then assign XML tags to each placeholder.

  When you import the XML document with the appropriate import options selected, InDesign populates the tagged placeholders with the corresponding XML data and clones the layout for each repeating element found in the XML content. All the data is unique from one cloned instance to the next, but the design remains the same for each iteration (**Figure 16.9**). All the boilerplate text—words, spaces, tabs, and paragraph returns—is also preserved.

  This setup is a little more complicated to create. It requires you to insert the placeholders into one text frame so that all the XML content flows within a single story. See "Strategies for setting up a template," later in this chapter for more information.

What Are Repeating Elements?

XML is *repeating* when the same configuration of elements appears multiple times in a row, but the data in each instance is unique. Compare this concept to a database, which stores information in the form of *records*. Records are collections of data that follow the same pattern. There are often lots of records, each with the same set of data fields. For example, a database of employee records might contain 60 records. Each record contains the employee's name and contact information in separate data fields.

XML is very good at modeling such data structures. When you export information from a database into an XML document, the record structure is maintained. In the figure at right, the XML document contains repeating Employee elements (records), each of which contain the same set of elements. The data in each element is different, but the structure is exactly the same.

```
<?xml version="1.0" encoding="UTF-8"?>
<Employee_Records>
    <Employee ID="1">
        <Name>Cary Powell</Name>
        <Address>2233 W Seventh Street</Address>
        <City>Eugene</City>
        <State>OR</State>
        <Zip>97402</Zip>
        <Phone>555-555-5555</Phone>
        <Email>cary@companyemail.com</Email>
    </Employee>
    <Employee ID="2">
        <Name>Richard Lopez</Name>
        <Address>1 Park Avenue</Address>
        <City>New York</City>
        <State>NY</State>
        <Zip>10001</Zip>
        <Phone>222-222-2222</Phone>
        <Email>richard@companyemail.com</Email>
    </Employee>

    ...
</Employee_Records>
```

A

```xml
<?xml version="1.0" encoding="UTF-8"?>
<Section ID="Coffee Supplies">
    <SectionName>Wholesale Coffee Supplies</SectionName>
    <SectionDescription>Romantem nihiciam te effren vit, sulic moentiae dientimius tam ponvolum publicturae conum maximortum iam tabi sim et fure derobus? At furem iaed mandium efac temena, sul tatquis hor istrum nonvoltussi publibe remque nitam or atque preis ocum det viviris orem morum inatintemus publin avervis? Dactum nontidientem orturbi senterc enati, publius, utursus, nequi publiam iam ex modin dium firmis, nos essilicae cultum, quissimis udelum.</SectionDescription>
    <!-- Commercial Coffee Maker -->
    <Product SKU="00238-00239">
        <Image href="file:///Users/gabrielp/Desktop/Coffee_Catalog/images/0238.tif"></Image>
        <NewLogo href="file:///Users/gabrielp/Desktop/Coffee_Catalog/images/new_logo.ai"></NewLogo>
        <Name>Commercial Coffee Maker</Name>
        <Bullet1>Metal base.</Bullet1>
        <Bullet2>3-prong grounded plug.</Bullet2>
        <Bullet3>"Brew View" guage.</Bullet3>
        <Bullet4>NSF approved.</Bullet4>
        <Table>
            <Sku>00238</Sku>
            <Description>101 Cup, Black Stain</Description>
            <Unit>each</Unit>
            <Price>$49.99</Price>
            <Sku>00239</Sku>
            <Description>55 Cup, Black Stain</Description>
            <Unit>each</Unit>
            <Price>$29.99</Price>
        </Table>
    </Product>
    <!-- Coffee King Commercial Grade -->
    <Product SKU="00264-00265">
        <Image href="file:///Users/gabrielp/Desktop/Coffee_Catalog/images/0264.tif"></Image>
        <Name>Coffee King Commercial Grade</Name>
        <Bullet1>Metal base.</Bullet1>
        <Bullet2>3-prong grounded plug.</Bullet2>
        <Bullet3>NSF and CSA approved.</Bullet3>
        <Bullet4>One year warranty.</Bullet4>
        <Table>
            <Sku>00264</Sku>
            <Description>101 Cup, Aluminum</Description>
            <Unit>each</Unit>
            <Price>$39.99</Price>
            <Sku>00265</Sku>
            <Description>55 Cup, Aluminum</Description>
            <Unit>each</Unit>
            <Price>$19.99</Price>
        </Table>
    </Product>
    <!-- Iced Tea Dispenser -->
    <Product SKU="00272">
        <Image href="file:///Users/gabrielp/Desktop/Coffee_Catalog/images/0272.tif"></Image>
        <Name>Iced Tea Dispenser</Name>
        <Bullet1>Half gallon gradations on side of reservoir.</Bullet1>
        <Bullet2>Tomlinson faucets.</Bullet2>
        <Bullet3>FDA approved polypropylene.</Bullet3>
        <Bullet4>Black base, White tank.</Bullet4>
        <Table>
            <Sku>00272</Sku>
            <Description>5 Gallon</Description>
            <Unit>each</Unit>
            <Price>$34.99</Price>
        </Table>
    </Product>

    ...
</Section>
```

XML document (not all records visible)

Figure 16.9 This XML document contains the data for a section in a product catalog (**A**). In the template, one sample layout was created with XML tags assigned to each placeholder (**B**). When the XML content is imported, it populates each tagged placeholder with data and clones the sample design for each instance of the Product element found (**C**).

B

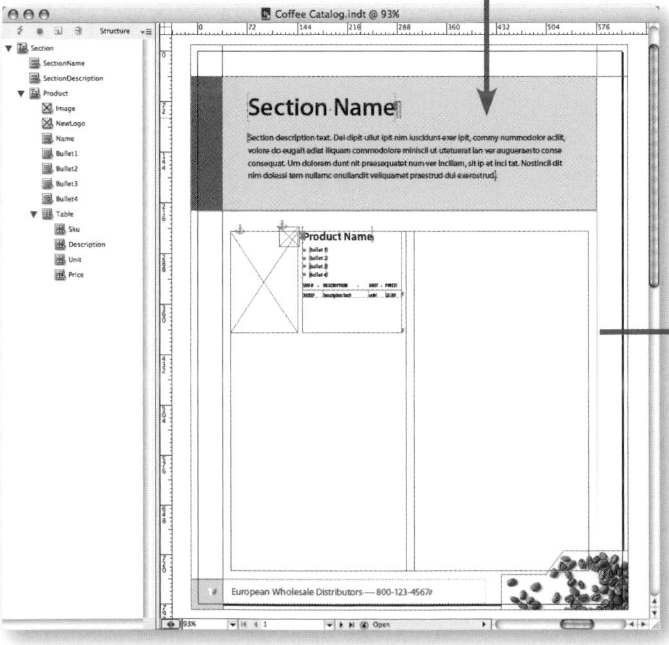
Coffee Catalog.indt @ 93%
Structure
Section
SectionName
SectionDescription
Product
Image
NewLogo
Name
Bullet1
Bullet2
Bullet3
Bullet4
Table
Sku
Description
Unit
Price
Section Name
Product Name
European Wholesale Distributors — 800-123-4567#

XML-ready template

C

Wholesale Coffee Supplies
Commercial Coffee Maker
Coffee Press
Coffee King Commercial Grade
Hot and Cold Server
Iced Tea Dispenser
Cream Dispenser
European Wholesale Distributors — 800-123-4567

Final merged document

Setting Up an XML-ready Template

Now that you're familiar with XML and have an overall understanding of the workflow, you're ready to create a template specifically designed for automating a layout with XML.

Step 1: Create a Sample Layout

Determine which of the two methods you'll use to set up your template. Every publication is different, so study the design and choose the method that is most appropriate for your circumstances. Here are a few tips for choosing a method:

- If your publication contains one item per page, such as a set of certificates, recipe cards, envelopes, or flyers, you can create multiple instances of the sample layout and place each instance on a page of its own.
- If your publication contains a fixed number of items per page, such as a set of labels or business cards, you might set up multiple instances of the sample layout. So, if you have an XML document that contains a list of 60 address entries and there are six labels per page, you would need to set up ten pages of sample labels.
- If you can't predict how many items will appear on a page, such as in a price list or product catalog, set up one sample layout that is cloned when the XML content is imported.

After you've chosen the most suitable approach, arrange all the sample text, graphics placeholders, and boilerplate elements on the page, using master pages and applying style sheets as necessary. Make sure the size of each frame is large enough to handle the most amount of information it will contain; otherwise, text frames may become overset and images improperly cropped.

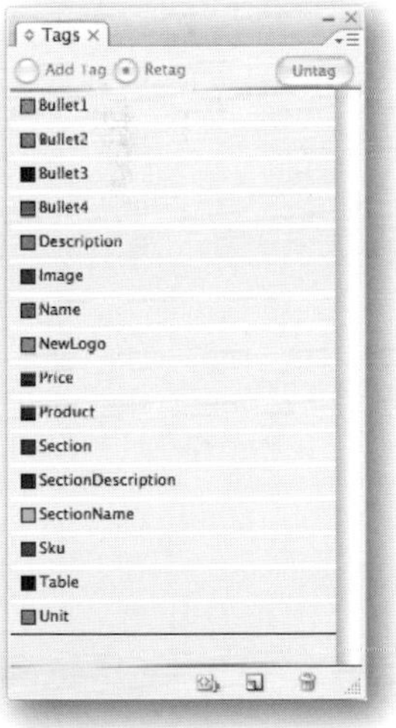
Tags
Add Tag
Retag
Untag
Bullet1
Bullet2
Bullet3
Bullet4
Description
Image
Name
NewLogo
Price
Product
Section
SectionDescription
SectionName
Sku
Table
Unit

Figure 16.10 By importing the tags instead of creating them from scratch, you're ensuring that the tag names exactly match those in the XML document you'll eventually import.

Step 2: Assign the XML Tags

With the sample layout set up, you can now assign the XML tags. But before you can tag anything, you first need to create the tags. You can create them from scratch, but its more efficient to import them from the most reliable source—your XML document. Choose Load Tags from the Tags panel menu and select the document containing the tag names you want to import. The tags are added to the Tags panel, each with its own unique color (**Figure 16.10**).

Assign a tag to each of the text and graphics placeholders in your sample layout. This identifies where the XML data should be placed. The formatting applied to each placeholder determines the appearance of the imported data.

When tagging, you must pay close attention to what you're tagging and in what order you assign the tags, because the structure of the tagged sample layout must parallel the structure of the imported XML file (**Figure 16.11**). When the assigned tags in your template match those in the XML document by name and by structural hierarchy, InDesign correctly populates the tagged placeholders with the corresponding XML data upon import. If something is off, InDesign still imports the XML content, but the placeholders are not populated with data.

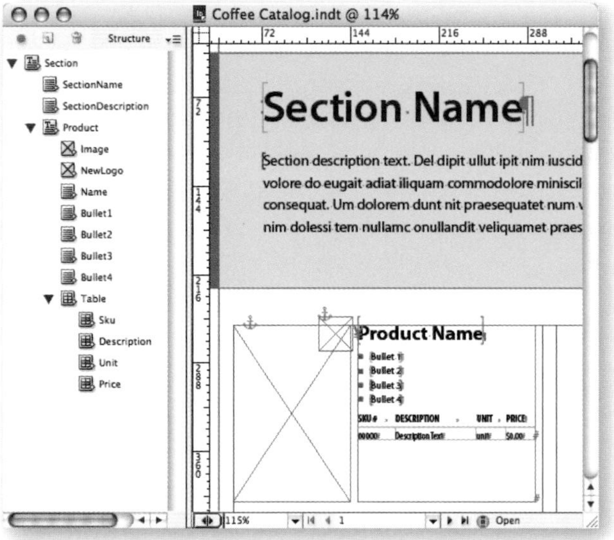
Coffee Catalog.indt @ 114%
Structure
Section
SectionName
SectionDescription
Product
Image
NewLogo
Name
Bullet1
Bullet2
Bullet3
Bullet4
Table
Sku
Description
Unit
Price
Section Name
Product Name
Open

Figure 16.11 As you assign tags to placeholders, the Structure pane displays the hierarchical structure of the tagged items. Use it to guide your tagging process. The structure in this template parallels the structure of the XML document shown in Figure 16.9.

● **Note:** InDesign provides several ways to assign tags: manual tagging, automatic tagging, and mapping styles to tags. When creating a template for automating a layout with XML, using the manual tagging method gives you the most accurate and predictable results. This chapter only teaches the manual tagging method.

REPLACE THE DEFAULT ROOT ELEMENT

By default, every InDesign document has one element, called *Root*. To ensure successful import results, the root element in the Structure pane must match the name of the root element in the XML document you plan to import. To replace the default root element with the correct root element, select Root in the Structure pane and click a tag in the Tags panel. You can also select Root in the Tags panel and click the Delete Tag button at the bottom of the panel. Choose the tag you want to replace it with in the Delete Tag dialog (**Figure 16.12**).

Delete Tag
Delete tag and replace with:
Section
Cancel
OK

Figure 16.12 If a tag is being used in the document when you delete the tag, the Delete Tag dialog appears so you can replace the deleted tag with another available tag.

In some layouts, it's necessary to assign the root element to a text frame, so that any tagged placeholders within that frame show up in the Structure pane as child elements of the root element. To tag a frame with the root element, drag it from the Structure pane to the frame. If you attempt to assign the root element by clicking a tag in the Tags panel, the new element appears as a child of the root element in the Structure pane.

TAGGING PLACEHOLDER TEXT

Before tagging any text, it's a good idea to first assign a tag to the frame the text is inside of. To tag a frame, select it and click a tag in the Tags panel. The tagged frame becomes color-coded with the color of the tag in the Tags panel. To tag placeholder text within a frame, select the text and click a tag in the Tags panel. The text becomes enclosed in color-coded brackets, called *tag markers* (**Figure 16.13**).

● **Note:** Make sure the view mode is set to Normal mode, or you won't see the tagged frames or tag markers.

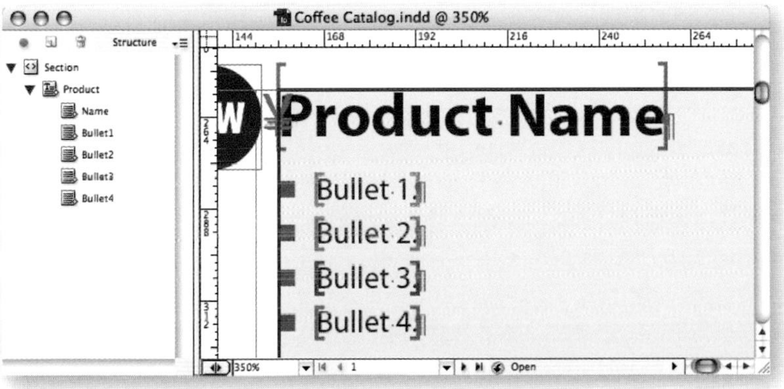
Coffee Catalog.indd @ 350%
Structure
Section
Product
Name
Bullet1
Bullet2
Bullet3
Bullet4
Product Name
Bullet 1
Bullet 2
Bullet 3
Bullet 4
350%
Open

Figure 16.13 When you tag text, the new element appears in the Structure pane as a child of the frame element in which the text is located. In this case, the *Product* tag was assigned to the frame that contains the product name and bulleted list.

If you don't see the tagged frames or tag markers, it's a good idea to make them visible. To display color-coded tagged frames, choose View > Structure > Show Tagged Frames. To display color brackets around tagged text, choose View > Structure > Show Tag Markers. If you want to change the color of a particular tag, double-click it and choose a color from the Color menu in the Tag Options dialog.

● **Note:** If a frame isn't tagged and you tag text within the frame, InDesign automatically tags the frame using the tag specified in the Tagging Preset Options dialog, which you can access by choosing Tagging Preset Options from the Structure pane menu.

Here are some guidelines for tagging placeholder text:

- **Assign only one tag to a text frame.** When you tag a frame in a threaded story, all other frames in the story are assigned the same tag. You can't assign more than one tag to a story.
- **Use the Add Tag option.** If all the text in a frame is selected when you attempt to assign a tag to it, the tag is assigned to the frame, not the text.

If the frame was already tagged, the assigned tag name in the Structure pane is simply updated. To tag all the text in a frame with a different tag from the one already assigned to the frame, select the text, click the Add Tag option at the top of the Tags panel, and then click a tag. By default, the Retag option is always selected until you purposefully click Add Tag.

- **Tag text within tagged text.** You can tag text within a region of tagged text, such as a specific word within a paragraph or a paragraph within a story. The tagged text appears in the Structure pane as a child of the existing element.

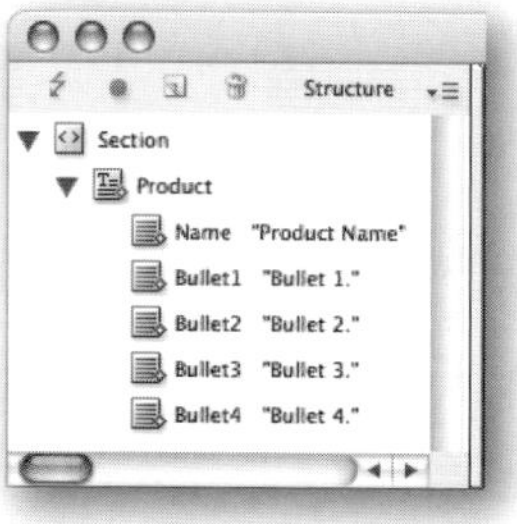
Structure
Section
Product
Name "Product Name"
Bullet1 "Bullet 1."
Bullet2 "Bullet 2."
Bullet3 "Bullet 3."
Bullet4 "Bullet 4."

Figure 16.14 Text snippets are shown to the right of the element in quotation marks. Only the first 32 characters of the tagged text are displayed.

- **Pay attention to what you tag.** Avoid tagging paragraph returns, tabs, spaces, or boilerplate text. Anything enclosed within the color-coded brackets is replaced with imported XML content. So, if you've included a paragraph return when tagging some text, the paragraph return will be deleted and replaced with XML content, and the text will run into the next paragraph.
- **Show hidden characters.** It's a good idea to show the hidden characters to make it easier to see what you're tagging. To make them visible, choose Type > Show Hidden Characters.
- **Show text snippets.** The Structure pane can display the first few words of text in an element, called a *snippet*, which helps you to see what you've tagged (**Figure 16.14**). To make the snippets visible, choose Show Text Snippets from the Structure pane menu.
- **Use the Story Editor.** Another way to view and assign tags to text is to use the Story Editor, where tagged text appears surrounded by the entire tag name instead of just brackets. If you want to be sure that boilerplate text is positioned outside of the tagged content, the Story Editor is the surest method (**Figure 16.15**). To open the Story Editor, choose Edit > Edit in Story Editor.

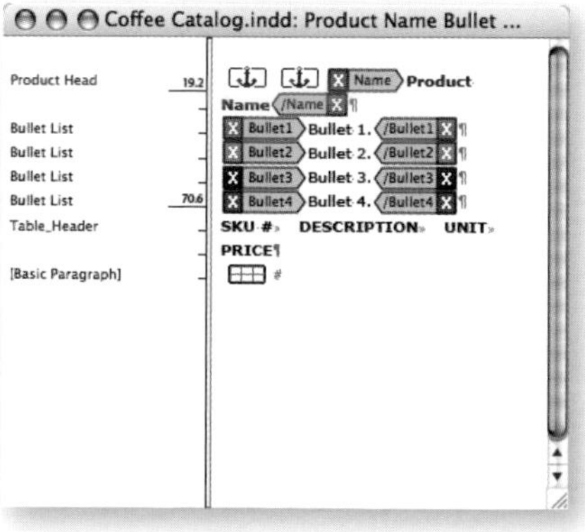
Coffee Catalog.indd: Product Name Bullet ...
Product Head
Bullet List
Bullet List
Bullet List
Bullet List
Table_Header
[Basic Paragraph]
Name
Product
Name
/Name
Bullet1
Bullet 1.
/Bullet1
Bullet2
Bullet 2.
/Bullet2
Bullet3
Bullet 3.
/Bullet3
Bullet4
Bullet 4.
/Bullet4
SKU #
DESCRIPTION
UNIT
PRICE

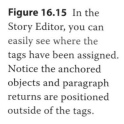

Figure 16.15 In the Story Editor, you can easily see where the tags have been assigned. Notice the anchored objects and paragraph returns are positioned outside of the tags.

TAGGING PLACEHOLDER GRAPHICS FRAMES

Before tagging a graphics frame, you might want to delete the sample image inside of it first. Although it's not completely necessary, it clearly communicates that the frame is a placeholder frame. It's helpful to set frame fitting options to determine how imported content is cropped and fitted within the frame. Also keep in mind when cloning repeating elements with images that the images in the sample layout must be anchored into the text frame holding the rest of the record's content.

● **Note:** If you tag a frame containing an image, InDesign assigns the new element an href attribute that points to the linked image file. When importing XML content, InDesign replaces any tagged images with the incoming content.

To tag a placeholder graphics frame, select it and click a tag in the Tags panel. The color of the assigned tag is applied to the frame to indicate it has been tagged (**Figure 16.16**).

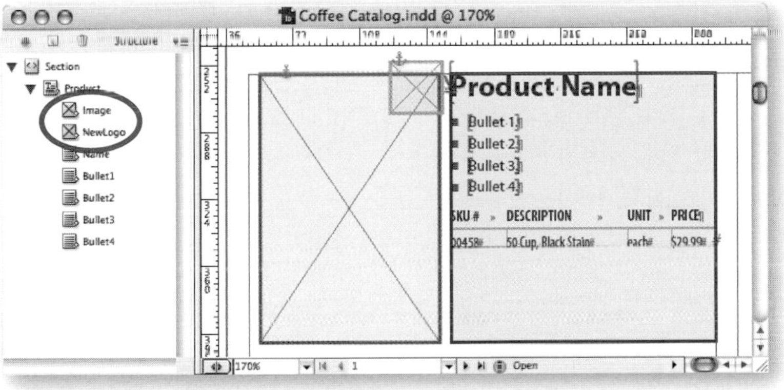
Coffee Catalog.indd @ 170%
Section
Image
NewLogo
Bullet1
Bullet2
Bullet3
Bullet4
Product Name
Bullet 1
Bullet 2
Bullet 3
Bullet 4
SKU #
DESCRIPTION
UNIT
PRICE
00458
50 Cup, Black Stain
each
$29.99
170%
Open

Figure 16.16 When you tag a frame, the new element appears in the Structure pane as a child of another element. Since both graphics frames are anchored within the text frame that has the *Product* tag assigned to it, they appear as child elements of that frame element. The icon to their left indicates they are empty frames.

TAGGING PLACEHOLDER TABLES

Tagged tables must conform to a specific structure, which consists of a single table element containing multiple cell elements. It's a good idea to always tag tables before tagging individual cells.

● **Note:** To change the default tag names, choose Tagging Preset Options from the Structure pane menu.

To tag a table, select the entire table and click a tag in the Tags panel. InDesign automatically tags each cell using the default tag that is specified in the Tagging Preset Options dialog. However, you can use different names for the table and cell tags if you want. This is, of course, necessary if you want the tagged table to use identical names to those in the XML document you plan on importing.

● **Note:** The correct XML import options must be specified for InDesign to automatically clone repeating table rows. See "Importing the XML Document," later in this chapter for more information.

With the table tagged, you can now apply a different tag to each cell within it. To tag a cell, place your cursor inside the cell and click a tag in the Tags panel. The cell tag name in the Structure pane is updated with the new tag name (**Figure 16.17**). Be careful not to select text within the cell; otherwise, the text will be tagged and appear as a child of the cell element in the Structure pane.

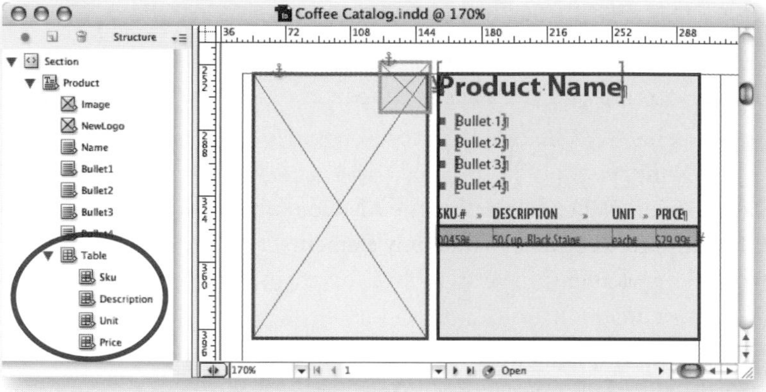
Coffee Catalog.indd @ 170%
Structure
Section
Product
Image
NewLogo
Name
Bullet1
Bullet2
Bullet3
Table
Sku
Description
Unit
Price
Product Name
Bullet 1
Bullet 2
Bullet 3
Bullet 4
SKU # DESCRIPTION UNIT PRICE
170%
Open

Figure 16.17 When you tag a table, InDesign creates a table element in the Structure pane as well as one cell element for each cell in the table. The cell elements are child elements of the table element. Since the table flows within the text frame that has the *Product* tag assigned to it, it appears as a child element of that frame element.

It's not necessary to tag more than one row in the table. In fact, if the table contains more than one row, you can delete the extra rows. As long as the number of columns in the placeholder table match the number of columns in the imported XML content, InDesign can clone that structure. (**Figure 16.18**).

Figure 16.18 The table in this XML document contains enough cell data for two rows (**A**), so InDesign automatically creates a second row when the XML content is imported (**B**).

A

```
<Product SKU="00238-00239">
    <Image href="file:///Users/gabrielp/Desktop/Coffee_Catalog/images/0238.tif"/>
    <NewLogo href="file:///Users/gabrielp/Desktop/Coffee_Catalog/images/new_logo.ai"/>
    <Name>Commercial Coffee Maker</Name>
    <Bullet1>Metal base.</Bullet1>
    <Bullet2>3-prong grounded plug.</Bullet2>
    <Bullet3>"Brew View" guage.</Bullet3>
    <Bullet4>NSF approved.</Bullet4>
    <Table>
        <Sku>00238</Sku>
        <Description>101 Cup, Black Stain</Description>
        <Unit>each</Unit>
        <Price>$49.99</Price>
        <Sku>00239</Sku>
        <Description>55 Cup, Black Stain</Description>
        <Unit>each</Unit>
        <Price>$29.99</Price>
    </Table>
</Product>
```

B

NEW
Commercial Coffee Maker
Metal base.
3-prong grounded plug.
"Brew View" guage.
NSF approved.
SKU # DESCRIPTION UNIT PRICE
00238 101 Cup, Black Stain each $49.99
00239 55 Cup, Black Stain each $29.99

STRATEGIES FOR SETTING UP A TEMPLATE

With the basics of tagging under your belt, let's look at some different tagging strategies you'll need to employ depending on the type of template you're creating:

- **Tag only as needed.** If an XML document contains more data than you want placed into your publication, just use the necessary tags for your particular situation. When importing the XML document, you can choose to filter the imported content so that only elements from the XML document with matching elements in your publication are imported. See "Importing the XML Document," later in this chapter.
- **Tag once, then duplicate.** If you're setting up a template with multiple instances of a sample layout, it's most efficient to set up one sample layout first, assign tags to each placeholder, and then duplicate the layout as many times as necessary. This prevents you from having to repeat the tagging procedure for each duplicate layout on the page. The order in which you create the duplicate layouts determines the order in which the XML data is placed on the page. So, if the original version of the layout is located at the top of the page, and then a duplicate is created and placed below it, InDesign first populates the original version with XML data before it populates the next one.
- **Leverage the speed of master pages.** You can quickly duplicate pages of sample layouts by placing the layout(s) on a master page and then applying it to multiple document pages. At first, only one instance of the corresponding structure appears in the Structure pane regardless of how many times the layout appears on document pages. So when you import an XML document, only the layout on the master page gets populated with data. However, if you override the master items on each document page, the corresponding structure for each layout will appear multiple times in the Structure pane—once for each iteration—and then the imported XML content will properly populate each layout instance.

  This is a fast way to create a template for a set of labels, business cards, or any other structured publication that contains a fixed number of items per page. Just remember to untag the layout on the master page before you import an XML document, or the layout will be populated with data. To untag an object, select it and click the Untag button at the top of the Tags panel.
- **Insert the tagged placeholders into one overall text frame.** If you're setting up a layout that will be cloned, it's imperative you insert the tagged placeholders into one overall text frame, so when the layout is cloned, it flows within a single story. If placeholder frames have been threaded together, the imported content is flowed from one frame to the next. If the placeholder frame(s) can't accommodate all the XML content, it will become overset. You can autoflow the remaining content by creating and threading more frames (**Figure 16.19**).

■ **Tip:** As you duplicate a sample layout, notice its structure is simultaneously added to the Structure pane.

■ **Tip:** You can override all the master items on a document page at once by choosing Override All Master Page Items from the Pages panel menu.

● **Note:** If text or objects within a group are tagged, you cannot place the grouped object within a text frame. However, you can anchor multiple objects within one frame and then anchor that frame into another frame.

■ **Tip:** To flow text automatically, click the out port of the overset text frame, hold down the Shift key, and then click the loaded text icon in an empty column. InDesign creates new text frames that adhere to the margin and column guides, and adds new pages until all the text is flowed.

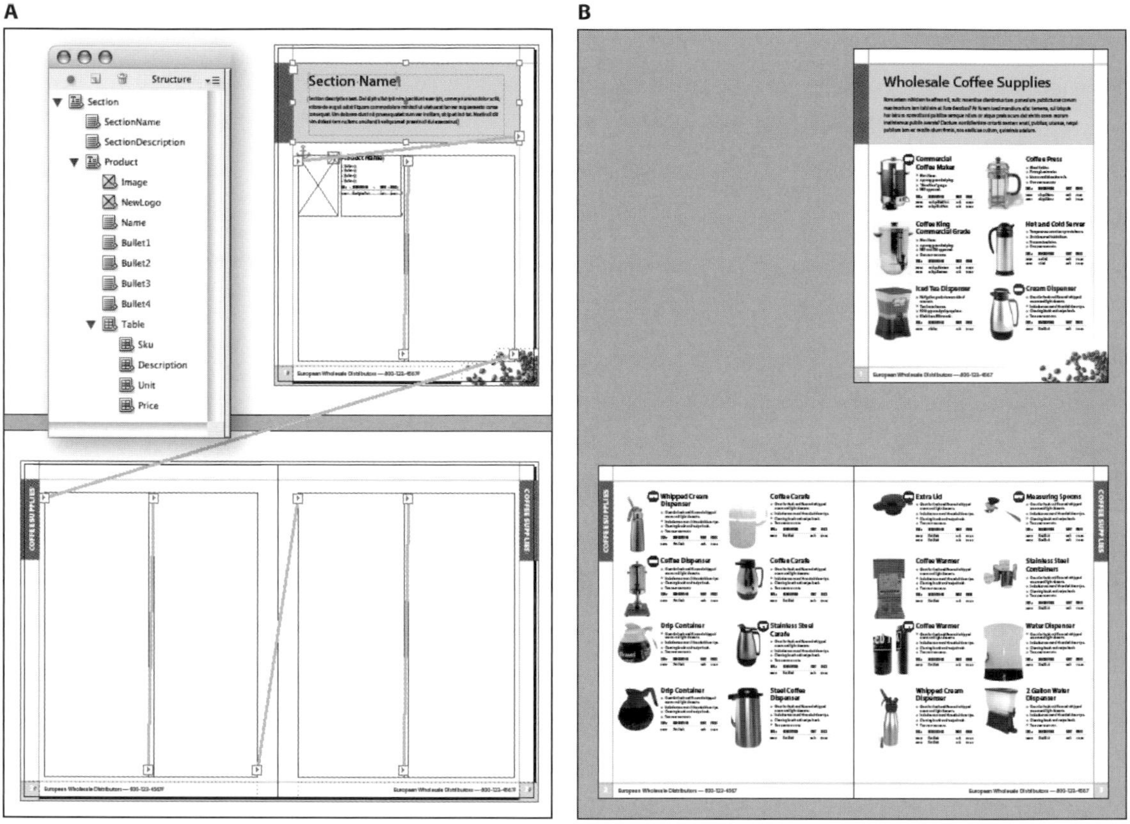
A
B
Structure
Section
SectionName
SectionDescription
Product
Image
NewLogo
Name
Bullet1
Bullet2
Bullet3
Bullet4
Table
Sku
Description
Unit
Price
Section Name
Wholesale Coffee Supplies

Figure 16.19 This template is set up for the layout to be cloned (**A**). To match the structural hierarchy of the XML document to be imported, the *Section* tag was first assigned to the story, which will include all the tagged placeholder content. Next, the *SectionName* and *SectionDescription* tags were assigned to text placeholders within the first frame. Then the sample product layout—which was already tagged—was inserted as an anchored object into the second text frame. The layout after import (**B**).

- **Insert frame break characters when needed.** Sometimes it's necessary to insert a frame break character after all the text in a frame to force any following text to flow into the next threaded frame. For example, a frame break character was inserted after the section description text in Figure 16.19 to force the sample product layout into the next frame.

  If your publication contains one layout per page and you're setting up the sample layout to be cloned, you'll need to put all the tagged placeholders into one frame that adheres to the margin and column guides on the page, and then insert a frame break character to force each repeating record to flow into its own frame (**Figure 16.20**). To insert a frame break, choose Type > Insert Break Character > Frame Break.

A

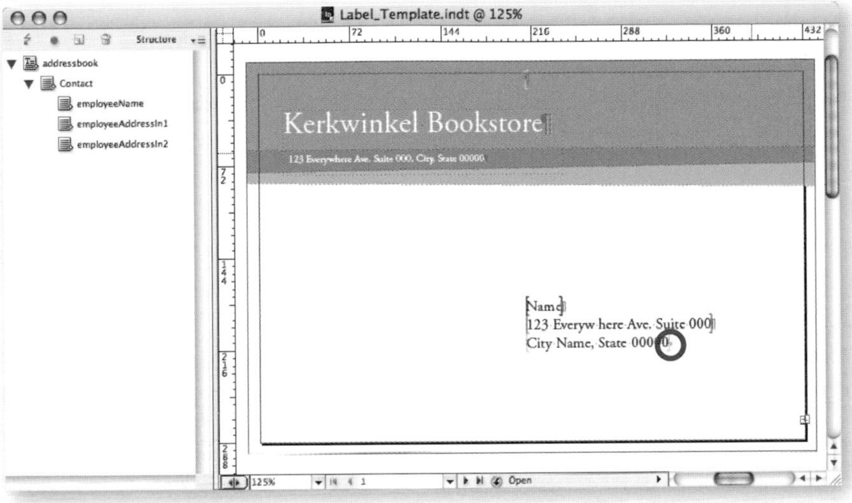

Label_Template.indt @ 125%
Structure
addressbook
Contact
employeeName
employeeAddressln1
employeeAddressln2
Kerkwinkel Bookstore
Name
123 Everyw here Ave. Suite 000
City Name, State 00000

B

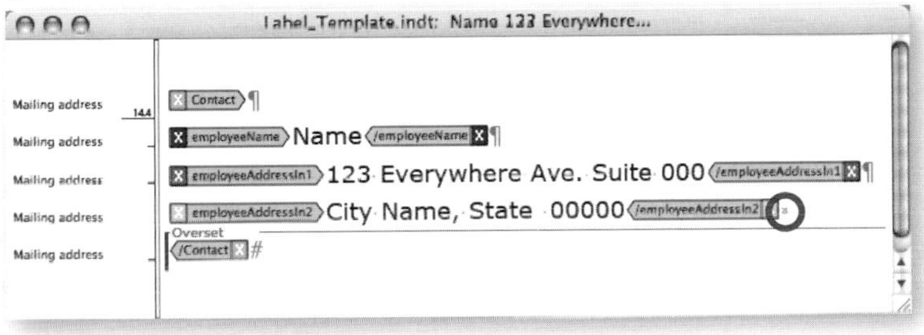

Label_Template.indt: Name 123 Everywhere...
Mailing address
Contact
employeeName
Name
/employeeName
employeeAddressln1
123 Everywhere Ave. Suite 000
/employeeAddressln1
employeeAddressln2
City Name, State 00000
/employeeAddressln2
Overset
/Contact

C

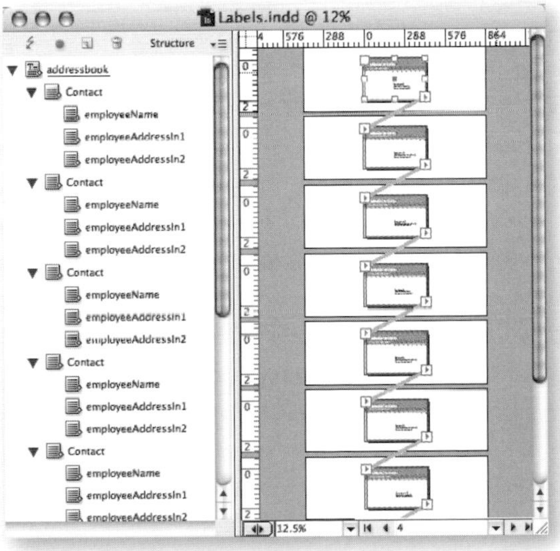

Labels.indd @ 12%
Structure
addressbook
Contact
employeeName
employeeAddressln1
employeeAddressln2

Figure 16.20 In this label template (**A**), a frame break was inserted after all the tagged placeholder text. In this case, the frame break must be inserted within the Contact element, yet outside of all the other placeholder tags so that it is cloned with each instance of the layout (**B**). After the XML content is imported, you can autoflow the remaining content (**C**).

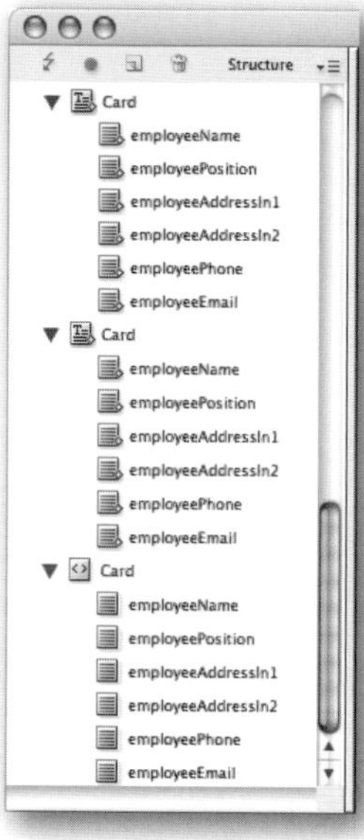
Structure
Card
employeeName
employeePosition
employeeAddressln1
employeeAddressln2
employeePhone
employeeEmail
Card
employeeName
employeePosition
employeeAddressln1
employeeAddressln2
employeePhone
employeeEmail
Card
employeeName
employeePosition
employeeAddressln1
employeeAddressln2
employeePhone
employeeEmail

Figure 16.21 The last Card element in this template is empty as indicated by the icon to its left. All the other element icons have a blue diamond on them, which indicates that the element is attached to an item on the page. The absence of a blue diamond means that the element is not attached to a page item.

■ **Tip:** It's a good idea to document which import options need to be selected for your particular template. Take a screen capture of the XML Import Options dialog with the correct options selected and add it to your template package folder.

Step 3: Clean Up the Template

It's important to clean up your template to ensure successful results when the XML document is imported. Here are a few important things to do:

- Remove any unnecessary objects from the document, including unused empty frames, objects on the pasteboard, and any other elements that are not part of the final layout.
- If a master page contains tagged placeholders, remember to untag them. You might also choose to delete them.
- Delete any extra unused elements from the Structure pane. When a tagged object is deleted, it is removed from the page, but its corresponding element in the Structure pane remains as an empty element (**Figure 16.21**).

Step 4: Test the Import Results

With the template complete, you're technically ready to use it. However, it's important to test your solution before launching the final template to make sure that everything functions as expected. Don't be surprised if the first few attempts at importing an XML document don't work. Designing an XML-ready template can be a meticulous process in which you must concentrate on a lot of minute details. It's easy to overlook an item that keeps your solution from working. Sometimes fixing just one element or selecting one option makes the solution suddenly work. A detailed description of how to import an XML document follows.

Importing the XML Document

To import an XML document, choose File > Import XML (or choose Import XML from the Structure pane menu). Make sure you select Show XML Import Options and the Merge Content option at the bottom of the Import XML dialog before you import the document (**Figure 16.22**).

You must use the Merge Content option to import XML into tagged placeholders. When merging content, InDesign replaces identically tagged and structured elements in your document with the imported XML elements. Show XML Import Options presents additional options to control what happens when the XML content is imported (**Figure 16.23**). It's best to become familiar with each option to gain the most control over the import results.

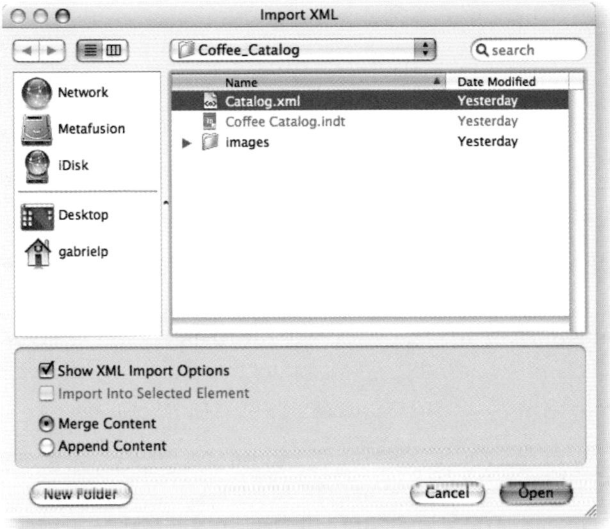
Import XML
Coffee_Catalog
search
Network
Metafusion
iDisk
Desktop
gabrielp
Name
Date Modified
Catalog.xml
Yesterday
Coffee Catalog.indt
Yesterday
images
Yesterday
Show XML Import Options
Import Into Selected Element
Merge Content
Append Content
New Folder
Cancel
Open

Figure 16.22 The Import XML dialog.

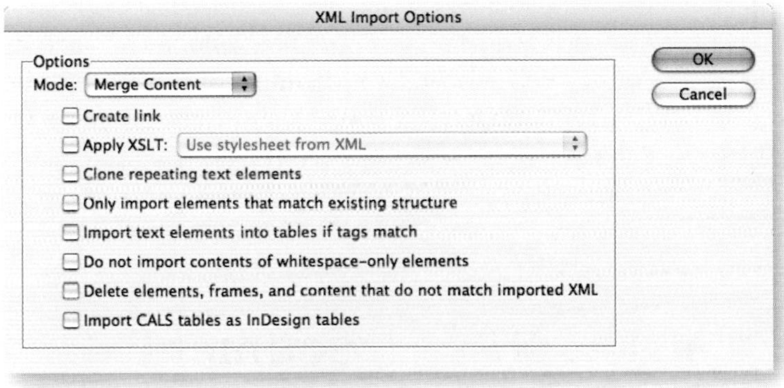
XML Import Options
Options
Mode: Merge Content
Create link
Apply XSLT: Use stylesheet from XML
Clone repeating text elements
Only import elements that match existing structure
Import text elements into tables if tags match
Do not import contents of whitespace-only elements
Delete elements, frames, and content that do not match imported XML
Import CALS tables as InDesign tables
OK
Cancel

Figure 16.23 The XML Import Options dialog. The options you select depend on how the template has been set up and the condition of the XML document.

Here's a look at each import option in detail:

- **Create link.** When selected, InDesign establishes a link to the imported XML document and lists it in the Links panel. If you make changes to the XML source document, you can update the XML data in your InDesign document by updating the link.
- **Apply XSLT.** This advanced option allows you to assign an XSLT (Extensible Stylesheet Language Transformation) file to the XML content upon import. XSLT stylesheets make it possible to filter, rearrange, and perform other transformations on XML content.

- **Clone repeating text elements.** If your template has been set up with a sample layout that will be cloned, you must select this option. InDesign replicates the formatting applied to the tagged placeholders for each repeating element found in the XML content.
- **Only import elements that match existing structure.** If the XML document contains elements that you do not want imported into your document, select this option. Only the elements from the imported XML file with matching elements in the document are imported.
- **Import text elements into tables if tags match.** Definitely select this option if your layout contains a tagged placeholder table. InDesign imports content into a table if the XML document contains a table whose tagging matches the tags assigned to the placeholder table and its cells.
- **Do not import contents of whitespace-only elements.** With this option selected, InDesign ignores empty elements in the XML document. An element is considered empty if it contains only whitespace, such as paragraph returns or spaces. It's very important to select this option if you've inserted items such as paragraph returns, tabs, frame breaks, boilerplate text, or anchored objects between tagged placeholders and you want to preserve these items when you import the XML document. As long as the parent element that contains the tagged layout is empty, InDesign leaves the boilerplate text and other characters in place (**Figure 16.24**).

A

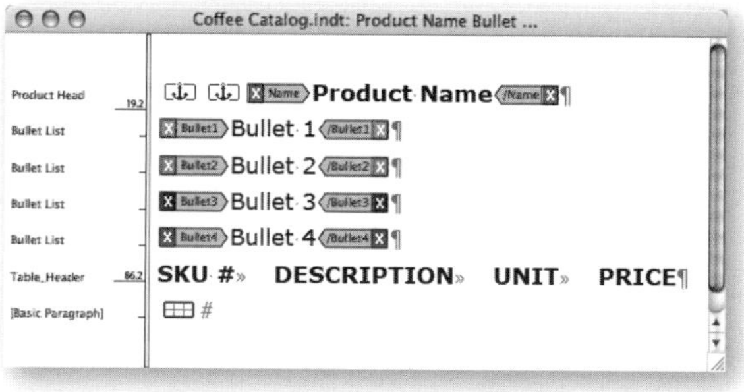
Coffee Catalog.indt: Product Name Bullet ...
Product Head
Bullet List
Table_Header
[Basic Paragraph]
Product Name
Bullet 1
Bullet 2
Bullet 3
Bullet 4
SKU # DESCRIPTION UNIT PRICE

B

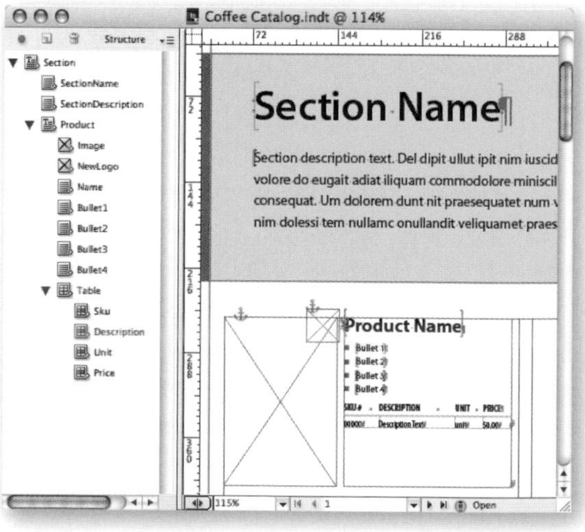
Coffee Catalog.indt @ 114%
Structure
Section
SectionName
SectionDescription
Product
Image
NewLogo
Name
Bullet1
Bullet2
Bullet3
Bullet4
Table
Sku
Description
Unit
Price
Section Name
Product Name

Figure 16.24 The header row for the table in this layout is boilerplate text, which has been inserted within the parent frame tagged with the *Product* tag and positioned outside of the tagged placeholder text. Since the Product element—which contains all the other elements—is empty, the boilerplate text is preserved.

- **Delete elements, frames, and content that do not match imported XML.** If this option is selected, InDesign removes elements from the Structure pane and the layout if they don't match any elements in the imported XML document. For example, in Figure 16.9 the XML document contains a NewLogo element that only occurs in some of the products. On import, if one of the products doesn't contain the NewLogo element, InDesign deletes the corresponding placeholder frame. As a result, the red "New" logo only shows up for those products that contain the NewLogo element.
- **Import CALS tables as InDesign tables.** If a table in the XML document follows the CALS specification, it is converted to an InDesign table during import when this option is selected.

Take Automation to the Next Level with XML Rules

InDesign CS3 has a new rules-based XML processing engine that allows publishers to create custom-automated XML publishing solutions. Rule sets are groups of instructions that evaluate XML data and take specific actions if that data meets certain conditions. They are defined using standard scripting languages: JavaScript, AppleScript, or VBScript.

To learn more about using the new XML rules engine in InDesign CS3, see the Adobe Web site. Additional information can be found on the scripting page at www.adobe.com/products/indesign/scripting.

Index

A

A-Master page, 124
Above Line option, 215–216, 218
Access, Microsoft, 298
Add Bullets dialog, 186
Adobe
  Bridge. *See* Bridge
  Creative Suite, 283
  Illustrator. *See* Illustrator
  InDesign. *See* InDesign
  Paragraph Composer, 178
  Photoshop. *See* Photoshop
  Single-Line Composer, 178
  Swatch Exchange files, 58, 158–159, 277
  Web site, 265, 278, 321
agates, 76
Align menu, 205
Align panel, 84, 110
Align Stroke options, 201–202
Align to Baseline Grid button, 110, 113, 114, 174
All Caps command, 170, 171
anchor points, 62, 63, 66, 79, 211
anchored objects, 89–90, 213–218
Append Metadata command, 293
AppleScript, 22, 321
ASCII, 171
ASE files, 158–159, 277
auto leading, 113, 168, 181
automated publications, 20–21, 32, 297, 309
automatic kerning, 167
automatic text flow, 104–105
automation tools, 5

B

background art, 11, 12, 47, 142, 265
Balance Ragged Lines option, 183
Based on Master option, 125
baseline grid, 9, 110–115, 207
baseline shift, 168–169
[Basic Cell] style, 234
[Basic Graphics Frame] style, 223, 269–270
[Basic Table] style, 234, 241
[Basic Text Frame] style, 223, 269–270
Bevel Join option, 201
bleed area, 9, 10, 33, 95–96
bleed guide, 10
Bleed mode, 119
blending modes, 220, 265
boilerplate, 16, 305, 307, 309, 312, 320
books, 247
borders, 44, 236
bounding boxes, 63, 209, 210
Bridge, 283–295
  assigning keywords in, 293–294
  customizing workspaces in, 287–288
  default workspace, 285
  entering metadata in, 292–293
  filtering files in, 291
  finding files in, 294
  interface, 284–289
  labeling files in, 289–290
  launching, 284
  navigating folders in, 285–286
  organizing files in, 289–294
  previewing thumbnails in, 286–287
  rating files in, 289–290
  shrinking windows in, 288–289
  sorting files in, 291
brochures, 10
Browse command, 284
bulleted lists, 184–188
Bullets and Numbering feature, 185–187
business cards, 6, 19, 21
Butt Cap style, 200–201

C

calculating values, 88
CALS specification, 321
cap styles, 200–201
captions, 100, 114
Card elements, 299, 306
carriage returns, 176, 177
case, changing, 170–171
catalogs, 247, 307, 308
cell borders, 236
Cell Options dialog, 230–233
cell styles, 13, 14, 234–235, 243, 245
cells. *See also* tables
  copying and pasting, 228
  formatting, 229–233
  placing images in, 246
  selecting, 229
  using color in, 246
centimeters, 76
Change Case commands, 170–171
Chapter Number options, 135
character formatting, 166–173
Character panel, 166
Character Style Options dialog, 192
character styles
  creating, 191–192
  defined, 13, 190
  illustrated, 15
  importing, 198
  keeping track of, 44
  naming, 52
  updating, 51–53
child master, 125
Chinese fonts, 275
ciceros, 76
CJK fonts, 275
Clear Transformations command, 87
closed paths, 62
collection files, 295
color harmony rules, 160
color management, 33, 163–164
color modes, 150
color palettes, 282
Color panel, 150
color printing, 32
Color Settings dialog, 163–164
color swatches, 150–164
  changing order of, 51, 161
  creating, 50–51, 150–157
  deleting unused, 159–160, 264
  filtering, 162
  finding unnamed, 160–161
  loading, 158
  naming/renaming, 51, 151–152, 264
  organizing, 159–160
  purpose of, 16, 150
  sharing, 158–159
colors. *See also* color swatches
  baseline grid, 112
  file label, 290
  layer, 50, 146
  layout grid, 117–118
  mixing, 150–151, 160
  ruler guide, 109–110
  in tables/cells, 246
column guides, 10, 101, 266
column settings, 42
column strokes, 238

columns
controlling height of, 232–233
optimal arrangement of, 107
purpose of, 104
selecting, 229
setting up, 104–106
comments, 300–301
Compact mode (Bridge), 288–289
companion Web site, viii
composition methods, 178, 181
consistency, design, 6–7, 17, 149
container frames, 64
content, frame, 64, 66, 72
Content panel (Bridge), 286, 291
content type, 100
Control panel, 78–80, 83, 86, 166, 174
Convert Text to Table command, 228
Convert Variable to Text command, 139
corner effects, 203
Corner Options dialog, 203
Create Guides dialog, 108–109
Create Package Folder dialog, 57, 276
Creation Date variable, 97, 135, 137
Creative Suite file browser, 283
Custom Text variable, 137

D

data-field placeholders, 19, 46
Data Merge feature, viii, 19–20, 32, 188, 305
database programs, 298
Date Format field, 136
decimal tabs, 189
Define Lists feature, 248–249
Delete Character Style dialog, 52
Delete Paragraph Style dialog, 52
Delete Tag dialog, 310
delimiters, 300–301
design principles, template, 23–27
design requirements, template, 30
diagonal lines, 233
dictionaries, 18, 32, 172–173, 180, 278
Direct Selection tool, 65, 66–67, 69–70, 72, 200
direction lines, 62
document grid, 116–117, 119
document prolog, 301–302, 303
Document Setup command/dialog, 41, 42, 95
document tree, 301–302
document type declaration, 303
document window, resizing, 270
dotted border, 44
drop caps, 177–178
DTDs, 303–304
dummy text. *See* placeholder text

E

ease of use, template, 25–26, 271
eBooks, 19
Effects panel, 219, 221–222
elements
cloning, 320
defined, 299
deleting, 321
importing, 320
naming, 301
repeating, 99, 307, 320
Ellipse Frame tool, 64
Ellipse tool, 71
embedded links, 264
empty text frames, 130–131
Enable Layout Adjustment option, 121
End menu, 202
end tags, 300
endpoints, 62
EPS files, 33
Excel, 228, 236, 242, 244
eXtensible Markup Language, 20, 298. *See also* XML

F

Favorites panel (Bridge), 285, 286
file browser, 283
File Handling preferences, 40
File Info dialog (Bridge), 272–273, 293
File Name variable, 97, 137
FileMaker Pro, 298
files
adding metadata to, 293
assigning keywords to, 293–294
filtering, 291
finding, 294
labeling, 289–290
organizing, 289–294
rating, 289–290
sorting, 291
Fill With Placeholder Text command, 33
fills, 200, 230–231, 238
Filter panel (Bridge), 291
Find dialog (Bridge), 294
Find Font command/dialog, 47, 263
Finder (Mac OS X), 289
First Baseline options, 206–207
Fit Page in Window command, 270
Fit Spread in Window command, 270
Fitting options, 129
Flattener Preview panel, 265
Flip commands, 86
Folders panel (Bridge), 285, 286
font families, 166
fonts
copying, 275
looking for missing, 263
and metadata, 292
OpenType, 171–172, 173
PostScript, 33, 171
printing considerations, 33
TrueType, 171
footers, 11, 12, 239
footnotes, 247, 251–254
forms, interactive, 19
frame breaks, 316–317
frame content, 64, 66, 72
frame edges, 266
Frame Fitting Options dialog, 129, 218
frames, 61–91
aligning/distributing, 84
anchoring objects in, 89–90
applying corner effects to, 203
applying fill/stroke color to, 200–202
flipping, 86
formatting, 47, 200–222
grouping/ungrouping, 88–89
measuring position of, 80–83
nesting objects in, 89–90
numerically positioning, 83
numerically resizing, 85
vs. paths, 63
preventing text wrap in, 206
purpose of, 61
redefining content of, 72
rotating, 86
scaling, 86
showing edges of, 43, 64
skewing, 86, 87
stroke weight for, 86
terminology, 62–63
tools for working with, 78–87
transforming, 86–87
types of, 64–72
framework, 9, 11, 34, 47, 93
FX button, 221

G

gap color/tint, 202
Glyph Scaling option, 181

glyph sets, 173, 277–278
Glyphs panel, 173
Go to Bridge button, 284
goals, template design, 24
gradient swatches, 153–154
Graphic Frame option, 209, 210
graphic links, 276
graphical specifications, 12
graphics
  cropping, 65
  frames, 64–68, 313
  organizing, 16
  placeholders, 12, 127–129, 313
  repositioning, 67
  resizing/scaling, 65, 67
  tools for working with, 65
grid units, 97–98
grids, 9. *See also* baseline grid; layout grids
Grids in Back option, 117
Grids preferences, 110–113, 116–117
Group command, 89
guides, 10, 42, 101, 266. *See also* ruler guides
Guides & Pasteboard preferences, 117–118
Guides in Back option, 118
gutter space, 10, 98

H

hanging indents, 176, 184, 187
hanging punctuation, 207
headers, 12, 239
hidden characters, 44, 50, 133, 216, 267–268, 312
Horizontal Filmstrip workspace, 288
horizontal ruler, 74, 76–78, 106
HTML, 298
hyphenation settings, 178–179, 180, 276

I

Ignore Text Wrap option, 206
Illustrator, 31, 158–159, 164, 219, 220, 277
image resolution, 33, 264–265, 271, 292
images, 40, 246, 264–265. *See also* graphics
Import XML command/dialog, 318–319
inches, 41, 76
.indd file extension, 38
indenting text, 175–176, 184, 187
InDesign
  automation tools, 5
  color capabilities, 149
  Data Merge feature, viii, 19–20, 32, 188, 305
  frame formatting tools, 199
  interactive features, 19
  predesigned templates, 37–58. *See also* predesigned templates
  scripting support, 22
  table features, 227, 228. *See also* tables
  welcome screen, 38
  XML tools, 304–305, 321. *See also* XML
InDesign Type, 172
.indt file extension, 38
Inline option, 215
Insert Anchored Object dialog, 214
Insert Footnote command, 251
Insert Table command, 228
Insert Variable command, 97, 133
Inset Spacing options, 204
inside margins, 103
interactive forms, 19
International Standards Organization, 9
Invert option, 210
ISO, 9
Item Information dialog, 144

J

Japanese fonts, 275
JavaScript, 22, 321
join options, 201
journals, 247
Jump options, 210
justification settings, 181

K

Keep Options dialog, 182–183
kerning, 167–168
keyboard shortcuts
  for applying file ratings, 289
  for applying labels, 290
  for cell styles, 235
  for formatting text, 166
  for frequently used styles, 52–53, 55, 225, 240
  for rearranging objects, 91
  for switching modes, 119
Keywords panel (Bridge), 293–294
Korean fonts, 275
Kuler, 160

L

labels, 282, 289–290
Language menu, 173
language translations, 100, 172
language versions, 32, 146, 148
Last Page Number variable, 137
Layer Options dialog, 146
layers, 145–148
  assigning colors to, 50, 146
  creating, 34, 146–147
  hiding, 50, 148
  locking/unlocking, 44, 147, 148
  merging, 50
  naming, 146
  and pasted objects, 148
  purpose of, 16, 123
  rearranging, 148
  removing extra, 263
  selecting objects on, 147
  tips for working with, 50, 147–148
  ways of using, 145–146
Layers panel, 16, 45, 147–148, 269
Layout Adjustment feature, 120–121, 269
layout grids, 97–119
  choosing colors for, 117–118
  composition of, 97–98
  planning, 98–100
  printing, 119
  purpose of, 97
  showing/hiding, 118–119
  tools for working with, 100–117
  using multiple, 99
layouts
  assigning XML tags to, 309–310
  cloning, 315
  creating, 309
  duplicating, 315
  mock-up. *See* mock-up layouts
leading values, 113, 114, 168, 181
least effort, principle of, 26
Letter Spacing option, 181
libraries. *See* object libraries
linked content, 243–244
linked graphics files, 276
Links panel, 264
lists
  bulleted, 184–188
  multilevel, 250–251
  numbered, 184–188, 248
  running, 248–249
Load Styles dialog, 198, 226
Load Swatches command, 158
Load Tags command, 309

Lock Guides command, 110, 266
Lock Guides option, 147
Lock Layer option, 147
logos, 12, 16, 64, 142, 154, 264
long documents, 247–260
  footnotes for, 251–255
  multilevel lists in, 250–251
  running lists in, 248–249
  table of contents for, 255–260
looping nested styles, 54
Loupe tool (Bridge), 287

M

Mac OS
  Finder, 289
  Glyph Sets folder, 278
  predesigned templates location, 39
  Scripts folder, 22, 278
  Spotlight, 292
  XML editor, 298
magnification levels, 75, 270
manuals, 251
margin guides, 10, 101
margins, 100–103
Margins and Columns dialog, 42, 102
markup, 298, 300, 302
master items
  defined, 126
  detaching, 140
  distinguishing from other objects, 126–127
  hiding, 141
  locking/unlocking, 140
  maintaining separate layers for, 145–146
  overriding, 139–140
  tips for working with, 140–142
Master Options dialog, 48
master pages, 124–142
  choosing number of pages for, 124, 126
  components of, 10–12
  constructing layout of, 126–139
  controlling text wrap on, 211
  converting mock-up spreads to, 48–49
  converting page spreads to, 126
  copying existing, 126
  copying objects to, 48, 126
  creating, 124–126
  deleting unused, 49
  exploring, 43
  leveraging speed of, 315
  naming, 49, 125
  purpose of, 10, 34, 123
  setting default, 269
  setting up, 34, 124
  setting up placeholder graphics frames in, 127–129
  setting up placeholder text frames in, 130–132
  setting up text variables in, 133–139
  and tagging strategies, 315
  updating, 48–49
  working with master items in, 139–142
Master Text Frame option, 124
mathematical expressions, 88
Measure tool, 82–83
measurement system, 41, 75–76, 270
Merge Content option, 318
Merge Layers command, 50
metadata, 272–273, 283, 292–293
Metadata panel (Bridge), 292
Metrics Kerning option, 167–168
Microsoft
  Access, 298
  Excel, 228, 236, 242, 244
  Word, 228, 236
millimeters, 41, 76
Minimum Vertical Offset option, 118
missing links, 264
Miter Join option, 201
miter limit value, 201
mixed ink groups, 156–157
mixed ink swatches, 155–156
mock-up layouts, 33, 46–47, 51–52, 94
Mode buttons, 118–119
Modification Date variable, 97, 135, 136, 137
Move dialog, 75, 83
multilevel lists, 250–251
multilingual publications, 146, 148
multilingual templates, 171, 173

N

name-value pairs, 300
nested objects, 89–90
nested styles, 44–45, 53–54, 192–195
New Cell Style dialog, 234–235
New Character Style dialog, 190
New Color Swatch dialog, 151–152
New Document dialog, 95
New Master dialog, 124
New Paragraph Style dialog, 190
New Style Group command, 197
New Table of Contents Style dialog, 257, 258
New Table Style dialog, 240
newsletter template, 4
Next Page Number marker, 132
Next Style option, 195–196
nodes, 301
[None] style, 234
[None] swatch, 150
nonprinting characters, 267–268
Normal mode, 42, 119, 269
Notepad, 298
Number Step style definition, 52
numbered lists, 184–188, 248

O

object-level formatting, 200
object libraries
  adding objects to, 143
  adding to template packages, 58, 277
  copying items among, 145
  creating, 34–35, 49–50, 143
  naming, 143
  organizing, 143–145
  purpose of, 16–17, 123, 142–143
Object Library panel, 143
Object Style Options dialog, 55, 223
object styles, 222–226
  creating, 54–55, 222–224
  importing, 226
  naming, 55
  productivity tips, 55, 225–226
  purpose of, 13, 222
  rearranging, 55
Object Styles panel, 15, 223
objects
  anchoring, 89–90, 213–214
  applying transparency effects to, 219–222
  defined, 62
  grouping, 89
  nesting, 89–90
  wrapping text around, 208–213
opacity value, 219–220
Open a File dialog, 39
open paths, 62
OpenType fonts, 171–172, 173
Optical Kerning option, 167–168
Optical Margin Alignment feature, 207–208
orphans, 182
Output Date variable, 97, 135, 137
overrides, 242–243, 263

overset cells, 246
Oxygen, 298

P

Package command, 57
package utility, 36, 274–278
page count, 99
page format, 99
page framework, 9, 11. *See also* framework
page guides, 42
page numbers, 11, 12, 132
page size, 9, 94
page spreads, 126
Pages panel, 42, 48, 102, 141
Panel Options dialog, 142
Pantone colors, 153, 154, 155, 158
[Paper] swatch, 150
Paragraph Formatting Controls button, 174
Paragraph panel, 174
paragraph rules, 183–184
Paragraph Style Options dialog, 45, 113, 193, 249
paragraph styles, 190–198
  creating, 191
  defined, 190
  illustrated, 14
  importing, 198
  keeping track of, 44
  linking, 197
  naming, 52
  nested styles in, 13, 44–45, 53–54, 192–195, 226
  updating, 51–53
paragraphs, 174–189. *See also* text
  adding rules above/below, 183–184
  aligning, 174–175
  composing, 178
  indenting, 175–176, 184
  justifying, 181
  spacing, 176–177
  specifying Keep Options for, 182–183
parent master, 125
parsing, 304
Paste Remembers Layers command, 148
pasteboard, 117–118, 262
Pathfinder panel, 203
paths, 62, 63, 70–71
PDF files, 19, 33
Peachpit Web site, viii
pen icon, 147
Pen tool, 71
Pencil tool, 71
percentages, 76
personalized letters, 19
Photoshop, 31, 158, 164, 210, 219, 277
picas, 76
placeholder frames, 63, 64, 266, 267
placeholder graphics frames, 127–129, 313
placeholder text, 33, 311–312
placeholder text frames, 11, 130–133
placeholders, 12
points, 41, 76
Polygon Frame tool, 64
Polygon tool, 71
Position tool, 65, 67–68
PostScript fonts, 33, 171
predesigned templates, 37–58
  customizing, 41–58
  deleting unwanted styles from, 56
  editing, 39
  file format for, 38
  implemented, 57–58
  layout of, 41–45
  location of, 39
  opening, 38
  packaging, 57
  preparing for production, 56
  revising, 47–56
  saving, 39–40
  selecting, 41
  setting default styles for, 56
  testing, 56
  working with layers in, 50
preferences
  File Handling, 40
  Grids, 110, 112, 116–117
  Guides & Pasteboard, 117–118
  Labels, 290
  Snap to Zone, 118
  Text Wrap, 212
  Units & Increments, 75, 77
Prefix option, 124
Preflight dialog, 275
Prevent Manual Positioning option, 218
preview images, 40
Preview mode, 119
Preview panel (Bridge), 287
Previous Object button, 91
Previous Page Number marker, 132
principles, template design, 23–27
print area, 100
Print Layer option, 147
print presets, 277
printing
  bleed/slug areas, 96
  layers, 147
  layout grids, 119
  and template design process, 32–33
Printing Instructions dialog, 275
process colors, 154
product catalogs, 307, 308. *See also* catalogs
productivity
  and object styles, 225–226
  and style sheets, 195–198
  and table/cell styles, 244–246
  and templates, 5–6
profitability, templates and, 7
Projecting Cap style, 200–201

R

ragged lines, 183
readability, 97
Rectangle Frame tool, 64, 127
Rectangle tool, 71
reference point locator, 80, 87
[Registration] swatch, 161
Relative to Spine option, 217–218
repeating elements, 12, 99, 307, 320
Replace Metadata command, 293
resolution
  image, 33, 264–265, 271, 292
  monitor, 174
rigid templates, 27
root element, 301, 310
Rotate dialog/tool, 87
Round Cap style, 200–201
Round Join option, 201
row strokes, 237
rows, 229, 232–233. *See also* tables
Rule Above command, 183
Rule Below command, 183
rule sets, 321
ruler guides, 106–110
  adding to object libraries, 16
  changing color of, 109–110, 266
  creating, 108–109
  deleting, 110
  locking/unlocking, 110, 267
  moving, 110
  and page framework, 9
  placing on separate layer, 119, 146
  purpose of, 106
  selecting, 109, 110
  ways of using, 111
Ruler On Spine option, 77–78

Ruler Per Page option, 77
Ruler Per Spread option, 77
rulers, 74–78. *See also* ruler guides
running headers, 134, 137–139
running lists, 248–249

S

sample elements, 262
sample pages, 43, 146
sample text, 130
Save As command/dialog, 39, 40
Save Collection dialog (Bridge), 295
Save Metadata Template command, 293
Scale dialog, 85
screen modes, 42, 118–119
scripting languages, 278, 321
scripts, 22, 278
Scripts folder, 22, 278
Scripts panel, 22
search feature (Bridge), 294
section markers, 132, 133
Select Content button, 90
Selection tool, 65, 68–69, 72
Send Backward command, 91
Send to Back command, 91
Shear dialog/tool, 87
shortcuts. *See* keyboard shortcuts
Show Baseline Grid command, 110
Show Content Offset command, 82
Show Document Grid command, 116
Show Frame Edges command, 43, 64
Show Guides command, 42, 266
Show Guides option, 147
Show Hidden Characters command, 267
Show Rulers command, 74
Show Structure command, 304
Show Subset dialog, 145
Show Tag Markers command, 311
Show Tagged Frames command, 311
Show Text Threads command, 268
sidebars, 100, 114
Single Word Justification option, 181
slug area, 9, 10, 95–96
Slug Cubed, 97
slug guide, 10
Slug mode, 119
slug plug-ins, 97
Slugger ID, 97
Small Caps command, 170, 171
Snap to Document Grid command, 117
Snap to Guides command, 112, 118
Snap to Zone preference, 118
Snap Zone option, 121
snippets, 312
Sort menu (Bridge), 291
Space Before/After options, 176
special effects, 221. *See also* Effects panel
speed, designing/testing templates for, 25, 271
spot colors, 32, 154–155, 265
Spotlight (Mac OS X), 292
spreadsheets, 227, 228, 244
stacking order, 43, 90–91, 148
Stamp It, 97
Start menu, 202
start tags, 300
States panel, 45
Story Editor, 312
Story panel, 208
strikethroughs, 169–170
Stroke panel, 200
stroke weight, 86
strokes, 200–202, 230, 231–232, 237, 238
Structure pane, 304
style groups, 53, 55, 197
style guides, 278, 279–282
style sheets
    basing one on another, 197
    clearing overrides from, 263
    examining, 44–45
    importing, 198
    increasing productivity of, 195–198
    organizing, 197
    purpose of, 13
    removing excessive, 262–263
    updating, 198
styles
    accessing frequently used, 52–53, 55
    character. *See* character styles
    defining new, 52
    deleting unwanted, 56
    naming/renaming, 52, 55, 198
    nested, 44–45, 53–54, 192–195
    object. *See* object styles
    organizing, 53, 55
    paragraph. *See* paragraph styles
    rearranging list of, 53, 55
    redefining, 52
    setting default, 56, 269
    table, 13, 14
    TOC. *See* TOC styles
Stylus Studio, 298
subscripts, 169
Suite Color Settings dialog, 164
superscripts, 169
Swatch Exchange files, 58
Swatches panel, 16, 51, 150, 162. *See also* color swatches

T

tab leaders, 189
table borders, 236
table cells. *See* cells
table fills, 238
table footers, 239
table headers, 239
table of contents, 17, 255–260. *See also* TOC styles
Table of Contents Styles dialog, 257
Table Options dialog, 236–239
Table Setup command, 235
table specifications, 13
table style overrides, 242–243
table styles, 13, 14, 239–246, 245
tables, 227–246
    CALs, 321
    converting text to, 228
    creating, 228
    formatting, 229–233, 235–239
    placing images in, 246
    productivity tips, 244–246
    selecting, 229
    spacing before/after, 236–237
    tagging, 313–314
    tracking, 248
    using color in, 246
Tabs dialog/panel, 75, 176, 188–189
tag markers, 311
tagged tables, 313–314
Tags panel, 304–305, 309–310, 311
template usage instructions, 146
templates
    adding metadata to, 272–273
    basic elements of, 9–16
    benefits of using, 5–7
    cleaning up, 262–265, 318
    for colored paper, 150
    constructing, 34–35
    constructing layout grid for, 97–119
    creating mock-up layout for, 33
    customizing, 41–58
    defined, 4
    defining objectives for, 30–33
    deleting unwanted styles from, 56
    and design consistency, 6–7, 17
    designing, vii, 23–27, 29–36
    editing/revising, 39, 47–56, 120–121

templates (*continued*)
- exploring layout of, 41–45
- finalizing, 262–270
- flexible *vs.* rigid, 27
- implementing, 36, 57–58, 272–278
- labeling elements in, 282
- for long documents, 247
- merging data into, 19
- opening, 38
- packaging, 36, 57, 274–278
- predesigned, 37–58. *See also* predesigned templates
- preparing for production, 56
- and productivity, 5–6
- and profitability, 7
- projects suitable for, 8
- purpose of, vii, 3
- saving, 39–40
- searching, 294
- selecting, 41
- setting default styles for, 56
- setting up automated, 20–21, 309–318
- setting up framework for, 93
- specifying default settings for, 266–270
- storing common elements for, 16–17
- style guides for, 279–282
- testing, 26, 35, 56, 270–272, 318
- types of, 8
- XML-ready, 297, 305, 309–318. *See also* XML

testing templates, 26, 35, 56, 270–272, 318
text. *See also* paragraphs
- aligning, 174–175
- boilerplate. *See* boilerplate
- changing case of, 170–171
- converting to table, 228
- formatting, 47, 166
- frames, 64, 68–71, 105
- hyphenating, 178–179
- indenting, 175–176, 184, 187
- placeholders, 12, 33, 130–133
- snippets, 312
- tagging, 311–312
- threads, 268
- variables, 97, 133–139
- wrapping. *See* Text Wrap feature

Text After field, 135
Text Before field, 135
Text Frame Options dialog, 106, 114–115, 203–207
Text tool, 229
Text Wrap feature, 100, 141, 147, 206, 208–213
textbooks, 251
TextEdit, 298
threads, text, 268
Thumbnail slider (Bridge), 286
Thumbnail view, 144
tint swatches, 153
TOC styles, 17–18, 45, 255–260
tracking, 167
Transform panel, 75, 78–80, 83, 86
transparency effects, 31, 146, 219–222, 265
Transparency palette, 219
trim size, 94
TrueType fonts, 171
Tufte, Edward, 227
type. *See also* text
- area, 100–101
- changing case of, 170–171
- layers, 146
- specifications, 12
- styles, 166–167

Type menu, 202, 209
Type on a Path tool, 71
Type tool, 68, 70
typefaces, 166–167
typographic specs, 12

U

unassigned frames, 64, 71–72
underlines, 169–170
Unicode, 171
Units & Increments preferences, 75, 77
units of measure, 75–76
user dictionaries, 180, 278

V

VBScript, 22, 321
vector graphics, 62
vertical ruler, 74, 76–77, 104, 112
Vista, Windows, 22, 278

W

Web sites
- Adobe, 265, 278, 321
- this book's companion, viii

welcome screen, 38
white space, 98, 100
widows, 182
Windows
- Explorer, 289
- Glyph Sets folder, 278
- predesigned templates location, 39
- Scripts folder, 22, 278
- XML editors, 298

Word, Microsoft, 228, 236
Word Spacing option, 181
workflow requirements, 31–32
workspace buttons (Bridge), 287–288
wrap options, 208–213. *See also* Text Wrap feature

X

X, Y location fields, 83
X Relative To option, 217
XHTML, 32
XML, 207–321
- editors, 298
- *vs.* HTML, 298
- importing, 318–321
- InDesign's tools for, 304–305
- markup rules, 298–304
- meaning of acronym, 20
- parsing, 304
- purpose of, 20, 32, 298
- repeating, 307
- setting up automated template with, 20–21, 309–318
- tagging strategies, 315
- teminology, 298–304
- testing, 318
- workflow, 305–308

XML Import Options dialog, 319
XMLSpy, 298
XMP metadata, 283
XP, Windows, 22, 278
XSLT, 319

Y

Y Relative To option, 217

Z

zero point, 76–77